MORE PRAISE FOR *THE GENIUS OF THE BEAST*

"Howard Bloom's newest book nails it once and for all. Hard to believe a book could clarify and illuminate everything swirling through and around our beleaguered selves, but this one does it!"
—Richard Foreman, MacArthur Genius Award winner,
founder of the Ontological-Hysteric Theater, and the man the
New York Times calls the "gray wizard of experimental theater"

"Howard Bloom's books on leadership are a gift to civilization. *The Genius of the Beast* is the best business history I've read, and I've read many. It does resonate to my frequency! It does."
—Alex Lightman, author of *Brave New Unwired World:
The Digital Big Bang and the Infinite Internet,*
CTO of FutureMax Group, and CTO of the
United Nations' Intergovernmental Renewable Energy Organization

"Riveting, brilliant, remarkable, distressing, optimistic, and beautifully written. A glorious tour-de-force history of the world. I found myself quoting facts from *The Genius of the Beast* to my friends and displaying a level of erudition far greater than they were accustomed to. A great book."
—Michael Zilkha, owner of Zilkha Biomass Energy

"Bloom is a brilliant synthesizer who connects the dots so the rest of us can see."
—Paul Herr, author of *Primal Management*
and inventor of the Horsepower Survey™

"If the world pays attention to Howard Bloom, the future of capitalism and the future of the world will change."
—Bob Krone, provost of Kepler Space University

"Bloom makes a culture rock 'n' roll as he blows away past myths, present cul-de-sacs, and future blind alleys. If the safest place in any crisis is always the hard truth, Bloom doesn't hesitate to tell us what's real, what works, and how we can escape the mess we are in. Pay heed!"
—Don Edward Beck, PhD, chairman of
Global Centers for Human Emergence and coauthor of
Spiral Dynamics: Mastering Values, Leadership and Change

"Read with delight this terrific book in which Bloom rewrites the history of the West and shows us what capitalism is really all about—or what at its best it demands of us and how it rewards our innermost natures. Bloom is a thinker of the order of Herbert Spencer or Henri Bergson—he tries to see the whole picture from the origin of the universe through the origin of life to the origins of humanity and the continuity of the creativity of the cosmos in our personal and social behavior. His insights along the way are mind-churning: his portrayal of Plato's real genius as a marketer is brilliant. The bacteria who poisoned their environment and thus moved evolution upward . . . what a metaphor. Columbus's greatest skill was marketing, not navigation; the role of tea rituals; and the tale of soap; all are wonderful. I've been writing about Max Weber and 'the spirit of capitalism' and it makes me even more aware of the brilliance of Bloom's argument about what is in the beast and how it can be tapped: capitalism does not just emerge from the Protestant ethic but from the nature of the human animal and its cosmic inheritance. Let's hope this side of the beast can win out over its parochial and narrow other self that longs for the safety of the tribe. But about the West at its best, he's right: Capitalism = Service. An amazing and brilliant book."

—Robin Fox, founder of the Anthropology Department at
Rutgers University, former director of research for the
H. F. Guggenheim Foundation, coauthor of
The Imperial Animal, and author of *Kinship and Marriage*

"The Genius of the Beast: A Radical Re-Vision of Capitalism is AMAZING!!!!"
—Steven Johnson Leyba, author of *COYOTE SATAN AMERIKA* and
The Last American Painter

"There is a resonating message in *The Genius of the Beast*. The human being is front and center in history. Front and center in the past, present, and future. That human being is our client. *The Genius of the Beast* explains the centrality of understanding our client's emotions. It explains the paramount importance of delivering outcomes that satisfy those emotions and of delivering those outcomes in an ethical manner. This message is fundamental in a time when there's a fracture in the investment business as we continue the shift toward retirement management. The old normal does not fit the current situation anymore. There are too many unsolved problems. There are too many unsolvable problems. The investment profession needs a new language. Traditional finance and economics described the client in terms of rational utility. That language is no longer good enough. We need new words that help us understand our clients' emotional needs. That's why we've put *The Genius of the Beast* in our advanced curriculum for retirement management analysts and have cited it in our own book, *RIIA's Advisory Process: How to Benefit from 'The View across the Silos.'"*

—François Gadenne, chairman of the board and executive director,
Retirement Income Industry Association, and coauthor of
*RIIA's Advisory Process: How to Benefit from
"The View across the Silos"*

"This book will simultaneously tease your brain, arouse your emotions, and motivate you as it probes deeply into the soul of man, society, and capitalism as the engine of Western civilization. The author gifts us with a counterculture manifesto that resurrects the goodness of capitalism while also connecting to the roots of humanity, of the human soul as a microcosm of the soul of society. . . . 'The future of the human race is hidden in our fantasies.' For me this book was science fiction in reverse, the lucid explanation of how good is bad, bad is good, and above all, the raw fact that every advance of civilization has been an advance of connectivity. The author joins William Greider and John Bogle as one of the moral wise men mentoring capitalism back toward its social purpose: doing well by doing good—satisfying individual natural emotional needs to reengineer society over and over again. . . . [*The Genius of the Beast*] will grab you by the throat and shake your fundamental perceptions of life."

—Robert D. Steele, number one nonfiction reviewer at Amazon.com, creator Marine Corps Intelligence Center, CEO of OSS.net, Inc., thirty-year veteran of clandestine, technical, and corporate intelligence, and author of *On Intelligence: Spies and Secrecy in an Open World*

"A delightful and insightful roller-coaster ride into the future of capitalism, ripe with Howard Bloom's trademark gusto for kaleidoscopic adventure on the frontiers of history, biology, physics, marketing, economics, and management."

—Nova Spivack, CEO and founder of Twine.com, the world's leading pioneer of semantic webs

"At last, a consistent, free-flowing, unmutilated vision for those who want to see the connection between physics, emotions, business, and society. Some Bloomian terms and concepts (like *reperception, messianic capitalism, cycles of boom and crash*, and *the universe feeling out for her possibilities*) have already invaded my everyday speech. This is exactly what we need: a science book meant for action and an action manual rooted in science."

—Pascal Jouxtel, partner, Eurogroup Institute, Paris

"In *The Genius of the Beast*, Howard Bloom achieves what he has set out to do—articulating a thoroughly secular call to what amounts to a spiritual mission. By tracing the capitalist impulse to innovate all the way back to its humble origins in bacteria and ants, Bloom conveys a powerful moral and evolutionary imperative for us to reinvent ourselves—and reinvigorate this system—for the sake of our collective future."

—Andrew Cohen, founder of EnlightenNext

"This book is beyond genius. It is genius. Genius new concepts, genius new visions, and genius new insights to bump our species up. . . . *The Genius of the Beast* arrived at a critical time in my life. . . . I was depressed and cynical about capitalism. With the new lens provided by this book, I went from a limited, news-based mind-set into a realm where I can see capitalism clearly from a microscope and from the Hubble at the same time. To get to know Marx as a capitalist is enough to turn my world upside down yet right-side up. To see Isaiah as a sort of Anthony Robbins means the new lens is working! I never thought I would want to read the book of Isaiah again. 'Without positives, nothing happens' is such a powerful and important concept and Bloom explains it beautifully. . . . Writes Bloom, 'If you serve others with all your heart, with all your soul, and with all your intellect, you may be loathed, you may be hated, and you may be mocked, harassed, and hounded, but you will succeed.' The fact that Bloom can state this and prove it time and time again with fascinating history and science leaves me with motivation, confidence, and peace. This book is causing a revolution in my brain and soul."

—Troy Conrad, comedian and creator of Comedy Jesus,
"Comedy's Answer to the Religious Right"

"Pure poetry, divinely begotten. It's a struggle of visions, wine and wafer, to become the real world's flesh and blood. I am convinced that Howard Bloom is the reincarnation of Plato. This beast is absolutely captivating. A godsend."

—Mark Lamonica, winner of the Southern California Booksellers
Association Nonfiction Award, author of
Rio L.A.: Tales from the Los Angeles River, Whacking Buddha: The Mysterious World of Shakespeare and Buddhism,
and *Junk Yard Dogs and William Shakespeare*

"I'm a Christian and Bloom is an atheist. But he brilliantly nails the divine nature that drives us toward creation and rest. *The Genius of the Beast* is a secular epiphany."

—Brace E. Barber, president and CEO, Decipherst, Inc.,
and author of *No Excuse Leadership*

"Howard Bloom personifies America's entrepreneurial genius; following him will lead us to a new world of wealth creation."

—Rich Kirby, president of Kepler Space University

THE
GENIUS
OF THE
BEAST

THE
GENIUS
OF THE
BEAST

A RADICAL RE-VISION OF CAPITALISM

HOWARD BLOOM

Prometheus Books
59 John Glenn Drive
Amherst, New York 14228–2119

Published 2010 by Prometheus Books

Inquiries should be addressed to
Prometheus Books
59 John Glenn Drive
Amherst, New York 14228–2119
VOICE: 716–691–0133
FAX: 716–691–0137
WWW.PROMETHEUSBOOKS.COM

14 13 12 11 10   5 4 3 2 1

Library of Congress Cataloging-in-Publication Data

Bloom, Howard K., 1943–
    The genius of the beast : a radical re-vision of capitalism / by Howard Bloom.
        p. cm.
    Includes bibliographical references and index.
    ISBN 978–1–59102–754–6 (hbk. : alk. paper)
    1. Capitalism—Social aspects. 2. Economic history. 3. Consumption (Economics)—Social aspects. I. Title.

HB501.B636 2009
330.12'2—dc22

                                                                      2009024994

Printed in the United States of America on acid-free paper

CONTENTS

6 CONTENTS

PROLOGUE

1

DOES SOUL BELONG
IN THIS MACHINE?

Why does capitalism need a radical re-vision?

The first decade of the twenty-first century gave the Western world one skull-cracking slap after another. The attacks of 9/11 and the downing of New York's World Trade Center, the slog in Iraq, the Great Crash of 2008, the implosion of major corporations like General Motors, Chrysler, Merrill Lynch, and Citibank, and the growth of China to superpower status—these were wake-up punches. They handed you and me—CEOs, researchers, artists, students, and thinkers—what may be our greatest opportunity and our greatest responsibility since the Great Depression and the Nazis threatened to topple the Western way of life in the 1930s.

Our civilization is under attack. But many of us don't want to defend it. Why? There's a void in our sense of meaning. We've been told that the "Western system" is one in which the rich stoke artificial needs to suck money, blood, and spirit from the rest of us.[1] We've been told that the barons of industry work overtime to turn us from sensitive humans into consumers—mindless buyers listlessly watching TV while growing obese on the artificial flavors, the chemical preservatives, and the cheap sugars of junk food. And some of that is true.

But the problem does not lie in the turbines of the Western way of life—it does not lie in industrialism, capitalism, pluralism, free speech, or democracy. The problem lies in the lens through which we see.

Emotional flows have powered our past and will drive our future, too. But we've never had the perceptual lens to bring them into view. Capitalism works. It works for reasons that don't appear in the analyses of Marx or in the statistics of economists. It works clumsily, awkwardly, sometimes brilliantly, and sometimes savagely. *The Genius of the Beast: A Radical Re-Vision of Capitalism* attempts to show us why.

The Genius of the Beast seeks to reveal the deeper meaning beneath what we've been told is crass materialism. It probes the mystery of how our obsessive making and exchanging of goods and services upgrades the nature of our species, gives us new powers, and endows us with the equivalent of new arms, legs, eyes, and brains.

The Genius of the Beast probes an untold secret of the Western system—we're not mere digits in a numbers game. We're feeling people woven in emotional exchange.

What is the *beast*? It's *Western civilization*. A monster with a peculiar metabolism—capitalism. Capitalism is a word that has become, to many, a curse. But beneath the surface, capitalism and the Western system hide astonishing abilities.

The Genius of the Beast stares a blunt fact in the face. Many of today's corporations are creatively and morally asleep. But you and I can wake them in a most ironic way—through a strange but vital upgrade in the richness of our lives.

Every culture needs a creation myth, a vision of how it came to be. That creation myth defines a culture's values and its aspirations. *The Genius of the Beast* is an attempt to provide a radically new creation myth—a factual creation myth, a creation story based on history and science. *The Genius of the Beast* is an attempt to give you and me a radically new way to understand our society.

The Genius of the Beast is a quick soar through a jet stream of stories that tell the tale of the rise of a strange creature—Western civilization—and of its capitalist digestive machinery. *The Genius of the Beast* explores the startling flipside of familiar tales—the way stone tools remade our genes, the way Paleolithic rouge and beads upgraded our ability to think, the way we invented the city, the king who invented money, the secret wonders of Phoenician trade, and the strange ways in which William Shakespeare, P. T. Barnum, J. D. Rockefeller, and the soap and cotton revolution upgraded humanity. Taken together, these episodes reveal an untold story of our origins, a new key to the quandaries of work and daily living, and a new view of our future in a world of instant change.

The Genius of the Beast is designed to give you pleasure. But if it succeeds in its mission, it will also give you something extra—a radically new way to see.

2

RAISING THE POOR AND THE OPPRESSED

Which Is the System That Does It Best?

Religions and ideologies promise to elevate the poor and the oppressed. But only the Western system delivers on that promise century after century. Here are four examples.

Barbara Annis, head of a CEO-coaching and corporate consulting firm headquartered in Canada, dropped by my Park Slope Brooklyn brownstone one evening for a meeting. A friend was sitting in who has started businesses in Azerbaijan, Hungary, Egypt, Jordan, Pakistan, and Haiti. The international entrepreneur leaned forward in the black reclining chair to my right and asked Annis a blunt question: "What do the CEOs you coach want the most from life?" The answer wasn't a doubling in stock value. It wasn't a leap in quarterly profits.

"What they really want," said Annis, "is to do something of value for society. They want to know that they've contributed to something bigger than themselves. Something with real meaning."

A few evenings later, I walked up the block to our neighborhood's major shopping street, Seventh Avenue, took a sharp right, went another few blocks, then barged into the Community Bookstore to ask its owner, Katherine, just how urgently a book is needed that radically morphs our perception of Western values, that turns our vision of capitalism on its head, and that shows us the moral imperatives hidden in our society. Should I really set aside my next two books of scientific theory and focus on a book about the meaning of our work, the meaning of our lives, and the meaning of the way we live, the meaning of our society?

Standing behind the counter of her coffee and pastry bar, Katherine stopped and thought for a moment. The question had struck something deep in her. You could see it in the way she almost closed her eyes.

"A friend of mine had guests from Germany a few weeks ago," she said. "Before they left, the Germans said they envied her. She didn't understand why." Germany has a social welfare system that defies belief. The Germans get nearly two months of vacation a year. And the Germans live under a government that doesn't make war in Iraq, that doesn't drop cluster bombs on villages in Afghanistan, that doesn't encourage greenhouse gasses, and that doesn't pervert a country like Nigeria just for the sake of its oil. Said the bookstore owner, "My friend's guests told her she was lucky. 'You Americans,' they said, 'have the best way of life in the world.' My friend called me in confusion to ask how in the world that could possibly be. What—if anything—is good about our society? No matter where I am, no matter who I meet, that sort of question has been nagging everyone I see."

* * *

If given a choice between earthly goods and emotional nourishment, humans will tighten their belts and go for emotional meat. In more than ten thousand "suicide bomber factories" worldwide, in more than ten thousand Wahabi madrassas, children are being taught to make holy war. The West, they're told, has nothing left to give the world but immorality and decay.

The teachers in these madrassas peddle passion brilliantly. They feed the hunger for meaning with the junk food of emotion—violence and righteous fury.

But could the madrassa teachers be right? Do we in the Western system have nothing worth struggling for? Do we have nothing that's worthy of idealism and belief?

In the years since 9/11, a steady stream of intelligent, socially responsible friends have told me that American civilization is

expiring, and that it deserves to die. Ours, they say, is the most violent culture in the history of humanity. It has raped the planet and tortured its captives of war. If it does not collapse under its own weight,
it should be executed for its crimes. These are people with influence.
One, for example, runs international seminars for a high-prestige
institute. Another is in the publishing world. (He's not, thank God,
affiliated with the publisher of this book.)

But here's a basic fact of the Western way of life, hard as we may
find it to conceive: Capitalism offers more things to believe in than
any system that has ever come before. Nearly every faith, from Christianity and Buddhism to Islam and Marxism, promises to raise the
poor and the oppressed. But only capitalism delivers what these ideologies and religions profess. Capitalism lifts the poor and helps them
live their dreams.

The proof is in the mega-perks we tend to take for granted:

- In the mid-1700s, cotton clothes were a luxury import that only
  the super rich could afford. The masses worked from day to day
  in stiff animal hair fabrics that housed insects and that scratched
  and tortured the skin. Changing into new clothes every few days
  or laundering them regularly was impossible. There was little
  sense in bathing if your shirt still carried last month's stench. In
  1769, capitalism introduced the power loom and changed the
  very nature of the shirts upon our backs. By the twentieth century, capitalism had made a T-shirt of cotton—the fabric of
  kings—the norm for even the poorest sub-Saharan African.
- In the nineteenth century, capitalism gave us another new universal—soap. Statistics show that Westerners grew dramatically
  healthier and added decades to their lives beginning in roughly
  the 1840s, when the soap and cotton revolution kicked in.
- In the early 1800s, sending an urgent letter to a relative on a
  distant coast took months or weeks. Then capitalist enterprises
  built the telegraph system, allowing messages to be sent across
  continents and seas in a matter of hours. In the 1990s, a mesh
  of multinational corporations took another leap. They built the
  mobile phone system and made it second nature to ring Taipei
  from Tampa and Bangalore from Boston while you were
  walking down the street.

- In the mid-1840s, a trip from New York to California took more than half a year by either wagon or by sailing ship.[1] Your odds of dying on the way were roughly one in five. Then in 1869 there came a capitalist masterpiece, the transcontinental railway, which snipped the trip down to a week. In the twentieth century, capitalism went even farther. It gave the average citizen jet wings and slivered the New York–LA trip from roughly a hundred hours to just five.

The Western system accomplished in three hundred years what it would have taken evolution over three hundred million to achieve—it gave us the equivalent of new arms, legs, ears, eyes, and brains.

No other civilization in the history of this planet—not that of the Egyptians, the Romans, the Muslims, the pre-1970 Chinese, or the twentieth-century Marxist Russians—has ever come close to lifting the downtrodden in these ways. None has ever done so much to elevate, empower, and create a brand-new category of humanity, a brand-new niche of comfort and prosperity—a massive and productive middle class.

The middle class is an economic engine that even Karl Marx, in his *Communist Manifesto*, praised for creating "wonders far surpassing Egyptian pyramids, Roman aqueducts, and Gothic cathedrals." Yes, the same Karl Marx who hated the middle class. The same Karl Marx who turned the word for middle class into an epithet—*bourgeoisie*.[2]

But the middle class is something we usually don't notice—a sea of humans that the Western System has raised from the ranks of the downtrodden for generations, a sea of humans who have left their poverty behind them permanently.

How have the Western system and its sidekick, capitalism, pulled off deeds of this magnitude? How has the Western system worked wonders without knowing its own nature? And if capitalism is such a miracle worker, why does it need a radical upgrade?

3

THE MESSIANIC IMPERATIVE

Your work, your daily life, and the economy are a lot
more than they seem to be.

The West does far more than it gets credit for, but that's nothing compared to what it can ultimately achieve. Yes, the capitalist system has
performed its share of miracles and its share of atrocities. But every
one of the dozens of corporations I've worked with uses only 10 percent of its brain. And most of us during the working day operate on
less than half a brain as well.

Some of us ache to jolt our dozing brain cells into action. And we
need to if we're going to keep producing new jobs while our old jobs
slide away. Those old jobs are being outsourced to India, China,
Mexico, Costa Rica, Poland, Russia, Hungary, the Philippines, and
South Africa. The Western system is spreading and upgrading entire
nations—Korea, Taiwan, Thailand, Singapore, India, and the really
big one, China. That spread of the Western way of life is a testament
to its power to change lives.

But to compete we need to bring our sleeping brains to full arousal.
Which brings us to an irony: to energize the industrious and analytic
potential of our minds, we need to find and engage our feelings.
Sensing our own desires, irritations, and fantasies can help us understand the unexpressed emotions of our fellow human beings. Strange

as it sounds, understanding our emotions—our passions and our depressions—can help us give others what they need before they even know they want it. It can help us create entirely new human powers— new technologies, new services, and new industries. Emotion is one key to creating new jobs, to raising incomes, to goosing the gross domestic product, to extending the escalator of upward mobility, to giving us satisfaction, and to giving us new meaning in life.

But there's more to it than that. There is an implicit code by which we in the West live—a code that demands that we uplift each other, and that we do it globally. It's a thoroughly secular call to be messianic. It's an economic call, a call to save thy neighbor.

* * *

We desperately need a re-vision, a reperception, and a reinvention of the system that has given Western civilization its long-term strength and its recent weaknesses. We need to wake up capitalism to its mission.

There's a place where we make meaning. But it isn't just in charities or in volunteer activities. It's in our daily work.

Business, commerce, and exchange are at the heart of Western civilization. They're also at the center of our daily lives. We spend more time at work than at any other waking activity. When we meet strangers, we tell them who we are by naming our trade, our way of making a living. Capitalism is what we do each day. But capitalism is not at all what we think.

The goal of this book is to take both you and me on a deep dive and a high flight—an exploratory mission into a secret that's right under our noses—into a set of moral imperatives and heroic demands that are implicit in the Western way of life. An exploratory mission into the secrets of our hidden magic, into the secrets of our unseen gifts, and into the secrets of our utopian capacities.

On the way, we'll tunnel into a cluster of mysteries. Why we are saviors who must wake up to our powers. Why consumerism—that wretched sin—isn't what it seems. Why frivolity is a search strategy in disguise. Why salesmanship, cash flow, profits, and marketing hide a strangely messianic core. *The Genius of the Beast*'s upcoming glide through the history of Western civilization is a retelling that hints at the rich ore beneath the slopes and plains of our history's terrain.

The Genius of the Beast aims to lay bare the emotional substance in what we've mistakenly labeled with a dehumanized vocabulary, the language of clods, lumps, stones, and numbers—the language of "materialism," "commodification," "consumerism," "derivatives," "utility maximization," "quarterly profits," "products," "markets," and "supply and demand."

People are the ones who demand. We do it because we desire, we hanker, we hunger, we're eager, we're roused. Or we're deadened, we're hurt, we're unsatisfied, we need. Wanting is an emotional thing. Value is emotionality. So is price. And so is profit. Coin is massed attention. Cash is emotional need.

It's not the plastic or the silicon in what we make that counts. It's the passion! It's the emotional boost, the emotional solidity, the emotional satisfaction, the emotional soar, the emotional swiftness, the emotional whisper, and the emotional roar.

Hold on to your seats. We're about to turn the conventional story of the Western system on its head. We're about to zip from the prehuman era to today in a way that musty preconceptions have hidden from our view. We're about to use a tool kit of new concepts:

- the evolutionary search engine
- the birds and the bees of boom and crash
- the cycle of insecurity
- stored vision
- microempowerment
- tuned empathy
- the hells and the heavens created by your neurobiology seven times a day
- the hungers in the fissures of your brain
- novelty lust
- identity tools
- creative capitalism versus criminal capitalism
- and management by walking outside

Get ready for a very strange trip, a very strange trip, indeed. You're about to step through the looking glass of capital. You're about to view nearly everything you take for granted from one of the strangest points of view you've ever seen. You're about to reperceive the core of history, business, creativity, and economics through the lens of emotions we don't normally comprehend, the hidden feelings driving you and me.

1

THE MYSTERY OF MANIC-DEPRESSIVE ECONOMIES

4

THE GREAT CRASH OF 2008

Why do economies collapse?

On December 6, 1974, the Dow Jones Industrial Average, the measure of the health of America's economy, was a sickly baby. It lay at a tiny 577 points. What's worse, it had just taken a huge spill and investors were in agony, terrified it might fall further. Thirty-three years later, on October 9, 2007, the Dow was a swaggering giant. It had rocketed to a level that few who experienced the financial hard knocks of the 1970s could have imagined. It scraped the sky at 14,164 points. If you'd invested $1,000 in 1974, your money would have grown to $24,547.66 by 2007, a stunning return on your savvy.

It was the equivalent of the sickly baby growing up to be fourteen stories tall.

What's more, many brokers and financial experts said that America would never have a major crash again. The new economy of iPhones and Google would soar, glide, and fly. Brokers at the prestigious investment house Morgan Stanley said that the Dow would soon reach 20,000. And modern economics, with its sophisticated fiscal and monetary tools, would stop any major dive before it could start.

The seers of perpetual boom were wrong. Very wrong. On October 9, 2007, the Dow Jones Industrial Average dropped a walloping 320 points in eight hours. But that was just the beginning. For over a year, the Dow continued its sickening slide, plummeting by hundreds of points at a time. In the two months between September 15, 2008, and November 25, 2008, the world's companies lost a total of $16 trillion in stock market value.[1] That loss was the size of the gross domestic product of China, Japan, and England combined. It was the size of the total output of roughly 1.4 billion of the world's most productive humans working for a full year. No wonder the worried heads of twenty governments got together in Washington in November 2008 to stop the plunge.[2] No wonder the US government tried to end the economic dive with over $7.7 trillion of bailouts and rescue plans by the end of 2008. But the Great Crash of 2008 would not be stopped. The result? In just one month, October 2008, 533,000 Americans lost their jobs.[3] And two of America's three automaking companies, General Motors and Chrysler, two mainstays of America's growth in the twentieth century, were bleeding to death and showing off their wounds as they begged Congress for a $36 billion cash transfusion.

What in the world caused this massive slide?

Every economic crash wears a disguise. On the surface, it looks unique—like something that's never happened before. On the surface, it looks like it was caused by big mistakes. By villains. By presidents and their duffle-headed economic policies. By parasitic speculators. By con men and cheaters. And by greed. But do villains and greed really cause panics, collapses, recessions, and depressions? Or do we become obsessed with sin and skullduggery when crashes come because that's how we are built—to react to catastrophe with blame? Are greedy cheaters, swindlers, and con men with us in both good times and in bad? And does something in our biology make us focus on them when things go awry? More important, does something in our biology trigger booms and crashes? And if booms and crashes are built into the very fiber of our being, why have they survived? Why do they continue to corkscrew through every economy we know?

In a Darwinian world, only the fit live on. Only what works remains. To hang in there for hundreds or millions of years, a strategy has to contribute to success. Could it be that boom and crash contribute to the success of human beings? If that's true, what in the world do they achieve? Equally important, what can you and I do to turn crashes into opportunities? Not just opportunities for ourselves. Opportunities for all of humanity.

The superficial story of the Great Credit Collapse of 2008 is a tale of overpaid executives milking the system. It's a story of modern bandits conning money out of you and me. It's a story of idealism starting a chain of events that led to ruin. And it's a story of good turned into accidental evil. Or that's the way it seems. But that is just the mask, just the disguise. The real cause of a crash is best explained by tales of bacteria and mice—our relatives on the tree of life. Bacteria and mice share a huge number of genes and internal machinery with you and me. They are relatives who, like us, go through boom and bust. And they do it without money. Why? Because the hidden roots of an economy go much deeper than they seem.

Like all economic crashes, the Great Credit Collapse of 2008 hid its real causes in an ocean of red herrings. Folks on the right think it was caused by one set of bad guys—people trying to do good. And folks on the left are sure the collapse was caused by the "greed is good" mentality of thieves in hand-tailored business suits: upscale robbers going for twenty-million-dollar paydays and for two-hundred-million-dollar golden parachutes.[4] But that, remember, is just the disguise. Under the surface, there was something far more primal going on.

Here's how the commentators on the right saw the origins of the greatest economic disaster since 1929. It was, they said, all the fault of the Left. Their story begins in 1994, when Congress gave the power to regulate mortgages to the Federal Reserve Bank. Idealistic political activists from community organizations like the Association of Community Organizations for Reform Now (ACORN) and the Neighborhood Assistance Corporation of America (NACA) put the screws on President Bill Clinton. The Federal Reserve Bank, the community organizers said, was protecting a nasty practice—red-lining, refusing mortgages to people in inner-city and low-income neighborhoods. So Clinton told his cabinet to wipe out this discrimination against minorities. The result was the invention of the NINJA loan, the No Income, No Job, No Assets loan.[5] In essence, Clinton was out to deliver on the motto of his 1992 campaign for president: "It's the economy, stupid."[6] Clinton's goal was messianic. It was to turn folks who had never before been able to own homes into homeowners. It was to make the working poor, the disenfranchised, and the folks normally forced to live in slums into property owners. Clinton's goal was to lift these oppressed masses into the middle class and to give them a stake in the stability of a vigorous, inventive America. His aim was to bring the disadvantaged into the circle of those who build equity with each monthly payment they make. But the NINJA approach meant loaning money to people with no savings, people who earned low paychecks, and some who earned no paychecks at all.

Clinton's dream was glorious. It was the latest upgrade of Franklin Delano Roosevelt's New Deal and of Lyndon Johnson's Great Society program. It was so compelling that Republican president George W. Bush continued the Clinton policy. He even expanded it.[7] But the NINJA strategy was also subtly diabolic. Why? It ignored the mandate of capitalism—be messianic. Save thy neighbor. But how can that be true? Clinton's plan was extremely messianic. It aimed to lift the poor to a stature they'd never known before. Right? Yes, but at someone else's expense. NINJA loans mugged Peter to pay Paul. They forced loan officers, mortgage brokers, and lenders to close their eyes to mortgage applications with phony income and asset claims. NINJA loans skipped the traditional process of careful scrutiny, the agonizing bureaucratic fact-checking of a borrower's ability to repay. NINJA loans took the money you'd deposited in your bank and that you'd set aside in your 401(k) accounts and gave it to people who couldn't give it back to you. Theft is not messianic. And this was theft from you and me, from investors big and small.

NINJA loans also had a downside for the family who received the loan. New forms of mortgages designed to meet the Clinton mandate tempted the poor with low initial payments. But they were mortgages with a wicked sting—they were *adjustable rate mortgages*. After thirty-six months of pampering you with pleasantly affordable interest rates, they underwent a Jekyll-and-Hyde transformation, slashing you with the vicious claws of far higher interest rates. One family in East Oakland across the bay from San Francisco, for example, paid a monthly $1,500 for their mortgage in 2005. They had that comfortably low rate for the first three years. Then came *mortgage resets*, and their interest rates swelled like tumors. The $1,500 payment soared to $6,000 a month.[8] The wallet shock was unbearable. Families like this were forced to rush to real estate brokers in the hopes of selling before their homes could be repossessed by the bank. They were forced to sell their houses at a fraction of what they'd paid for them. If they could sell them at all. But bank foreclosure was the fate of a disturbingly high percentage of the NINJA loan recipients. By December 2008 one out of ten homeowners in America was in foreclosure or was late on mortgage payments. In California and Florida, entire neighborhoods took on the look of ghost towns seemingly overnight—with empty houses and for sale signs on what felt like nearly every lawn.

Why the extraordinarily high interest rates? Was it the greed of bankers and fat cats on Wall Street? Yes. But it was also your greed and mine. When we'd put our savings into money market accounts or mutual funds, we'd wanted the highest interest rates we could find. NINJA loans kicked in with these high rates after their first three years because the money they doled out was yours and mine, and we wanted to earn a nice return on what we socked away. If usury was involved, you and I were among the usurers.

NINJA loans, high-risk loans, liar loans—loans based on falsified income and asset statements—and subprime loans helped fuel a real estate boom. From 2001 to 2005, the prices of homes rose at a rate that would theoretically have doubled their value every seven years. The 73.8 million American families who owned their own houses looked richer and richer on paper every year.[9] And everyone wanted to get in on the real estate boom. Everyone wanted to crowd into the express elevator that whisked you up to instant wealth. Feature stories, get-rich-quick Internet schemers, and late-night infomercial hucksters told of cab drivers, hairdressers, and single moms applying for NINJA loans to buy property in their own neighborhoods and even houses in distant cities, convinced that the buildings would soon double in price. The craving to make money this way spread with astonishing speed. It even spread to England, where it seemed that nearly every member of the working class was buying flats, renting them out, and speculating over the dinner table or in the pub about which neighborhoods would rise the fastest. We had a bubble. And bubbles have a nasty habit. They burst.

5

WHO TOPPLED THE TITANS?

Thud, after thud, after thud. The tale of the falling banks.

By 2006, there was trouble in real estate. According to Florida congressional candidate Paul Rancatore, the NINJA "loan market" in 1995 "was nonexistent." By 2008 "it represented over 25% of all mortgages."[1] By the end of 2006, foreclosures had hit a record level. People were driven out of their homes by their inability to pay the pole-vaulting monthly charges, and the banks were taking mini-mansions and starter homes back and auctioning them at ridiculously low figures.

That's when the giants began to fall. Those giants were our key financial institutions, the vertebrae in the backbone of our economy, the girders of the economic infrastructure that allows you and me to whip out our credit card or our checkbook and to buy everything from this week's groceries to a new car. The first to go was a company that specialized in NINJA loans—New Century Financial. In the early 2000s, New Century Financial was a probe on the bold new frontier of high-risk mortgages, NINJA mortgages—mortgages known widely as subprime because they were below the lowest level of credit worthiness normally considered acceptable in the investment business. But on April 2, 2007, New Century went into Chapter Eleven—

bankruptcy—and fired more than half its staff.[2] The fall was shocking. Most of us had never seen a major financial institution go under before. But financial collapses of this kind were about to become the order of the day.

In July 2007 the fifth-largest bank on Wall Street, Bear Stearns, made an announcement that hit the headlines like a sledge hammer. Two of its hedge funds had imploded. If you or your mutual funds had money invested in these Bear Stearns ventures, your hard-earned cash had just done a disappearing act. Eight months later, on March 17, 2008, Bear Stearns went completely under. J. P. Morgan, the $2.3 trillion financial services firm,[3] saved the day by scarfing up the Bear Stearns wreckage at a sub-bargain basement price—buying an $18-billion company for $240 million. That's the equivalent of buying a three-hundred-dollar mini-laptop for four dollars. But there was worse to come.

When America twitched, France and England showed signs of cerebral palsy. On August 9, 2007, French investment bank BNP Paribas informed investors that two of its funds had become will-o'-the-wisps thanks to a "complete evaporation of liquidity." The cost of credit jumped, and heavy-duty anxiety hit the financial community worldwide.

A quiet process of emergency rescue—of government bailout—began. The European Central Bank pumped a humongous 203.7 billion Euros into the banking sector. That's enough money to buy every man, woman, and child in Manchester, England, three houses.

Once upon a time, a single billion was nearly inconceivable. In 1861, just before the Civil War, the entire federal budget of the United States was a mere $67 million. At that rate, one measly billion would have sustained the entire government of the United States for close to fifteen years.

But in 2008, the billions were about to pile up like pennies. On February 20, 2007, the G7 leaders—the leaders of the seven biggest industrial nations in the world—came out with a projection of losses from mortgages and from the investment vehicles that had been built to raise money for NINJA loans. The figure was shocking—four hundred billion dollars—enough to fund America's space program for more than twenty-three years. But that projection was way, way too low. In August 2007 a German bank that had plunged big time into

American NINJA mortgages—Sachsen Landesbank—showed signs of collapse and was saved by a merger with one of its biggest rivals, Landesbank Baden-Wuerttemberg.[4] In September 2007 the British bank Northern Rock imploded. It went secretly to the Bank of England for emergency funding. When the BBC leaked the news of Northern Rock's trouble, worried depositors rushed to the bank to grab their cash. Those panicked depositors pulled a billion pounds out of Northern Rock before the government saved the day by assuring depositors that if Northern Rock failed to give them their funds, the government would.

In October 2007 a top-tier bank in a nation of bankers—Switzerland—announced $3.4 billion in losses. The shuddering bank was UBS. And UBS was not some tiny local bank. It was a global player, with branches in fifty countries.[5] The chairman and CEO of UBS resigned. Then Citigroup, one of the world's two biggest banks,[6] with 12,000 offices in 107 countries and a staff of 358,000, sprang a leak. It announced that $3.1 billion had gushed from its coffers—$3.1 billion in dead loss. But that was only a prelude. The following week Citigroup announced another $5.9 billion in losses. Six months later Citigroup's publicly announced losses had mounted to $40 billion—enough to give every adult in Chicago an SUV. But that was just a taste of things to come.[7]

In October 2007, the trouble hit Merrill Lynch. Merrill Lynch was a titan. It had assets of over half a trillion dollars—$681.05 billion to be precise.[8] And Merrill Lynch was literally the symbol of Wall Street. Its branding device was a bull, and it paraded that symbol in the most emblematic place of all—in the form of a seven-thousand-pound giant bronze bull smack in the middle of the Wall Street district.[9] Why was Merrill Lynch's golden calf in the financial district's heart a bull? The muscular animal was more than just an arbitrary symbol of power. It said that Merrill Lynch was bullish on Wall Street. And it said it in an unforgettable way. So when Merrill Lynch's head resigned over $7.1 billion in bad loans, America's average, everyday investors got their first inkling that they were in for serious trouble. The trouble was so serious, in fact, that on December 6, 2007, President George W. Bush announced that he had a plan to bail out more than a million homeowners whose mortgages were about to go into foreclosure. It was the right move from the wrong man. Bush's credibility had been brought down to zero by eight years of blunders, including the war in Iraq, which had proven to be a shabby, costly, and morally disturbing embarrassment.

Worse, our economic gurus had given us the false sense that catastrophic crashes like the Great Depression of 1929–1939 would never happen again. Why? Economists had cracked the code of the business cycle. They had found the secrets that stopped slides from becoming nosedives. Their tools? Raising and lowering interest rates, and knowing how and when to become financial saviors—"lenders of last resort." Economists like Federal Reserve Bank chairman Ben Bernanke, an economist who had spent a good part of his professional life studying the Great Depression, felt they knew how and when to "helicopter" cash.[10] How and when to drop bails of money into trouble spots and calm them. How and when to be catchers in the rye with big safety nets, big bundles of money.

But in 2008, helicopering money into trouble spots did not do the trick. Nor did raising and lowering interest rates. The Fed, which bills itself (accurately) as the Central Bank of the United States,[11] began its emergency interest-twiddling on September 18, 2007, by cutting the rate at which it loaned money to banks by half a percent to 4.75. The meaning in English? This rate shift was supposed to free up more money by giving the retail lenders of greenbacks—banks—a cheap supply of cash that those banks could loan to you and me. Money they could sell us in the form of home loans, auto loans, refinanced mortgages, loans for vacations, student loans, and loans to pay off credit card debt. Interest rate changes theoretically also freed up money that the banks and brokerage houses could lend to corporations to cover payroll and inventory.

Did the tweak of interest rates work? Within six weeks of this careful interest adjustment, the giants of banking and investment— Citigroup and Merrill Lynch—had begun to teeter. Four months later, on January 22, 2008, the Fed made a rate cut so out of the norm that it was designed to startle us into economic health. Instead of a mere quarter of a percent or a bold half a percent, the Fed cut its rates by a shocking three-quarters of a percent—the biggest rate cut in twenty-four years. Did this fresh blitz of interest rate shock and awe make a difference? No. For a minute things looked hopeful. A few of the world's stock markets swung upward. Briefly. Others slid further into the abyss. Then, a mere nine days later, a little-known company called MBIA announced that it had lost $2.3 billion in only three months.[12] That's enough money to buy all the grocery stores in Kansas.

Losses of this size would put most companies out of business instantly. But MBIA had a special importance. It was part of the hidden machinery designed to keep the investment companies that handle retirement funds from going belly up. It was the world's biggest bond insurer.[13] MBIA was part of an invisible safety net. And the securing lines of that safety net were in danger of being snipped.

MBIA blamed its troubles on, guess what? NINJA loans, aka subprime mortgages—theft from the lender.

The notion that modern economists can solve all problems with fiscal and monetary policy[14]—emergency money drops[15] and interest rate adjustments—took it on the chin again on April 20, 2008, when the Bank of England followed the US Federal Reserve Bank and lowered rates a quarter of a percent to 5. The effect was that of a popgun in an artillery barrage. To journalists reporting on the scene, it appeared that nearly everybody in England had been investing in real estate. Barbers, butchers, bakers, and candlestick makers had been buying flats, renting them out, and dreaming of flipping properties. But there was trouble in Real-Estateville, even in England. Despite the Bank of England's heroic lowering of interest rates on loans, the prices of houses, which everyone had bet would double or triple, dropped for the first time in twelve years. The fall was a mere 1 percent. But it came as a shock, an alarm bell that no one thought would ever ring. And within twelve days of the Bank of England's magic rate cut, 850 companies had gone belly up in Britain—going "into administration"—the rough equivalent of our bankruptcy.[16] The interest rate fiddling had failed, but the trouble wasn't limited to the United States and England. On May 22, 2008, the Swiss bank UBS, the bank whose former CEO and chairman had resigned over less than $4 billion in losses a mere six months earlier, confessed that the bank had lost ten times that amount—a whopping $37 billion. The money had gone down the drain of America's subprime mortgage implosion. UBS tried to give itself a lifeline by raising $15.5 billion in a "rights issue." But sophisticated insiders and investors were frightened of investment. And money was drying up.

The modern miracles of economic theory were not working. Nor was another, far more ancient approach—scapegoating, the blame game. The FBI tried to give those whose confidence was quivering a boost by finger pointing, shaming the villains, the greed-mongers, the bad guys who had caused the debacle. On June 19, 2008, the bureau arrested 406 people, including real estate developers and brokers. The impact? None. Six days later one of the biggest and most august banks in England, Barclay's, began to crumble. The cracks in its foundation were growing so fast that it asked for help from Qatar, a tiny Persian Gulf oil nation at the sandy lip where the deserts of Arabia meet the Indian Ocean. Qatar had socked away a ton of oil money. The government-owned Qatar Investment Authority bought a full 7.7 percent of Barclay's—enough to have a major influence on the bank's policy for decades to come. The Qataris picked up this slice of one of the world's top banks for a mere 1.7 billion pounds, turning London, a city where Arabic was almost as common a language as English, just a tad more into what author Melanie Phillips called Londonistan. As if to demonstrate that the downslide was impervious to any remedies yet invented by economists, on July 9, 2008, one of the biggest stock markets in the world, Britain's FTSE, a mainspring in the global system, went into a sickening plunge, dropping a gut-wrenching 20 percent.

On July 13, 2008, a mere three months after Bear Stearns—Wall Street's fifth-largest bank—went down, the mortgage lender IndyMac dropped in its tracks. IndyMac wasn't small potatoes. The IndyMac collapse was the second-biggest bank failure the United States had ever experienced. And IndyMac's collapse proved contagious. It set off a financial plague. A plague of perception. A plague of emotion and belief. Investors panicked over the fate of all mortgage-based investments. The day after IndyMac's collapse, investors bailed out of Freddie Mac and Fannie Mae. The prices of Freddie's and Fannie's stocks plunged. Freddie and Fannie owned or guaranteed 5 *trillion* dollars' worth of American mortgages. That's trillion with a T. More than the entire annual output of Japan, the world's third-largest economy.

As Mathew Tombers, a TV producer in New York, said in his weekly update to his friends, "This is the week when the trillion became the new billion."

From August 2007 to January 2009 the economists would continue to apply their theories. There would be many more interest rate adjustments. And many more attempts to "helicopter" cash to financial firms that were on the verge of collapse. Would these techniques work? No way. Why? Why did economics prove so useless? Why was monetary policy so helpless to stop the downslide?

Because economic crashes are not the fault of bad guys. They are not the result of obscure things like credit instruments and subprime mortgages gone hog wild. They are built into our biology. They are driven by a mass emotional engine. A mass perceptual engine. A search engine with which the cosmos feels out her possibilities. Booms and crashes are driven by a breakthrough generator—a transcendence engine.

What is a *transcendence engine*? It's a mechanism that takes the ephemeral and turns it into hard and fast reality. In the inanimate universe a transcendence engine takes what's imminent from nothingness into the realm of being. Among humans, a transcendence engine turns the whisperings of the spirit—visions and imaginings—into everyday things, into commodities. A transcendence engine is a secular mechanism that does the job often credited to a divinity.

Booms and crashes make you and me the agents of an evolutionary engine—a thoroughly secular engine—that does something only gods were once thought to do. The act of creation.

6

THE MUSIC OF
BOOM AND CRASH

How the Great Depression of 1929 became a singing
ghost.

What's a depression? Something your parents argue about for the rest
of their lives. Or that's the way it looked to me growing up in Buffalo,
New York, in the 1940s and 1950s. My dad had come to Buffalo
from his hometown of Asbury Park, New Jersey, to seek his fortune
during the darkest days of the 1930s, in the middle of the Great
Depression. But 25 percent of American workers were unemployed,
and fortunes were as hard to come by in a stunned steel-making and
Great Lakes shipping city like Buffalo as they'd been back in the
beach town resorts of New Jersey. The children's clothing store my
father's cousins had founded had, apparently, not worked out. And
that was the store in which my dad had come to work. According to
my mom, my dad slept through the Depression. She did not approve
of unemployed men who slumbered until ten a.m. After all, *she* was
working. She had a good government job as a secretary to the head of
the New York State Liquor Authority. And the Depression had not
stopped the residents of New York State from drinking.

Despite my mom's carping, my dad insisted that he'd made it
through the tough times since 1929 by restricting his diet to canned
beans, meals in which he also claimed he ate the labels and the cans.

In 1964, when I was twenty-one years old, I wanted to help defeat conservative Republican bogeyman Barry Goldwater, the man many of us were convinced would start the first nuclear war. (We were probably wrong.) So I volunteered to work for whatever Democratic political candidate would have me. First, the campaign of Buffalo congressional candidate Max McCarthy put me to work writing position papers on the war in Vietnam. When I moved to New York City in September to start college at New York University, I switched to the campaign of another Democratic congressional contender, Ted Weiss. The Weiss campaign asked me to research the investments that had held their value through the Great Depression. What was the answer I came across while spending day after day buried in the stacks of the New York Public Library? The investment that had held its value through that ten-year slump was real estate. That and my parents' arguments were my first introductions to the subject of boom and crash, the subject of depressions.

Seventeen years later, in 1981, America endured the greatest recession since the 1930s. By that time I was doing fieldwork in mass behavior. I'd founded my second successful entrepreneurial company in the world of pop culture—The Howard Bloom Organization, Ltd.—the biggest public relations firm in the music industry. The economic downturn was so bad that companies in the music biz were laying off staffers by the hundreds. Not mine. How did we beat the recession? That's a story for another time. But this was another lesson in boom and bust, another lesson in depressions. A supremely practical lesson.

The smash of 1981 raised questions. What *is* a depression? Why does a depression start? How do you keep a depression from happening? And how do you climb out of a depression once it's flattened you? I ended my science project in pop culture in 1988, went back to science full-time, and began the research for my first book, *The Lucifer Principle: A Scientific Expedition into the Forces of History.* And I researched crashes and booms, business cycles, bubbles, and depressions. After all, when you slice open the cycles of war and peace you often find boom and depression just beneath the skin. And when you cut even that layer away, you find something even more basic— the naked patterns of mass behavior. And that's my territory, the mass behavior of everything from quarks to human beings.

Then came word of an appealing insight into boom and crash from MIT,[1] an insight based on a revival of the work of Soviet economist Nikolai Kondratiev[2]—the man who had headed the Institute for the Study of Business Activity in Lenin's bloody new Soviet Union. Kondratiev had been sentenced to death in 1938 by Stalin for his unconventional views (and for his loyalty to Stalin's chief rival, Trotsky). What were those heretical ideas? Kondratiev's concept was called the *Kondratiev wave*, or the *long wave*. Some called it the *supercycle*. Boom, said one interpretation of the Kondratiev wave, came when you pioneered a new technology, when that new technology took hold big time, and when you were the primary source of supply for that new technology's products.[3] Bust—depression—came when the technology you supplied had peaked, was in decline, and when other folks had developed the ability to make your once-hot new gadgets on their own. The nation that rises from the ashes of depression and that rules the world, the Kondratiev wave implied, was the nation that controls the new technology of the day. The nation that goes down is glued to the technology of the past. I bought it.

I was researching England's rise and fall in the nineteenth century at the time, and the Kondratiev wave model fit perfectly. Why? Until roughly 1830, the clothes on your back were among the most expensive pieces of property you owned. The aristocrats of Florence, Italy, spent 40 percent of their income on clothes. Just one spectacular outfit could cost "more than a good-sized farm out in the Mugello."[4] So you could make a fortune weaving, transporting, or retailing cloth and clothes. My father couldn't make a fortune with a children's clothing store in Buffalo, New York, in 1938. But if you were living in, let's say, Europe in 1550, you could. William Shakespeare's dad was in the wool business. Sir Isaac Newton was born in a hamlet named for the same fabric—Woolsthorpe-by-Colsterworth. Anton van Leeuwenhoek, the inventor of the microscope, was a cloth merchant.[5] The Medicis, the folks who financed Michelangelo, augmented their banking activities with a wool business.[6] And since roughly 1360 CE, England's king had sat on a bag of wool—the official woolsack—as a symbol of the source of his island kingdom's wealth.[7]

Then came a hot new technology. In 1769, an Englishman invented a gizmo-system beyond belief, an interlaced cluster of new devices that could allow a single unskilled worker to turn out goods that had previously taken the blood, sweat, and tears of a dozen highly skilled arti-sans.[8] The innovator's name was Richard Arkwright.[9] He'd gotten his start in a radically different kind of fiber business—barbering and wig-making. But cloth production fascinated him. Arkwright invented a carding process to comb out cotton, a spinning machine to make thread, and an automatic weaving machine to weave cotton fabric. He also invented new ways to power these machines—driving their gears with horses in the beginning, then powering them with the rush of mountain streams. When Arkwright put all these innovations together, he'd created something new—the factory. Arkwright planted factories all over England and Scotland. His 1776 factory in Cromford, Eng-land, was an astonishing seven stories tall.

Meanwhile, in 1784, a Scottish mathematical instrument maker named James Watt perfected yet another magical invention, a machine that could do the work of two, three, four, or four hundred horses, a machine that could take up less space than the distance between a single horse's front and rear legs, a machine that could work twenty-four hours a day without the bother of horse manure or hay. That gizmo was the steam engine.[10]

When the Brits and an occasional American hooked steam engines to automatic weaving machines, installed steam engines on ships, and put steam engines on railroad trains, they transformed the world. For the next seventy years people from six continents clamored to get English goods—cotton fabrics, clothing, thread, railroad tracks, rail-road trains, and steam engines. The English ruled the world. They ruled its finances and they ruled a passel of its nations, expanding into one of the biggest empires the world had ever seen. Just as the Kon-dratiev wave predicted, the British ruled because they dominated the hottest new technologies of the day. Then the technologies with which Britain had conquered and controlled peaked. Everyone who needed new clothes had them. Everyone who wanted a steam engine or a rail-road train was nicely equipped with one and only needed a new model from time to time. What's more, *import replacement* had taken place.[11] Britain's old customers had learned to make steam engines and inexpensive cloth on their own. The result? A depression. The world economy tanked in 1873. It tanked hugely.

The downslide was extremely hard on the Brits. England entered a gloom of a kind it felt it had never known before. It bogged down in a depression that seemed to last for the next twenty years. It was a depression so massive that it held the title of *The* Great Depression until another economic plunge stole that title in 1929.

Why had the British gone into such a massive slump? And why had the British lost their lead of the world when they came out of their depression? The Kondratiev wave seemed to hold the answer. England had pioneered the creation and mass marketing of the hot new technologies for a seventy-year-long period. But then new technologies had arisen, technologies the British had created but hadn't bothered to mass-produce, to market, or to promote. What were those sizzling new technologies? Steel, electricity, and the products of the chemical industry. All these had been created by clever Englishmen. But the Britons hadn't commercialized them. Who had developed steel, electrical, and chemical gadgets and mass marketed them? Two unlikely backward nations—Germany and America—two nations that would rule the next century.

There was a lesson in all this for the Americans. To come out of a depression on top, you have to produce and promote the hot new technologies of your century.

The Kondratiev wave of boom and crash seemed on target. So did the concept that depressions happen when an old technology is falling and a new one is about to arise. Do the arithmetic on four centuries of recent history and you discover that recessions happen every 4.75 years and great depressions strike once every 67 years, roughly once in a generation.[12] That's remarkably Kondratiev. There was just one problem. The Great Depression of 1929 to 1939 didn't fit the model. America did *not* go into depression because its technologies were old and in decline. Far from it. Five hot new technologies were rising in 1929—automobiles, airplanes, radio, electronics, and the wiring of homes for 24/7 electrical access. Count 'em, five. Every one of these techno-innovations would expand dramatically once the Depression was over. But every one of these was put on pause by a global crash.

When a new technology was still climbing toward its peak, the Kondratiev model predicted a boom. Yet the global economy had *crashed* in 1929, when autos, planes, radio, electronics, and the electrical wiring of homes were just starting their rocket ride to the top. Why? The MIT-Kondratiev model failed to answer the question. Was there another model that would?

At the end of another twenty years of research, I'd found an answer. Depressions don't come from our technologies. They come from our biology. They come from our emotions and our perceptions. They come from the way we feel and see. What's more, depressions come from the biocycles we help make when we are part of a group. They come from the soul of a society.

There was one more revelation. Boom and bust cycles are not unique to human beings. They arose when life itself began 3.85 billion years ago. They showed themselves among our first ancestors, bacteria. Then they reappeared in every other beast that lived in flocks, swarms, colonies, crowds, and herds. Why? Because boom and bust—the cycle of good times and depressions—performs a vital function for a society. That purpose? Exploration, consolidation, and repurposing—using something old in a very new way. Learning, thinking, and creating. Functioning as an evolutionary search engine that does something only the gods were once thought to do. Functioning as an evolutionary search engine that brings new creations into being. Functioning as a *secular genesis machine*.

What's a secular genesis machine? Genesis happens every day. New things come into being. And from time to time the cosmos invents something radically new—the first flood of atoms, the first flood of stars, the first flood of galaxies, the first flood of black holes, and the first flood of human beings. *A secular genesis machine is the mechanism that brings radically new creations into being without the hand of a deity.*

7

THE WORLD WIDE WEB
OF 1931

**The Great Knock-On Effect: How your investments
got caught in the domino stack.**

You heard the same thing repeated over and over again after the Great
Crash of 2008 began. For the first time in history, the world is Internetted and World Wide Webbed. Our modern electronic interdepen-
dence is dangerous. Even worse, it's a cause of the 2008 crisis.
Singapore is too closely tied to Germany. When Moscow twitches,
Mexico City has a convulsion. Brokers in Japan can use the Internet
to trade shares on the British stock exchange before most Britons are
awake. Englishmen and women can watch commodities in Chicago
rise and fall in real time and place their bets as if the global financial
market were a giant casino.

But a global economic mesh is not new. We've been World Wide
Webbed and Internetted since Rome began to import silks from China
in roughly 200 BCE.[1] Credit collapses have been global since at least
1720, when England's South Sea Bubble and France's Mississippi
Bubble collapsed within months of each other.[2] The Mississippi
Bubble's main mover was a British financial whiz and convicted murderer (he killed an opponent in a duel for insulting his mistress)
working in Paris, John Law. In 1717, Law convinced the regent for
the seven-year-old king of France, Louis XV, to give Law's creation,

the Mississippi Company, a twenty-five-year monopoly on trade with the Mississippi territories of North America.[3] This included a monopoly on the Canadian beaver trade, exclusive right to trade with Asia, exclusive right to trade with the East Indies, a monopoly on the tobacco business, and the exclusive right to mint coins for all of France.[4] These projects were as far as twelve thousand miles away from Paris. They were global.

So was England's South Sea Company, which raised funds for trade between London and South America.[5] What started out as promising business propositions triggered speculative manias that defied belief. Mississippi Company stocks rose to five times their starting price, then ten times, then twenty times. Invest a thousand dollars and you got back twenty thousand. Who could resist? Normal people like you and me became frenzied speculators, convinced that if they could get their hands on Mississippi Company or South Sea Company stocks, they would become rich. Demand grew so feverish that stocks were issued just for the right to buy more stocks—options. Prices flew sky-high. Then one day the public switched from manic enthusiasm to depressive paranoia. And the price of Mississippi Company and South Sea Company stocks went down to nothing. High-placed politicians, super-rich civilians, and ordinary men and women who thought they were on their way to wealth and luxury discovered they'd lost their shirts or blouses. That's a bubble. That's how bubbles burst. And bubbles, even three hundred years ago, were threads in a global mesh.

To see the pre-Internet World Wide Web at work, take a look at the credit collapse of 1931, the credit collapse that kept the Depression of 1929 going and made it far, far worse.

The beginning of the credit collapse of 1931 can be pinpointed to a single day—May 8, 1931—when executives at a bank in Austria called on their government for help in handling a small problem. Things had been going badly in the world economy since the New York stock market crash of 1929 two years earlier. Investments in businesses, buildings, and land that had looked solid as could be, investments that had made their owners feel secure and wealthy, had melted away like the morning haze, evaporating into the ozone, their value gone utterly. The Austrian bank had lost 140 million schillings. It had lost 85 percent of all that it had, 85 percent of its equity—the equivalent of losing your shirt, pants, and underwear in a strip poker game but still having your shoes and socks. The troubled Austrian bank was called Creditanstalt. Creditanstalt's problems should have been a minor incident. They were difficulties at a single bank you never heard of in the anonymous midriff of Europe, trouble in a land that had been beaten just a few years earlier in World War I. Trouble in a day long before wi-fi, an era of telephones nailed to the wall, an age of typewriters that worked with levers and not electricity, and trouble in a time when emergency messages were still sent by telegram. Not a serious problem, right?

In fact, Creditanstalt was more important than it seemed. Viennese academician Aurel Schubert, an economist at the Austrian National Bank and author of the definitive book *The Credit-Anstalt Crisis of 1931*, calls Creditanstalt a "superbank."[6] A legendary theorist of history who happened to be alive at the time—Arnold Toynbee, considered one of the greatest minds of his age and author of the twelve-volume masterwork *A Study of History*—took time out from his ponderings to explain that Creditanstalt was not just a local enterprise. It was, he said, "an integral and important part of the financial structure of the world."[7] Creditanstalt controlled an amount of money that equaled the budget of Austria's government. And Creditanstalt had a hand in a hefty percentage of Austria's major industrial companies.[8]

But the economists of the day felt they'd long ago learned to fill in potholes like the one Creditanstalt had just hit. These economists were not mere bumpkins tumbling from the turnip truck of elementary algebra. They had access to the advanced math of Albert Einstein's relativity. They lived in the age of the fancy equations of quantum physics. They were graced with the formulae of modern statistics and probability. And they could tap the wisdom of modern wizards like Britain's economist, mathematician, diplomat, and intellectual superman John Maynard Keynes. The Austrian government knew exactly what to do. It huddled for the weekend in top-secret meetings.

The ministers running Austria were antisocialist, but they decided to make an exception to their rules. They decided to rush in and "socialize the losses." They did what the governments of the seven biggest industrial nations in the world—the G7—did in the Great Crash of 2008. They injected money to keep Creditanstalt standing. They "helicoptered" cash. They took money from government funds and arranged a special rescue package backed by one of Europe's

leading banking families, a family that specialized in loans to governments—the Rothschilds. Then the Austrians tried to spread the risk.
They went international. They hit up the British central bank for
money. The British turned them down. If there was going to be a
domino effect and banks around the world were going to collapse one
after the other, the Bank of England did not want to be one of the
falling domino tiles. So the Austrian government turned elsewhere. It
went to the Bank for International Settlements in Switzerland.

The Bank for International Settlements was a stratospheric force.
It had been established a year earlier in 1930 by seven nations, seven
of the biggest financial powers on the planet—Belgium, France, Germany, Italy, Japan, England, and the United States.[9] But the Bank for
International Settlements only agreed to inject a sum that amounted
to pocket change—less than 100 million schillings.

And there were delays—not a good thing when the confidence of
the world is quivering. Finally, after two weeks of glitches, the Bank for
International Settlements came through with a cash transfusion for the
Austrians. The trouble should have ended there. The *Wall Street
Journal*, in fact, was sure that the ruckus had been brought to a dead
halt. The world's financial system was now crash-proof, the *Journal*
crowed with triumph. The Creditanstalt crisis, it declared, had proved
to be just "one more sore spot" that the decisive powers of modern government and finance had healed before it could break out in a rash. One
more mess the economic maintenance team had "cleaned up."[10]

But this upbeat self-confidence lasted less than seven days. Before
the week was out, the public and five other Austrian banks had
yanked their deposits from Creditanstalt. And money had started to
gush from banks in Hungary, Yugoslavia, Germany, and the Free City
of Danzig. The problem was spreading! So the Bank of International
Settlements jumped in to help once again, shoveling money into the
empty Eastern European bank vaults and trying to plaster banknotes
over the leaks. But the shivers spread, and the forces of government
and high finance turned to another strategy that we would try in the
Great Crash of 2008—massive global cooperation. One hundred and
thirty foreign banks chipped in to keep the global credit system afloat.

Now even England was nervous. It tossed 150 million schillings
into the pot. But that was nowhere near enough. Creditanstalt's
stumble flung the Austrian government from power. Austria's minister

of the interior was virulently against "a prolongation of the agony of Creditanstalt for two years, at the price of losing her financial freedom." He apparently could see the cataclysm that was about to arrive. He resigned four hours after an agreement was signed. That forced Austria's prime minister and his entire cabinet to resign. The old government imploded. A new government came in and guaranteed Creditanstalt's liabilities, all 1.2 billion schillings of them. If you were a Creditanstalt depositor (and a lot of Americans were), the Austrian government would make sure you could always withdraw your money. But that promise was not enough to create public confidence. The Austrians had just proven that in a credit collapse, even governments come and go. Not to mention government promises.

The withdrawals continued. And the new Austrian government tried mightily to make good on its word. It pumped out cash until its foreign reserves were sucked down to nothing. Then it got an extra bit of bad news. Creditanstalt had finished doing its books. Its losses were not its previously estimated 140 million schillings—no matter how massive that figure was. They were worse—1.2 billion schillings! Savers and investors yanked their money out of anything Austrian, including the schilling itself, and the Austrian currency collapsed.

It was time for more global muscle. The League of Nations—the early version of the United Nations—kicked in. It guaranteed a loan of 300 million schillings. But the League of Nations was, alas, a bureaucracy. The loan took a year to come through. The Austrians didn't have that kind of time. Nor did the world's economy. The banks in Hungary and Yugoslavia continued to quake ominously. So Germany jumped in to save the day. But the crisis sapped money so fast that Germany's equivalent of Fort Knox—its official government gold reserve—ran out of precious metal. German banks refused to pay depositors who showed up with their bankbooks and tried to take out their cash. Technically, it was called a *suspension of payments*. And suspensions of payments lead to bank runs—days when every depositor shows up before sunrise and scrambles for a place in a line that snakes around the block, a line of people hoping to withdraw what they can before the bank's last pfennig runs out. Suspensions of payments lead to panics.

In 1931 London was the banking center for the world. It held deposits from super-rich individuals and from big companies all over the globe. But the German banking cataclysm led to a run on Britain's impregnable fortresses of finance. The Brits shut down the boiler before it could explode. They froze credits. If you asked for your money, you got nothing. That amplified the panic.

Meanwhile, the Germans turned to the French and the Americans. The result? Between 1929 and 1933, two out of every five American banks collapsed—10,763 out of 24,970 banks went down. Many of those were swept away by the tidal wave that began with the dive of the Creditanstalt in Austria in 1931. There was no Internet in sight, but the financial system of the planet was already World Wide Webbed.

* * *

Only the banks of one European nation survived the Creditanstalt collapse intact. That nation was Italy. Italy was led by a fascist dictator—Benito Mussolini. And Mussolini was a master of public perception and mass emotion. He was a master of the force that turns the wheel of the business cycle. Mussolini knew the cues you have to send when times are tense. He went behind the scenes, met with his bankers in secret, and pumped cash into the Italian banks' vaults and tills. This is exactly what other government leaders had done, but there was a potent difference. Mussolini never let the trembling of his banks show. He flashed what animal behavior experts call *dominance cues*. He gave the impression that Italy's financial institutions stood strong and fearless in the storm. He worked the levers of emotion and perception. And emotion and perception are the keys to boom and crash. Emotion, perception, and the forces that shape them—the cycles of biology.

The result? If you'd just yanked your money out of a bank in Austria, Germany, England, or the United States, if you'd just pulled your savings out of a bank in a nation trembling with panic, to what nation would you send your money for safekeeping? Italy. Mussolini understood that emotion and perception are the core of economics. And he used the forces of the natural oscillators that move emotions the way the waves of the sea raise and lower a cork. Those oscillators? Cycles of exploration and digestion. Cycles of gamble and structure creation. Cycles driven by the pendulum of repurposing and the flywheel of insecurity. Cycles of creativity. Cycles that power an evolutionary search engine. Cycles that propel a secular genesis machine.

8

WHY X-RAY A BOOM?

Crash and boom are primal powers in disguise.
When you strip their mask, what do you see?

The Great Depression of 1929–1939 was not a local event. The economies of the world were Internetted and World Wide Webbed long before the introduction of computers and the invention of programmed trading. So even eighty years ago, flawed local decisions could go global. And those decisions could shape the mask with which the cycle of boom and bust hides its real face. In the late 1920s, President Calvin Coolidge was afraid of rampant inflation.[1] The US government had printed and issued paper money to make it through World War I. But Coolidge had no confidence in paper. The only real money, he felt, was gold.[2] Coolidge was determined to get us back on the gold standard. A standard that says to governments and to banks that you can only print a ten-dollar note if your vault holds ten dollars' worth of gold.

To put this conservative money strategy in place, the Coolidge economic team ratcheted up the price of credit.[3] America's Federal Reserve Bank raised the interest rate it charged for loans to American banks. Government banks—central banks—around the world followed the American example. That kind of move makes commercial banks—the banks that supply cash to big businesses and that give loans to you and me—leery about lending. When central bank interest rates go up, loans become hard to get. When businesses can't get loans to make it through their dry spells, they are sometimes forced to tighten their belts, to get "lean and mean." That can mean layoffs. In other words, a tightening of credit can put a tourniquet around your neck and mine. It can get us tossed out of our jobs.

Credit tightening can also trigger what psychologists call *emotional contagion*.[4] The contagion of what former chairman of the Federal Reserve Board Alan Greenspan famously called "irrational exuberance," contagion of the frenzy that powers a boom,[5] or the contagion of mass panic, the frenzy that triggers a bust. And these emotional contagions easily spread worldwide.

In 1928, after President Calvin Coolidge notched up the cost of American credit, the German, Brazilian, and Southeast Asian economies turned sickly.[6] They were soon joined on the sick list by a small crowd. In 1929, the economies of Poland, Argentina, and Canada caught a cold. Then came the big sneeze. In 1929, the American stock market crashed. On Black Monday and Black Tuesday, October 28 and 29, US stocks took a stomach-clenching dive.[7] They lost a quarter of their value. The plunge wiped out thirty billion dollars in value, a chunk ten times the size of the US government's budget. Wealthy investors became poor overnight. Some couldn't take it and committed suicide. Urban legend reports that in Manhattan hotels, when businessmen asked for rooms, the clerks behind the check-in desk asked, "Will that be for jumping, or will you stay overnight?" Over the next four years, America's total output of goods and services, its gross national product, fell a staggering 30.9 percent. One out of every four American breadwinners was out of work. And in one typical farm state, Mississippi, one out of every four farms was seized by banks for unpaid debt and put up for sale.[8]

But this crash was not confined to America. Emotional contagion went global. On Black Tuesday, Japan's Nikkei stock market lost 15 percent of its value, as if the Japanese were picking up the panic in New York via telepathy.[9] As things got worse, stock markets all around the world came to the brink of collapse.[10] And American banks, sliding downward rapidly, were forced to call in their loans to the banks and businesses of Europe, pulling the plug on fragile countries like Germany, which was still trying to recover from World War I.[11]

When economists tell you the story of the Great Depression, they point to America's tightened credit and to the Coolidge government's tight-money policies, then they point to what happened next. They say that one caused the other. They may be wrong. They may be suffering from what Nassim Nicholas Taleb, a Lebanese-American market trader and author of the influential book *The Black Swan*, calls the *narrative fallacy*, the notion that by telling the story of the events that happened before and after a market boom or crash you explain it.[12] Taleb feels that a more powerful pattern may underlie financial upheaval, a pattern that has very little to do with the tale of what was happening in the months and days before the market went through a mega-flip.

In fact, the tightening of credit in the late 1920s and what happened afterward may just be symptoms of a far bigger shift, a biological shift from what evolutionary biologists call one *phenotype* to another. A shift in the *wet-ware* and in the software that runs your body and your brain. A shift in your neurohormonal receptors. A bio-shift from exploration to digestion and from ebullience to fear. A backswing in the pendulum of repurposing and a forward flick from the flywheel of insecurity.

Why do we have crashes? And what can we do about them? Step one: understand them, and in the process, understand far more about who and what you and I are. Even more important, in the process of understanding booms and crashes, understand what we mean to each other. Through boom and crash we can understand what we achieve for each other. We can see how deeply we are connected to each other's hungers, insecurities, restlessness, fantasies, delights, and needs. What's more, we can see *why* we are so important to each other. We can see what our interconnections achieve. We can see the invisible amazements that you and I with our insecurities, our panic over decisions, our itch for entertainment, our need for the warmth of others, our ferocious hunger for attention, and, most important, our daily labors, bring into being. And we can understand how emotion, perception, passion, and soul are the primary forces of that seemingly soul-less machine called a capitalist economy.

We can see the workings of something we've never made out clearly before, something that has been there right in front of our eyes. We can see the operations of the ultimate breakthrough generator. We can see the clockwork of an utterly secular miracle maker. Through crash and boom, we can see how you and I are part of an evolutionary mechanism that ratchets forward relentlessly. We can see how that mechanism turns daydreams into realities, then uses these new realities to generate a quantum-shift, a radical upgrade, in the level of the next generation's fantasies. Through crash and boom we can see how you and I contribute to a system that seizes on that new level of fantasy and once again generates something from nearly nothing, a system that creates the next utter transformation of the everyday.

II

THE BIRDS AND THE BEES
OF BOOM AND CRASH

9

THE PENDULUM
OF REPURPOSING

The really big picture—the boom and crash of the cosmos.

What's *repurposing*? It's a word invented in 1984 for a radical change in the use of something. Using an unabridged dictionary as a doorstop is repurposing. Turning a fin into an arm is repurposing. Turning a water-swimming tadpole into a land-hopping frog is repurposing. Turning you from a Big Mac maker into a software engineer and me from an author into a pauper is repurposing.

One secret to booms and crashes is the *pendulum* of repurposing. It's an ancient oscillation between mania and depression, exploration and digestion, expansion and consolidation, explosion and contraction, proliferation and pruning, binge and purge, gluttony and self-denial, confidence and fear, individualism and centralization, and between invention and selection. Like the hands of a clock, the pendulum of repurposing drives something crucial in just one direction—forward. Its pulse powers our entire cosmos. The pendulum of repurposing drives our universe through the generation of astonishments, new things and new processes that no swatch of time or space has previously seen. The pendulum of repurposing powers an evolutionary mechanism that feels out the invisible possibilities of the future and turns the present into something new. It drives a secular genesis machine.

When did the pendulum of repurposing begin to swing? It showed up in rough form long before the birth of life. It showed up in the transformation of space and time into matter in the first microflick of the big bang 13.73 billion years ago. It showed up in the cyclical oscillation of photons, particles of light that flip back and forth from expansion to contraction at maniacal speed. But the real story begins 5 billion to 6 billion years ago, when a small herd of midsized stars entered their old age, grew dim and red, then exploded.[1] They left a vast spread of gas, gravel, and meteors, a confused clutter of garbage, a mob of pellets, a 27,000,000,000,000-mile-wide spray of mountains tumbling end over end, a cloud of dust, rock, and water.[2] But this outspread mist of matter was flipped from one phase to another—from expansion to contraction and back again—by the pendulum of repurposing. The vast scatter was seized by the itch to consolidate. The stones and the icy chunks were independent entities, yet they whispered to each other with a force called gravity. And that seductive social force—gravity—impelled them to forego their outstretch and to consolidate. To come together in a central mass. To squeeze together in a ball so enormous that it crushed the atoms of the matter it swallowed, ignited their atomic forces, and forced them to scream out photons and gleam with light. One of those flaming balls, those raging central cores of nuclear energy, was our sun. Rocks and dust had been repurposed—they had become the inferno at the heart of a star. The solar system had flipped from expansion to consolidation and from outstretch to structure formation.

Surrounding the sun was a ring of stray stones and snowballs that had escaped the great consolidation. But that disk of independent rocks and slush balls was hit by another wave of the great consolidating force, gravity. It clumped into a blob that gained in size. And every time the lumpy sphere fattened, it upped its gravitational power to kidnap, incorporate, and seduce. The result was a massive globe of matter—our planet, the Earth. Another secular act of creation, another material miracle of genesis, brought to you by the pendulum of repurposing.

Gravity clenched vast scatters of space garbage together in seven other balls big enough to be called planets. And gravity squeezed together a few other megahunks close to planetary size—planetesimals and planetoids. Cycles of expansion and consolidation, scatter and structure formation, and explosion and gravitational pull had formed something new—our solar system. These cycles rolled to the beat of the pendulum of repurposing.

On the surface of this third rock from the sun came yet another wave of expansion, consolidation, and structure formation. Dead atoms clumped and clustered in strange new ways, making molecules of a size that would have seemed awesome if you and I had been alive and shrunk down to the size of an electron to see them form. These new atom teams were the nano-equivalent of pyramids and sky-scrapers. They snaked together in ropelike twists and bends. The most aggressive of these megamolecular cables were a staggering 240,243,785 atoms in size.[3] And like the molecules and balls of rock that had clustered in suns and planets, these molecules consolidated. They came together in societies. They intertwined in teams.

Some formed another gift of consolidation and of social organi-zation—fatty envelopes enclosing micropools of water. Those envelopes were formed by quintillions of atoms weaving themselves together in waterproof, waxy membranes that formed the walls of tiny bubbles, tiny spheres. These oilcloth mini water bags were the ancestors of your cell membranes and mine. At this minute, the descendants of these cell walls give solidity to your hands, your skin, and even the eyes with which you are reading this word.

Inside the protective walls of these watery pouches other mega-molecules, other mega-atom teams, consolidated. And these massive molecules had bizarre new properties. They were molecular factories, assembly plants that did not wait for transport deliveries but enticed their raw materials into coming hither and delivering themselves. The ropelike exteriors of these construction plants were like the arrays of LED advertising displays in Times Square or Tokyo's Ginza district. They had the ability to dazzle other passing atoms. What's more, the megamolecular factories could twist and shout.[4] They could practi-cally turn some parts of themselves inside out.[5] They could reveal millions of empty atom shells calling for connection and they could hide millions of others in their interior. This gave them an electro-magnetic, digital vocabulary. A language of attraction and repulsion cues. With this push-pull vocabulary, these knotty fibers of one hundred thousand to more than one hundred million atoms could persuasively flash vast advertising scripts.

The electromagnetic allure of these megamolecules had the power to inveigle, lure, bait, and persuade stray atoms and smaller molecules. But they used that power to give themselves a very special ability—the capacity to make copies of themselves. These vain and egotistical molecules fathered, mothered, and constructed spitting images in their own likeness, images able to go out and make new copies of their parents. What's more, these ropelike makers of form, these ace consolidators, these ace inveiglers, were the ancestors of your gene team. They were the foremothers of your DNA. They were the inventors of the sort of megamolecular, spiral-twisting strings that make you you. Your collection of their megamolecular great, great grandchildren 3.85 billion years down the line are still seducing and recruiting, still flashing their electrochemical scripts and using them to entice atoms and smaller molecules into their schemes. They're your attention-glomming ropes of 24,000 genes.[6] Braided together, they go under the formal name of a *genome*. These massive gene teams—your genomes—command every one of your hundred trillion cells. And they are masters of repurposing.

Where's the cycle of boom and crash in this story? Where's the cycle of spread and clench, mania and depression, exploration and digestion, scatter and structure making? Where's the evolutionary search engine and the secular genesis machine? And where's the pendulum of repurposing? All over the place. From a dispersed mass of gas, there slowly formed billions of galaxies. Consolidation! Within those galaxies formed billions of stars. Structure making and repurposing! The life of a star is a pendulum swing, a pulsation of megaforce structure building. Megaforce creativity. A first-generation star has only three kinds of atoms to chew on—hydrogen, helium, and lithium. But that star is an innovator. It's a new atom maker. It crushes the virgin atoms of hydrogen, helium, and lithium in its heart. And it fuses the nuclei of those simple atoms into astonishing new collusions, making teams and particle societies of a kind this cosmos has never seen. A compressing, condensing, and digesting star creates bizarre new atoms like iron, carbon, and oxygen. That's the star's period of boom. But a living star is an evolutionary search engine, a genesis maker, a transcendence engine, a breakthrough machine, spewing forth light and forms of matter. It moves from boom to bust, from expansion to consolidation and back to expansion once again. The death of a star is a crash of catastrophic proportions. So is the expansion—the explosion—that spreads the crumbs of that crash through space. Then comes the next clench, the consolidation that makes the next star. A more advanced star. A star built on the foundation of its forerunner's legacy. A star shot through with the newest elements—iron, carbon, and oxygen—elements the previous star left in its wake. That's repurposing. New atoms, new stars, and new solar systems are all built by boom and crash. And new stars will someday die, explode, and spread again. Their transformations and radical upgrades come to us courtesy of the pendulum of repurposing.

But the birth of our star—the sun—and its planets is not the real story. It's a mere prelude. A prelude with a basic pattern that will continue to ebb and flow in whole new ways once macromolecules of astonishing size and complexity give birth to life.

* * *

The most amazing story of boom and crash, the most amazing tale of the cycle of repurposing, begins a mere 400 million years after our new sun and our planet pulled themselves together and began to explore their possibilities.[7] It begins when the vain and egotistical molecular ropes that could make others in their own image pulled another impossible act of consolidation and creation—making the first life-forms, the real Adams and Eves. Actually, just the first Eves—males hadn't been invented yet. These first feminine cells were our foremothers. Yes, the ancestors of all man and womankind were single-celled organisms huddled together in huge communities. And they were female. They were bacteria. Germs, bacteria, were the founding ancestors of our family tree. They were the kick-starters of our genealogy.

These bacteria were ferociously imperialistic, colonialistic, and entrepreneurial. They had to be. They were up against a deadline. There have been 142 mass extinctions on this planet. Mass extinctions caused by our planet's passage through dust, spiral arms of the galaxy, and cosmic rays in our solar system's 235,000,000-mile voyage around the black hole at our galaxy's heart.[8] (Yes, Virginia, nearly every galaxy has a black hole at its core.)

The mandate of bacteria was to explore, expand, and invent. To find as many niches as possible before the next planetary crisis. To find enough new forms so that if ninety-seven species were wiped out, three would remain to continue the grand enterprise of life. To achieve this, bacteria had to seduce, kidnap, and recruit as many inanimate atoms as possible and harness them in a project that would transform nature and would change the universe—the project of greening a barren rock swinging around the waist of a midlevel sun, the project of biomass, the start-up and the odyssey of life.

10

IS THE BUSINESS CYCLE
IN YOUR DNA?

Why bankers are like bacteria.

What causes boom and bust? Does economic catastrophe come from money, capitalism, speculators, overpaid CEOs, and greed? Does it come from conspiracies of illuminati and of power-grabbing families? Does it happen because of mistakes at banks like Creditanstalt? Does it ooze from the wreckage of wrongheaded fiscal policies like those of Calvin Coolidge? More than three billion years ago, bacteria already had a cycle of boom and bust built into their DNA. They were driven by the pendulum of repurposing.

Bacteria, like you and me, are astonishingly social. They cannot live alone. Take one bacterium away from its neighbors, away from its colony, put it in a Petri dish, and what will it do? If there's food, it will divide seventy-two times a day. It will multiply, surrounding itself with 144 daughters every twenty-four hours. Each of those daughters, in turn, will divide seventy-two times a day and surround herself—and her founding foremother, the first lonely bacterium—with progeny. If the bacterial colony could find all the food and housing it needs, that one lonely mother in theory could have 5.2×10^{151} kids, grandkids, and great-grandkids in a week. That's ten with one hundred and fifty-one zeros, more than all the atoms in over a million universes. At least that's what bacteria could do in theory. In fact, within a week your one solitary bacterium will have surrounded herself with something much smaller but stunning in its intricacy—a megalopolis, an entire colony.

A colony of bacteria is not a dumb or primitive crowd. It is one of the biggest and most complex societies this planet has ever seen. A single bacterial colony the size of your palm is so thin that you can't see it with your naked eye. Yet it contains seven trillion individuals— seven trillion citizens—more than all the human beings this planet has ever seen. All working in concert. All pooling their talents and their data. All communicating with a chemical vocabulary. And all working to solve the problems of the minute and the puzzles of the day. Working together to find new food. Working together to invent new ways to turn garbage into gourmet delicacies, wastelands into succulent buffets, tragedy into opportunity, to outrace and to outpace their rivals, and to win when competition turns into war. That's why bacterial metropolises are discovery machines and breakthrough generators. That's why they were the first life-forms to experience boom and bust.

The first bacteria followed the mandate of nature. They helped each other reinvent themselves. They helped each other discover their possibilities. They helped each other pull together a clutter of antique atoms in whole new ways. They helped each other advance the enterprise of secular creation and the operation of the evolutionary search engine. They helped each other advance the family of cells and DNA.

A bacterial colony is a search machine and a research and development team. It has to be. Put yourself in a bacterium's place. Today's food will soon run out. You and I will eat it down to the last drop and crumb. Tomorrow we will need new groceries. Tomorrow our colony will need its equivalent of new potatoes and meat. Imagine that you and I are the bacteria called *Caulobacter crescentus*.[1] We live in an immense puddle of fresh water, a lake far from the sea.[2] We are big eaters. We are sweet-tooth dessert devourers. We go for junk food— sugars—xylose, lactose, and galactose, high-energy treats. We have four big jobs in life—eating, multiplying, finding new food and housing, and communicating our experiences, especially our extreme experiences, our life and death experiences and our lottery-winning experiences. Oh, and we occasionally innovate.

How can we find new food before hunger kills you, me, and our community? Boom and bust. The cycle of repurposing. You and I are comfortable adults. We look like translucent string beans with, conveniently enough, a long string attached. That string is a thin, flexible tube like a soda straw that rivets us to our food. And I do mean rivet. Our straw is called a "stalk" because it looks like the stalk of a tulip. At the end of our stalks is a superglue so powerful that someday humans will be tempted to imitate its properties. And we're up against a problem. Soon we will slurp up every tasty molecule in the bit of lake bed we've sucked up to. What will save us? Boom and bust. The pendulum of repurposing. And the way boom and bust reshapes our kids. Our children can be born as Cain or Abel, as hunters or settlers, as explorers or homesteaders. Yes, like you and me, our kids will look superficially like translucent string beans with long threads. But in reality they will be born in two different forms—as spreaders or consolidators. As rebels or conservatives. As searchers or structure makers.

We old-timers are built to stay in one spot and glom up the goodies. We are built for boom. We do very poorly when the food supply goes bust. But some of our kids are natural-born bust escapers. They are born to be dissatisfied, born to say good-bye to our sedentary lifestyle and to our parcel of tasty property. Their "strings" are shaped for a restless quest. They are born to seek their fortune. How do we know their goals? Their "purpose in life" shows up in their physiology. Where you and I have stalks, our kids have propellers. They have whips—flagella—twirled by molecular rotary motors. With those high-speed rotors the young shoot and scoot. We old-timers are built to hang on tight, but our kids are built to swim through the waters and hunt new food and territory. They are built to explore.

No bacterium explores the landscape on her own. It takes a group of roughly ten thousand to cut a path across the lake bed that hides new food. So from the dot of a colony that you and I have founded, our daughters swim outward in armies, forming circles around us like the bands of a target surrounding the bull's eye. Those bands travel in deprivation and poverty. They forgo the luxury of reproducing and of normal comforts.[3] When they find food, they settle down. And when they settle, they throw away childish things. They throw away their flagellar propellers and put down roots.[4] They develop stalks and root themselves to the food bed of their new territory, their new home, just like you and I did once upon a time. Then they reproduce. Some of their kids are born as restless rebels, curious discoverers who will spread outward even more. In the process, the armies of impatient youth, the masses of restless seekers, grow our colony. They grow it massively.

Cycles of boom and bust, cycles of repurposing began with the cycles of a bacterial economy. An economic cycle was built into your foremothers' biology. Is that cycle built into you and me?

* * *

What flicked the timer of the bacteria's economic cycle—the timer of the bacteria's equivalent to a business cycle? Was boom and bust triggered by real-world scarcity? Was crash triggered by greed and mistaken policy? No. Even when the food supply is terrific, *Caulobacter* go through the equivalent of an utter loss of confidence in the riches they have known and a need to strike out, to explore, then to consolidate once again in a new home. *Caulobacter* bacteria cycle even when the underlying basics of their economy remain strong. They behave like you and I do when we've eaten too much of a rich dessert and have grown sick of it. Their perception shifts dramatically. Even if the food supply is bulging, the bacteria with travel-whips lose their taste for the sweets under their noses and are driven to find something new.

The story of the *Caulobacter crescentus*'s twitch from boom to bust and back to boom again is a tale of *two* timers. In *Caulobacter*, sometimes the cycle of boom and bust is switched from high-risk exploration to digestion, from spread to clench, and from the equivalent of irrational exuberance to panic by *internal* timers. Sometimes it's switched by the *outside* prod of bounty or scarcity. Both time clocks—the internal and the external—seem able to trigger the twitch from rise to fall and back again. Your sleep cycle is like this bacterial tale of two clocks. Sleep is a product of two timers. One of your sleep timers is tuned to the outside world. It switches as the sun sinks and as the world around you darkens from day to night. Another of your timers is totally internal. It can put you to sleep at three o'clock on a Sunday afternoon when the sun is bright as can be.

Caulobacter have an internal timer that drives them to switch from stalks to propellers and back again. And they apparently have an outside timer, the timer of feast and famine. Those two timers are apparently often out of synch. What happens when two timers drive a cycle? When two timers make waves? When two timers raise peaks and troughs in *Caulobacter* or in you and me? Two waves overlapping make an interference pattern. At some points where they meet the two waves add to each other's strengths and pile up their powers, making peaks. At other points, they cancel each other out and create peculiarly positioned valleys. Overlaid cycles—overlaid waves—can make things look random and chaotic.[5] But under the mask of randomness, two very simple time clocks are at work.

The irregularity of two overlapping cycles may explain the seeming unpredictability of boom and crash. The spikes and troughs of the two timers may help explain why the Kondratiev wave theory of boom and crash, the hypothesis that technology-waves bring big swings in the financial cycle, is only sometimes right. Thanks to internal timers, our biological clock can flick us into panic even when a new technology has many decades to go before it peaks.

If a cycle we've inherited from our bacterial ancestors is, indeed, alive in us today, what does that mean for the boom and bust of 2008 and for the bubbles and busts yet to come? How does it help us understand past cycles—the Tulipmania Crash of 1637,[6] the South Sea Bubble and Mississippi bubbles of 1720, the panic of 1797, the depression of 1807, the panic of 1819, the panic of 1837, the panic of 1857, the Great Depression of 1870,[7] the panic of 1873, the panic of 1893, the panic of 1907, and the Great Depression of 1929–1939? What does it mean for the changing global economy of today? Does the wrongheaded fiscal policy of a president like Calvin Coolidge really set off a global crash? Do NINJA loans really cause a worldwide economic collapse? Or does the cycle of boom and bust happen for reasons radically different than the ones economists conceive? And if something more basic is at work, what does that mean to you and me?

* * *

Boom and bust is not unique to capitalist economies, industrialized societies, or even to creatures who meet, greet, trade, and gamble with money. The cycle of boom and bust is shot through all of life, from the most primitive level to the most complex. Population boom and bust appear in protozoa, mollusks, amphibians, reptiles, insects, fish, and mammals.[8] Red grouse in England go through a four-to-eight-year cycle of boom and crash. Parasites called *Trichostrongylus tenuis* that feed on the red grouse go through crashes and booms as their meal supply of grouse increases in numbers then declines.[9] Snowshoe rabbits in Canada go through a ten-year cycle of population expansion and contraction. So do the lynx that feed on the snowshoe rabbit. Other animals that endure booms and crashes include Darwin's finches in the Galapagos Islands, reindeer on islands in the Bering Sea, lemmings in the Arctic, and hives of honeybees. The snowshoe rabbit and its predator, the lynx, go through a ten-year boom and bust cycle. The vole, a mouselike rodent of Finland, tunnels through a three-year cycle. The lemming of the Arctic goes through a four-year cycle of boom and crash, as does the animal that feeds on it, the short-tail weasel. And the side-blotched lizard of Santa Cruz, California, goes through a two-year cycle of good times and bad.

Boom, bust, and the pendulum of repurposing show up in an even stranger biological workplace—in you and me. They make you and me who we are today. Right now boom, bust, and the pendulum of repurposing are making us who we'll be tomorrow. Let's go backward in time to your very early days in your mother's womb, sixteen days after a sperm and egg first joined up to embark on the huge collaborative project called you. As a sixteen-day-old embryo, you were smaller than a period on this page, 0.44 millimeters, less than a fiftieth of an inch.[10] So was I. Despite your minuscule size, you were a tiny handbag of cells with an interior lining. And you were already being shaped by the pendulum of repurposing and by the cycle of exploration and consolidation—by the cyclical strategies of the evolutionary search engine.

Some of your cells itched to achieve more than the mere shape of a purse. They ached to become your nervous system, your skull, and your face.[11] That group of cells with high ambitions was located in a thin groove on the top of the bag that was you, a groove where the opening of a closed handbag is usually found. That groove is called the *neural crest*. How did the ballsy cells of that neural crest strive to achieve their goals? They divided and gave birth to exploratory armies, then they sent those soaring squadrons of cells out to explore on their own. Like the *Caulobacter* bacteria with tails, these search parties migrated away from the home of their birth to spots in the growing embryo of you, spots that were brand new. If they traveled to a destination where they were needed and found a hookup that seemed enthusiastic about their arrival, they stayed and became nerves. If they found no welcome, they were pared away. Ruthlessly. They were forced to literally kill themselves off. They were forced to use a molecular self-destruct mechanism called *apoptosis*, one of the most intensely studied biological phenomena of the late twentieth century. Apoptosis is otherwise known as preprogrammed cell death. It's a molecular kit for cellular suicide. And nearly every cell is born with it, including the cells with which I'm writing these words and the cells with which you're reading them.

Back to the embryo. New hordes of exploratory neural cell wannabes continued to set off on journeys through the developing you for months after your sixteenth day. If they received enthusiastic signals from the cells of their destination, they took root in the new territory. And they destroyed themselves if they'd ended up in a spot that didn't need them. That's the cycle of exploration and consolidation. That's the cycle of speculation and structure-making. That's the pendulum of repurposing. And that's the cycle at the heart of boom and crash.

11

THE SECRET OF
YOUR INNER FISH[1]

The tale of the adventurous cells and the mystery of
your mood swings.

Thanks to the pendulum of repurposing, you changed mightily in
your early days in the womb. You were repurposed over and over
again. According to the nineteenth- and early twentieth-century
German biologist and philosopher Ernst Haeckel, you went through
a series of radical transmogrifications, fast-forwarding through the
3.85-billion-year evolutionary history that shaped you.[2] First you
looked like a fish, then a salamander, a tortoise, a chick, a hog, a calf,
a rabbit, and finally, a human being. Or, to put it in the words Haeckel
handed down to us, "Ontogeny recapitulates phylogeny."[3]

Developmental biologists—unknowingly following the cyclic
rules of the evolutionary search engine—have scrapped and squabbled
about how precisely you resembled a rabbit, a calf, a chick, and the
rest of Haeckel's barnyard beasts when you were growing from the
size of a comma to the bulk of a football. In the last 120 years,
Haeckel's concept has gone from boom to bust and is ripe to swing
back to boom again.[4] But the fact remains that you and I once had
what looked like gills and tails. Our hands and feet were webbed. The
pendulum of repurposing carried us from one stage to the next,
sending out the cells that formed gill pouches and gill-like slits, then

prodding those cells that didn't fit the next stage to commit suicide and to make room for the next batch of cellular adventurers, entrepreneurial settlers who would turn one gill bar into your lower jaw, another into your ear, then would close the gill slits so that you'd no longer look fishy when you emerged from the womb and first looked your mother in the eye.

Eyes, too, were built using the pattern of exploration and consolidation, the pattern of high-risk speculation and structure making. Eyes were fashioned by the pendulum of repurposing. Out of every hundred cells that set out to become the interior of your eyeball, eighty were pared away and died. Only those that managed to hit precisely the right target remained.[5] The cells that made the mistake of migrating eagerly to become your tail or to find employment as tissue in the webs between your fingers were ruthlessly pared away. All were given the signal to kill themselves off in the name of making you into a human being. This is the pendulum of repurposing asserting itself in a major way. Like *Caulobacter* bacteria, the cells constructing you once set out to explore a new frontier. They were high-risk gamblers and speculators. They were probes into the unknown. Then they changed from explorers to homesteaders and settled down to munch the nutrients and to process the communicative chemicals they found. This is the pendulum of repurposing. This is the cycle of expansion and consolidation. This is the cycle of exploration and structure building, of search, sort, and boil down. This is the evolutionary search engine imposing its wheel-like strategy.

Expansion and consolidation power more than a bacterial colony and a developing embryo. They drive the cycle of boom and bust. They power the phases of a gestating, metamorphosing, changing, and growing economy.

First new companies, new entrepreneurs, new financiers, new speculators, and new nonprofit organizations multiply. They set out to explore the unknown of a new generation's opportunities. They set out to probe the possibilities opened by new lands, new technologies, new habits, new concepts, and new forms of society. These searchers, these antennae of society, overshoot their target. When the bust comes, some of the new endeavors prove vital. Some do not. Those that do not have three choices:

1. They can be absorbed by existing organizations, the big ones, organizations that have been through this pruning before and have survived. Wal-Mart, Exxon Mobil, Goldman Sachs, Google, Microsoft, or General Electric, for example.
2. They can scrimp, save, and live off their reserves and new financing.
3. Or the new enterprises can die.

Meanwhile, crash brings new central forms of organization, new controlling organizations, and new government organizations to life. Then the cycle goes back from bust to boom, and the next generation of entrepreneurial organizations and speculators sets off to test the power of its dreams.

You and I are cells in this enterprise. We tend to ride high during the boom. Then crash arrives and we discover that we're expendable. If we lose our jobs and are out of work for a long, long time, it softens us up. For what? For repurposing. For a new role when the next boom arrives.

12

BIONOMICS

Is Crash and Boom *in* Your Fingertips?

What do slime mold and your credit card have in common?

Bionomics is a word first used in the 1880s by insect specialists. It focused on ecology—the study of the relationships of a blister beetle, a mosquito, or a whitefly to its environment.[1] In 1990 Michael L. Rothschild, a Harvard graduate with degrees in law and business, used the term differently. In his *Bionomics: Economy as Ecosystem*, he proposed that biological models could revolutionize our understanding of economies.[2] Rothschild established the Bionomics Institute. Then the Russians took up the cause and founded the International Bionomics Institute to drive home the notion that "Bionomics is [the] economics of the Third Millennium."[3] In 2005 the head of the Russian Bionomic Institute, Igor Flor, took things a step further. He wrote his own Russian language take on bionomics, *Bionomics: Analysis Based on Bioeconomic Analogies*, a book complete with sections on "anatomy (structure), physiology (metabolism), psychology (behaviour), [and] evolution (natural selection)."[4] Were Rothschild and Flor on to something?

Every one of your cells has a skeleton, a rigging of tubules like the steel framework that holds up the walls, the floors, the ceilings, and the elevator shafts of an office building. How does that cellular skeleton come to be? The cell uses the biological mother of boom and crash. It uses the cycle of search, then consolidate. It uses the cycle of explore, then digest. It uses the cycle of speculate, then make structure. It uses the cycle of the evolutionary search engine.

First, a hub called a *centriole* sends out tentative shoots in random directions, thin tubes made of a temporary material called *tubulin*. If the tubes find their way to another cellular structure—to an energy-producing mitochondria, to the sorting-and-transporting endoplasmic reticulum,[5] to the membrane that holds the cell together like a balloon filled with water, or to the nucleus at the cell's center[6]—in other words, if the tubes find a destination that needs them—they're rewarded with a jolt of a chemical that toughens them up and makes them permanent. If they don't find a welcoming junction point, the pipes of tubulin dissolve and fade away. That's the cycle of exploration and consolidation, of high-risk speculation and structure building. That's the mother of boom and crash. That's the pendulum of repurposing.

Here's another pattern of bio-boom and crash that comes to us courtesy of the evolutionary search engine and the pendulum of repurposing. A slime mold—a *Dictyostelium discoideum*—is a bacterial spore that lands on a wet spot in a forest or a meadow—such as a puddle in a pile of leaves. If that wet slick is rich in the stuff that a slime mold likes to eat—bacteria, fungi, and the micro-bits of chaff and dandruff that plants shed—the spore explodes into a mob of one hundred thousand individualists eager to gamble their lives on an exploratory journey.[7] These liberty-loving pioneers are single-celled animals, amoebas. Each one shoots out from its birth spot raring to search the puddle's outskirts and to feast. None of the tens of thousands of amoebas sent out by the initial spore seems to sense that it has any purpose on this planet except self-indulgence and the good life. This is boom. Then a strange thing happens. The hundred thousand freewheeling bacteria begin to run out of food.[8] First one sends out a chemical distress signal—a broadcast of an alarm molecule called cyclic AMP. The hungry amoeba's report of danger is ignored. Then a few more run out of food and send out their reports of trouble. They, too, broadcast cyclic AMP. Soon the number of trouble chorusers grows too insistent to ignore. This is bust.

How does the slime mold respond? The bacterial freedom lovers go through a radical mass mood swing. They no longer feel like eating, drinking, and being merry. They no longer exult in the freedom to wander and to explore on their own. Instead, they panic and rush back to the center from which they all sprang. Then they cluster together and take their places in what looks like a slimy slug, a naked snail with a long neck that pokes up like the neck of a giraffe. Many die on behalf of this collective enterprise. They kill themselves off so their bodies can be used to toughen the underside of the slug, the belly on which the group emergency rescue project crawls. Others kill themselves off so they can offer up their corpses to toughen the neck that lifts the slug's head to the skies. The self-sacrificers' goal is to save the colony's genes. To save—and spread—the colony's precious seed. So the slug switches from consolidate back to explore. It manufactures spores like the spores that gave it its first burst of life. And it sends those spores into the breeze as high-risk gambles, as speculative investments in the future. Those spores spread randomly, carried by the wind. Some land in dry spots and never return to life. Others land in wet spots on leaves or branches and explode with energy. They are fruitful and multiply. The result is a mob of individualistic discoverers once again on a rampage to explore. This, too, is the cycle of expand, then consolidate. The cycle of discover, then digest. The cycle of mass mania and depression. The cycle of speculate, then structure-make. This, too, is the cyclic strategy of the evolutionary search engine. This, too, is the mother of boom and bust. This, too, is the pendulum of repurposing.

Here's another example of biological boom and bust. Two adolescent mice—a male and a female—find their way to a silo that their tribe has not yet occupied. The harvest has just ended, and the massive storage cylinder is filled with grain. The mice eat, drink, and are merry, indulging their sexual appetites. The result is ten mouse pups at a time—over five hundred in a lifetime.[9] Each of the pups who survives will explore the silo in a few weeks when he or she is grown. Each of these explorers who survives will mate and help bring her own five hundred pups into the world. Like the slime mold amoeba, the new mice will spread out, probe the silo's spaces, and provide antennae for the group, new probes for the mouse genome, discovering new pockets of food and new places in which to make a home. This is boom. One mouse, her children, and her grandchildren can produce three thousand probes into the unknown of the storage cylinder. Add in great-great and great-great-great-grand-pups, and the arithmetic is beyond me. These are the generations of explorers. Then the pendulum will swing in the opposite direction. The mice will generate so many offspring that they'll hit the carrying capacity of the silo—the limits of space, food, and the patience of the silo's owner. In fact, it's likely the mice will discover those limits by overshooting them. This is bust.

How will the mice respond? They'll give out their own equivalent to the slime mold amoeba's alarm chemical. A shrill sound so high in pitch that we humans can't hear it.[10] Or a molecule other mice can smell—a pheromone.[11] Both the community of mice in the silo and the individual mice will go through a mood swing, a phase change. They will go through a panic. They will move from the raucous eat, drink, and be merry approach to one of self-denial. They will move from what population biologists call R (think reproductive) to K (think conservative). That is the cycle of explore and consolidate. That is mass mania and depression. That is rodent boom and bust. That, too, is the pendulum of repurposing.

The pendulum of repurposing is a driver of an evolutionary search strategy. It's an algorithm in nature's bio-Googling. It's the timer of a landscape-and-opportunity exploration approach called the *fission-fusion strategy*, a strategy named by human observers of baboons and chimpanzees in the wild.[12] What's a *fission-fusion search strategy*? Fission-fusion strategies are the ways in which nature, animals, and humans explore and consolidate information. Fission-fusion strategies are simple. Fission means splitting apart. Fusion means coming together. The underlying rule of the fission-fusion strategy is spread apart then come back together again. Reach out, explore, then come back home and compare notes. Taste the new, then digest, and consolidate.

The chimp fission-fusion search strategy shows itself every day. Chimps spread out after sunrise to check the trees in the neighborhood for new fruit and to comb the undergrowth for plants that may be new.[13] They spread out to look for food.[14] Then the chimps come together again during the day to socialize and at nighttime to build their sleeping nests and to get some rest.[15] The females are stingy and keep their discoveries of tasty plants to themselves. But the males share information about food.

Nature uses the fission-fusion search strategy, the strategy of explore, then consolidates it in far more than chimps, mice, and your cytoskeleton. She uses it, for example, in your visual system to help you see. Look at the wall across from you. Seems pretty solid, doesn't it? And it looks like you've got it firmly in your sights. But your sights are much more wobbly than they seem. In fact your eye flicks back and forth over the wall roughly seventy times a minute. Your eye darts from side to side a hundred thousand times a day.[16] Why? Because of a search strategy. Your eye is always scanning, scouting, and probing, always exploring, always overshooting, always testing to see if there's something unexpected, something new. The consolidation that makes both the wall and your view of it seem so solid merges data from more than five visual processing centers in your brain.[17] The image you see is a unity made from the input of a scatter of probes and processors. That's the strategy of explore and consolidate, of speculate then structure-make. That's the fission-fusion strategy.

The clam is a solitary individual rooted in place. It has what's sometimes referred to as a foot. But it's really a clump of muscle that's more like a big tongue. The clam can poke that parcel of tissue out of her shell, and if she's lucky she can move herself a few feet a day across the sea floor.[18] A total of a few hundred yards in a lifetime.[19] But everything changes when it comes time for sex. The clam does what the *Caulobacter* bacteria do. She uses the fission-fusion strategy. And the pendulum of repurposing. Her genes change the form of body they generate. The clam sends out tiny travelers, larvae,[20] that are built to race and glide.[21] These young clams come complete with propulsive whips similar to those of the *Caulobacter*. Why? So the traveling clams can search for new food and a new home. So these speedy youngsters can find a rich new place in which to extrude a shell and go from explore to homesteading mode. That's the fission-fusion strategy. That's the search strategy that underlies the cycle of speculate and consolidate. That's the search strategy that underlies the pattern of boom and crash. And that's the search strategy at the heart of the genius of the beast.

13

THE TALE OF THE
JOBLESS BEES

You're not the only one who gets depressed.

Does the pendulum of repurposing drive your emotions? Does the fission-fusion search strategy explain your depression if you're laid off and your elation if your savings triple in value during a bubble? Do your depression and elation and mine help drive the massive search-and-breakthrough engine of society? For answers, let's visit the bees.

The search strategies of bees are a matter of life and death. So are the bees' cycles of explore and digest, of gamble and structure-creation. Bees generate what Cornell University honeybee researcher Thomas D. Seeley calls the "Wisdom of the Hive,"[1] a "colony of mind" and a "thinking machine."[2] They form a collective intelligence with a job to do—to find the exit doors before the next disaster. To explore their way beyond the range of the next catastrophe.

On a good day in May or June, in the fields of Ithaca, New York, near Cornell University, honeybees (*Apis mellifera*) find a plethora of flower patches—a banquet of potential sources of food. They have to make a collective decision about which food sources are worth the investment of hundreds of thousands of bee-hours[3] and millions of cumulative miles of bee travel.[4] These calculations have to be on target. Why? Bees are up against a deadline. And that deadline is a matter of life and death. If the bee society doesn't gather the raw materials for a stockpile of twenty kilograms (forty-four pounds) of honey by the end of the pollen season,[5] the bees won't have enough food to make it through the winter. The entire bee colony will die in the cold, dark months of January, February, or March. And the season for gathering is brutally short—ten weeks!

What's more, the food supply is so unreliable that even in the best of times—the lush months of spring, for example—a colony can be smacked by famine. Cornell University bee researcher Thomas Seeley weighed an entire bee colony day after day for three years. In mid-May of 1986 the dandelions were in bloom and the colony made out like a bandit. The bees bathed in the bliss of boom. But by the end of May, the dandelion bonanza was over. The result was starvation. Crash. The colony lost half a kilogram—over a pound—a day. For a colony whose twenty thousand bees tip the scale at a mere four pounds, a loss of a pound a day in stored food is staggering. It's the equivalent of a 160-pound human losing 40 pounds in twenty-four hours.

Then, in June, the black locust trees bloomed. Wham. Suddenly the colony was rich again. It went from bust back to boom. The result? The colony gained up to three times its bee weight—13 pounds—a day!

How do bees make it through boom and bust, through flower shortages and blossom bonanzas? How do they beat their deadline for honey making? How do they pull off the high-IQ mass deliberations it takes to win in the brutal game of life? The answer? They use the most fundamental search party strategy of the cosmos. Boom and bust. Exuberant optimism and panicked conservatism. Speculation and consolidation. Exploration and digestion. Emerge and purge. Search, sort, and boil down. They use the basic pattern that moves even photons—spread then crunch, then spread again. Oscillate. Cycle. They follow the search strategy of your eye when it flicks back and forth seventy times a minute,[6] overshooting on either side to see what you might be missing. The bees use the trick of stretching out, then gathering together and sifting through what they've found. They use the fundamental algorithm of the evolutionary search engine. They use the fission-fusion strategy.

How do bees pull this off? Brace yourself. They do it by using an insect equivalent of pop culture. They do it by using entertainment as an information transmission device. Yes, entertainment—something many of us think is useless—is a key tool for collective information processing among bees.

Entertainment? An animal equivalent to pop culture? And this supposed insect diversion acts as the informational drive train of the beehive's collective mind, as a power train of its group IQ? Surely that's an absurd anthropomorphism. Or is it? You be the judge.

14

BREAKDANCING
WITH ALL SIX FEET

How "mindless" entertainment boosts a hive's IQ.

Just like you and me, bees need attention to keep their spirits high. And just like you and me, bees need a sense of direction, a mission in life. In fact, the two—a sense of direction and the attention of others—are tightly linked. Both are crucial to apian search strategies.

Imagine that you are a forager bee. First off, you're a female. All the working bees in a hive are females—whether they're explorers, foragers, or maintenance workers. Males sit around and do nothing. Their laziness has gotten them a bad name—*drones*. But back to you, the forager. You've just flown out to a patch of linden flowers and have returned with your hip pouches filled with bright yellow, red, brown, or blue balls of pollen.[1] You get your attention—or fail to get it—just inside the entrance of the hive, a territory that serves as an unloading dock. On that dock are unloader bees, bees that grab incoming cargo from you and your fellow foragers and shuttle it into the catacombs of the hive. The unloader bees that greet you (or ignore you) know the needs deep inside the interior. They know the gut-level hungers of the colony. They know when the hive has more pollen than it can process but needs more nectar, or when it has its fill of nectar and needs to switch back to pollen harvesting.[2]

On hot days, if the temperature inside the hive shoots too high, the larvae, the young still in their eggs, will die. And the wax of the honeycombs is in danger of melting down utterly. The bees working inside the hive have to go into emergency mode, slapping water on the wax walls of the hexagonal cells inside to air-condition the place. But that takes a big water supply. So on a hot day when you, a humble forager bee, arrive with your honey sack filled with water,[3] the unloaders rush over like groupies and crowd around you, eagerly drinking in your cargo. They stroke you eagerly with their antennae and treat you like a superstar. The result? You feel great. You fly out with enormous energy to bring back more water.

But when evening comes and the hive cools down, if you show up with water you're wasting your time. The air-conditioning emergency is over. The hive needs pollen or nectar again. If you show up with a load of H_2O, the unloaders ignore you. They act as if you and your cargo don't exist. If you do manage to get the attention of an unloader, she sticks her tongue into your mouth to find out whether you're carrying water or nectar. When she discovers it's only water, she yanks her tongue out of your mouth, turns her back on you, and walks away. No wonder Thomas Seeley calls this "rejection."[4] An unloader bee's switch from curiosity to coldness is brutal. Think of what being ignored or rejected when you arrive with what you think is a gift does to you. Think of how you feel when you show up at home with what you think is a hot piece of gossip and your mate listens to your first sentence, then turns his back on you. At the very least it depresses you. It does the same damned thing to a bee.

Things get even worse if the fashionable flower patch of the moment is running out of pollen and nectar. When you, a forager bee, set off to follow the crowd to a barren raspberry patch and you come back with your cargo pouches nearly empty, the unloaders pass you by as if you were dirt. Attention means everything in the world of human fads and fashions. One reason you and I go with the trend is to get others to look at us admiringly. That's true of you and me. It's equally true of bees. Being ignored hurts. It hurts deeply.

When you, a worker bee, are shunned at the unloading dock, you don't give up easily. You return to your tapped-out flower patch for roughly half a bee workday—the equivalent of a year in a human lifetime. You act as if you just can't believe that your old source of a paycheck has dried up. But your pep is gone. You travel more and more slowly. When you come home, you "crawl" into the hive and are forced to beg for food. When you go back out to your old flower patch, you explore the blossoms at a sluggish pace and spend more and more time inside the hive. Finally you give up and join the ranks of what Seeley calls the "unemployed."[5] You stagger around as if you are stunned—or more as if you have lost your sense of purpose, your sense of meaning. Even your body temperature goes down. You downshift into a mode that eerily apes what University of Tennessee ethologist and neuroendocrinologist Neil Greenberg calls *subclinical depression*.[6] You slip into a misery that suits the needs of the group's explore and consolidate strategy, a funk determined by the pendulum of repurposing. And you're not alone. Crowds of discouraged forager bees like you wander around inside the hive looking for some way to lift their spirits, some way to energize themselves, some way, well, to "entertain" themselves.[7] And these mobs of what Thomas Seeley calls the "unemployed" find what they are looking for. How? In the speculation-and-consolidation strategy, the explore-then-digest search strategy, the fission-fusion strategy, the evolutionary search strategy of the hive.

A beehive has its conformists and its hippies, its everyday laborers and its creatives, its conservatives and its speculators. Ninety-five percent of the forager bees trail along with their sisters. They mine the popular flower patch of the day, go along with group decisions, and stick with "common sense," a shared consensus that's far more than a mere figure of speech.

But 5 percent do not follow the crowd. What does this minority do? It defies convention. Each bee in this bohemian batch acts appallingly self-indulgent, takes off on her own, follows her own tastes, opts for a seemingly meaningless waste of time, and flies an erratic, self-inspired path to and from what seems like nowhere.[8] That path can carry an explorer bee over a looping, twisting ramble as far as eighteen miles long. Strange as it sounds, the wanderers and the time wasters are the hive's eyes and ears, its saviors, its discoverers, and its scouts.

In bad times, the number of scouts, the number of seemingly aimless wanderers, the number of searcher bees, can more than triple. So the hive can raise or lower the proportion of its income it invests in curiosity, in speculation, and in exploration. But, like all of the hive's gambles, miscalculations can be fatal.

Back to the tale of you, the discouraged worker bee wandering around in the hive, seemingly looking for something to dispel your lethargy. What seizes your attention when the cargo you've brought back to the unloaders no longer gets you an enthusiastic welcome? What galvanizes you when your contributions have been persistently ignored?

Here's where a centralized data exchange, an information consolidator, a primitive precursor of pop culture, enters the mix. Five or six of the oddballs, the curiosity driven, the speculators, the nonconformist explorer bees, have accidentally bumbled into new flower patches or new water puddles.[9] And they are not shy about advertising their discoveries.[10] Like street buskers or soapbox preachers, they fly back to the hive and dance their news. Five or six compete on the inside wall of the hive in a spot near the entrance, a location Thomas Seeley calls "the dance floor." The dancing scouts duke it out for an audience like the break dancers who vie for your attention at Times Square. First they bribe the crowd by spitting a bit of whatever good stuff is in their throats into the mouths of the audience members. This gives a solid (or liquid) sense of what they've found. Then they kick into the famous Waggle Dance, a dance that Karl von Frisch won a Nobel Prize in 1973 for discovering.[11] The Waggle Dance pattern resembles an 8 laid on its side, an 8 with a long line where the two circles are squashed against each other. The scouts run forward, wriggling their equivalent of hips and buzzing their wings. At the end of this straight run, they turn left, loop back to their starting point, and do another straight-line run, buzzing and hip-wriggling as they go. But this time when they reach the end of their straight run, they turn in the opposite direction, right, and circle back to the start again. A dancer's straight-line run points out the direction of the promising flower patch. The dancers' distance from the hive's entrance and the length of her straight run tells how far away the discovery is and how hard or easy the trip is.[12]

The dance repertoire, its communicative vocabulary, is a very complex language for a bee with only a tiny number of brain cells.[13] The Waggle Dance figure eight doesn't convey its information in the form of a simple map. Instead, it fixes direction by the angle of a patch of flowers or of a water puddle relative to the sun. The sun constantly moves across the sky. So to decode the dance, you, an average worker, have to calculate an angle that shifts second by second and minute by minute. Which means the bee language—the message you're getting through the "trivia" of bee entertainment—is based on the equivalent of a dynamic calculus and trigonometry,[14] a math of nonstop change, an equivalent to what you and I would only be able to calculate with a downloaded program that performs "dynamic geometry"[15] and with a good computer. And this math is summed up in muscular movements. It's summed up in a dance! (Which makes you wonder what other ultracomplex information is summed up in the body language, entertainment, and trivial pursuits of human beings.)

But back to you, the downhearted bee. You and a bunch of other discouraged foragers, a milling mass of the dejected and the "unemployed," gather 'round to watch the dancers flash and flaunt. Now the most important signals become just what they are on a human stage or screen—conviction, energy, and endurance. Some explorers dance more enthusiastically than others. The most outrageous enthusiasts attract the biggest crowds. And, says Seeley, in a hive that's been cooped up for eight days by rain and cold, a colony that hasn't been able to forage, "a colony starved for pollen," a scout bee that finds a rich patch of pollen will dance as many as 257 waggle runs, carrying out a half-hour-long performance that impresses more than just bees. Even Seeley, a human observer trying to be as objective as possible, finds the display "extremely powerful."[16]

You, the unemployed and listless worker, crowd around one of the most potent persuaders, rubbing her with your antennae while she dances and following behind her through a dozen or more of her twists and bends. Your antennae are your odor detectors. By rubbing the dancing bee with your long feelers, you pick up the scent of the flower patch that the dancer is promoting. That sweet perfume of food makes an impression that will help you locate the dancer's find if you become sufficiently roused to follow her recommendation. And the dancer tries to guarantee your interest by turning around every once in a while, giving you the bee equivalent of a tongue kiss, and feeding you a bit more of the nectar she carries in her "honey stomach."[17]

Meanwhile, her enthusiasm is contagious. She lifts you from your lethargy and your depression. She excites you.[18] She apparently can raise even your body temperature. If her dance is sufficiently persuasive—which means if the bee dancing the message hoofs, hot-steps, and figure eights longer than her competitors, if she just won't give up—a few of your fellow conformists will catch a bit of the figure eight shimmier's enthusiasm and go out and check her report.[19] If the fact-checkers are impressed by what they find, they will come back and do a little jig when they arrive. Or they'll go to the dance floor and join the dance.

Finally, you help one of the advertisers for the richest patch take over the dance floor. How? You, too, fly out to check the scout's report, find a bounty of riches, come back loaded with goodies—pollen, nectar, or water—and are sent into ecstasy by the star-of-the-moment treatment that you get from the unloader bees when you fly back to the hive. How do you respond to the attention? You, too, step inside the hive, enter the dance floor, and dance your little abdomen off. Then you fly away to get another load.

The more dancers for a high-profit site, the fewer the bees who dance for competing sites. The winning site gets the greatest number of back-up dancers, and the greatest number of foragers. Finally, you and your fellow unemployed workers pick the prize-winning dancer, ignore her competitors, and follow the winner's recommendation. That's how the beehive makes up its mind!

Just to make sure that everyone gets the message and can find the hot harvest of the day, when you fly to the patch of blossoms you're mining, you leave a satisfaction report. You bumble through up to a hundred blossoms per trip, harvesting each one. If you like what you find, you mark your trail with a scent that tells others this is the sweet spot, *the* place to show up, the high-payoff site of the day. Satisfaction reports add up. They are centralizers, consolidators. They keep hundreds of foragers focused on the same target. A mix of defiance and conformity, a mix of going along with the crowd and of rebelliously going off on your own, a cycle of fission and fusion, of exploration and consolidation, of speculation and investment in what's proven and safe, is a highly efficient way to gather what the beehive needs.[20]

The payoff for you, the individual worker, on the other hand, is a massive emotional boost. When you come back home with your pouches full of dandelion pollen or nectar that the hive needs to beat its honey deadline, the unloaders once again rush to you, make a fuss over you, and unload your cargo as quickly as they can.[21] You and your fellow foraging conformists get what you need most, attention. You are a star. You sharpen up as if you have a sense of purpose, a sense of mission, and a sense of meaning again. You get a boost of energy. How do we know? Even your body temperature rises.

Meanwhile the explorer bees—the bee world's Warren Buffets, Paul Allens, George Soroses, Bill Gateses, Steve Jobses, Michael Jacksons, Albert Einsteins, and Henry David Thoreaus—go back to their self-indulgent flights and buzz off the beaten path, selfishly pursuing their trend-bucking rambles again. Many of them, like human rebels, are youngsters fresh from the nest, newbies who have never seen the outside world before. Many of them have not yet found their place in life. Thanks to their wanderings and to the wanderings of more-experienced but equally eccentric adults, the hive acts as a search engine,[22] a web of intelligent, autonomous sensors feeling out every nook and cranny of a territory that can cover an astounding 168 square miles![23]

The hive survives thanks to the insect equivalent of boom and bust, of mass mood swings and mass emotion—the equivalent of elation, conviction, enthusiasm, mania, depression, and most important, a sense of direction, a sense of purpose, and a sense of meaning. The hive survives thanks to emotion's control over a prime focuser of information flow—the hunger for attention. The hive also survives thanks to the bee's equivalent to personal emotions. The hive beats the honey deadline and acts like a group brain thanks to the way that personal emotions are knit into a search rule, a search algorithm, a search strategy. A group and a multigroup search strategy. And, on the really big scale, a planetary and a cosmic search strategy. A strategy with which the universe feels out her potential. A tactic with which the cosmos probes her possibilities. The fission-fusion strategy. The strategy of the evolutionary search engine.

* * *

The cycle of boom and crash, of speculate and consolidate, is vital to the survival of bees. It's vital to the survival of mice in a silo. It's vital to slime mold. It's vital to chimpanzees. It's vital to bacteria. And it even shows up in the life and death of stars. It's not just any evolutionary search strategy. It's *the* evolutionary search strategy. And here's what's really weird. In the beehive, the cycle of boom and crash translates into an intensely personal emotional exchange. And that emotional exchange is at the heart of an economy.

That emotional exchange helps explain why current economics just doesn't get it. That emotional exchange helps explain why the Kondratiev cycle comes close to elucidating the ups and downs of economies, but doesn't quite cut the mustard. And that emotional exchange helps explain why a monster like Benito Mussolini understood far more than a good-hearted, brilliant man like Ben Bernanke.

III

HOW PASSIONS POWER THE EVOLUTIONARY SEARCH ENGINE

15

YOU AND ME AND THE CYCLE OF INSECURITY

When you get upset, you turn to a friend, right?
Here's the reason why.

The pendulum of repurposing changes *Caulobacter* from home-steaders with straws to explorers with propellers. It changes bees from enthusiastic harvesters to sluggish, unemployed entertainment seekers. And the pendulum of repurposing is hooked to another mechanism in animals with psyches, no matter how primitive those psyches may be. That additional device is the cycle of insecurity.

You are a harvester ant in Arizona.[1] An ant researcher has decided to experiment on you and your ten-thousand-member family, your colony.[2] She's decided to pluck you and your sisters[3] out of the net-work of six-foot-deep tunnels you call home, cart you to unfamiliar territory, dump all ten thousand of you in this vast unknown, and see what happens. You and your 9,999 relatives mill around in a big circle, clinging to each other for comfort.[4] But you're very vulnerable. You have no food. You have no shelter. You have no protection from birds and other ant eaters. And you haven't got a clue about the perils or prizes available in this unfamiliar land of dust and grass. How do you get a feel for the lay of the land? How do you find stuff to eat and a place to get some sleep?[5] You are driven by the cycle of insecurity.[6]

Imagine that you're on the outer edge of this turning wheel of

97

ants. Eventually you get bored, restless, and curious. You scoot away from your sisters into the unknown of the new wilderness. You get less than an inch. Then you are seized by fear and discomfort. You feel you've literally gone too far.

How do animal behaviorists know how you feel? All they have to do is watch. After your brief trip into the unknown, your quick probe into the terra incognita beyond the colony's outer edge, you scuttle back to your sisters as rapidly as your six legs can carry you. What do you do next? You are desperate for affirmation, desperate to be comforted. So you look for someone you can talk to. Someone who can calm you down. You look for someone who will give you the ant equivalent of a shoulder to lean on plus hugs and rubs.

Sounds silly, right? Hugs and rubs among ants. But that's precisely how you communicate. You find a receptive sister. She touches you all over and you touch her all over, too. In the process you answer the question of how are you and what you have been up to. You deliver a report on where you've been and what you've found. How? You and your welcomer rub antennae.[7] She picks up on the chemical composition of the specks of matter you've carried back from your brave scouting expedition. She picks up on any hints of food or a safe place to bed down.

But that's not your only way of sharing information. It's not the only way you deliver a report on where you've been on your travels. And it's not the only way your welcomer lets you know how things have been in the milling circle of ants while you've been gone. Ants have an additional way of saying, "Fine thanks, and how are you?" It's called *trophylaxis*—mouth-to-mouth communication. We've seen it among bees. Imagine I'm the sister you confide in. You spit a bit of what you've eaten on your travels into my mouth. And I, being polite, spit a bit of what's in my "social stomach" into your craw, too.[8] Now I really know whether your half-inch voyage of discovery has landed you in a dusty emptiness or has shown you the location of a piece of cake. And if it's cake, I know precisely how sweet it is. If "a piece of cake" is, indeed, the message I've gotten from you, I send out a chemical bulletin that tells our crew that, eureka! you've struck gold . . . or pastry. And mobs of our sisters rush over to follow you to the hot food spot.

In your curiosity, you've extended the eyes, ears, and antennae of our group. And in your moment of hesitation, of self-doubt, and of uncertainty, you've been forced to bring the message of what you've discovered back to the group and to me. That's the cycle of insecurity.

Meanwhile, now that I've hugged you, rubbed you, and have paid attention to your dispatches from the outer limits, you get restless again. Once again you stop circling with the rest of us, and you rush out to make another half-inch foray over the horizon of what the rest of us know. Then you get insecure again and your fear sends you rushing back to report on what you've smelled, tasted, and seen. That's the cycle of exploration and digestion, the cycle of speculation and consolidation, the cycle of fission and fusion. That's the cycle of insecurity.

Are ants the only ones who act as each others' discoverers and mapmakers? Are they the only ones forced to touch base and report on their adventures, forced to give and get reports by the need for comfort, hugs, and rubs? Are they the only ones forced into a data exchange by a shudder of fear, by a loss of confidence, by a sense of discomfort, by an absolute need to touch base? Not by a long shot. Curious chimpanzees bravely march off on their own to explore the territory outside the campground of their group. Then they become extremely uncomfortable and rush back to the clan for hugs and rubs.

Baby human beings do the same. Mary Ainsworth did a classic series of experiments in the 1970s to explore the bonds between babies and their mothers. If you had been one of the babies, here's how the experiment would have gone. It's 1973 and you are a one-year-old. You and your mom arrive on the campus of Johns Hopkins University in Baltimore, Maryland, and go to the building that houses the Psychology Department. You're ushered into a midsized, windowless room with a two-way mirrored wall, three chairs, and toys on the floor. You are given a few minutes to sit with your mom, play with the toys, and get used to the place. Then a strange woman comes in through the door and plays with you. Your mom leaves. You cry. And eventually your mom comes back. Then both your mother and the stranger leave the room and you are all alone. Finally, the stranger returns alone, followed by your mom. What's the point? As a baby, you go through a cycle when you encounter the unfamiliar, the strange. First you are upset. Then you become curious. Then you get upset again. Your mom puts you on the floor. At first you cling to her shins. Then, once the contact with her warmth comforts you, you do what the ant does. You probe the unknown. You crawl two feet toward the stranger. But that's as far as you get before insecurity hits you. So you do a U-turn and scoot back to your mother's legs again. After more hugs and mama's warmth, you get your courage back. This time you crawl four feet in the stranger's direction before you whip around and head for the safety of your mom's ankles and calves. Then you set out on another voyage to the stranger, getting another two feet. You finally reach the unfamiliar woman, but only after losing all confidence and rushing back to your mom half a dozen times. Ainsworth calls your cycling back and forth the *attachment exploration balance*.[9]

Like the ants, babies alternate between courage and fear, between exploration and digestion, between the urge to speculate and the collapse of confidence. So do you and I. Why? Because we are part of something bigger than ourselves. A collective intelligence. A group IQ. The cycle of insecurity turns a mob into a team that searches its possibilities, explores them vigorously, then grows fearful and rushes back to its mother's shins. The cycle of insecurity drives us to indulge in our hopes then to indulge in our fears. It drives us to explore then test what we've discovered or what we've made. It drives us to toss aside the new projects that don't seem to pan out. It drives us to weigh what we have and to throw away our mistakes. It drives us to jettison ventures into the unknown that don't seem strong enough to hold up on the stormy side of a cycle of belief and doubt, a pivot triggered by a cycle of insecurity. The cycle of insecurity drives us through the emotional and perceptual flips that power boom and bust. And it drives us through the moods of boom and bust that cycle within us every day.

* * *

In humans the cycle of insecurity is linked to a vital trick of survival—our need to predict the future with the highest degree of accuracy mere brains can achieve. You can see this most vividly in a love affair. You have an unexpected argument with your mate. What do you do? You are like the disconcerted ant, the curious chimp, and the bawling baby after a trip into the unknown. You are upset. And there's only one way to calm you down. Like an ant in need of hugs, rubs, and a mouth-to-mouth swap of prechewed food, you need to spit it out. You need to talk to a friend.

Let's think about this for a second. The part of your brain that's most upset is your emotional center, your limbic system—a knob of neural tissue that sits at the center of your brain like a pit in a plum. And the parts of your brain that talk things out are behind your left eye and above your left ear. They're called Wernicke's Area and Broca's Area. Theoretically, if your emotional center wants to work things out with your speaking self, if it wants a comforting cliché with which to grasp your situation, it only has to travel four inches. But, no, your aching emotional center insists on working things out with your speech centers by making a phone call to your best friend from high school, a friend in Honolulu. You build a bridge between your aching emotions and your store of wise sayings ("Tell her you need your space," "Don't let her control you") by reaching out five thousand miles. Why? Because your brain isn't built to simply ease your pain when you step into stormy territory. It's built to use your pain to connect you with at least one other human being and share. If the story of your battle with your girlfriend is utterly amazing, your friend will tell it to five people he knows, even if you begged him not to. In turn, those five people will tell it to five others. And your fight may produce yet another way to understand the wild frontier of relationships for humans all around the globe, a story passed around the human hive.

Like the bacteria, the bee, the baby, the chimp, and the ant, you and I act as probes into the unknown. But what does this have to do with predicting the future? For the answer, I recommend a visit to *Othello*.

16

WHY JEALOUSY DRIVES YOU CRAZY

The Othello Effect

The movie theater in your mind. Or how to drive a friend insane.

Why do we have the cycle of insecurity to begin with? When we're in a new relationship, why do we go from ecstasy to hell? When we fall in love, why do our minds become movie theaters running what seem like twenty scenarios a minute? Scenarios of what life together in our late twenties, our thirties, and our forties will be. Scenarios of what togetherness will be like when we're sixty-four? Why do we see the potential glories—the passionate things we'll do in bed, the house we'll buy, the children we'll have, and how proud we'll be when the kids graduate from Harvard? And why do we see three times as many scenarios of betrayal and disappointment? Why do we go through one of the most vicious examples of the cycle of insecurity, the *Othello effect*?

Shakespeare's fictional Othello was a Muslim general who converted to Christianity and fought on the Christian side in confrontations like the real-life battle of Lepanto, the biggest bout of naval warfare the world had ever seen. The engagement involved 428 warships manned by 87,000 sailors and soldiers in 1571—an epic battle between the navy of Islam and the navy of Christendom in the Mediterranean Sea.[1] Othello's fictional victories won him the respect of Venice's most powerful families. In fact, he married Desdemona, the daughter of one of these Venetian aristocrats. This was not simply an arranged marriage designed to bring together allies—the sort of marriage that happened all the time in the power circles of societies from China to Chile. Othello was in love with Desdemona, and as Shakespeare demonstrates, the cycle of insecurity shows itself most vividly when you're in love.

When the play opens, Othello has complete confidence in his relationship with Desdemona. But that soon changes. Othello has an enemy who wants to see him fall—Iago. And Iago knows exactly how to tumble a man in love. Turn up the power to the insecurity circuit. Play on Othello's inner theater, his scenario projector. Give him every vision of betrayal you can conceive. If you play on the cycle of insecurity, your victim's brain will work overtime for you. Why? Because we test romantic relationships by using the same emotions that thrust us into boom and bust. We test new romantic relationships by alternating between wild enthusiasm and uncontrollable doubt. We test new romantic relationships by imagining every future we can foresee. We test new romantic relationships by creating vivid visions of what can be, vivid visions of the future. Including visions of nightmare rejection and pain. Visions twisted by panic or exuberance. We test new romances by flipping through the cycle of insecurity.

Why? Why does romance put our future-scenario machinery into overdrive? The answer comes from the field of evolutionary psychology. A romance can last anywhere from a month to a lifetime. So imagining each scene and deciding which vision is most likely helps us with one of the biggest decisions we will ever make: the investment in a lifelong relationship that will tap all of our productive energies and that will produce our kids.

In the end, Iago pulls off a perception shift. He switches Othello's imagination from visions of paradise with Desdemona to visions of hell—the two poles of the cycle of insecurity. Iago prods Othello into one of the most dire visions of all, that Desdemona is cheating on him. Why? Othello is black and Desdemona is white.[2] Othello is from a strange society and Desdemona wants the familiar. Othello simply isn't good enough.

All of this is imaginary. But most of what we think we know is in the imagination. Right now the wall behind your head exists for you only in your memory. It exists only in your beliefs. Swivel your head around to check that it's still there, and you'll have to rely on memory to be sure this page still exists. Reality is a matter of belief. So losing his belief in Desdemona repurposes Othello as dramatically as the shift from a stalk to a propulsion whip repurposes a bacterium. Othello turns from a lover to a murderer.

To avenge his shame in the Muslim manner, says Shakespeare scholar Adam Hall, Othello smothers the woman he loves. And with that act he destroys his alliances and torpedoes his own life. Why? Because his future-testing mechanism has run amok, something it does in all of us when we're in love. Othello chooses the wrong scenario of what is happening outside the realm of what he can see. He chooses the wrong picture of the invisible world. He chooses the wrong vision of the payoff that will come from his relationship in the future. He chooses the wrong vision of what could be.

A boom is a period when we're at the top of the cycle of insecurity, at the ebullient peak where we see only the glorious possibilities. We become antennae of the group. We eagerly rush to feel out brand-new things. New speculations, new stocks, new commitments, new investments, new gadgets, and new status symbols. And in a crash, we hit the bottom of the cycle of insecurity. We are slammed by the Othello effect. We see only the risks and the potential cataclysms. We bail out.

We also test what we've got. We see what's big enough to survive. And we cluster around it. We become testers and selectors. And we become centralizers and new-structure creators, pulling together new institutions to help us weather the storm. But like the cycle of insecurity in ants, chimps, and babies, the cycle of insecurity in humans isn't just an individual mood swing. It's a social thing. As Charles Mackay implies in the title of his definitive 1841 classic on crashes, panics, and manias, *Extraordinary Popular Delusions and the Madness of Crowds*, "extraordinary popular delusions" are not just individual things. They are manifestations of the "madness of crowds."[3]

Is there a sanity to this madness? What does the cycle of insecurity in humans achieve?

17

GOOGLING THE FUTURE

The Fabulous Russian Gets It Wrong

The story of the explanation for everything, the Kondratiev wave.

The cycle of boom and crash is like the fin of a shark skimming just above the water's surface. It's not an independent creature. It's just the visible portion of a larger beast, a part of the body of something far bigger beneath the waves. The shark itself, gray, sleek, massive, and hungry, cuts through the dark waters beneath the crests and ebbs in the quest for food. But you and I can't see it. If we're standing on the beach, all we spot is a moving triangle—the fin.

What's the invisible body of which boom and crash is a mere fin? Depressions and good times are a manifestation of a cosmos Googling her potential. They're a manifestation of a universe feeling out her future and wrestling the impossible into reality through tools like you and me. Crash and boom is a fin moved by a search strategy, the search strategy of fission-fusion, the search strategy of explore and digest, of gamble and test, of growing bold then losing your confidence, the search strategy of the cycle of insecurity built into your biology and mine. But this primal search pattern takes on a whole new meaning when it asserts itself among us human beings. In bees, the cycle of spread and clench, of reach out then digest, runs over and over again, week after week, year after year, and century after century.

So does the beehive's boom of spring and the beehive's bust of winter. But the structure of beehives remains the same. Honeycombs are still made of wax. Each cell in the honeycomb is still hexagonal—it still has its familiar six sides. And the social structure of the hive—with a queen, her retinue, her nursemaids, her interior workers, her unloaders, her outdoor foragers and her explorers—stays the same. That's not true in societies of human beings. The cycle of boom and crash in humans brings social breakthroughs.

Let's go back to the Kondratiev wave. Kondratiev wave theory says the rise of new technologies brings boom and that the petering out of old technologies brings crash. Is this always true? In 31 BCE, the Roman Empire was split by a civil war between the armies of a thirty-two-year-old named Octavian and the army and navy of Mark Antony and his politically brilliant girlfriend, Cleopatra, queen of Egypt.[1] The battle was over expansion strategies. Over speculative tactics for feeding the next boom. Octavian wanted to keep the focus of the empire in Rome with its eye on expansion in Europe.[2] Meanwhile, it looked like Cleopatra had convinced Mark Antony to move the center of the Roman Empire east and to look for expansion in the Middle East and Asia.[3] No matter which direction Rome faced, east or west, its technologies remained the same. Rome raised its cash by using the warship, the shield, the sword, and its highly disciplined army to seize new lands and to bring home the loot.[4] Rome raised yet more money by collecting whopping annual tributes from conquered territories such as Greece, Spain, and France.[5] It fattened its treasuries with twenty-five thousand drachmas a day of silver from Spain's super-rich silver mines and with a flood of silver from the mines of Laurium and Macedonia.[6] And Rome took in its food by raising it on huge industrial-sized farms planted on conquered land and worked by slaves, *latifundia*,[7] or by importing it on cargo ships that crossed the shipping lanes that Rome had expropriated when it seized control of the Mediterranean Sea from the Phoenicians in 146 BCE.[8]

There are often crashes when wars are over. Why? Wars are forms of exploration. They test your reach. They show you just how far you can go. What do you do after your aggressive expedition outward has landed you more food? Or less? You repurpose. You sit down and digest what you've found. Or you stew over your losses. One way or the other, you consolidate. Recessions and depressions happen not when technologies peter out, but when the group shifts from fission to fusion, from stretch to clench, from exploration to digestion. Recessions and depressions are powered by the pendulum of repurposing.

Exploration and outstretch focus the energies of your group on its periphery, its outskirts, its new frontiers of possibility. Digestion centers your group on your collective core, on testing what your group has found, on throwing out what seems weak, and on pulling together the discoveries that pass the test—on solidifying the winners in new and stronger ways. In you and me, digestion takes the comfort foods and the new treats we've discovered in our multimile exploratory expeditions through the aisles of grocery stores and corner shops, chews it, sends it down our esophagus, focuses it in a single churning ball in our stomach, separates what fuels us from the stuff we can't use, sends the useless and the harmful sludge down our intestinal pipes on their way to the pit of porcelain in our flushing room, and sends the good stuff into our bloodstreams to be fashioned into the megamolecules that keep us functioning for the next few days. These molecules are used as fuel or fused into muscle, fat, and bone. That's consolidation. That's repurposing.

But digestion doesn't just maintain the status quo. It also feeds a process of radical change, of fresh creation, of extreme repurposing. You and I change every day and every year. Once you were an embryo. Then a zygote. Then a baby. Then a toddler. Then a child. And you continue to change as you read this page. Ten billion cells of your body die every day,[9] and you replace them without knowing how you pull off this act of creation or without knowing you are creating at all. Your body has never experienced middle age or old age before, yet the community of cells that make, rebuild, repair, and constantly change you will find their way to reshape you as an older person as surely as they found their path to making you an embryo a long, long time ago. How they manage to follow this master plan when there are no blueprints and no master planner, we still don't know.[10] Despite enormous achievements in genetics. The one thing that we can clearly see is the cycle of expand and consolidate, of explore and digest, of speculate then test and toss away, in our developmental biology.

Modern social organizations find their way forward using this evolutionary search strategy. Crash and boom work as an exploration-engine that generates breakthroughs, an exploration-engine that drives social change. Crash and boom usher in new institutions.

Let's go back to Rome. The Kondratiev wave says that major depressions arrive when hot new technologies cool down. Rome's technologies weren't chilling in 30 BCE when Octavian won the "final war of the Roman Republic" and when Mark Antony and Cleopatra killed themselves. Yet there was an unmistakable downturn. Why? In all probability, the depression was an example of the pendulum of repurposing at work, doing something it does over and over again—bringing recession after a war. Why recession after war? Because huge numbers of men are no longer needed as soldiers. Octavian dismissed a hundred thousand soldiers to slim the army down from sixty legions to twenty-eight.[11] And according to Tacitus, Octavian was up against a problem. He needed to "apply soothing medicine to the spirits of the soldiers, that they might be willing to endure peace."[12] Octavian had a hard time coming up with the funds to pay the dismissed soldiers their discharge bonuses—bonuses equal to thirteen years of pay.[13] The result was a near mutiny. Octavian settled as many soldiers as possible on lands seized from the conquered.[14] But it's not easy to repurpose soldiers as farmers. Incompetent farmers are lucky if they can feed themselves, much less others. While they wait for their crops to come in, they live as inexpensively as they can. They don't buy. They hang on to their bits and pieces of leftover plunder. They don't send consumer dollars—or Roman denarii—whizzing through the economy.[15]

What's worse, if they grow frustrated, former soldiers can return to what they know best. Picking up their arms and fighting. This time not for the state but against it, as rebels. The former soldiers are like the dazed and confused bees whose old jobs are no longer paying off. They need repurposing. Even in ancient Rome.

In its postwar recession, Rome's focus turned inward. Rome went through a perceptual shift. Its future projectors, its scenario generators, its Othello mechanisms, no longer focused excitedly on fresh opportunities. Rome's fantasies focused on problems. On the ways things could go wrong. On the ways you could lose your toga, rather than the ways you could win a whole new wardrobe. The poetry of Horace, for example, was filled with visions of the end of the world, visions of the fall of the Roman Empire.[16] These visions of apocalypse were false. In fact, Rome would thrive and grow for at least three more centuries. But Rome's projections of doom were as vivid and as persuasive as our modern apocalyptic scenarios—global warming, the destruction of nature, and the end of resources on mother earth.

Rome went from binge to purge, from exploration to consolidation, from hunting and gathering to digestion. Rome shifted position in the cycle of insecurity. Instead of crawling out to explore the strange, Romans rushed to the comfort of their mothers' shins again. The result? Rome gave new powers to its central institutions. In the Romans' moment of emotional crisis, they strengthened the central structures they felt could save them.

When Octavian took power, he renamed himself Augustus. He declared himself emperor. And he moved a process forward that had begun under his great uncle, the man who had adopted him as a son and had willed him his property, Julius Caesar, seventeen years earlier. Octavian shrank Rome's democratic institutions down to fig leaves. And he built the powers of a central regulator, a central controller—himself and the institution of emperor, an institution he dramatically advanced. He turned from an explorer to a consolidator. One of the most important consolidators in Western history.

While he was at it, Augustus reformed the government. Under the previous system, taxes were collected by "tax farmers"—entrepreneurs who were allowed to set tax schedules as high as possible. These tax gougers turned over the bulk of what they collected to the state, then they were permitted to pocket any extra money their extortionate rates pulled in. Tax farming was vicious, and Augustus needed as much good will as possible. He was about to raise taxes.[17] So Augustus abolished tax farming. He also established policies that favored free trade, private enterprise, and private property. And he built or rebuilt roads and harbors, opening the way for an upgrade of multicontinental trade.[18]

How does the Roman crash of 30 BCE fit the Kondratiev wave? It doesn't. The crash wasn't triggered by a formerly young technology grown old and gray. But the Roman crash *does* fit the model of the fission-fusion strategy. It followed a period in which two potential Roman rulers—Octavian and Mark Antony—tested the limits of their possibilities by warring with each other. And the Roman crash of 30 BCE was a period of digestion and consolidation. It was a period of returning to roots. Augustus even went on a campaign to restore the ancient values of the early republic, including the old-time religion and the old family values.[19]

Was Augustus's institution building and centralization in a time of slump or crash an exception to the rule? No. Not at all. The panic of 1819 in America was blamed on wildly speculative new technology and pathologically enthusiastic exploration of new opportunities. It was blamed on "overinvestment" in manufacturing and "wild speculation" in western land. But that placement of blame was false. It turned out that the "wild speculators" were right. Their manic dreams of giant payoffs from factories and from western acreage accurately predicted the future. Manufacturing had by no means peaked in 1819. In fact, the growth of industrial production would go on for another two hundred years with no end in sight. And the western lands that the investment enthusiasts were scarfing up for less than a dollar per acre would sell for $2,350 per acre 189 years down the line.[20]

But in 1819, American society's manic-depressive cycling from frenzied belief to doubt, panic, and blame, American society's immersion in the Othello effect, *did* shift the American herd into a different kind of creativity. It drove Americans to craft new centralizing institutions. It led to the spread of the savings bank to help the poor pile up their pennies so they could make it through the next panic.[21] And it led to the creation of manufacturing associations to support the new factory founders. The panic of 1819 shifted America from exploration and expansion to consolidation and structure creation. From hunting, gathering, and shopping to digestion.

Eighteen years later, America was hit with the panic of 1837. Again, exploration of new opportunities—wild speculation and overenthusiasm about new lands and new technologies—were blamed. But were technologies really going from exuberant youth to elderly decay in 1837? Were they following the pattern of the Kondratiev wave? Far from it. In 1825, the Erie Canal was opened. That revolutionary man-made 363-mile-long waterway brought the riches of the Middle West's iron mines and wheat fields into the economy of the Atlantic seaboard. The Erie Canal replaced the perilous journey from the wilderness of states like Michigan, Wisconsin, and Minnesota with a mere cargo-boat ride to New York City, Boston, Philadelphia, and the other bustling cities of the East. The Erie Canal also put the Midwest an ocean-boat ride away from Europe. When harvests failed and England and France were threatened with famine, Europe soon learned to send its gold to the United States in exchange for Erie Canal–transported grain.

The opening of the Erie Canal also added a new layer to the infrastructure of fantasy. It fired the imagination of a tall, gangly sixteen-year-old kid in Kentucky who read schoolbooks by firelight at night and who put himself through a course in the law, became a politician, then eventually became president. This audacious outsider dreamed of an upgrade on the canal's miracles—a transcontinental railroad, another wild scheme criticized as a techno-boondoggle. That kid who fixated on the Erie Canal was Abraham Lincoln. It was Lincoln's passion over the new techno-transport technologies that led him to become a railroad lawyer. And it was his hero worship of the Erie Canal's main creator, New York governor DeWitt Clinton, that impelled Lincoln to try his hand at politics.

Was enthusiasm over canal building a crazy fever of irrational exuberance? Not exactly. The Erie Canal was a goose that laid golden eggs at a machine-gun pace. From 1825 to 1883, the canal produced a profit of $42 million—the equivalent of over a billion 2007 dollars. Dollars that fattened the treasury of New York State.[22] And the Erie was just one of seventy-nine canals in the United States.[23] Yes, some canal firms like the Morris Canal and Banking Company in New Jersey failed. But in 1837, the profits from the technology of canal building were just getting started.[24]

Which brings us to the other techno-bubble supposedly behind the panic of 1837—railroads. The borrowing and investing in railroads was frenzied in the years before 1836. The dreams of railroad investors were huge. In England, superengineer Isambard Brunel, newly hired as chief engineer of Britain's brand-new Great Western Railway, looked out over England's mere 955 miles of track and planned a railway system that would cover tens of thousands of miles. Brunel was convinced that railroad lines would reach all the way to North America. Was Brunel's enthusiasm and that of the speculators behind him wrong? Yes and no. Railroad tracks would never stretch across the Atlantic from England to North America. But rail lines had by no means reached their peak in 1837. When the panic of 1837 arrived and the "railroad bubble" was decried as an insane fantasy, there were less than two hundred miles of track in the United States.[25] Over the next sixty years, the miles of track would increase to two hundred thousand.[26] And those webs of track would make big money for the investors who stuck with them.

Nor had canal technology come anywhere near a peak in 1837. Canal building would go on producing profit and bringing America together in unbelievable new ways until 1907, when the construction of canals finally petered out. What's more, canals and railways would be social transformers, making America an interknit nation of a kind the world had never seen before. The canal and the railroad would be engines of both exploration and consolidation. Engines of creation. And carvers of new social forms.

For example, the system of personal timing that you and I use evolved because of railroads and telegraphs. When the transcontinental railroad and the transcontinental telegraph line connected me in New York to you in Seattle in the 1870s, I could contact you almost instantly. To coordinate our work and our schedules, we needed to formalize and synchronize our sense of time.[27] And the railroads needed the same thing, a formal, coordinated time structure to schedule trains so they wouldn't collide head on. Railroads also wanted to let passengers know when to show up for an arrival or a departure. What's more, if you were commanding an army in one of the two great railroad-enabled wars—America's Civil War or Europe's Franco-Prussian War of 1872—you needed synchronized time to make sure your troops were coordinated. This wasn't easy when a state like Illinois had twenty-seven time zones and Wisconsin had thirty-eight.[28]

How did we pull off a rearrangement of the very foundations of our day? We used a piece of European technology whose modern mass production was invented in Connecticut and Massachusetts—the inexpensive watch.[29] We kept track of time in hours and minutes measured by our pocket watches.[30] And we learned to show up promptly at nine a.m. for work and at eight p.m. for a late-dinner engagement. In 1883, when railroads could no longer stand the confusion of hundreds of discombobulated local times, they divided America into four time zones and presented the dithering government with a fait accompli. Those zones allowed us to have our own local noon when the sun reached its peak in the sky and our own local midnight when darkness was at its height.[31] Those zones also allowed us to synchronize our watches by a linked system of minutes and hours. Railroads and the telegraph pulled off a fundamental change in the hidden structure that patterns our thinking and lays out our days. Railroads and the telegraph pulled off a fundamental reconstruction of our scaffold of habit. But more on the scaffold of habit in a few minutes.

All of that was in the future in the panic of 1837. But only the visionaries saw it. Only the speculators nurtured these mad dreams. Which brings us back to Mr. Kondratiev. Peaking technology did not trigger the panic of 1837. But the panic of 1837 was followed twenty years later by yet another crash blamed on overenthusiasm for railways and canals, the panic of 1857. American Henry Carey Baird complained, "Our railroad system has cost more than $1,000,000 and has brought ruin upon nearly everyone connected with it, the nation included."[32] His gloom was misplaced. The world was yet to see just how gigantic the fortunes amassed in the railroad business could become. A mere thirteen years later, railroads would build the fortunes of fabled magnates like rail maker and former railroad executive Andrew Carnegie,[33] railway consolidator J. P. Morgan, and railway owner Commodore Vanderbilt. These men garnered some of the biggest treasure heaps ever piled up by human beings. And they pulled their profits from the creation of a transportation system that would knit together a continent. A transportation system that would give humans new comforts and new powers. A transportation system that was blamed for one bubble after another. A transportation system that exceeded even the wildest speculators' dreams.

18

WHAT DOES CRASH CREATE?

Why Mother Nature loves collapse.

Let's surf back once again to Nikolai Kondratiev's wave.

Kondratiev and his interpreters said that surges of technology bring cycles of boom and crash. When a new technology takes hold, economies rise, then soar. And when technologies peak and slump, economies peak and slump, too. But a peaking technology does not explain most economic collapses. Something very different is at work. What? A creative search strategy. A producer of material miracles. A secular search engine. A secular genesis machine.

Economic collapse brings new social structures, new central solutions, new social forms. The panic of 1857 helped usher in one of the most important acts of centralization and institution building in American history—the Civil War. In that war Abraham Lincoln, the railroad attorney, preached a radically new form of social consolidation. A form we take for granted today but that was utterly new in Lincoln's time—the modern "nation." "A new nation conceived in liberty and dedicated" to a "proposition." A cluster of humans pulled together not by the divine right of kings, not by their ancestors' possession of one piece of land for hundreds of generations, and not by race, but pulled together by a common set of secular beliefs and a voluntarily accepted heritage of ideas.[1] The Civil War took America from what Lincoln called a mere "association of states," from a voluntary federation of thirty-four states and eight territories, to "a more perfect Union" and "a national government" with an "organic law," the Constitution, at its core.[2] When Lincoln said "organic," he meant it. Removing a state was like amputating a limb, he explained.[3] The United States was one body and would remain so for as long as men remained dedicated to the proposition that "government of the people, by the people, for the people, shall not perish from the earth."[4] The Civil War was consolidation and institution building in one of its most extreme forms.

The Civil War also led to crucial acts of economic structure creation. It brought us the greenback, America's first national currency. It produced federal regulation of banks. And it triggered the invention of the checking account.

Are these examples exceptions to the rule? Have other crashes refused to follow the Kondratiev model? Have other crashes broken Kondratiev's rule and arrived when a new technology was still on the rise? And have other crashes led to centralization of power and to new institution building?

The answer to all these questions is a resounding yes. The panic of 1857 and the postwar recession that came on the heels of the Civil War were followed by the Great Depression of 1873. In America, pundits and their readers blamed the depression on another railroad bubble. They blamed the crash on irrational exuberance over a new technology. But railroads had not peaked. They would continue a dizzying rise for another sixty years. On the other hand, the Great Depression of 1873 led to digestion—to centralization and structure making—in a staggering way. From it came new forms of mortgages and new financial instruments. From it came a movement to make the greenback permanent, and something else that gave radical new powers to American citizens. The North American railroad sprawl was like the exploratory spread of bacteria, ants, bees, cells in the embryo, and tubules in the cell. It was a hodgepodge, a tangle. Visionaries, entrepreneurs, and speculators had taken a chance on building railroads to ten-house towns in the hope that the easy access created by the tracks and trains would do for these nowhere-villes what the Erie Canal and the railroads had done for one obscure hamlet in the great unknown of the Midwest. That sleepy little village was Chicago, a town built from nearly nothing to an amazement by the new transport technologies.

Chicago was so scrawny that it scarcely even qualified as a village before the building of its first rail line. The name "Chicago" comes from a word of the Native American Illinois and Miami tribes for a wild leek, *shikaakwa*. Chicago was a mere spot where a bunch of Indian trails met. Nineteenth-century mapmaker, historian, and Chicago resident Rufus Blanchard describes the unpromising early Chicago like this: "At the close of the war of 1812 James Galloway, a native of Pennsylvania, emigrated to Erie Co., Ohio, in this way, where he lived till 1824. He then resolved to try his fortune on the Illinois prairies at or near Chicago, where the ague was less prevalent than at his home in Ohio."[5] Galloway bought a wagon, packed it with everything he owned including a gun, a tomahawk, ammunition, blankets, and a bag of corn meal, hired a trapper as a guide, and set out on a dangerous ride through Indian territory following a narrow Native American trail.

How many inhabitants did Chicago have when Galloway finally arrived? A hint comes from the following: "Mr. Galloway and his companion took the Chicago trail. It led principally along the sands of the lake and brought them directly to the spot by a better road than the average path through the wilderness. Here Mr. Galloway made the acquaintance of Billy Caldwell and Alexander Robinson, two notable Indian chiefs . . . and a Scotchman named Wallace."[6]

But don't be deceived into believing that Chicago's total population was a mere six. There were more. "Besides these," writes Blanchard, "Mr. Galloway mentions Mr. John Kinzie, Dr. Wolcott and Ouilimette as permanent residents, and several others who were only transient visitors at the place." That was it. A population of roughly nine. Concludes the author, "Such was Chicago, late in the autumn of 1824."[7]

By 1833, when Chicago was officially incorporated, the population was still a pathetic 350.[8] Then, in 1848, the first rail line to Chicago, the Galena and Chicago Union Railroad, opened for business. That same year the Illinois and Michigan Canal began its operations, connecting the Great Lakes to the Mississippi River.[9] The result of this confluence of ultra-high-tech transport technologies was a material miracle, an act of secular genesis. By 1858 Chicago, a poorly marked spot on an Indian walking path, was up to 91,000 inhabitants.[10] That's right. Chicago went from three hundred and fifty inhabitants to ninety-one thousand in a mere ten years. A nowhere had become a somewhere. All because of the railroad and the canal.

Meanwhile, what happened to the speculators and the entrepreneurs who had gambled their money and their credibility on a line to nowhere, on the Galena and Chicago Union line? In 1864, the Galena and Chicago Union merged with the North Western in what was considered one of the biggest deals in the history of American finance, a deal "talked about from the Atlantic to the slopes of the Missouri River" and "the first really important railroad consolidation that had taken place in the United States."[11] The men who invested in the Galena and Chicago Union got filthy rich.

The result? There were railroad lines erected by competing firms that paralleled each other. There were more hopeful lines to nowhere. Lines to towns that were in suspended animation before the tracks were laid and towns that remained in a coma once the new lines to them had been put in place. All this was the fruit of speculation, expansion, and exploration. Speculators had acted like sperm, like cells with propellers taking pay-packs of money to spots where it might or might not be needed. In building tracks wherever they thought there might soon be a need for them, speculators had acted as feelers testing the landscape of future possibility. And laying down society's bets. Speculators had acted out stage one of the fission-fusion search strategy—spread out and explore. Even when exploration is a risky gamble.

The resulting railroads needed the pendulum of repurposing. They badly needed the swing from expansion to consolidation and from exploration to digestion. They needed pruning. And that's what they got. Megafinancier J. P. Morgan ruthlessly pared, pruned, and connected, turning the tangle of rails into a national system, a system on which you could travel from one coast to another and to whatever major city you chose. That's the fruit of the switch from bacteria with tails, bacteria built for exploration, to bacteria built for digestion, bacteria that suck up the landscape with stalks rather than sailing over it at top speed. That's the fruit of speculation. From 1790 to today, the explorers—tycoons, speculators, and entrepreneurs—have carried money, energy, and excitement to the outskirts of American civilization and have explored new frontiers of possibility. Speculators have acted like the tails of bacterial explorers, of clam infants, and of migrating cells of the neural crest. They've been the propellers carrying money to spots where they hoped it would receive a welcome. And the few who've succeeded have been paid outrageous sums to compensate for the fact that they risked failing more than 99.9 percent of the time.

Meanwhile, consolidators and centralizers have pulled the threads together. They've grasped the lines that the entrepreneurs and speculators laid in place and have tied them together in whole new ways. And they've created new central institutions along the way. J. P. Morgan was one of the most important structure makers America has ever seen. But more on Morgan in a few seconds.

First, it's important to understand something strange. In Western economies, just as in the embryo, the cycle of boom and bust is not a wheel that stays in place. It is not like the Buddhist cycle of the universe—birth, maturity, and death, then begin all over again from the very same starting place. The modern Western cycle of soar and crash has been a wheel that's rolled forward. It has been a wheel of creation. A wheel of expansion, exploration, pruning, and new form generation.

The crash of 1907 was typical of the cycle of boom and crash. Like the eighty years of crashes before it, it was blamed on the usual suspect—a railway bubble. But railways still had a long way to go. Over the next forty years the railway system would be transformed and expanded with stations that rivaled the Taj Mahal (Grand Central Station in New York City, Union Station in Washington, DC, and the Thirtieth Street Union Station in Philadelphia, among others) and with trains built to set new speed records.[12] The Kondratiev wave would once again prove wrong. Railroad technology was not peaking. What would prove right? The cycle of exploration and digestion, the cycle of spread and consolidate, the cycle of entrepreneurial exuberance, wild speculation, and sober central institution building. The cycle of the evolutionary search engine.

What central institutions did the panic of 1907 generate? The crash hammered home a key concept in modern economics—the lender of last resort—a person or institution with a massive hoard of cash and credit that could bail the system out when it sprang leaks, when it hit the consolidate end in the swing of the pendulum of repurposing.[13] The panic of 1907 would lead to the creation of the Federal

Reserve system, the ultimate lender of last resort, the main savior in the Great Crash of 2008.

Twenty-two years after the panic of 1907 came another bust that built new institutions, another swing from exploration to consolidation—the Great Depression of 1929–1939. Were peaking technologies behind this humongous economic catastrophe? No. Automobiles, electricity in every home, forced-air central heating, radios, and a host of other electronic appliances were on the rise and had much, much further to go. On the other hand, did the Great Depression lead to central structure building? You bet. From the Depression of the 1930s we got the Securities and Exchange Commission, the Federal Deposit Insurance Corporation, the Glass-Steagall Act, and Social Security. We got the Securities Act of 1933, the Securities Exchange Act of 1934, the National Labor Relations Board, and the stabilization of unions as a key part of the American industrial system.

* * *

From the Great Depression of the 1930s, we also got a new ritual that radically changed the battles between labor and management. In the Homestead Strike of 1892, seven Pinkerton guards and eleven strikers were killed. In the Pullman Strike of 1894, fourteen thousand troops faced off against workers. The face-off turned violent and thirty-four strikers died of bullet wounds. In Pennsylvania's 1897 Lattimer Massacre, nineteen striking coal miners were killed. And in Colorado's Ludlow Massacre of 1914, nineteen strikers died, including two women and twelve children. Until the depths of the Great Depression, strikes were pitched battles waged with guns. As recently as the 1931 strike in Harlan County, Kentucky, and the Dearborn, Michigan, Ford Motor strike of 1932, strikers and the troops who opposed them had died over the pay and hours of workers. The Great Depression of the 1930s brought us a ceremonial act that eliminated the use of bullets—peaceful striking. To mediate strikes and to guarantee labor-management peace, the Great Depression brought us the National Labor Relations Board, a government arm that settled disputes between labor and management with words, not violence, and that made sure even the most massive strikes remained peaceful.[14]

The Great Depression of the 1930s also brought us the Federal

Housing Administration and the retail, thirty-year fixed-rate mortgage. It created the institutions that would power our continued growth in the twentieth and early twenty-first century. The Great Depression acted like the slime mold slug with a giraffelike neck—like the central congregation of independent slime mold cells gelled into a single body, a central survival project in which many cells died to make the base and neck of the bigger beast. But in the case of us humans, there were very few deaths. And there was a bottom line. The great crash of 1929 to 1939 led to the creation of institutions this earth had never seen.

If technocycles don't power the cycle of boom and crash, what does? Why do "great depressions" happen over and over again? Why did we have the Tulipmania crash of 1637,[15] the South Sea Bubble crash of 1720, the Mississippi Bubble of 1720, the panic of 1797, the depression of 1807, the panic of 1819, the panic of 1837, the panic of 1857, the panic of 1873, the panic of 1893, the panic of 1907, the post–World War I recession of 1918– 1919, the Great Depression of 1929–1939, the recession of 1953, the recession of 1957, and the 1973 oil crisis downturn? Not to mention the recession of 1981, the recession of 1990–1991, the Nikkei Bubble of 1991–2005, the dot-com bubble of 2000, the recession of 2001, and the Great Crash of 2008? Could it have been a pattern built into our biology? A pattern that's 3.85 billion years old? Or older? A pattern we can even see at work in the early cosmos? Could the cycle of boom and crash be propelled by the pendulum of repurposing? Could it be a manifestation of a search-and-create strategy? The fission-fusion strategy? The cycle of stretch out, explore, then pull back and digest? The cycle of reach out to discover your possibilities, then pull inward to weed out what doesn't work and to create new structures to cushion risks? The cycle of exploration and digestion? The cycle of insecurity? Could it really be that you and I are part of a search engine of a universe probing her possibilities? Could boom and bust really be turns in the wheel of an evolutionary search engine, a secular genesis machine?

19

THE BATTLE OF THE BIG MEN

Pigs, pies, puddings, and wizards of finance.

When crash comes and most of us go down, who's left standing, and why? In New Guinea, men are just like they are everywhere else. They want admiration, attention, and status. They want to be at the top of the social totem pole. And they want sex. How do the lucky few get all of these? Surplus. Savings. Piles of treasure. And what does treasure amount to in a society without money? In some societies, treasure is gold and jewels. In some, it's cattle and sheep. In some it's fish oil and copper. In some it's shells. In others, its armor and weaponry. In yet others it's clothes and blankets. And in almost all, it's art and amazing rarities. But in New Guinea, it's pork, pies, and puddings.

How do you rise in the pecking order in New Guinea? You become an entrepreneur. You become a maker of social organization. You come up with a dream and you sell it with all your heart to your relatives, your friends, and strangers, persuading them to work with you on a project that will take you to the top—raising pigs, the source of pork. And raising taro, the raw material of pies and puddings.

You and the staff you recruit work like maniacs all year to pile up as many pigs and as much taro as you can. You make sure of that. You motivate, inspire, and bully your team. If you have to, you shame them. Or you listen to their ideas and use the ones that work the best.

You do everything in your power to maximize productivity. Why? Because when the harvest is over, you'll make your big move, your play in the status game. You'll challenge an established big man, a man with a team that has won the production competition year after year after year, a man who humbles others with his achievements, a man who abashes others with his reputation and dignity.[1]

You'll invite him over for dinner. And when he arrives you will feed him and give him gifts. You will offer him one pork dish after another until the variety and the quantity stagger him.[2] Then you will pile on the taro pies and taro puddings. If you awe him with more helpings of food than anyone can possibly eat and with more gifts than he and his team can carry away, he will fear for his high position. Why? Because if he can't top what you've achieved, you'll move up on the status ladder. And he will be forced to move down. In New Guinea, he who can pile up the surplus wins the status game.

Why? What does this rule of the status game achieve? It turns New Guinean society into a productivity machine. It also turns New Guinean society into a collective intelligence, a group IQ, a social learning machine. It harnesses the pendulum of repurposing and the cycle of insecurity. It harnesses the wheel of exploration and digestion, the wheel of expansion and consolidation. It turns an island of competitors into an evolutionary search engine, a bio-Googling team.

Each young contestant in the pork and pudding contests goes out to test the potential of new lands—or of old lands cropped in new ways. Each one is forced to come up with new and better ways to motivate his neighbors to pitch in and achieve. Then each is forced into a competition. He is forced into the digestion stage. He who has the most toys, the most extra stuff to play around with, wins. And that person is he who has the greatest gifts for social organization. And he who has the greatest surplus in his pockets—or in his storage heaps.

What does this have to do with a modern economy? What does it have to do with you and me?

20

THE BRILLIANCE OF THE ROBBER BARONS AND THE J. P. MORGAN BLUES

Can a monster be a messiah? And if so, how?

An economic crash is like the pork and pudding contest. He who has the most is left standing. Why? Because he who has the most is often he who has the greatest powers of social organization. It's he or she who manages to pull together the most effective team.

Evolution is vicious. She tests us with crashes to discover who is the greatest social structure maker. To survive, a society functions as a productivity engine that uses people shamelessly. A productivity engine with a collective intelligence, with a group IQ. A productivity engine with ingenuity. Where does that collective cleverness come from? From the hidden rule at work in the embryo when would-be neural cells migrate to a new spot, don't find a welcome, and kill themselves off. From the hidden rule that makes would-be tubules in the cellular skeleton reach out for a connection point that needs them, and if they don't find one, dissolve away. From the hidden rule that makes a bee come home with a load of what she hopes the hive needs, and, if no one wants what she brings, thrusts her into a stupefied depression. And from the hidden rule that generates the cleverness of computer learning machines called complex adaptive systems—Darwinian and neural-net-based learning machines. It's a rule enunciated by Jesus when he made a paradoxical and uncharacteristically harsh

127

statement: "To he who hath it shall be given. From he who hath not, even what he hath shall be taken away." It's a rule summed up in the title of the old blues tune "Nobody Loves You When You're Down and Out." And it's a rule that Columbia University sociologist Robert Merton calls the Matthew effect because Jesus's quote on the subject is found in the Gospel of Matthew.[1]

The Matthew effect, the law of "nobody loves you when you're down and out" and of "from he who hath not, even what he hath shall be taken away," is the key rule of clever machines,[2] the key rule of machines that learn from experience and innovate. It's the rule behind the genius of evolutionary search engines. And it's despicable. But "nobody loves you when you're down and out" turns entire societies into thinking machines with an intelligence that transcends your smarts and mine. Thinking machines that take on problems that are often too big for you and me to see. Problems like how to fix the flaws in an economy.

Society's collective intelligence is not always brilliant. But nature has a way to make sure this group IQ is as smart as can be. That method? Testing. Testing in competitions between societies. Testing in peaceful competitions of commerce. Testing in violent competitions of war. Or testing in competitions between the groups *inside* a society. Testing in competitions between subcultures. And testing in competitions between individuals. Which is where crash and boom come in.

How do the battles of the big men and the rule of "nobody loves you when you're down and out" sharpen the collective puzzle-solving capacity of a society? How do they advance the workings of an evolutionary search engine? One answer lies in the tale of a man often referred to as a "robber baron," a man accused of running an insidious, conspiratorial scheme to control and milk America, a "money trust"—J. P. Morgan.[4] Morgan was one of the greatest consolidators and structure makers of all time. And he was the one big man left standing head and shoulders above the rest in two of America's biggest crashes, the panic of 1893 and the panic of 1907. A few minutes ago we caught a glimpse of Morgan at work pulling the exploratory threads of a disorganized railroad expansion together and tying them into a national railway system. Morgan consolidated the promising sprawl that seventy years of entrepreneurial exuberance had produced. And he turned that sprawl into a national railway system.

J. P. Morgan's mastery of the art of social organization and structure creation was awesome. In 1869 Morgan wrestled with two other titans over control of the Albany and Susquehanna Railroad and won. In 1885 he reorganized the New York, West Shore & Buffalo Railroad, then persuaded the New York Central Railroad to lease the result from him. In 1886 he reorganized the Philadelphia & Reading Railroad. In 1888, he did the same to the Chesapeake & Ohio Railroad. Then the government passed the Interstate Commerce Act of 1887, establishing the Interstate Commerce Commission, the first government commission to regulate an industry, a commission designed to clamp down on skullduggery and rate-fixing in megabusiness, a commission that was aimed specifically at skullduggery and rate fixing in the railroad industry.[5] J. P. Morgan took advantage of the opportunity to call together a group of folks who had never met face to face before, the wildly competing presidents of thirty of America's most powerful railroads.[6] Morgan pulled this passel of squabblers and dirty fighters together for conferences in 1889 and again in 1890, showing them how to work together rather than at cross purposes. The result? Morgan made high-speed, long-distance travel for people like you and me simple, reliable, and affordable.

In 1892, Morgan "Morganized" yet another new high-tech business—the budding electric power and appliance industry. He merged two of the key players—Edison General Electric and the Thompson-Houston Electric Company. The result was a high-quality giant—General Electric.

Then came the panic of 1893. The public mood switched from mania to depression. Folks who had been entranced by visions of wealth a few months earlier now had fantasies of disaster and poverty dancing in their heads. The Philadelphia & Reading Railroad, the Northern Pacific Railway, the Union Pacific Railroad, the Atchison, Topeka & Santa Fe Railroad, and the National Cordage Company all failed. But as in many other economic catastrophes, America saw the rise of new social structures. Among them were new forms of public expression, new forms of protest. In 1894 there was the nationwide Pullman strike, the Great Northern Railroad strike in Martinsburg, West Virginia, and the Bituminous Coal Miners' strike in Birmingham, Alabama. Then came the Haverhill Shoe strike in Massachusetts in 1895. And Coxey's Army, a protest against unemployment in which one hundred jobless men set out on foot from Massillon, Ohio, on March 25, 1894, and paraded to Washington, picking up another four hundred protestors along the way and capping the event with a fire-and-brimstone speech from their leader, populist Jacob Coxey, on the grass in front of the nation's capitol. Coxey's Army helped lay the base for the antiwar protests of the twentieth and twenty-first centuries.

In the panic of 1893, the pendulum of repurposing showed that it could do for humans what it does for bees—yank them out of a failing productivity team and plug them in where new wealth was flowing. Jobless people pulled up stakes in the East, headed west on the new railroads to find a way to make a living, and ended up in struggling new towns like Seattle, Portland, Salt Lake City, Denver, San Francisco, and Los Angeles, towns the railroads helped put on the map.

Here's where the New Guineans and their food competitions come in. The cycle of boom and bust triggers big man competitions: displays of who can produce the most surplus, demonstrations of who can produce industrial societies' equivalent of pork, puddings, and pies. Those fighting to remain standing in the panic of 1893 included railroad tycoon Edward Henry Harriman, oil king John D. Rockefeller, banking maestro Jacob Schiff, and another master of finance, Francis H. Peabody.[7] Who would win the right to save the day? Who would show he could produce the biggest surplus? Who would benefit from the rule of "to he who hath it shall be given" and from the law that "nobody loves you when you're down and out?" Who would benefit from the Matthew effect? Or, to put it a bit differently, who was J. P. Morgan and why did he come out on top?

John Pierpont Morgan was born into the banking business. His grandfather had been in on the ground floor of two daring new companies in Hartford, Connecticut. One was the super high-tech Connecticut River Steamboat Company. The other had more global potential—the Aetna Insurance Company, a firm that now rakes in over $27 billion a year.[8] The Aetna Insurance name now sounds old and stuffy, but it was a company whose line of business was risk—selling protection from death, hazard, accident, and catastrophe. J. P. Morgan's dad, Junius, had been an intersociety splicer, a part of the system that made the economy global even in the nineteenth century. Morgan's dad had gone to London in 1854 as a banker. His specialty? Raising money to back a still-new republic, the United States. Raising funds to turn this new territory's murderous wilderness into a source of riches. Selling fantasies of what America could be and routing speculative money from the Old World to the New. Junius's son, J. P.—Pierpont to his friends[9]—was what many of us men dream of being but never quite achieve. He was tall, powerful, and a people person. He had a fertile mind and was a terrific persuader. And he loved numbers in a way few others do. He spent his vacations from school working in the back offices of banks, offices called "counting houses." Why? Because he loved the inner workings of finance.

Pierpont had a strange romantic history. When he was twenty-four years old, he fell in love with "a frail girl with an oval face and hair parted down the middle," Amelia Sturges.[10] But there was an obstacle. She was dying of tuberculosis. Yet Pierpont insisted on marriage. He carried Amelia down the stairs of her parents' Fourteenth Street, Manhattan, house for the ceremony. Then he carried her to a carriage waiting outside the door and whisked her off to a European honeymoon. The result was inevitable. His bride died four months later while they were still in France, leaving Morgan in grief. Some say this strange affair and Morgan's intense commitment to it was a sign of Morgan's love of the dangerous and the difficult, not to mention the impossible. Morgan was willing to challenge death itself. For his second marriage, Morgan settled on the secure but unexciting, a cold but normal high society wife. Then he satisfied his needs with a succession of mistresses.[11] His equivalent of the New Guineans' multiple wives.[12]

But most important was Pierpont's ability to see a future that did not yet exist, to believe in his vision, to sell it powerfully, to back it financially, and to organize other men and existing institutions in brand-new ways. Pierpont's specialty was doing what the big men of New Guinea do—splicing people together in new kinds of productivity teams. He organized other entrepreneurs on a scale that the New Guineans could not have conceived. He was a structure maker in an economic web that spanned continents.

When Morgan reorganized businesses, they showed a miraculous ability to produce profits for their stockholders. And thanks to the labors of his grandfather and his father, Morgan was rock solid financially. His competitors often depended on borrowed funds to manage their high-finance industrial ploys. Morgan was different. He actually had money in the bank.[13]

In 1895, the US government was in trouble. It was running out of gold. Running out fast. Could Morgan do for an entire nation what he had done for the railroad and for the electric industry? A new president, Grover Cleveland, thought he could. The crash of 1893 had turned the Democrats out of office and had brought a landslide victory to the Republicans, sweeping Grover Cleveland into office in 1894 with a big mandate. In 1895, Cleveland begged J. P. Morgan to help fill the rapidly emptying Treasury of the United States with new gold.

Morgan was up for the challenge. He floated a bond issue, then followed the path that his grandfather had pioneered. He went to Europe to sell the citizens of England and the Continent on the American dream.[14] Times were not as tough in the Old World as they were in the new. Europe had recovered from its twenty-year-long Great Depression in roughly 1894, just as America was sliding into the financial abyss.[15] Wealthy Europeans with excess money in their pockets for the first time in two decades were anxious to invest it. But they did not believe in the monetary soundness of the US government. Whom did they believe in? J. P. Morgan.[16] So Pierpont pulled off the impossible. He raised $100 million and filled the US Treasury with gold. Morgan had won one bout of the big man contest. There would be more.

In 1896 America went back to work. It shifted once again from bust to boom. In 1901 J. P. Morgan pulled together another new industry, steel, the miraculous new metal that kept railroad tracks from curling and stabbing their uplifted ends into passing railroad cars and killing dozens of passengers. First Morgan helped bankroll a new steel company—Federal Steel. Then he persuaded the emperor of steel, Andrew Carnegie, to sell his business.[17] Morgan merged Carnegie's massive firm with Federal and with a passel of smaller steel companies, creating the United States Steel Corporation, the company that would dominate the steel industry for most of the twentieth century. In 1902 Morgan once again demonstrated his knack for making structure in revolutionary new fields. He helped launch the modern farming revolution when he bought the McCormick Harvesting Machine Company and the Deering Harvester Company, fused them with two smaller tractor and harvester companies, and created International Harvester.[18]

Then, in 1907, it happened again. The cycle of insecurity shifted from confidence to fear. Panicked citizens lined up outside of banks to grab their cash before the banks could collapse. Businesses were failing left and right. Another big man contest, another swing of the pendulum of repurposing, and another consolidation and structure creation phase was in the offing. Once again J. P. Morgan won the competition of the big men. On October 23, 1907, he pulled together ten leading bankers at his office on the corner of Wall Street and Broad.[19] These giants of finance sat in one room while Morgan and four banking magnates he trusted sat in another. The odd thing, he told his fellow titans of finance, was that, like the railroad kings he'd pulled together in 1889, the ten banking heads in the room next door had never met each other before. During that evening and the days that followed, Morgan accomplished the impossible. He pulled together money from commercial financial institutions, from the US Treasury, and from the wealthy (John D. Rockefeller kicked in $10 million—$220 million in 2007 dollars). And once again, Morgan brought in gold from a panic-shaken Europe—an impossible feat.[20] Morgan used this kitty to keep the stock market open, to shore up banks on the verge of collapse, and to save even the city of New York from bankruptcy.

Morgan's initiatives led the nation to see the power of a "lender of last resort." In an attempt to turn Morgan's role into a permanent part of America's financial structure, the government put together the Federal Reserve Bank. The expansion and exploration of a boom had given way to centralization, consolidation, digestion, and structure building. A bust had turned out to have a creative side. It had turned out to be another roll forward by the wheel of the evolutionary search engine, another chug forward by the secular genesis machine.

Why had J. P. Morgan won the big man contest? Because he had cash from his family and cash from his own astonishing achievements. Because he had surplus. And because he proved that he was an organizer, a crafter of productivity teams par excellence. He was an inventor of new structures that worked brilliantly.

21

THE POET AND THE
ESCALATOR OF COMPLEXITY

The ratchet in the gears of crash and boom. Or
crash, boom, chemicals, and crayfish.

In the end what does the cycle of boom and bust do to earn its keep
in the evolutionary game? It puts us on an escalator of complexity, an
escalator that's moved upward since 1776, when the living standard
of the West rose to that of ancient Rome for the first time since the
empire of the Latins began to crumble in 410 CE.[1] In 1795 the poet
William Blake wrote three poetic prophecies on the economic depression going on around him.[2] Europe had just gone through one of the
worst winters it had ever seen. The result was famine.[3] Thousands or
tens of thousands of people died of hunger in France and England.
There was no official count. Mass death was a normal part of economic downturns in those days. But it would not stay that way.

When the famine of 1795 was over, the British government established a system that paid low-wage workers extra money to cover the
price of bread.[4] And a London magistrate, Patrick Colquhoun, began
to advocate something new, "soup kitchens."[5] These safety nets were
designed to make sure no one would ever starve in an economic stall
again. The English did not do this out of charity. They did it out of
fear. The starving massed in the streets and rioted. Mobs like these
had just pulled off a revolution in France and had taken nobles like

the ones in Britain's parliament to the guillotines. Britain's political rulers wanted to keep their heads. Chalk up a victory for the pendulum of repurposing.

The evolutionary search engine and the secular genesis machine aren't picky about their fuel. They feast on fear. And they sometimes use it to create. The results can be impressive. By the panic of 1907, so many social nets had been put into place that few feared starvation. Now you panicked because your bank failed and you lost your savings. During the Great Depression of 1929–1939, the US government invented the Federal Deposit Insurance Corporation, an institution that guaranteed your savings even if your bank went down in flames. The result? By the Great Crash of 2008, you could even trust the soundness of the credit system. It didn't feel that way, but in fact your credit cards and mine still worked. We still had cash to buy a sandwich, to grab a coffee at Starbucks, and to make it through the week. And we had another innovation put into place during the Great Depression—unemployment insurance.[6]

But human nature is stubborn. We're convinced that each new downturn is the greatest economic catastrophe that has ever been. We felt emotionally clobbered by the Great Crash of 2008, just as clobbered as the folks of 1795 had felt when their crash arrived. But we failed to count our blessings. Our period of deprivation would look like paradise to a subsistence farmer in Ireland or Scotland in 1795 whose crop had failed and who had nothing to eat.[7]

So why did we feel we were just as threatened and smashed as the folks dying of starvation over two hundred years ago? Because of the perception shift, the mass mood swing, and the personal emotion flip that makes the cycle of boom and bust work. Because our moods of irrational exuberance in good times and our dread and doubt when things are bad change us physically. Shifts from manic to depressive shift our hormone balance. They literally reset our physiology.

Let's go back to the mysterious secrets of biology. Nearly every form of multicellular animal we know competes for dominance in a pecking order. That includes lizards, lobsters, puppies, and you and me. Two crayfish go up against each other to see who can raise his head the highest—an instinctual ritual so universal that lizards and chimpanzees use it too. The crayfish literally have showdowns over "standing," over who can stand the tallest. The crayfish that wins goes through a massive central nervous system shift.[8] His nerve cells' receptors for the neurochemical serotonin are altered by his triumph. (Serotonin is the hormone boosted by the human antidepressant Prozac.) The victorious crayfish's reworked receptors interpret serotonin as the ambrosia of the gods, an ambrosia that gives him confidence and dignity. His serotonin receptors give him a positive way of seeing the world around him. That positivity shows up in an erect posture, a posture of leadership and majesty. In the victor's body the neural settings of good times, the neural settings of mastery, and the neural settings of boom strut their stuff.

But the serotonin receptors in the loser go through the opposite of boom—they bust. They are changed as completely as the canvas of a pointillist painter who decides to paint over an existing scene in sunny daylight and to turn it into the same scene in the gloom of night. The loser's rearranged neural receptors interpret serotonin as a signal to abase himself, to crawl humbly before his betters, to grovel, and to fear. Thanks to a radical remake of his hormonal receptors, the loser interprets the world as being in depression.

In technical terms, serotonin becomes a stimulant for the top animal and an inhibitor for the crayfish he's just defeated.[9] What's more, the loser's system is shot through with octopamine, a chemical that makes him timid.[10] The winner's perceptions, his confidence, and his resistance to disease rocket him to the top of his form. The crayfish that loses also goes through a radical emotional and perceptual shift. But in his case, it's a downgrade. His rejiggered serotonin receptors trigger the equivalent of misery. And his system is flooded with stress hormones.[11] Those hormones make his perceptions sluggish, his emotions dreary, his body slumped, and his attitude one of bleak acceptance.

The researchers who discovered this chemical boom and bust remarked that it's as if each crayfish—the winner and the loser—have gone through a brain transplant.[12] My colleague and sometime conspirator in the generation of new ideas, evolutionary biologist Valerius Geist, professor emeritus of environmental science at the University of Calgary and president of Wildlife Heritage Ltd., calls this a change in phenotype, a body-shift.[13] It's also a shift that can happen to you and me when we win or lose. Especially when we lose big-time because of economic cycles that eliminate our jobs and wipe out our savings. But in cycles of boom and bust, you and I are never alone. A vast mass of humans around the globe share our ebullience or our gloom. And many share our central nervous system changes, our upshift or downshift, our changes in phenotype.

Control is another central nervous system shifter.[14] Another resetter of our physiology. When you feel you are in control, your perceptions, your energy, your confidence, your immune system, and even your posture are shifted to high. But when control slips away, watch out. You are hit with glucocorticoids—stress hormones. Stress hormones are picker-uppers, energizers, when they come in short, sharp spikes. But the floods of glucocorticoids triggered by helplessness and lack of control are·long and often lasting. And glucocorticoids in long doses are poisons. They trigger apoptosis—preprogrammed cell death. They force some of your key brain cells to commit suicide. They also lower your ability to perceive solutions. They lower the activity of your immune system. And in extreme cases, they kill you.

If you feel that you have no control over your fate and if that depressing view dogs you long enough, you may slide into an even more appalling physical state—learned helplessness. Not only will your body cave in, but you will lose your will to dodge your agony even when there's a clear avenue of escape—like a guaranteed job you could get if only you could muster the courage to make a phone call. In learned helplessness, your own body conspires to destroy you. The guilty hormone is called *substance P*.[15] And, like glucocorticoids, it's a self-destruct chemical produced by your very own cells.

Why does biology boost you physiologically when you show you have control? Why does the evolutionary search engine upshift the vigor of the individuals, cliques, and nations that have a handle on things? And why does your physiology reward you when you can accurately predict the next big blow? Why does your body punish you when you haven't a clue?[16] Why does the evolutionary search engine give bonuses to those with ideas that seem to pay off, to those with an approach that seems to offer control over fate and circumstance? Why does the evolutionary search engine give hormonal boosts to the members of the group who are mastering the moment? And why does biology spurt hormonal poisons into the bloodstreams of those who are flailing and failing? Why does the evolutionary search engine give those who are on top of things a regal posture and saddle those who are flummoxed with a slouch and a slump? Why is the evolutionary search engine so appallingly cruel?

The answer hauls us back to computer simulations of neural nets and Darwinian algorithms, simulations of successful learning machines. In clever machines, success and the ability to adapt are based on a cruel rule—the Matthew effect—"To he who hath" and "nobody loves you when you're down and out."

Sounds pretty grim when we hit the downslide, doesn't it? So, again, what do we get out of being components of an evolutionary search engine, if anything? We build institutions that protect us. But we also build something more subtle. We build a tool of extraordinary powers. We build a *symbol stack*.

What is a symbol stack? Imagine that you're Ivan Pavlov in 1905. You have a hunch about how animals are trained. And you are perfectly willing to be cruel in the interests of science. First you demonstrate that a dog will salivate when you give him food. Then you ring a bell when the dog's food arrives. After time has passed and the bell has accompanied the food over and over again, you ring the bell and don't deliver the food. The dog salivates anyway. Says Pavlov, the dog has come to associate the bell with food. But what you've actually done is something more. You've demonstrated that a dog can be trained to recognize a symbol—the bell that stands for food. Let's call a bell-equals-food symbol a first-order symbol, the first layer of symbols in the symbol stack.

Is there a human equivalent to the bell that stands for food? Yes. Gold and silver. We love gold and silver because they are pretty. We love them because they boost our status. But we've also loved gold for roughly 2,600 years because it's a symbol. It stands for something. Four thousand years ago in Mesopotamia, if you raised sheep and I raised barley, I'd eventually get hungry for meat. So I'd trade you fifteen sheaves of barley for one of your sheep. To pull this off, I'd go to the marketplace with my barley and you'd go with your sheep. And we'd trade the goods on the spot. Then came a first-order symbol in the symbol stack. You and I would both get used to the idea that gold and silver could stand for grain and meat. Yes, we'd stubbornly refuse at first. We'd suspect that this new-fangled method of exchange was too dangerous, too displeasing to the gods, and too much of a con game. But after a few generations, the association of the symbol with the real deal would become a part of our scaffold of habit. Then, if we were making a really big deal, I'd go to the market with a few bits of my gold and you'd show up at the market with a few bits of yours. You'd give me gold for something that was nowhere in sight—my barley. And I'd give you gold for something equally invisible—the sheep you were grazing in the countryside. We'd be on a par with Pavlov's dog. We'd be at level one of the symbol stack.

In Babylon in roughly 3000 BCE, the symbol stack rose even higher. Scribes invented small clay tokens that represented barley and sheep. When you and I made a deal, we'd soon discover that six months later when it came time to deliver the goods, we remembered the arrangement we'd worked out differently. I thought you owed me thirty lambs. You were sure it was twenty. And I thought I'd said I'd give you two hundred sheaves of wheat. You remembered with absolute certainty that I promised to give you three hundred. So we learned to make our deals in front of a scribe. The scribe made a clay envelope. He put three hundred tokens representing barley sheaves into the clay pouch to record my side of the deal. He put thirty tokens representing lambs in to keep a record of your promises. Six months later when we squabbled, you and I would go to the scribe and he'd break open the envelope and show us what we'd actually committed to.

Eventually an inventive scribe would press the tokens into the outer side of the clay envelope and leave a permanent indentation, a permanent mark, so that he wouldn't have to break the clay open to see the contract we'd made. The idea of making an imprint in clay turned into a huge breakthrough in the symbol stack—writing.[17] And it turned into the written deal—the contract.

Would there be an advantage to using symbols instead of real goods? To using gold and imprints on clay instead of sheep on the hoof and grain ready to take home and eat? Yes. We might, for example, make our deal long before my barley had become ripe and long before your new season of lambs had been born. To put it in economic-ese, we might make a futures contract for our commodities. Or you might be in Athens and I might be in Chersonesus, a town on the Black Sea, over 650 miles away. I might want your absolutely wonderful olive oil and you might covet my massive sheaves of wheat.[18] Using symbols—gold and contracts—you and I could make a deal to supply each other year after year. Our symbols could represent something invisible and risky, the stuff of Othello's dreams and nightmares—the future.

What symbols have we gotten as a result of crashes, manias, and panics?

- The dollar in the crash of the 1780s
- The savings book—a book that represented the money you socked away in a savings bank—courtesy of the panic of 1819
- The government-backed banknote, created by the Free Banking Act of 1838[19]
- The concept of the idea-based nation (the panic of 1857)
- The greenback (also the panic of 1857)
- The check (the crash of 1865)
- And the fixed-rate thirty-year mortgage, a gift of the Great Depression

How high has the symbol stack risen? Gold is a first-order symbol associated with real goods and services—real sheep and barley. Paper money is a second-order symbol, a symbol that represents a symbol. Paper money represents gold. A savings book and a check are symbols of a symbol of a symbol—symbols of greenbacks, which are symbols of gold, which are symbols of sheep and barley. Pretty complicated, right? But symbols are like levers. The higher the order of a symbol on the symbol stack, the more it can accomplish. You can make much bigger deals in much less time with a handwritten letter of credit on paper than you can with a pile of gold. And you can make even faster (and more-complicated) deals with a computerized fund transfer.

But there's a problem. The higher the symbol on the symbol stack, the harder it is to understand its positives—and its risks. Crashes often come when we are dealing with a new symbol that's just been slid onto the top of the symbol stack—like a hedge fund, a US dollar index future contract, or a credit default swap.[20] Crashes often reveal the dangers hidden in the use of a symbol. And crashes often force us to create institutions or regulations that can dampen the damage.

Over time, use of the symbols enters our scaffold of habit. What's the *scaffold of habit*? And what does it have to do with boom, bust, and capitalism? The scaffold of habit is the toothpick tower–like lattice of little things we do in our daily lives, little things from which the walls of a social structure are built. It's the time we go to bed at night, the time we get up in the morning, the routine of three meals a day, the side of the plate on which we expect to find our fork, the attention we pay—or don't pay—to the clock or to sunrise and sunset, the distance we stand from each other when we talk, the way we phrase our emotions, the emotions we display and the feelings we hide, the embarrassing things we tuck away, and the clichés we fall back on. It's the heap of stones with which the fortress of our society is built.

In Polynesia, men dance in two rows, moving their arms in a strangely familiar motion, moving them with swiftness, with control, and with precise group synchrony. Why? That motion is what shoots a Polynesian outrigger boat forward on the ocean when these men go off on a fishing expedition or when they make war. The dance exercises the scaffold of habit. It exercises precisely coordinated rowing. In Muslim society men get together in a group five times a day, lay out their prayer mats, and recite prayers while they bow to Mecca. Five times a day—more frequently than you and I eat meals. Why? They are practicing the habit of a *jamaat*—a congregation of men.[21] A congregation whose unity serves them well in politics, in peace, and in war.[22] Many an Islamic militant group making war against you and me today uses the word jamaat in its formal name—Jamaat-ud-Da'wah,[23] for example, in Pakistan, the group accused of involvement in the November 2008 Mumbai, India, attacks on the Taj and the Trident luxury hotels that killed 195 and wounded 295.[24] What's the importance of these five daily prayer ceremonies? They exercise the scaffold of habit, the scaffold of group solidarity.

Says British-American military historian Hugh Bicheno, "The 'how' of battle hinges on weapons and the habits they require of the men who use them."[25] Underneath a successful military campaign there lies a scaffold of habit.

In India there is the Bharatanatyam dance. Archaemetallurgist and Bharatanatyam dancer Sharada Srinivasan at the National Institute of Advanced Studies in Bangalore, India, one of my friends, has made a video (it's on YouTube)[26] showing how the elaborate, aesthetically rich but seemingly useless dance rehearses the key muscular patterns of metal making the ancient Indian way. What does the dance achieve? It strengthens the scaffold of habit that once underlay a key ancient Indian technology.

In South Korea in 1973 entrepreneurial dictator Park Chung Hee wanted to establish a steel industry. He turned to the World Bank for funding.[27] But the World Bank was less than enthusiastic about the project. Nearly every tin-pot dictator on the planet had erected a steel plant as a useless status symbol. The world was awash in so much excess steel-making capacity that Korea didn't stand a chance of getting into the international steel business.[28] Said the World Bank, Park's notion of an "integrated steel mill in Korea was a premature proposition without economic feasibility."[29] In other words, it was a stupid idea. Park responded by getting the Austrians and the Japanese to train 597 workers in steelmaking. Then he put his men to work in an empty Korean field, where they pretended they were standing at the machines needed for modern steel production. Every day, Park had these workers rehearse precisely the movements they would need to operate "a sintering plant, a coke oven, a blast furnace, a basic oxygen furnace, an ingot-casting facility, and a plate mill." Sounds absurd, right? But, says MIT political economist Alice Amsden, "Each stage demanded a different set of technical skills. . . . The correct mixture and quality of raw materials, the balancing of capacities, the scheduling of material flows, and the relieving of bottlenecks."[30] When South Korea was finally able to build its steel plants, it snatched the low-cost steel business away from the United States and Japan and put itself on top of the steelmaking heap. What was Korea's secret? Determination. Persistence. Utter dedication to a vision. And the scaffold of habit.

What happens when the scaffold of habit can't keep up with a rapidly shifting reality? Americans rebelled against paper money and the greenback over and over again from 1788 to 1884. They weren't in the habit of using it. Paper wasn't real money, they said, unless they could convert it to gold. Little did they seem to realize that gold, too, is just a symbol. Just a token that stands for goods and services. It took a hundred years of anti–paper money upheavals before the habit of viewing paper money as, well, *real* money took hold. Then Americans panicked over something new. This time, they lost faith in a symbol of a symbol of a symbol—in the bank books and checks that stood for greenbacks. The bank books and checks that stood for paper money. And what did the paper money stand for? Gold. And what did gold symbolize? Haircuts, horses, hand soap, buggy whips, and Model Ts.

A new layer in the symbol stack was dependent on a scaffold of habit. The habit of using paper to buy things. Which is where repurposing comes in. The cycle of boom and crash, the pendulum of repurposing, makes us desperate in periods of crash. And desperation makes us willing to embrace new things. Desperation helps drive new habits home. Some say that the real savior of America in the Great Depression of 1929–1939 wasn't Franklin Delano Roosevelt's New Deal. It was an act of desperation . . . World War II. And what's a war? A radical swing in the pendulum of repurposing. In a war where survival is at stake, a war of total mobilization, men are willing to do something they would resist with all their might in peace time. They are willing to leave the comfortable habits of home, work, and family. They are willing to leave their cities, congregate far away in unfamiliar kinds of teams, and have drill sergeants bark, bully, and humiliate them into a very different routine from any they've ever known before, a routine that rehearses them in group organization, a routine that inculcates a radically different scaffold of habit.[31]

Then comes the ultimate big man contest, the war itself, a competition to see which nation has the greatest surplus, the greatest command of natural resources, the greatest cleverness, invention, confidence, and the greatest ability to produce not just tanks, ships, and planes, but to produce human beings, to raise children who can be used as cannon fodder, the greatest ability to produce young men and women who a nation can feed into the war machine. Yes, in war we offer up the lives of young men and women the way a New Guinean big man offers up his pork and pies.

Does any of war's repurposing stick? Does a scaffold of habit pounded into a soldier change the way he acts in times of peace? Sociological pioneer Max Weber[32] and postmodernist historian and philosopher Michel Foucault[33] are sure the habits stick very solidly indeed. They say that everything from the hospital system and the modern corporation to government bureaucracy is built on the base of habits first hammered into men's brains by the sort of drilled-and-disciplined armies that arose in the days of Prussia's Frederick the Great.

In America, when we shifted from Great Depression to full-fledged war mode in 1941, many women abandoned their role as homemakers and went to work in giant industries making the weapons their men would expend so carelessly on the battlefield, weaponry that would form one heap of wreckage after another. The daily appearance of women at the workplace helped boost the powers of a movement that had been struggling ever since the suffragette days of the late 1890s—the movement for women's rights. World War II rehearsed Americans in the daily habits of real female equality. The habits of daily discipline also helped World War II veterans when they finally left the service at war's end in 1945 and went to college on the GI Bill. Those habits helped produce the deeds of what NBC news anchor and author Tom Brokaw calls "the greatest generation."[34]

***

By the year 2000, Americans had come to believe in their banks and in the newest Lego on the symbol stack—a piece of plastic called a credit card. The ritual of whipping out your plastic and signing a charge receipt had "become routine"—it had been added to the scaffold of habit. Another symbol had been added to the symbol stack.

These days we take paper money for granted. It's finally settled into its place on the symbol stack. It's finally built its cross-braces in our scaffold of habit. And these days credit cards are symbols of paper money. Symbols of a symbol of a symbol. Third-order symbols for those of us who can keep count (I'm not one of them). Treasury Secretary Henry Paulson kept our credit cards working in the Great Crash of 2008 by propping up the banks that issued the cards. He shored them up with close to $8 trillion in rescue funds.[35]

Did we really get benefits out of the cycles of boom and crash that plagued us from 1795 to 2008? Did catastrophe prove to be opportunity in disguise? Grim and harsh opportunity? Yes. We no longer had to worry about starvation. Crashes no longer came with famines attached. In fact, crashes were often accompanied by food surpluses. We no longer had to worry about our savings. Those were insured by the government. And we no longer had to worry about the total disappearance of that third-order symbol without which we could not live—Visa or MasterCard. Or at least that's the way it appears at the moment I'm writing this—in 2009. You can never quite be sure.

But certainty or not, one thing is clear. We've moved up on a device that only rarely (and temporarily) runs in reverse. We've moved up on the escalator of complexity.

* * *

Your heart and mine will each beat roughly three billion times in our voyage from the womb to the grave.[36] During that time we will be put together, taken apart, and put together again without noticing it. We will dance to the beat of the pendulum of repurposing. Remember, first we were constructed as embryos. Then we were reconstructed as infants, repurposed as children, radically remade as teenagers, dramatically reshaped as young adults, re-created as middle-agesters, reshuffled as oldsters, rejiggered as doddering postsenior citizens, discarded as corpses, and finally we will be taken apart again and repurposed as bacterial cells, cells that are eaten by worms that are eaten by birds. The birds will relieve themselves as they fly over farmlands. Their intestinal wastes will help make the corn that feeds our children and their children beyond them. Repurposing.

Ten billion of your cells and mine die each day to keep you alive.[37] Ten billion a day die to move you from the stage you are at now toward the stage you'll reach next month and next year. And ten billion new cells find their place in the always slightly different you. Even after death, our molecules keep cycling, spreading, exploring, consolidating, and dying for the greater cause.

That cause? This is a universe spreading her arms to explore her possibilities, a cosmos feeling out the darkness of the future with her fingertips. Like you and me, she is changing constantly, evolving into forms she has never experienced before. And the sensory cells of the fingertips with which she explores include you and me.

This gives us a responsibility. We are parts of an evolutionary search engine, components in a secular genesis machine. We are among nature's tools for reconstructing herself in flamboyant new ways. Economies are also among nature's tools of creation. But when nature creates, she destroys to make new things. She creates by driving us with strange forces—discontents, desires, and dreams. We do nature's work when we turn those restless dreams into realities, realities that amplify the powers or elevate the lives of our fellow human beings.

IV

TRUTH IN THE
CORRIDORS OF POWER

22

THE TRUTH AT ANY PRICE INCLUDING THE PRICE OF YOUR LIFE

Honesty has clout. A story of soul power from my
early corporate days at "Engulf & Devour."

The genius of the beast lies in the brilliance of the evolutionary search engine. The genius of capitalism and of the Western system lies in the creative powers of the secular genesis machine.

And the genius of the beast lies in the Western system's way of pursuing the fission-fusion search strategy, the strategy of exploration and digestion, of speculation and consolidation, of gambling, discovery, and structure formation.

Strange as it may seem, the genius of the beast is not at its best when it blindly follows just one principle, the principle of profit—"buy cheap and sell dear." The genius of the capitalist system is at its best when it follows two fission-fusion search rules, two exploration-and-consolidation search rules, two search rules with their roots in a strange place. With their roots in our personal passion and in our commitment to each other.

What are those two search imperatives? They're two rules from a long-lost book. They're rules that book called the first two rules of science: (1) The truth at any price including the price of your life, and (2) look at things right under your nose as if you've never seen them before, then proceed from there.

What led me to this peculiar conclusion? My background was in theoretical physics, microbiology, and psychology. But from 1968 to 1988, I did fieldwork in mass behavior, fieldwork in pop culture. During those two decades in the corporate world I helped generate $28 billion in revenue (more than the gross domestic product of Oman or Luxembourg) for companies like Sony, Disney, Pepsi-Cola, Coca-Cola, and Warner Brothers. And I was a member of the teams that built or sustained the careers of figures like Prince, Bob Marley, Bette Midler, Michael Jackson, Billy Joel, Paul Simon, Billy Idol, Peter Gabriel, David Byrne, John Mellencamp, and Queen.

Here's the story.

* * *

The year was 1973. I was a scientist five years into a twenty-year-long Voyage of the Beagle, an expedition into the world of corporate and popular culture. I'd landed in a place I'd never expected to be—a twenty-third-floor Manhattan conference room at Gulf & Western Industries.

Gulf & Western was one of the mightiest conglomerates of the mid-twentieth century. Corporations were in a feeding frenzy. They swallowed smaller firms alive, discarded the parts they felt were unimportant—like the people who'd built the firms from nothing—and either kept the remains or sold the dismembered pieces for a profit.

Time magazine called it the era of "Voracious, Inc."[1] The worldwide business community summed it up with an even more threatening nickname: "Engulf & Devour."[2] The term "Engulf & Devour" was coined specifically to describe one of the worst of these megapredators—the company in whose offices I was ensconced: Gulf & Western Industries.

Gulf & Western had chewed up a venerable giant of the film business, Paramount Pictures. Along with the meat had come the feathers and the beak. One of those feathers was a music lightweight called Paramount Records.

Music was a hot property in 1973. It was the boom-time of psychedelia and rock. CBS was making a fortune off of tie-dyed stars like the recently deceased Janis Joplin. RCA was hauling in profits from Jefferson Airplane and was still riding high on the greatest solo rock 'n' roll revenue producer of all time, Elvis Presley. Atlantic Records was getting rich with new albums from a beachhead act of the British Invasion, the Rolling Stones, and with Led Zeppelin, the central band in an even newer movement, heavy metal. And Capitol Records was raking in profits from the foursome that had landed the British Invasion on American shores—the Beatles.

Teenagers were the fastest-growing market on the planet. Since 1968, platinum-priced executive newsletters had sprung into being, promising to explain this puzzling cash explosion, the emerging "youth phenomenon."

The forces underlying the youth explosion were simple. America had just been through the longest peacetime period of prosperity in its history. The trickle-down effect had carried the wealth from the pockets of parents to the allowances of their kids. Kids have no necessities to spend on, so every cent a teen received was squandered as "disposable income."

What were the first things teens with money in their pockets plunked down their coins and dollars to buy? Usually those antique twelve-inch vinyl music Frisbees called LPs (short for long-playing records) with roughly ten songs apiece.

So a foothold in the music business was a necessity for a conglomerate, especially for one dedicated to engulfing and devouring. Paramount Records, Gulf & Western's entry to the music industry, was scarcely even a single toe-rest, much less a solid footing. Paramount Records had once been a firm that sold the soundtracks to Paramount's movies. But soundtracks had stopped selling way back in the mid-1960s. Now, in 1973, Paramount Records had just one lonely star—a singer/songwriter who'd sold tons of records in the late 1960s but was on her way to oblivion. Her full name was Melanie Safka Schekeryk, but she went under just her first name, Melanie.

As Melanie sank from her former heights, the only Paramount Records replacement in sight was a band the press loved but the public did not, Commander Cody and His Lost Planet Airmen.

So Gulf & Western acquired the distribution of another thirteen record companies. And it plucked a president to run this operation from the golden nest of CBS—one of the most successful firms in the twentieth-century music business. (We'll poke into the mystery of CBS's incredible levitation . . . and of its eventual fall later.)

That CBS executive, Tony Martell, had made his name by aiding in the launch of a most-unlikely success story—a strange "concept record" with an even stranger subject matter. The "concept" was a holy grail several had striven for but none had yet been able to achieve—a "rock opera." The music's writer was the twenty-three-year-old son of a church organist from London's All Saints Church. He had staged a minor musical called *Joseph and the Amazing Technicolor Dreamcoat* in a London School at the age of nineteen.[3] Now he'd moved into something seemingly even more alien to the music of the day: a rock 'n' roll version of the story of Christ from the point of view of Judas Iscariot. The upstart composer without a band and without an electric guitar in his hand was Andrew Lloyd Webber. His preposterous project was called *Jesus Christ Superstar*.

And *Jesus Christ Superstar* sold like crazy.

That may have been an accident.

I was at ABC's flagship New York FM station, WPLJ, one afternoon in 1970 when one of PLJ's most popular DJs—Dave Herman—stood chatting with his arm resting on a tall stack of promotional albums that had come in that week's mail. When a pause arose in the conversation, Dave looked down to see what his left elbow was propped on. The album cover caught his eye. "What's this?" he said, his eyebrow lifting with curiosity. He picked the album up, read the title on the front jacket, slid the record halfway out of its sleeve, skimmed the list of songs on the label, and said, "Hmmmmm, it looks interesting. I think I'll play it as soon as I get on air." Then he slid the LP back into its sleeve again. Fifteen minutes later *Jesus Christ Superstar* made its radio debut on Dave Herman's turntable. The rest is history.

Jesus Christ Superstar went to number one on *Billboard*'s charts. And its composer, Andrew Lloyd Webber, went on to write musicals like *Evita, Phantom of the Opera,* and *Cats*, productions that would earn him a knighthood and that would land him a fortune of over a billion dollars.[4]

The idea of music about Jesus Christ as a rock singer of sorts, a superstar, had fired an influential DJ's imagination. Was this Tony Martell's sly work? Or was it just a fluke? In business, many make the mistake of crediting you with a success you didn't create. They fall into the *narrative fallacy*. They fail to ask whether you were one of those who had built and driven the train or whether you were merely along for the ride.

Gulf & Western had snatched Tony Martell away from CBS and had made him the president of its struggling and straggling flock of fourteen record companies in the hope that he could replace the tin in its music with platinum. And Tony Martell had been kind enough or crazy enough to hire me.

At the time, I was a twenty-eight-year-old who had no legitimate credentials for a place in the corporate world or in the music business. I'd been involved with science since I was ten. My obsessions were cosmology, microbiology, geopolitics, and psychology. At twelve, I'd helped conceive a computer that had won a regional science prize. At sixteen, I'd been a lab assistant at the world's largest cancer research center, the Roswell Park Cancer Institute in my hometown, Buffalo, New York. Before my freshman year of college, I'd designed and implemented research on Skinnerian programmed learning at Rutgers University's Graduate School of Education. And by the age of twenty, I'd edited conference proceedings for the psychologist Sol Gordon, head of New Jersey's Middlesex County Mental Health Clinic and an author who would go on to sell several million copies of his books. Mine was not a stunning business bio.

Like most kids I'd become a music addict at the age of thirteen or so. But I'd listened to all the wrong stuff—Mozart, Beethoven, Rachmaninoff, Bartok, Errol Garner, Dave Brubeck, Miles Davis, and Stravinsky—not to rock 'n' roll.

Even my real reasons for being in pop culture and the world of conglomerates were suspicious. My only claim to even the faintest hint of legitimacy was that I'd edited a national rock magazine and had increased its circulation 211 percent in two years.

And I had one other thing going for me. When science had seized me at the age of ten, the book that had inspired me spelled out its author's version of the first two rules of science. Rule 1: The truth at any price including the price of your life. To illustrate, the book told the tale of Galileo, and told it wrong. In this book's version, Galileo demonstrated that the Earth revolved around the sun then stood by this truth despite the threat of a fiery death at the stake, a threat that came directly from Pope Urban VIII. In fact, Galileo had compromised with the pope, who happened to be a former friend and patron, not a deadly enemy. Galileo abjured his truth and lived under house arrest for the last nine years of his life.[5]

Thank God the book told the tale wrong. I needed the inspiration of a man who wouldn't compromise when it came to the most important insights in life, insights that you feel can save and upgrade your fellow human beings.

Rule 2 of science as the book told it? Look at things right under your nose as if you've never seen them before, then proceed from there. Look at things you and everyone around you take for granted as if they were alien implants, things from another planet, then pursue the questions that tumble from this Martian point of view. Once again, the book gave an example. It told the tale of Anton van Leeuwenhoek, the draper in Amsterdam who took a startled second look at the magnifying lens he used every day to examine the weave and threads of the cloth he bought and sold.[6] Van Leeuwenhoek had the kooky notion that his ordinary magnifier could be souped up for use in a radically different way. So he ground lenses that could magnify objects to three hundred times their real size and created the microscope.[7] Then he turned his new device on two realities right under his nose. One was merely mundane—pond water. The other was unspeakable—sperm. What did van Leeuwenhoek discover? Living things as strange as aliens from another galaxy. *Animalcules*— living, moving, twirling, microscopic beasts—in both the pond water and the semen.[8] Then van Leeuwenhoek discovered bacteria, blood cells, and capillaries. What the Dutchman found right under his nose and what Galileo found in the sky above his head utterly changed the way we see the world around us. Van Leeuwenhoek and Galileo played potent roles in the cycle of speculate, explore, and consolidate, in the forward movement of the evolutionary search engine, in the upshift of the secular genesis machine.

What do the first two rules of science have to do with business? Everything, as I was about to see.

At thirteen years old I realized I was an atheist. Yet all the people I knew, from my parents and their friends, to my Sunday School teachers and every tribal people I'd ever read about, from Africa and Asia to Scandinavia and North America, had their gods. And those gods had the power to grip us with emotions utterly beyond our imaginings. Emotions like those that seized Macumba dancers in Brazil and made them fall to the floor foaming at the mouth and writhing in the film *Black Orpheus*.[9] Emotions like those the African American author James Baldwin wrote about in his novel *Go Tell It on the Mountain*, the falling-to-the-floor ecstasies his protagonist experienced in his "Holy Roller" church in Harlem.[10] The Macumba dancers felt they were seized by the spirits of their ancestors. And Baldwin was convinced that his body had been taken over by Christ. Something had possessed these men and women in an extraordinary way. But if there were no gods outside of us, then where were they? *Inside* of us. Not just right under our noses. Right *behind* our noses. In other words, the gods were fair game for the second rule of science. Look at things right under your nose as if you've never seen them before, then proceed from there.

That put me on the track of a mystery. What are the gods inside of us? What are our elemental passions—our glints of what we call divinity? How do we manage to reach them? How can we explain them in the language of science? What's the role of the passions in a constantly evolving cosmos? How can we harness our most intense and transcendent emotions—the gods inside of us, our primal passions—to increase the power and the intensity of our daily lives?

The answer, it seemed, did not lie in the ivory tower, that great devourer of scientific researchers and of college professors—a prison I'd been destined to end up in since the age of ten. The answer, I was convinced, lay in the real world of getting and spending, of profits and losses, of making a living, and of the modern myth-making machine.

Charles Darwin had found the secret to evolution in a five-year voyage that took him out of the confines of Cambridge and Oxford, where the high priests of mainstream science were caged. He'd found the finches that gave him his clue in a spot way off the map of science, the Galapagos Islands. I was convinced that the next Galapagos Islands, the islands of personal passion and of mass emotion, lay in a twentieth-century terra incognita, in a place where no scientist I knew of had tried to mount an expedition—in the media and in its companion, the star-making machine.

Over at Gulf & Western, they didn't care what my motives were. They didn't care what sort of fieldwork I'd done so far in five years of TV, advertising, publishing, and graphic design. They didn't care that by a fluke I'd landed on the cover of *Art Direction Magazine*. The folks at Gulf & Western only saw that I'd made money in mass quantities for a magazine and for its publisher.

So they asked me to create from scratch a public and artist relations department, a new team to keep singers happy, to build careers, and to garner publicity. Again, they didn't give a hoot that I'd never done one whit of public relations in my life. They had a company in a nosedive. Any source of profit would be just fine.

When I first arrived at Gulf & Western's music operation and was given an office with three windows overlooking Central Park, this HQ of tunes was a most peculiar place. There were no staff meetings—ever. There were no lists of the records we were putting out. No one gave us any sense of what to do from day to day. Heck, there wasn't even a list of the names and addresses of our fourteen record labels.

Our company was by no stretch of the imagination a team. And one thing intuition revealed quickly: it takes teams to make stars. It takes teams to make companies. Twelve of our fourteen labels had no teams—none at all. Even the presidents of the labels seemed elusive, as if they'd been invented by some lowly staffer on LSD.

But there were two gems in our stack of chaff and dandruff—two companies with teams that had a work ethic and a passionate determination to succeed. One was Seymour Stein's Sire Records—the company that would eventually sign and build careers for Madonna, The Ramones, Talking Heads, The Smiths, Tom-Tom Club, Depeche Mode, Echo and the Bunnymen, Ice-T, Pet Shop Boys, and Brian Eno's collaborations with David Byrne. The other was Dot Records—the number-three company in country music, a company with a team spirit that was ferocious, driven by a fierce desire to climb to number one.

So I tried to give the singers and musicians from Sire and Dot that extra boost they needed to succeed and used simple correlational studies and other scientific techniques to figure out exactly what made careers in the record business go to the top. Then I applied every lesson—and there were many.

When the Paramount Records talent scout, its A&R (Artist & Repertoire) guy came into my office frothing with enthusiasm over whatever surefire star he'd found that day, I loved his buoyancy. But when he left, I went back to work strategizing, directing my growing staff (the only staff that was mysteriously given budgets to hire new employees while other departments were told to slim down), landing roughly six hundred stories a month for Sire acts like Renaissance and the Climax Blues Band, and getting feature stories in a new magazine called *People* for folks like Donna Fargo and Roy Clark—now-forgotten entertainers who paved the way for country music's charge from its hideout in the Bible Belt into the mainstream of American culture.

Then one day the Paramount Records' A&R guy trapped me. His gonzo-megastar tale of the day, told with his usual wild excitement, concerned a thirteen-year-old girl from Crown Heights in Brooklyn— a very marginal neighborhood. This kid, his new discovery, was going to be a monster, a superstar, a gorilla, a smash. Sure, just like Augie Meyers and the rest who'd slipped into invisibility. "And guess what," the A&R maestro said, "I've set her up to do a showcase at the Plaza Hotel tomorrow at noon."

Yikes. This was a smart bomb I couldn't dodge. The Plaza Hotel was just a short and pleasant walk away. I was the head of the Public and Artist Relations Department. That meant that on the rare occasion when a singer or musician who didn't come from Sire or Dot managed to actually make it to a nearby stage, I had to be there to make the artist feel we were paying attention to him or her. If the company was doing nothing for a singer, I told him so. But still, I owed him or her the courtesy of my presence.

So the next day at fifteen minutes to noon, I left my office and my growing staff and walked at top speed along the lower margin of Central Park, not stopping to take in the springtime scenery, straight into the white-with-gold-trim elegance of the Plaza Hotel, into one of the Plaza's nightclubs, and sat down at a small, round table, expecting to hear some unfortunate kid who couldn't carry a tune if you put it in a bucket and Krazy Glued the handle to her palm.

The room darkened. The lights came up on the small semicircular stage. Out came a squashed-looking African American adolescent, a mere 4'8" tall with a microphone in her hand. Her eyes swept the room, seeming to peer with intensity directly into my face and into that of everyone else in the miniamphitheater-like curve of nightclub tables. There was something ferocious and commanding about those eyes, as if she'd reached through your skin, grabbed you by the esophagus, pulled your nose up to hers, then given you a silent command to sit, to stay, to pant, and to obey.

Then she opened her mouth and sang. For half an hour she gripped you and everyone else your peripheral vision could see. Her hold on your ears, eyes, and throat extended to your body and to those gods of bone-deep passion I'd been hunting for. She dragged you at high speed through hell and heaven, through the exaltation of being dipped, thrown, lifted, and flown.

The team it would take to turn this exquisitely controlled raw power into a career did not exist. Paramount Records, her label, was a name on paper, not a thriving company. But two minutes after she began to sing, I opened a space for her in my priority list—a very big space indeed.

Meanwhile, Dot Records and Sire Records were steadily upping their revenues, their profits, and their prestige. But our other twelve labels remained anonymous sinkholes into which maintenance dollars flowed never to be seen again. And the company that Gulf & Western Industries had swallowed when acquiring us, Paramount Pictures, was a giant in the film industry—a studio run with deftness, precision, and artistry.

So Paramount's president, Frank Yablans, did a bit of maneuvering, and one day, roughly two weeks after I first saw Stephanie Mills, I came to work and discovered that our president now answered to a new boss. From this day forward, Tony Martell would be slid under the thumb of Paramount Pictures' president Frank Yablans.

* * *

I'd never seen Frank Yablans. None of us on the twenty-third floor of the Gulf & Western building had. All we knew was that he had a reputation akin to Adolf Hitler's and Attila the Hun's. Gossip implied that intimidation was his game and that he could turn you into ash and powder simply by looking your way.

The news of this move down, this earthquake on the corporate organization chart, brought about something unprecedented—a meeting of our department heads.

This meant that we, the chief honchos, seated ourselves at eleven o'clock one bright morning around a big, previously unused conference table in a windowless, unused conference room. Before us we discovered a neatly typed list of records the company was planning to release during the next few weeks, all disks none of us had heard of. Our president seated himself at the far end of the table, cleared his throat, and prepared to take charge. Then the door opened. You had the feeling that laser lights and the sound of trumpets had streamed into the room. And, as if walking on a path of lightning bolts, in strode a small man with a four-thousand-dollar suit and an expression masterfully contrived to strike terror into even a titanium-armored heart.

As this multimegaton Napoleon walked the length of the room, our president, Tony Martell, slumped back in his chair until his chin seemed to dip below the line of the conference table's top. When the mini-Napoleon reached the conference table's head, Martell slid out of his seat like a flattened jellyfish. Then the newcomer took over the power chair from which our noble leader had just oozed.

This was the human Godzilla we'd all heard of, Frank Yablans. Yablans glanced at the list of upcoming releases on the table in front of him, picked the first one, turned to the executive on his left, and said, "You. What are you doing to promote this record?"

In reality, nobody was doing more than a whisper to promote any record, much less a record not a soul had heard. But I don't think the executive upon whom the withering stare was fixed wanted to admit that. So he mustered all the brain cells he had used in college to answer essay questions about matters he'd never studied and made up an elaborate story on the spot, a fictional saga of his heroic efforts.

Then Yablans turned to the next executive in line, opened his Howitzer mouth, and fired the same question. Executive number two followed executive number one's creative example. He made up a story. About four executives later, Yablans finally got to me.

Now remember, I was new to the corporate world. Science was my religion, and the first commandment of science as I'd learned it is, "The truth at any price including the price of your life." Galileo had spent his last nine years under house arrest, and the Italian astronomer Giordano Bruno had died at the stake so that I might have the privilege of infiltrating the corporate world.

"I'm not doing anything about this record," I said. "In fact, I'm not doing anything about ANY of the records on this list. Ninety-nine percent of the music we sign doesn't stand a chance of success. Working on it would be a waste of effort and of time. But there's a girl one of our labels has just signed who is getting forty percent of my attention." And I proceeded to describe the thirteen-year-old wonder from Brooklyn, Stephanie Mills.

When I finished, Yablans abruptly walked out of the room, his face frozen, leaving five executives unquizzed but still quaking like the Oakland Overpass during an earthquake. A top vice president grabbed me by the arm with a grip designed to take my humerus bone to the breaking point and hissed, "You fucking **nun**. If you ever do that again, you're fired."

When I arrived back at my office, my secretary told me that I'd received a phone call. It was not my exit notice. It was Frank Yablans's secretary. Mr. Yablans had set up a meeting for the next day at noon with all of his East Coast vice presidents and department heads. He wanted me there. And he wanted me to bring Stephanie Mills.

Thus began an expedition into the power of sheer honesty. An expedition into the power of the first rule of science: The truth at any price including the price of your life.

* * *

From that point on, the Paramount Pictures people treated me as a member of their staff, calling me in whenever they were planning campaigns to break major films. They put me in charge of their campaign for a record by supermodel and later film and television star Cybill Shepherd, a record masterminded by her boyfriend, director of the fabulously successful film *Paper Moon*, Peter Bogdanovich. They let me architect a music-press assault for the soundtrack orchestrator of Robert Redford's *The Great Gatsby*—Frank Sinatra's legendary arranger Nelson Riddle. And they gave me full control of the press effort for *The Life and Times of Sonny Carson*, directed by Frank Yablans's little brother, Irving.

No one at Paramount dared get near *The Life and Times of Sonny Carson*. Why? They thought Frank had simply tossed his brother a few million dollars of production money to keep him out of trouble. What's more, the film was about a controversial black activist. But the little brother, Irving Yablans, would eventually make a fortune creating *Friday the 13th*. Sonny Carson would resurface in the early 1990s as a leader of the anti-Korean, anti-Semitic movement in the

New York black community.[11] And I'd become the leading "black" publicist in the music industry. But that's a story for another time.

The corporate VP who'd threatened to fire me for being "a fucking nun" was tossed out of the company two weeks later by Frank Yablans (which sickened me, since beneath this VP's gruffness was a deep commitment to his people and to his work).

Ten months later, Gulf & Western finally tired of the music business. It sold its record holdings to ABC Records. ABC flew a vice president to New York from LA. He gathered all fifty-seven employees in the New York office, told us to go on working in our normal manner, and promised us that our jobs were safe. "No blood," he said, "will flow in the corridors of this company."

On the following Friday, everyone in the company, everyone in that room, received a pink slip in the mail. Everyone with a single exception —me. And I resigned. Why? The company had fired my staff. Without the team I'd built there was no way I could accomplish anything.

The VP who had made the "no blood in the corridors" speech appeared unannounced in my office the morning after I tendered my resignation, having taken the red-eye in from the LA. He laid a blank piece of paper on my desk, told me to write my name at the top, to write the names of all the employees I wanted to keep, then to fill in the salary I wanted for myself and the salaries I wanted for the members of my team. I gave us all a modest raise and went to work for ABC.

A year later I got a call from the attorney who had negotiated the sale from Gulf & Western to our new owners. "You know why ABC was willing to pay so much for Gulf & Western's record holdings, don't you?" he said. I confessed that I didn't have a clue. "The reason," he said, "is you."

This was preposterous. I was a novice in the corporate world. I was a scientist learning the hard way that the politics around me only made sense if you saw them in terms of wolf packs—with alpha males, beta males, and small, competing, carnivorous teams whose members were bound to each other by instinctual loyalty. I told the attorney he was wrong. There was no way I could have triggered a profitable sale of a company.

His answer: "No, listen carefully to me. What did you do for Dot Records? And what did you do for Sire? You increased their cash flow, their profits, and their market share. I'd say you doubled or tripled their worth." The rest of his explanation suddenly made the puzzle pieces fall into place.

Why had ABC not fired me? Because, the lawyer explained, "The president of Sire Records, Seymour Stein, and the president of Dot Records, Jim Foglesong, both flew out to California to meet with Jay Lasker, the president of ABC Records. Do you know what they told him?" As usual, I didn't have a clue. "That without you they would bolt . . . they'd find a way to leave ABC."

Those were the wages of truth in the days of Engulf & Devour. Those are the wages of truth today.

* * *

As for Stephanie Mills, our department got her into everything from the *New York Times* to *Seventeen Magazine*, with a whole bunch of television shows in between. Then she landed the lead in the Broadway production of *The Wiz*, the first black-written, black-produced Broadway musical. A musical based on *The Wizard of Oz*. A brilliant idea. My staff and I did most of the publicity for *The Wiz*, using it to pull in a landslide of additional press for Stephanie.

Stephanie never became the household name I would have liked. But the base for Stephanie's career was well laid. Mills would have three number-one R&B records in the late 1980s—"I Feel Good All Over" (1987), "If I Were Your Woman" (1987), and "Something in the Way (You Make Me Feel)" (1989). She'd also have three gold albums and would sell several million LPs and CDs.

And I came away with a lesson. Rule of science number one, the truth at any price including your life, was a powerful tool in business. I'd soon learn more about why.

23

HOW TO GAIN
THE POWER OF THE FORCE

Use your core emotions. The tale of the speech that
saved Prince's *Purple Rain*.

The truth at any price including the price of your life.

If you crusade for the people that you serve, if you find their feelings deep inside yourself, and if you let that self-discovery bring new
parts of you to life, you can have what Obi-Wan Kenobi promised to
Luke Skywalker in the *Star Wars* movies.[1] You can have a power that
feels eerily like *the Force*. And you may even prove that you can play
a role in the cycle of explore and consolidate, in the forward movement of the evolutionary search engine, in the upshift of the secular
genesis machine.

The year was 1984. By now I had my own company—the largest
public relations and career strategy firm in the record industry—with
a two-story office in a Victorian building at the corner of 55th Street
and Lexington Avenue in New York. The office of the Howard Bloom
Organization, Ltd., was distinctive, with its chocolate brown walls, its
natural wood trim, its sunken lights, and its circular staircase. The
one thing that didn't quite fit the elegance was me. My desk was a
huge burl-wood-and-chrome affair. Its aircraft carrier deck–sized surface was a crazy heap of papers. There were seven Rolodexes spread
out in a phalanx, despite the computer monitor next to my left elbow,

part of a cybersystem I'd designed in 1976 and that we'd finally been able to afford in 1983—thus making us the first firm of our kind worldwide to computerize.

Far more strangely, there was a bulging, bright red nylon knapsack propped against the mocha wall behind my office chair. When you walked in and saw the knapsack hidden behind my high-backed throne, you wondered whether you were meeting with a CEO or a college student.

The backpack was there for a reason. It held a neatly folded extra shirt, a toiletries kit, and one of the first laptop computers, a one-pound TRS-101 with a memory of 24K. Periodically a frantic call would come in from LA, Indiana, Atlanta, Houston, London, or Germany, usually around four in the afternoon. The sky was about to cave in. A client was about to make a big mistake. "You've got to be out here tonight," the caller would say. "You're the only one that (fill in the blank with names like Michael Jackson, John Mellencamp, Billy Idol, or Run DMC) will listen to. You're the only one who can change his mind."

There was no time to take a cab home and pack. There were just enough spare minutes to ask a receptionist or an account executive to call our car service and to get me an airline reservation on the next flight to the city I'd been summoned to. Then I had to strap on the backpack and run.

One day I got a call of a far more leisurely kind. It was four o'clock in the afternoon, but I would not be needed on the Warner Brothers studio lot in Hollywood to rescue the project in distress until eleven a.m. the next morning. Ahhhhh, breathing space.

Here's the situation. I'd been working with Prince since he was nineteen years old. He was an amazing human being. He'd been an A student in a Minneapolis high school while running two musical careers simultaneously. When he was roughly fourteen, he'd organized a band that toured the Minnesota bar circuit, putting Prince onstage in places where he was far too young to buy a drink. (He wouldn't have purchased a cocktail anyway. Prince led a sober, serious life.)

Prince had long since taught himself to play every musical instrument you'd find in a rock or R&B band. And he could sing. So he worked out a deal with a studio that made music for local radio and television commercials. He offered to record all the musical tracks on the studio's projects for free—thus saving the studio a small fortune in musician fees. In exchange, Prince wanted use of the place, of its recording equipment, and of its instruments late at night after the work of the day was complete. This studio time would have cost Prince roughly a thousand bucks an hour in 2007 dollars, something no high school kid could pony up, even if he did have income from his live performances.

When Prince did his homework, I do not know. But by the age of fifteen, he'd recorded an entire demo album and was about to graduate high school early and with honors. He flew into New York during a summer vacation, stayed at his sister's apartment, and took his record around to every record label and production company he could find. Two production companies wanted to sign him. Both said they could make him a star. But there was a hitch. He was just a fifteen-year-old kid. The owners of the production companies said Prince should stop worrying about the details—they'd tell Prince what name to use, how to dress, what graphics to put on album covers, how to orchestrate his music, and what songs to sing.

Fifteen-year-olds who have the audacity to dream of stardom will normally jump at anything that sounds, looks, or quacks like a contract. Not Prince. He wanted to control his own clothing, the art direction of his albums, the orchestration of his songs, and every word and note he sang. In other words, young as he was, Prince had a vision. He wanted to live that vision. And he wanted control over everything. So he did the impossible. He passed and went back to Minneapolis.

Three years later a local Minneapolis manager, Owen Husney, landed Prince a recording contract with Warner Brothers Records that made Prince the youngest musician in history to gain total creative control over his own albums and over every photo and design used on his album jackets or in his publicity campaigns.

Not long after, I got a call from Prince's new manager, a powerful LA-based manager Prince had brought on board to shoot for stardom. The new manager, Bob Cavallo—known for his work with bands like the Lovin' Spoonful, Earth, Wind, & Fire, and Little Feat—asked if I knew who Prince was. I did. Prince was a nineteen-year-old who had just scored a platinum LP that no one in the music business had paid attention to. Why? Because Prince was black. His album had shown up only on the R&B record charts—the black record charts. And in those days it was unhip within music business culture to work with a black act if you were white.

Which meant I worked with black acts all the time. They deserved a champion and there's no better way to make impossible things happen than to throw yourself heart and soul into a crusade that you believe in. The truth at any price including the price of your life. Prince became one of my new crusades.

Three years and a lot of hard work passed. By 1984, Prince was very well known indeed. He had a small slew of gold and platinum albums up his sleeve. But now Prince was possessed by an idea that was as cockily absurd as his notion of total control over his music had been when he was fifteen. Prince wanted to make a movie. Not a movie like the ones Elvis Presley had made in which someone else had come up with the idea, had written the script, and had simply told Elvis where to stand and what to say or what to sing. Not a movie like the Beatles' films—improvised, high-class home movies laced with the whimsies of high-profile directors like Richard Lester. Prince had a feature film inside of him and felt it kicking to come out. He wanted to write the script. He wanted to control the movie's shape, the way it looked and felt. He wanted to get his message from that space between his ribs and spine, where the unborn film beat with a rhythmic drive straight to his audience, to the people he saw face to face whenever he performed onstage.

The idea was outrageous. Movie budgets make album budgets look smaller than a seahorse trying to ride a whale. Roughly 99 percent of the folks who graduate with film degrees never get to make a feature picture. Folks with no training or track record in films don't stand a chance. Especially kids who are known for just one thing—their music. And most especially kids who are black.

Bob Cavallo—Prince's LA manager—had never made a film either. But he had a few advantages. He dared to appreciate the outrageous. He dared to nurture it. And he was brilliant at it. As I just mentioned, his firm, Cavallo, Ruffalo, and Fargnoli, had made its name handling anything-but-normal bands with genius, bands like Little Feat. Cavallo was also an inspired and inspiring assembler of teams. And he did a superb job of motivating team members. Including me. So Cavallo and his partners went for it. They raised what looks like nothing today but was a fortune way back then—$9 million—to give Prince his film, and the freedom to make it his way.

That money went into renting every room in a motel in Minneapolis, pulling in a film crew from LA, and getting a director fresh out of film school who was willing to do things Prince's way. The funds also went into flying me to Minneapolis for four days so I could get to the heart of the key people involved—the director, Prince's new female protégés Wendy and Lisa, who played important roles in the film, and quite a few others—then write it all up for a forty-page press kit. When that crash immersion was over, I went back to New York and kept track of the rest of the film-making process by phone.

When the four p.m. phone call came in telling me I had to be on the Warners lot the next morning to see the finished film, the despair in the voice from LA was not what I'd expected. "We've failed," it said. "We've done everything we could. We've cut and edited what we've got in every conceivable way. And there is no way we can make it work. It's not a film. Please get out here fast. See the movie tomorrow morning with us when we show it to Warner Brothers' executive team and tell me what you think."

By then I'd had twelve years of film experience. I'd done statistical analyses of the film audience. I'd done correlational studies and anthropological field expeditions into teen culture—the culture most films aim for. I'd dissected the relationship between music and film using the tools of science and of history. I'd studied all of this information mathematically, conceptually, AND intuitively, using my own emotions, tuning my guts and my heart.

The result: I'd been there with the Paramount Pictures staff when they had watched one of Burt Reynolds' first movies—*The Longest Yard*. They hated it. I loved it. It went on to win an Academy Award. I'd been there when a publicist friend ran a screening for New York's snootiest cinema critics and had asked me to come along to hold her hand. The reel of celluloid she handed to the man in the projection booth featured a bodybuilder who had the audacity to think he could act. The movie's name was *Pumping Iron*. My publicist friend hated it. So did the critics from the *New York Times* and the *Village Voice* who sat in the room with us. I loved it. There was something about the weightlifter/actor wannabe you couldn't resist. His name was Arnold Schwarzenegger.

All of these experiences had wetted my feet in film. I gained an additional edge thanks to a scheduling accident. Instead of the usual six p.m. flight to LA, I had the leisure of taking a plane at nine a.m. the next morning. When the flight attendant walked up and down the aisles offering headphones to watch the movie, I don't know why, but I took one. I normally work on planes—that's why the laptop was in the backpack. And I've never felt like watching films early in the morning. But this was an exception—again, I didn't really quite know why.

On paper the movie the flight attendants were about to roll should have been sensational. A powerful new audience had emerged in the mid-1980s—single, white, middle-class working mothers, the products of premature divorce or, in some daring cases, of women aware that their fertility clocks were running down and who were determined to have a kid with or without the benefit of a wedding ceremony and a live-in man. This film was about this "target demographic"—it zeroed in on a single, white, middle-class mom's romantic trials and tribulations. Its female star was very hot—Susan Sarandon. Its male star had come off huge successes in George Lucas's *American Graffiti* and Stephen Spielberg's *Close Encounters of the Third Kind*. He was also one of my personal favorites—Richard Dreyfuss. From the very first instant, I could feel the position papers that I would have written to promote this film within a company like Paramount Pictures or Twentieth Century Fox. I could feel the way I'd have pitched the film at a meeting of the marketing, promotion, and publicity teams.

I wanted to like it. I *knew* I'd like it. But I didn't. The movie—*The Buddy System*—lacked something critical . . . heart. It lacked a factor I suddenly realized isn't spoken of in the sciences or in the entertainment industry. It failed to make my throat clench. It failed to bring a tear to the corner of my eye. It failed to sweep me into that very private realm of feeling whose aftermath leaves you wishing that the lights wouldn't go up in the theater and that you wouldn't have to march up the aisle and out the door with other people who could catch a glimpse of your face. After a really moving film, you don't want anyone to see you because you are as emotionally open and vulnerable as a clam without a shell.

After *The Buddy System* I was in perfect control of my emotions. Why? The movie had flunked the lump-in-the-throat test. It hadn't tugged at the gods inside. Which means that by the time the plane landed at LAX, I'd learned a new lesson in movie measurement.

So when my cab pulled into the gate of the Warners lot and I found my way to the screening room, Bob Cavallo was waiting with a crowd of roughly forty other people. I declined Bob's invitation to sit with him and one of his partners. Instead, I found my way to a seat at the back, far from anyone else. There was a solid reason for this antisociality. If Prince's movie was going to score on the clenched-throat-and-tear-duct meter, I didn't want my business associates to see me. I didn't want to be embarrassed.

What's more, I didn't want to feel inhibited. I wanted my emotions to make the judgment. Those intimate feelings that might have stayed in hiding if I'd sensed that my reactions were on review.

Ninety minutes later, I knew we had a wonderful movie, a film I'd be willing to fight for no matter what. *Purple Rain* worked my emotional core into exquisite twists. I had never, ever seen a film like this—a movie with a rock soundtrack that did for me what I suspect the Broadway musicals of Lerner and Loewe had done for my parents—delivered its emotional punches and its uplifting feelings through the power of its music.

When the film was over and we had a solid five minutes to recompose ourselves, we—the Warner VPs, the Warner department heads, and the producers, Bob Cavallo and his partner Joe Ruffalo—marched into a large but strangely arranged conference room next door. What was strangely arranged? The conference table's head was to our left and its foot off to our right. Normally a door looks out over the table's tail or head. And your positioning at a conference table can be crucial.

The mood once we all trooped in and found places to sit was funereal. I was seated at the table's center, facing the door. Officially the folks at the table's head and foot should have been the focus of attention and authority. But the spot that faces the door has an unofficial power status no matter where the head may be. Again, these details of leadership are worth observing.

One of the Warner executives allowed a bit of chit-chat—most of it discretely focused on failure—then gave the company's official position. "We have a plan for this film," he said. "We're going to roll it out in six theaters in Arizona and see how it does before we take it national." Those words were not what they seemed. They were a secret cinema world cliché, a ritual death spell. Warner Brothers had just said that it was going to can the film, chuck it, abort it, and destroy it. That's what the "six theaters in Arizona" speech means. I was furious. This was literally one of the best films I'd ever seen.

So I barged in and gave a speech that in a sense I didn't give at all. It was a lecture that spoke itself through me. Even the demeanor with which it delivered itself came from a place that isn't normal—it came from a place of Charlton-Heston-as-Moses-parting-the-Red-Sea intensity. It came from the gods inside.

"This film," I said, "cannot be killed. It is a milestone in movie history. It hits you where it counts—right in the gut, right in the throat, right in the corner of your eye. And it does that for a reason. It says something with emotional power, something so charged and potent that there's no way to sum up its message in words. The picture captures something everyone in this room can feel but none of us can define. It captures something every human in America who loves rock will feel as well. It succeeds at something Aeschylus, the Greek playwright, worked his ass off to achieve—catharsis, a twist and cleansing of the passions that you can't write up in a memo, that you can't explain in a pitch. A message more potent than words is a message too potent to kill."

The speech that grabbed the folks in that room by their throats relied on more than just personal emotion. It pulled from a solid knowledge of the past of the film and of the entertainment industry. "Once upon a time," I said, "you had musicals like Jerome Kern and Oscar Hammerstein's *Showboat*. The musical films of the 1930s, 1940s, and 1950s must have done something powerful in their time, because they're still alive and will keep on selling in video for many decades to come. They amortized their costs a long time ago. Now every copy they sell is pure profit for their owners. This film is as radical a step today as the composer Arthur Freed's fist-in-the-face-of-authority was when he slipped around every obstacle MGM's executives could throw at him and starred an unknown, Judy Garland, in a film that pulled in almost zero initial profit in 1939, *The Wizard of Oz*."

There was intense emotional conviction to this speech. But there was something else—*saturated intuition*—intuition soaked in a sense of the history, present, and future of the entertainment industry. The gumption fueling the speech was based on something else we'll sluice into later in this book—tuned empathy—a deep knowledge of the audience whose right to see this film I was fighting for, a love of these kids, and an effort to find their interests in myself, being able to place myself emotionally in their running shoes and tie-died t-shirts.

That knowledge of the audience was based on statistical studies and on something far more important—months of weekends spent with suburban kids in Connecticut digging into the secret culture they didn't let their parents see, getting a first-hand feel for the enthusiasms and subtleties of a generation ten to twenty years younger than anyone in that Warner conference room, including me. How I got the opportunity to dive into the hidden depths of private teen subculture is another tale we'll leave for later.

"The old-style musicals of the 1930s, 1940s, and 1950s," I said, "don't reach me. They don't reach the kids who are moved by modern rock. But this music **does** reach me. It tells me the movie's story. It tells it to my gut. It reaches my generation. It reaches generations younger than mine, too."

"This film," I explained, "can be a watershed in pop culture. Until 1965, songwriters in Tin Pan Alley wrote the hits. Singers were just puppets who put those songs across. In 1955, Elvis Presley had the audacity to throw his hips into the act. But even he was only singing other people's songs. It took the Beatles in the 1960s to set singers free so they could do something outrageous, write their own songs and sing them. Which means that when the Beatles sang, they sang with all their heart. They opened up something potent in themselves, something the emotional selves in us responded to. Now Prince has taken that a huge step further. He's the first musician to write not just his songs, but his own film.

"*Purple Rain* is more than actors on a screen. It's Prince's insides writhing. This movie screams to you. It cries to you. It brings your own screams and cries to life. This is a film you cannot shelve. This is a film you cannot hide. It's a film you have to open as wide as you possibly can."

People respond to facts. They respond even more to passion and conviction. They respond to the truth at any price including the price of your life.

It's easy to kill a film. It's easy to kill a project of any kind. If you say something negative in a meeting, you seldom lose. A snide remark, if delivered in just the right way, makes you look like you know something others have missed. It's the conference room version of a parlor trick.

On the other hand, if you say something positive, you make yourself a target. Others can show how savvy they are and how stupid you are by tearing you down. But without positives, nothing happens. When you feel a truth as powerfully as Moses did when facing Pharaoh, it can change the mood of a room full of executives. It can change the way they see the value of what they're doing. It can energize them. It can lift them out of the trenches and send them charging across the battlefield.

That speech, in its own small way, helped save *Purple Rain* from the coffins of filmdom. That, plus a series of miracles wrought by Bob Cavallo. Not to mention one more tiny act of subversion, which Cavallo catalyzed to do the trick. Warners ran a sneak preview of *Purple Rain* in San Diego. I wasn't supposed to know about it. Cavallo slipped me the word. If I sent press down to see it, Warners would be furious. Warners had threatened to put me out of business once before, and they could easily try it again.

But when you're on a crusade, barriers are invitations to a breakthrough. I had my staff call three key critics in LA—Michael Gilmore from *Rolling Stone*, Robert Hilburn from the *Los Angeles Times*, and David Ansen from *Newsweek*. Each went down to San Diego knowing he absolutely wasn't supposed to be there. This gave each of these writers something vital, an ego-stake. Before Warners could make its final marketing decisions, *Rolling Stone*, the *LA Times*, and *Newsweek* all broke with reviews riddled with quotes like this one from David Ansen's *Newsweek* piece: "As a movie star, he's unprecedented. Prince may find himself anointed as the screen's newest and most singular idol. Prince is one of the handful of performers who've restored the urgency and danger—and the beat—to the rock scene. And *PURPLE RAIN* gets that excitement on the screen." Warners changed its attitude. The film was rolled out nationally. It was rolled out in a promotion that tied the movie to MTV, the first film-tied promotion in MTV's then-brief history. Roughly six months later, *Purple Rain*, the movie that had cost $9 million to make, had grossed $95 million dollars—over ten times its production budget. (That's $187 million in 2007 dollars.)

Look, I was an ordinary human being just like you. And I was an alien in the business community. So why could I sometimes see what others couldn't? When I spoke, why was it occasionally magical, as if *the Force* were with me? The answer involves three potent tools—tuned empathy, saturated intuition, and truth. Tuned empathy is your ability to tune your emotions to those of your customers, to be able to feel as if you were living in their skin. Saturated intuition is a gut sense based on knowing the details and daily flow of your business as if it were the flow of your own breath. And the ultimate force-giver is "the truth at any price including the price of your life."

Now let's dive into the story of why these things matter to you and me. Let's dig down to the roots and see how these tools overturn the standard ideas you and I grew up with, the standard notions about business, work, emotion, reason, and human exchange. Let's do it by tunneling into the history of the human soul, the history of daydreams, and the history of turning phantoms into hard and fast realities. Let's do it by diving back to the beginning, to the very start of capitalism and of its companion, the Western system. Let's do it by diving to the secret core of the evolutionary search engine and of the secular genesis machine.

V

THE GREATEST HITS
OF HISTORY . . .
AND HOW THEY
GOT TO BE THAT WAY

24

PLATO AND THE NAME GAME

How a Greek entrepreneur 2,400 years ago succeeded mightily but made a big mistake.

Passion, commitment, idealism, and honesty often sound out of place
in conversations about business. Yet these qualities, plus gut sense,
intellect, and intense conviction, helped gross hundreds of millions of
dollars for Stephanie Mills, for Prince, for Warner Brothers, and for
Gulf & Western Industries.

The rules that made for this success in the world of corporations,
politics, and even the scientific community were these:

- If you champion the interests of millions of people outside the
  picket fence of your friends, your co-workers, and your family;
- If you seek truths others don't see, if you find them, if you question them, if you test them, and if, when you sense they are
  solid, you battle for them;
- If you know that unseen truths are not just logical;
- If you know that tracking truths takes both emotion and
  reason;
- If you know that truth feeds off of supersaturation—off of
  unconventional study and minute-to-minute immersion in your
  field;

- If you know that your instruments for divining truth are:
  your gut feeling
  PLUS your intellect
  PLUS continual contact with folks outside your social sphere
  PLUS the sum of all you've learned by following every curiosity that's in you,

Then you will outdo your competitors. Why?

Because serving others is the real purpose of the deadened institutions in which so many of us have become like deadened cells. If you serve others with all your heart, with all your soul, and with all your intellect, you may be loathed, you may be hated, and you may be mocked, harassed, and hounded, but you will succeed.

And you will do more. You will advance the cause of the evolutionary search engine. You will advance the cause of the secular genesis machine. You will advance the cause of a cosmos feeling out her possibilities. You will do it by using your emotions to feel out the soul of your fellow human beings.

So why do we often think that business is a field in which commitment and personal passion are out of place, a field in which idealism is the wrong way to go, and a field in which creating something of lasting meaning is an impractical dream? Blame it on a long line of misguided thinkers. Blame it on the Greeks.

The time was over four hundred years before the Christian Era. The place was Athens. A small group of entrepreneurs were shaping a lucrative new form of intercontinental commerce—a society-advancer par excellence—the idea business, the perception trade, and the publishing-and-higher-education industry. These pioneers of commerce were doing something more. They were shaping the perceptual lens through which you and I look at our world today.

But there was a catch. The legacy these founders of the knowledge industry left to us was marred by a glassy flaw, a bit of fraud, a swirl of gray that blocked our sight. The founding fathers of the thinking trade pondered society and its ethics, but they overlooked some of their own most important tools, tools that made their own enterprises thrive. One of those founding fathers of the wisdom trade acknowledged that a city-state needed its craftsmen, its artists, its importers, its exporters, its merchants, and its retailers if it was going to live a rich and varied life.[1] But in his twenty-seven existing works, this sage only devoted three brief passages to the necessity of business skills, then he moved on. What's worse, he denied that the techniques of a salesman—the methods that a stall owner in the marketplace used to persuade a shopper to favor the olive oil from one island over that from another—had anything to do with him.

That key figure in the development of the Western way of thought was Plato, the philosopher who many modern experts credit with opening the gates of insight to every basic issue the modern mind has ever conceived.[2] Plato did something crucial. He invented a phrase to describe the product he claimed he wasn't selling, the commodity he believed towered over all the others. He called it "the food of the soul."

Plato used the concept of "merchants of the food of the soul" to ridicule his archenemies, the Sophists, who, he implied, were hawking something for drachmas that should never be bought and sold.

Plato wouldn't stoop that low. Or so he led his customers to believe. But he sinned against the rule of the truth at any price, including the price of your life. He failed to leave a treatise about one of his greatest talents—something he did better than any of his competitors—promotion and marketing, keys to the way that he himself sold concepts that expanded the reach of the soul and that multiplied the powers of those who pursue meaning.

Why did Plato fail to explain an art so crucial to his life and to ours? Why did he neglect promotion, marketing, and sales, skills he had mastered to the nth degree? Because Plato came from a society that despised its merchants and its practical businessmen. Plato wanted his potential clients to regard him as far loftier than a simple vendor in the marketplace. He wanted to jack up his own price.

In other words, Plato was blinded by snobbery. And he passed that blindness on to you and me.

But make no mistake about it—Plato was a great salesman. And he had an advantage. He wasn't building from scratch. He had two hundred years of product development behind him. In roughly 600 BCE, a full 173 years before Plato first emerged from the womb, a thinker from the Greek trading city of Miletus came up with a new substitute for an old wholesale and retail item, religion.

Religion claimed it could keep you from disaster and give you luck by placating the gods. Thales of Miletus—the man who invented philosophy—offered to untie you from the apron strings of the capricious deities. He developed a new technique that could protect you from cataclysm and clue you into opportunity by helping you understand far more than just the whims of Zeus and his wife, Hera. Thales' new approach to thought could help you see the cause and effect behind mere ordinary things . . . things like stones and suns, plants and animals, politics, truth and justice, ideas, and your fellow human beings.

Religion demanded faith. Thales' new approach gave reign to other emotions—calm analysis and blazing curiosity. Religion's tools were ritual and revelation. Thales' tools were multicultural concept gathering, debate, and reason.

Thales called his new approach to understanding and control "the love of wisdom and sagacity"—*philo* (love) plus *sophos* (wisdom and sagacity). Thales had invented *philosophy*.

Thales and the philosophical thinkers who followed him were in a field very similar to that of food processors like Sara Lee or of clothing makers like Gucci today. They imported ideas, reworked them, upgraded them, then retailed and promoted them. They built their public image, their brand, and their alliances step by step, spreading the popularity of their finished goods.

One of the coups that made Thales famous won him the title "the father of astronomy." Herodotus, the first Westerner we know of to write a history, reports that the Medes and the Lydians had been battling for six years and nothing seemed capable of stopping the blood bath. Then one afternoon "day was on a sudden changed into night."[3] Apparently the darkness in midday scared the armor off the combatants, who stopped stabbing and hacking at each other and screamed for mercy from any god who was listening. The fright was so great that the commanders hastily patched together a peace treaty.

Had the Ionian Greeks been on the battlefield, they would have known that this darkness in midafternoon was nothing to be afraid of and they would have beaten their panicked enemies. Why? Thales had predicted this disappearance of the sun.

How did Thales know an eclipse was coming? He had more than reason on his side. Merchants and the commercial shipping industry made the Greek society tick. Greek merchants wove a web of exchange in tin, wine, wheat, pottery, and wool from Spain to the

Black Sea, a mesh whose commerce threaded through five hundred Greek city-states. Greek colonies—most of them seaports—stretched the 2,400 miles from Massilia in France (now known as Marseilles) and Hadrumetum in North Africa to Dioscurias, Theodosia, and Phasis in present-day Turkey, Georgia, and the Ukraine. The Greeks treated their merchants with disdain. But it's the merchants and their profits who would someday give Socrates his bread (made from imported Ukrainian wheat) and Plato his inspirations. Inspirations based on the imported ideas Pythagoras had developed in his academy at Crotona in Italy. And inspirations based on the imported model of the Spartan constitution and state, the model from which Plato had gotten the notions of political structure he proposed in his dialogue *The Republic*.

Thales was the son of Phoenicians who had moved to the Greek shipping hub of Miletus. Only one people rivaled the Greeks at trade—the people of Thales' parents' native land, Phoenicia.

What does this have to do with eclipses and philosophy? Thales was the equivalent of a searcher bee. He traveled the sea lanes—probably on trading ships—looking for ideas. He'd picked up the technique of eclipse prediction in Egypt. He'd refined his mathematics using techniques from Babylonia.[4] Then he'd worked these into his own concepts of a cosmos based on material substances like water. In other words, Thales was in the idea export, import, retroengineering, upgrading, and repackaging biz. He was a living embodiment of the key rule of the evolutionary search engine—search, stretch, speculate, then digest and consolidate.

A hundred and fifty years later, the center of Greek trade and power had moved from Miletus to Athens. In that town another walking Cuisinart of imported knowledge abandoned his father's craft—sculpture—and spent his days in the marketplace asking cagey questions. Those questions made his reputation. His name was Socrates.

What were Socrates' thought-stumping questions based on? The native Athenian blended ideas from earlier Greek philosophers: Parmenides, Heraclitus, Anaxagoras, and Zeno. All these men were foreigners whose notions had entered Athens via its routes of trade. Parmenides was from Elea. So was Zeno. Heraclitus was from Ephesus. Anaxagoras—who may have come to Athens and have been

Socrates' teacher—was from Clazomenae. Socrates, like Thales, was an ace concept consolidator.

By the time Plato was born, Socrates was a legend. If you can believe Plato's later accounts (and you'd be wise to hesitate before trusting them entirely), Socrates had received the ultimate rave review from the critic beyond all critics—the Delphic Oracle, the woman in a holy trance who spoke on behalf of the god Apollo. Demonstrating that you can take men away from the gods but you can't take the gods away from men, the Oracle had proclaimed Socrates "the wisest man in Greece."[5]

Socrates had also won notoriety for his influence over the young, especially over youngsters like Alcibiades, a fabulously rich kid who had captivated all of Athens with the success of his racehorses, with the cleverness of his quips, and with his ability to amuse the highly visible, highly popular head of state, Pericles.[6] Alcibiades had worked out a plan for making war on Syracuse, then was held back from leading the army by a scandal. Athens was dotted with statues that celebrated the holy power of the male erection.[7] One dark night, someone knocked the statues' penises off. Word of mouth said the culprit was Alcibiades.

Without Alcibiades leading the charge in Syracuse, the war he'd planned was lost. Alcibiades was threatened with punishment for the penis stunt. In revenge, Alcibiades turned on Athens, joining up with Athens' foes, the Spartans, then switching sides again and offering his services to another Athenian enemy—Persia.

Despite this questionable behavior, Alcibiades was called back to Athens to lead a successful naval campaign. Then he fell out of favor with the public again when he lost big-time to a new Spartan commander, Lysander, the year after Plato became a student of Socrates. In other words, many Athenians saw Alcibiades as a troublemaker . . . one whose mischief sometimes threatened the city's very survival. Keep this story in mind. It plays a part in Socrates' demise.

Plato was the son of a very prominent, very aristocratic family, one that traced its roots to Athens' former kings. The money that gave Plato the freedom to think for a living probably came from the labor of the farming families who worked his ancestral land. The freedom from daily chores that gave Plato even more thinking time came from "subhuman" Robovacs, who didn't rate high enough for thought—slaves.

When he was twenty years old, Plato signed up as one of Socrates' students.[8] Eight years into the relationship between the two, Socrates pulled off the ultimate personal marketing and publicity stunt—martyrdom. Few embark on this course deliberately—though one of Socrates' predecessors in philosophy, Pythagoras, had done it—dressing in an all-white suit then tossing himself into a volcano. In modern times martyrdom has led to a permanent place in memory for Abe Lincoln, John F. Kennedy, and Martin Luther King Jr. Martyrdom has group-bonding power. It also grabs a vital space in our respect and our memory, even when, like Lincoln, Kennedy, and King, you do not seek it out.

Socrates was condemned by Athens' authorities for leading the youth of the city—youth like Alcibiades—astray. The philosopher accepted his death sentence with grace. And at the ripe old age of seventy, he drank a fatal cup of poison, hemlock, while, if Plato's accounts are accurate, giving one of his finest speeches.

This set the stage for Plato's rise. The twenty-eight-year-old cashed in on the fabulous name value Socrates had left behind and packaged what he claimed was Socrates' philosophy in over twenty books.

Plato may well have put his own ideas into Socrates' mouth. However, Plato presented these volumes as authentic re-creations of Socrates' greatest hits—his most important dialogues. Then Plato attached the names of famous men to these bids for literary influence. Plato named one dialogue for Cratylus, a philosopher who'd gained fame long before Plato had come along. Cratylus had studied under one of the founding fathers of Greek thought, Heraclitus, the philosopher of change who (according to Plato) said, "you can never dip your foot into the same river twice."[9] Plato had attended Cratylus's lectures in his youth as a mere member of the audience. Now Plato used Cratylus's name to pole-vault himself up to Cratylus's level and beyond.

Plato used the name game once again when he named another of his dialogues *The Critias*.[10] Critias was a superstar who would be dubbed by the 1898 edition of the *Harpers Dictionary of Classical Antiquities* as "one of the most accomplished men of his time"—a quadruple threat—a philosopher, a poet, an orator, and a politician. Critias would eventually become one of the Thirty Tyrants—the aristocratic strongmen who would seize control of Athens after it lost a twenty-seven-year-long war with the Spartans in 403 BCE. In other words, Critias was an attention-getter. And he was more than simply famous. He was also Plato's uncle. In essence, Plato snatched Critias's reputation and used it for a double-duty task—to build the star power of his own writings and to boost his family's reputation. This was salesmanship and marketing.

Then there was the dialogue Plato wrote in which he portrayed Socrates debating one of Plato's archrivals for influence, Gorgias, the man known as the father of the Sophists, an inter-city-state celebrity who made a fortune in lecture fees and in fees for teaching how to make politically persuasive speeches. Public demand kept Gorgias on tour so many days of the year that he was famous for upping his profits by evading taxes. How? He never stayed in one place long enough to be counted as a resident. Gorgias was also the expert who literally wrote the book on rhetoric (titled, with great wit and originality, *The Handbook to Rhetoric*).

When Plato used Gorgias as a character in one of his dialogues, it made a ballsy statement—that Plato and Socrates were not only on a par with Gorgias, they were far higher. As an author, Plato had the power to whisk Gorgias into a "historical reenactment" of an incident from Socrates' life, to portray Gorgias as a very bright man, to make sure that Socrates seemed even brighter, to guarantee that Socrates came out as the real master of the debate, then to shuffle Gorgias off-stage again. Gorgias may have been great, but Socrates—and by extension, Plato—were greater.

The use of the names of the famous was a marketing technique of the sort we see today in celebrity endorsements. Add the name of a celebrated person to what you're selling, and you give your product that leading light's candlepower. The trick may seem shabby, but it works.

Why have 2,500 years of thinkers forgiven Plato for this cheap trick?

One: because it's a trick that all of us in the "food of the soul" trades use. We do it every time we cite an expert, every time we hark back to a legendary sage like Plato, Aristotle, Kant, Hegel, Darwin, or Einstein, and every time we write a footnote.

Two: the meat of the matter is in the validity of what we have to say. What's more, as we'll see in tales that come up a few chapters down the line, if you have something you believe in, it's your obligation to sell it. If you fail to sell what you feel can uplift others, you let your fellow humans down.

And three: invoking the names of the great and using them to validate what you're selling may speak to something deep in our instinctual tool kit—it may speak to an attention swiveler built in by the evolutionary search engine.

It's been a popular intellectual sport for centuries to find the unique qualities that put humans above all other animals. Once it was said that man alone made tools. Then a school dropout and former British secretary named Jane Goodall went to the forests of Gombe and found chimpanzees stripping the leaves from twigs and using the denuded sticks to fish termites and ants from nests. Other chimp researchers discovered that some of these hairy relatives of ours also set up stone anvils and hammers to break open the shells of nuts.

Birds are good at tool use, too. Darwin discovered that woodpecker finches use cactus spines to pry insects out of holes.[11] Jane Goodall, the chimp expert, also discovered that Egyptian vultures use stones to crack open ostrich shells.[12] Others found that ravens and the seabirds known as oystercatchers use tools too. So Man the Toolmaker was no longer Man the Distinctly Different.

Then it was said that man alone had language. But researchers studying patas monkeys in Africa found that these lowly beasts use different "words" to tell each other whether to look below them for a snake, to look to either side for an approaching leopard, or to look up into the sky for a diving bird with its talons aimed at patas monkey meat. Ten years or so later, researchers found that chickens have a similar lexicon of warning sounds. Meanwhile, gray parrots demonstrated in the lab and out of it that they can master not just 150 words or so of human vocabulary, but that they can also grasp some of the abstract concepts that go with those words. If you asked a gray parrot named Alex, a parrot studied by the University of Arizona's Irene Pepperberg, to pick a square shape from a batch of wooden toys, he could do it. If you asked him to switch gears and to pick something blue from the same batch, he would get your drift and find you something painted a nice cerulean hue. What's more, if he got grouchy, Alex told Pepperberg, "Don't tell me to calm down."[13]

Meanwhile, a naturalist who studied prairie dogs even claimed that these chatty beasts have a "vocabulary" of 220 words. There went language as the Great Human Differentiator.

So what does distinguish humans from oystercatchers, chimps, chickens, patas monkeys, and prairie dogs? It's the knapsack of accumulated knowledge we carry with us from toddlerhood to death—our culture. And what instincts persistently shovel new material into the cultural backpack? Ancestor worship. Legend loyalty and celebrity fetish.

We find these three in nearly every culture.[14] To validate an argument, we refer back to our ancestors—or to someone who, while still alive, has already garnered the sort of authority only ancestors normally have. A Frenchman may cite the support for his ideas in the works of Racine or Rousseau. A dictator in Eastern Asia like Malaysia's Mahathir Mohammed or Singapore's Lee Kuan Yew will justify "Asian Values" by citing Confucius or the Koran. An American will cite the Founding Fathers—Thomas Jefferson and Ben Franklin—or the work of a popular expert, from Sigmund Freud to Dr. Phil. And we'll all cite the authority of a person who was a legend in times past or is a living legend today.

Americans, Frenchmen, and virtually all Europeans will go back further and pull citations from four key ancestral knapsacks—the Bible, the Koran, the Vedas, or the Greek and Roman classics. To make a point, we unwittingly keep legendary figures, both living and dead, alive in our vocabulary—and alive in the minds of our friends, our employees, our bosses, and our families. We are ancestor worshippers in disguise.

What advantage does this mental equivalent to a knee jerk give us? It's a conceptual structure maker and a conceptual consolidator. It provides us with a portable stash of useful notions that other species would forget. It provides us with bits of wisdom (and of fallacy) from a history that's at least eight thousand years old.

Look, for example, at what you're reading now—the tales of ancestors and of living legends, all evoked to give you (and me) new insights into what should be obvious but isn't—the value of what we do each day. The name game plays on this wisdom-gathering instinct, this fixation on the rich, the famous, or the great. The name game plays on our compulsive fixation with the big men and the big women of history.

The use of names to persuade—the name game—was only the start of Plato's promotional campaign. Plato pulled off the ultimate social contribution—and the ultimate promotional gimmick: he established an institution that lasted eight hundred years, the Academy.

And he established a reputation, a brand, that has held up for 120 generations. How did he do it?

Plato founded an elite school in a suburb of Athens, the above-mentioned Academy. And, though he claimed he was not a merchant, Plato set up a money-making system that kept the Academy running for eight centuries. That money-making technique is known today as bringing in endowments. Here's how it worked. Plato cherry-picked his students, gifted kids from families of mega-wealth and mega-influence. These were youngsters who already had more than a fair head start at becoming agora movers and Parthenon shakers. One of Plato's goals was to persuade the parents of alumni to leave their money to the Academy. A second target was to maximize the odds that graduates would become renowned and would boost the Academy's fame and prestige.

It worked. Plato achieved what he set out to do. And he deserved to. He sold what he believed would better his fellow human beings. He put his whole life into developing his ideas. He put all of his intellect and all of his passion into his books. He put his soul into his work. He sold new ways to think. And he sold new ways to work out what an ideal state should be.

Plato did far more than simply sell to a local and an international market. He sold his ideas to a future audience, an audience he would never live to see, an audience that existed only in vision and imagination, the audience of future readers like you and me, the audience of posterity.

Why should this matter in a world of bottom lines? Plato's promotional flair gave him stature, power, and money. But selling to audiences who appeared long after he was dead didn't net him a cent. When publishing houses like Penguin put out the Greek classics today, Plato doesn't get a royalty check. So what profit it a man to lose his life yet speak to you and me?

The payoff comes in something the Greeks were shooting for even if they wouldn't be around to enjoy it—immortality. That's what being a part of something higher than yourself is all about. We humans are paid not just in money but in recognition and in knowing that we've made a difference. This payoff, in fact, is more satisfying than cash. Permanence is more than just the ultimate coup in marketing. It's the ultimate act of digestion and consolidation. The ultimate act of structure making. It's the ultimate social contribution.

Plato failed in only one thing. He said nothing about how he built his career. He didn't explain how he constructed the launchpad that put his concepts into a lasting orbit.

Plato sold "food for the soul" magnificently but refused to reveal the secrets of this achievement. He left us thinking that the work of a promoter, the work of a marketer, and the work of a merchant were violations of the purity of soul. Plato, more than anyone, should have known that's not true. Soul is at the heart of what those in business do.

* * *

For all he gave us, Plato robbed us of the dignity of our labors. He taught us to downgrade what we do to earn our daily cappuccino. He stopped us from seeing how our work, like his, can tap into our deepest passions and can inject lasting meaning into others' lives.

Here are some of the questions Plato dodged, some of the questions whose answers he knew but hid. What is buying and selling all about? Why does this capitalist process work? What does it achieve? Why is it so central in our lives? How do we make contributions as potent and as lasting as Plato's work turned out to be?

The story of where capitalism came from and of where it's going next yields a heap of very strange answers to these questions. So check your oxygen tanks. We're about to dive deep into the underwater caves of Western history. This is not the snorkel trip they took you on in high school or in college. Capitalism's history has been radically misperceived. The real history of capitalism, its hidden history, is a tale that started with a pile of stones, a bit of mud, maniacal persistence, and a batch of lunatic daydreams. It's the untold tale of an astounding evolutionary search engine and of an unbelievable secular genesis machine.

25

THE STONE TOOL EVOLUTION OF CAPITALISM

What's in a Flake?

> The first secret of capital: we're a species that reinvents itself.

> The Industrial Revolution and its consequences have been a disaster for the human race. They have greatly increased the life-expectancy of those of us who live in "advanced" countries, but they have destabilized society, have made life unfulfilling, have subjected human beings to indignities, have led to widespread psychological suffering (in the Third World to physical suffering as well) and have inflicted severe damage on the natural world. The continued development of technology will worsen the situation.
>
> Theodore Kaczynski
> *The Unabomber's Manifesto*

Literature, philosophy, and magazines have told us for 150 years that one wing of the Western system is twisted and broken—capitalism. TV shows and movies have made greedy corporate executives and real estate developers their villains. Street marchers from Seattle to Thessaloniki have called for capitalism's end. Capitalism, we're told, is a game in which the rich manipulate the rest. Capitalism steals the very soul and replaces it with artificial needs. Capitalism, say deconstructionists, postmodernists, postcolonialists, anticapitalists, and other rulers of intellectual fashion, is a game of vampirical greed. Capitalism's not the answer, it's the enemy.

And guess what? As we'll see, this segment of the intellectual elite has played a vital role in the very system it critiques. But few of the intellectual leaders who rail against capitalism have spent years in the office suites of major corporations. Few know capitalism's real traps. And few know capitalism's hidden gifts. Even fewer know what capitalism can produce if it makes a perceptual shift.

The anticapitalists have framed the terms of the debate. We use their language and buy into their tale of capitalism's rise. We trot out sneering catchphrases like "consumer culture," "rampant materialism," "commercialism," "manipulation," and "exploitation." We take the contempt in those terms for granted. We don't stop to ask whether the assumptions hidden in these syllables are true. We have been too lazy or too unaware to know that our language determines the way we see our roots, the way we nurture our ideals, and the way we aim toward long-term goals.

History and catchphrases go hand in hand. Histories are our modern myths. They are the molders of our belief. They are the source from which we take our zeal and our sense of meaning. So it's time to straighten out the twisted tale of the history of humankind. It's time to find the real roots of the Western system. It's time to find the real roots of capitalism.

Why? Because the tale that the anticapitalists tell is only a half truth.

Yes, capitalism has often has been a bone and a heartbreaker, a nut crusher, and a human trash compacter. Conquest and disease killed between 10 million and 70 million Native Americans when the Western system elbowed its way into the New World from 1492 to 1890.[1] The Triangle Shirtwaist Fire in New York City in 1911 killed 146 women—most of them younger than twenty-three years old—in less than fifteen minutes.[2] In 1984 a nighttime leak of forty tons of methyl isocyanate gas from a Union Carbide pesticide factory in Bhopal, India, sent a toxic cloud crawling across a forty-square-kilometer residential area housing half a million people. The result was death for 28,000 and lasting illness for another 120,000.[3] And by 2001, one San Antonio, Texas, company, Clear Channel Communications Inc., had offices in 63 countries and owned 1,200 radio stations, 135 clubs, theaters, arenas, and stadiums, 19 television stations, and 770,000 outdoor advertising displays. In 2004 Clear Channel was on the verge of bridging the gap from the free market to monopoly and was capable of determining what information you and I do and do not get to see.[4]

More examples? The digging of the Hawk's Nest Tunnel in Virginia in 1930—a tunnel designed to give power to a new chemical plant and to give jobs to men tossed out of work by the Great Depression—led to the deaths of over 475 workers.[5] Silicosis—the industrial disease that killed those workers—has also killed an uncountable number of sandblasters, stonecutters, pyramid builders, and foundry workers laboring for pharaohs and for Mayan kings, or slaving away for Maoist, Marxist, and Dengist regimes. Mining accidents alone kill 10,000 Chinese workers a year today. And the worst industrial accident in history, the Chernobyl nuclear power plant fire of 1986, killed 15,000 emergency clean-up workers and irradiated 5 million Ukrainians, Belarusians, and Russians, innocent victims who lived under a socialist, Marxist regime.[6]

So the carnage of material progress isn't confined to capitalism, to Marxism, or even to the industrial world. In Mexico, long before Westerners arrived, the Native American Aztecs not only built their pyramids at a cost of the lives of hundreds of thousands of workers, but they deliberately killed up to eight thousand people a day on those pyramids' steps. Aztec priests ripped open the chests of their sacrificial victims with obsidian knives and, while the men and women were still alive to feel the agony, held their beating hearts up to the sky. Then the Aztec citizenry supped on the flesh of their victims.[7]

The Aztecs took pride in the deaths they caused. Bernal Diaz was a conquistador, a fighter, a writer, and a man who came from a Spanish feudal society so bloody that it burned its heretics in public squares. Yet even Diaz was horrified in 1519 by the racks of skulls he saw displayed in the centers of Aztec cities like Xocotlan, where he estimated the number of heads in a single pile came to 100,000.[8]

Some say we should all go back to the paradise of hunting and gathering. But the bones of six prehumans who were hacked up with stone axes and knives 800,000 years ago in a cave in Atapuerca, Spain, hint that we were already killing—and eating—each other in our primeval hunting-gathering days.[9] What's more, the murder rate among one of the world's most studied and admired living hunter-gatherer tribes, the !Kung San of the Kalahari Desert, is nearly twice as high as the killing level in New York City.[10]

The history of capitalism, of the West, and of every tribal, indigenous system humans have ever contrived has been riddled with cruelties.

But there is something hidden in capitalism that it's up to us to see, something that demands an end to cruelty and that challenges us to invent new Edens, to achieve new glints of paradise. It's capitalism's hidden commandment, a silent ethic that rewards those who uphold it, an ethic that gives you and me the power to upgrade the nature of our work, the richness of our lives, and to open new horizons for humankind. That ethic says: "Serve thy neighbor. Empower her, console her, and delight her. Carve out new frontiers for her, new forms of human feeling, new ways of seeing, and new tools of mastery." Be messianic.

Saving others is the key to cash flow, meaning, zest, creativity, and success. But to save our neighbors by the millions, we'll need to shift the way that we use passion, empathy, and reason in our working lives. More on that change later.

Meanwhile, there is a capitalist story that it's unfashionable to tell. Since its first beginnings capitalism has been a liberator, an emotional upgrader, and a full-speed-ahead creator of new forms of empowerment and of whole new worlds of human possibility.

* * *

The first human industry began 2.5 million years ago, when one of our ancestors, probably *Australopithecus garhi*, improved on what may have been a chimpanzee invention.[11] In 2002 the first archaeological dig to focus on chimpanzee technology showed that chimps in the Tai National Forest of the Ivory Coast, 375 miles west of the country's capital, Abidjan, had been making stone tools from granite, laterite, feldspar, and quartz for a hundred years. What's more, the evidence hinted that chimps may have been making these tools for the last 5 million years or so.[12]

The Tai Forest chimps used tree roots or tablelike rocks firmly fixed in the ground as anvils to hold hard-shelled nuts, then they pounded away for up to five hours, smashing one golf ball–sized coula nut or oil palm nut after another with sharp stone hammers.[13] These techno-savvy chimps dragged their hammer stones from one tree to another over distances of a mile or more. They were picky about the rocks they added to their nut-cracking tool kit and put together a collection of the best stone implements from hither and yon. But they stuck with the same anvils generation after generation.

If you didn't know these tools had been fashioned by chimps, you might have thought they were made—and pulled together in a kit— by early human tool crafters. So what was the difference between the toolmaking invented by chimps and the toolmaking done by early humans?

The difference between notches in a stick and a Blackberry.

Humans are the most pathetically helpless species this planet has ever produced. We were born naked, without the fur that allowed mice, mammoths, and sabertooths to easily endure the summer heat or the freezing cold. And we were born with a lust for meat but without the fangs and claws it took to bring down fast and muscular prey. So we were tossed a challenge—to use our oversized brains to invent our own coats, fangs, and claws. To use our heads to invent our own outboard slashing teeth.

Eagerness and exaltation must have flowed like manna two and a half million years ago, when a man or woman could abandon a clumsy, blunt slammer and could chip at flint or limestone or obsidian to make a blade. What new horizons were opened to humanity by the ability to use a sharpened edge to cut? What new powers spilled from this forward move of the cycle of explore and consolidate, from this turn of the wheel of the evolutionary search engine, this forward flick of the secular genesis machine? Despite the drawback of their stubby teeth, prehumans armed with cutting stones could do more than merely slice a carcass into steaks and chops. They could skin the pelt in a single piece and use it for clothing, carrying bags, baby slings, tents, and huts. They could give themselves the fur of more luxuriously clad animals and travel to cold lands up north, then comb the edges of glaciers for meat and outwit the frost of eleven long ice ages.

A human with a chipped stone tool was no longer a weakly muscled, upright, naked fool. He was a radically different beast—one who had made his own fangs, claws, coat, and slashing teeth.

Was there joy in these new abilities? Was there celebration of this newfound mastery? Were there games to see who could make the best stone blades and who could skin the fastest? Did fans and clans feel passion as they urged their champions on? The tools remain. The cheers are gone. But I suspect they happened.

One thing we know for sure. The ability to predict your destiny and to control it changes hormone flows in your body and your brain. It ups the activity of your immune system, hikes the level of your health, lengthens your life, tweaks your ability to see and think, and makes you stand up straighter. Stone tools were humanity's first hand-made hormone boosters. They were humanity's first bionic control upgraders.

What's the point? We are the pistons of a secular transcendence engine. Our material goods are extenders of our humanity. They upgrade our powers and our creativity. They sometimes change us utterly. Make something that you really want, and what you create may remake you. Make something that you really want, and it may remake others too.

26

FLASH ISN'T FRIVOLOUS—
WHY WE NEED
THE IDENTITY BIZ

Three hundred thousand years ago we came up with another breakthrough—makeup—a clue to our deepest needs.

Cosmetic goods infiltrate the imagination, and the bank accounts, of women across classes and regions, rich and poor, urban and rural. . . . [This is] a renewed imperialism, a colonialism by other means. [Through it] we understand the insidious credo of globalisation: that of creating needs where they don't exist.

Nancy Adajania, *The Hindu*, India[1]

Very often, our "wants"—and even many of the things considered "needs" in affluent societies—are the result of ideas of the "good life" created by the media and advertising industries.

UNESCO's Consumer Education Curriculum[2]

It's time to take the "superficial" seriously. "Trivial" wants may well propel the advance of humanity.

What does capitalism demand from you? What does it ask of you if you want to make a living and if you want to enjoy the work you do? Does the Western system order you to create artificial needs and to stoke them to a frenzy? Or does it count on you to find real needs and feed them brilliantly?

Supposing the needs you cater to are new. Which did you really do: manufacture them or ease their birth and serve them when they cried out for a feeding?

Our species is still brand-new in evolutionary time. Our tools of understanding are even newer. The word *psychology* wasn't invented until 1590, when it was introduced in the universities of Germany by the philosopher Rudolph Goclenius and his pupil Otto Casmann. The thinker who really put psychology on the map, Sigmund Freud, was still alive in 1939.

There are needs whose point we're still too ignorant to see. Human hungers we downgrade may play key roles in the larger scheme of things. Goods and services you and I think are hollow may have a deeper meaning.

Makeup came long before basics like fishing hooks, sewing needles, plows, and trade. We invented rouge and powders two hundred thousand years before we devised these seemingly far more basic tools of food, clothing, and shelter. Why? Why did we need reddeners and flashy skin colorers more than mere practicalities? Why was blending in but being different so very important? Why has makeup and its function survived until today? Why has it done more than survive? Why has it thrived? What is its function anyway?

Prepare for a seemingly preposterous truth. Makeup plays a key role in the evolutionary search engine. It plays a crucial role in the secular genesis machine. Makeup brings us together with the others of our tribe. If the members of your tribe paint their faces red and the members of mine don't paint their faces at all, telling one of you from one of us becomes easy. But here's the real trick. Makeup also slivers us ever-so-slightly apart. It advertises the uniqueness of our personality.

What's the value of setting us apart? In biology, there's a fundamental process called *lateral inhibition*. Technically, lateral inhibition is an "antagonistic neural interaction between adjacent regions of a sensory surface."[3] But lateral inhibition is much more. Lateral inhibition is a boundary maker. Lateral inhibition digs a ditch, a trench, a canyon between clumps, clusters, and individuals. It sets us apart from each other. And lateral inhibition, like exploration and speculation, is crucial to a search strategy. How? Lateral inhibition stretches us out like the fingers you spread apart to comb a shag rug when you search for a lost contact lens. Lateral inhibition specializes us. Lateral inhibition turns us into members of a search team.

Here's how lateral inhibition works in the photoreceptor cells with which you see.[4] These sensory cells are located on the retinas of your eyes. And they all compete to make a picture out of an incoming stream of light. When one sensory cell gets the hang of a new incoming flow of photons, when it names the tune of that flow, it shouts eureka to its neighbors.[5] It shouts the equivalent of "I've got this ball!" Yes, a signal works in the eye the same way a shout works when the left fielder and the center both try to position themselves to catch a fly. It means "stop running and step aside." The signals sent by the sensor that successfully interprets the meaning of the incoming stream of light tells its neighbors to shut up, to leave space, to let the winning sensory cell interpret this one by itself, to let the winning photon catcher send its message to the cable that goes from the eye to the brain—the optic nerve.[6] This sort of "don't get in my way" shout creates a small but crucial distance between cells, organs, and organisms like you and me. And it makes different groups pursue slightly different approaches to food, clothing, shelter, ideas, metaphors, and worldviews.

Many things produce the spacing of lateral inhibition. One of the most effective is a sense of identity. A sense of where we belong and of our strategy for standing out within our crew. We call the cluster of strategies with which we distinguish ourselves and try to get attention our "personality." For example, Frank Sulloway, a visiting scholar at Berkeley's Institute of Personality and Social Research, explains that generally if you are a first child, you become the "good kid."[7] If you do things the way your parents like most, you get attention and praise. But if you're the second child, watch out. When you arrive the "good kid" slot is already taken. So how can you get attention? How can you become the focus of your parents' gaze? You become the "bad kid," the rebel, the creative, the revolutionary.[8] You get attention by breaking your parents' rules. You are forced to set a distance between yourself and your older brother or sister. Why? To find a niche in the landscape of your parents' emotions. To find a slot for yourself, a way to capture your dad's and mom's attention. The separation you are forced to create between yourself and your brother or sister is lateral inhibition.

What does your rebellion do for your family? What does lateral inhibition achieve? Aside from causing havoc and grief? It gives your parents a gang of kids each of whom will explore the world in a slightly different way. It gives your family eyes and ears that are alert for different things. It gives your family a diverse search team. It spaces you out from your siblings the way you separate your fingers when you probe that shag rug for your contact lens. It spaces you out the way you'd spread out if you were in a search party combing a field of chin-high corn for a lost child. Lateral inhibition provides a dragnet of outspread probes for the search engine of more than just your family. It provides a search net for your society.

On the grander scale of things, what helps set our group apart from the groups of others? Once again, lateral inhibition. A set of signals—the way we wear our hair and beards, the way we color our faces and our bodies, the style of the clothes we don, and even the foods we eat and the distinctive smells those foods give to the members of our separate families, clans, tribes, nations, and civilizations.

On the cosmic scale, separate identities, slightly different specialties, are vital to the evolutionary search engine. They turn each of us into probes into the impossible, probes into the familiar, and probes into the unknown.

So the trivial, the vain, the frivolous, and the seemingly wasteful often play a role we fail to see. They turn us into antennae of a search and innovation machine. And the fact that we denigrate "the superficial" hides a blunt fact—that we don't understand the function of the frivolous. And that we haven't even made the effort to ask. But in our labors, in emotional capitalism, in the capitalism of passion, we need to respect the role of the trivial, the frivolous, and the vain if we're to serve the yearnings of the human soul. In fact, serving needs like these is central to the capitalist mission. What's more, serving yearnings like these is uplifting. It's messianic. It can help save others from being invisible in the eyes of those whose attention they need to survive. We humans, like bees, need attention to feel alive.

Remember the second rule of science: look at things right under your nose as if you've never seen them before, then proceed from there. That rule turns you, me, and every Nobel Prize winner on the planet into probes of the search and innovate machine, probes of the evolutionary search engine, probes of the secular genesis machine, probes of a creative drivetrain to whose operation we've been far too blind. That engine works through play, novelty, entertainment, awe, curiosity, and surprise.

One strong hint to the role of things we denigrate is a simple fact we alluded to a few minutes ago. That before we invented fishing hooks, sewing needles, plows, and trade, we invented one of the first emotion-manufacturing enterprises. It specialized in superficiality.

The time was roughly 300,000 BCE—a full 100,000 years before we finally evolved the bodies and the brains we have today.[9] That's when we created the identity business—the makeup industry. Why at such an early date did we invent the trivial dusts—the cosmetics and the pigments—with which we colored ourselves and with which we colored our lives?

First came a biological upgrade—a growth spurt in a gulley in the skull—the *foramina*.[10] The trench of the foramina guides nerves to the face. In other words, a boost in nerve power equipped our lips and eyes to put on a show of smiles, frowns, scowls, smirks, pouts, and the many other looks with which we humans flash the meekness or uniqueness of our personalities.

Then came a new way to show off your pretty or your frightening face, your peace face or your war face, not to mention your delectable or your terrifying body: face and body powders and paints.[11] It started with the trick of grinding—putting something you wanted to crush on a flat, fixed stone, in some cases a stone into which you'd carved a shallow valley so that whatever you pulverized wouldn't roll or sift away. With another heavy stone you'd heave your weight back and forth over the nugget you intended to crack and crunch. In the end, you'd have a puffable dust, a smearable powder.

Based on this stone-mashing technique, the cosmetics industry first reared its head in Terra Amata, France, and in the Hungsi Valley of India 300,000 years ago.[12] At Hungsi our prehuman ancestors stashed reddish brown iron oxide pebbles they apparently intended to pulverize. At Terra Amata other early relatives of ours left seventy-five pieces of stone of the sort they crushed to produce a palette of colors vivid with reds, browns, and yellows.

Crushing stones to colored powders wasn't just a passing fad or a flimsy, artificial hunger shoved down the throats of gullible cave-dwellers by unscrupulous capitalists. For 100,000 years, from 270,000 to 170,000 years ago, our prehuman relatives used the caves at Twin Rivers, Zambia, in Southern Africa, as a central processing plant for makeup. They brought in rocks from two or three miles away, rocks that yielded shades of powders from yellow, brown, and red to purple, bluish black, and pink.

The variety of rouges we prehumans produced in this single Zambian cave rivals those at department store makeup counters today. If you sat at one of the most popular rock grinding spots—a cave opening that looked out on the terrain—in your makeup manufacturing cavern 270,000 years ago at Twin Rivers and ground specularite, you got a purplish red pinpricked by sparks of light. If you ground hematite, you got a dull-surfaced reddish brown. If you ground limonite, you produced a yellow green. If you chipped or hammered at dolerite to get to its core, you could add yet another yellow green to your palette. And if you wanted to put in yet more sweat and toil, you could carve your colored stones into portable coloring sticks that archaeologists call crayons.

The folks who powdered and shaped these pigments went for glitter. Nearly 89 percent of the weight of the 108 pieces of pigment in just one section of the Twin Rivers dig was the twinkling, purple specularite. And that percentage of sparkle seems the norm.

The prehuman cosmetics makers also went for quantity. Archaeologists calculate that thousands of fragments of raw materials for pigment making remain to be sifted from the Twin Rivers site alone.

Once the mass-production of makeup kicked off in the cradle of modern man—Africa—it never stopped. The Karo, a tribe of a thousand near the Omo River in Ethiopia, still make their own body paint today. And the photos of their body art are amazing.[13]

But why slather yourself with makeup? Why turn yourself new shades and tints? Why break your back to paint your cheeks, your nose, your arms, and feet? Why make yourself unnatural? Why not go with the skin that you were born with—whether it was black, red, yellow, or pale white?

Were ochre and hematite rouges used 300,000 years ago to improve the natural pink that makes a woman seductive or to highlight the bright red that accompanies a mano-a-mano battle? Were they used to ape the sort of flush, the sort of quickening of the blood that raises the body temperature of bees that are on to something in short supply, something others find absolutely vital?[14] Were they used, as they are today, to amplify the social cues of sexual fertility? The "youthful glow" of beauty? We don't know. And we don't know the exact meaning of yesteryear's bluish black and glitzy yellow green body and face decorators either.

But the evidence from modern hunter-gatherers hints that humans used skin paint to fill a basic craving—the hunger for identity—the desire to both blend in and to stand out—the need to show that I'm a part of this group, I'm one of you, but I'm also someone special you must pay attention to. I'm me. Fashion and makeup still serve these deep identity needs today, the need to prove that you belong and the need to prove that you also stand out. In fact this need is one of the most basic drives that power the capitalist machine. It is also one of the most despised because it is the least appreciated, the least respected, and the least understood.

You can see your identity needs at work when you're flicking through mp3s on the Internet or buying a new pair of shoes. Let's say you belong to the symphony music crowd. When you skip over the country category you detest or when you loathe the alligator loafers with the tassels, you may tell yourself that you are making judgments in terms of raw aesthetics. But in your heart you know that something more is going on.

The country and western music you shun makes you think of hay-seeds down on the farm who support the wrong political candidates and cheer for all of the wrong causes—or of semiliterate truckers in some seedy bar guzzling enough beer to kill a cow, then making a pathetic attempt to cheat on their wives and ending up in a sloppy fight. You don't want to identify with these lowlifes. You don't want anybody else to think you would associate with them either. So the thought of listening to the twang and whine of country music sends a shudder down your spine.

Hidden in that shudder is the premonition of the sneers you'd get if your friends and neighbors felt you were a part of the country music crowd. You pass by the hip-hop sites even more quickly. The contempt that your friends would have for you if you grew to like rap music would be beyond belief. Finally you settle for Vivaldi. This is something your fellow patrons of the classics could listen to with pride. Though they might regard even Vivaldi's *Four Seasons* as a bit plebeian, a bit too well-loved by the vulgar masses.

In the privacy of your home, you might listen to Garth Brooks, Johnny Cash, or Loretta Lynn—giving yourself a guilty pleasure you carefully hide most of the time. But your public tastes are guided by a shrewd and semiconscious calculation of your social position.

You make your decision about shoes in the same way. You briefly picture a parade of those who would admire you and those who would loathe you for each pair you glance at in a shopping mall window. You calculate which social circle the subtleties of each shoe's design would help you penetrate and which cliques they'd get you bounced from. Once again, an internal social calculator reigns over what you and I prefer to think of as our taste.

What role has this social calculator played in our evolution and in our history? What role does it play today? Should we really cater to it and why?

Is our contempt for "vanity" a mistake? Should we, indeed, take "useless," "superficial" needs more seriously?

The sheer antiquity of our obsession with the external tools of social positioning hints that the answer may be yes, identity tools may be crucial to our humanity. In fact, the need for vanity and identity are critical to a drive we normally deride. They're central to an evolutionary propellant that's gifted us with upgrade fuel since the days when we still had big, brutish brows. Vanity and identity are part of what makes us, in the phrase of the Dutch historian Johan Huizinga, not just *Homo sapiens*, man the knower, but *Homo Ludens*[15]—man the player, man the gamester, man the competitor, man the species that fools around.[16]

Fighting fish show how they fit in but aspire to be better than the rest with a blaze of color on their chests. Dolomedes triton water spiders are more creative. They show how they fit in yet stand out by outdoing each other in a collective fad, the mating dance. But among all the animals, only humans show that "I am one of you but I am me" with such a gush of fresh inventions and with such a flood of new twists on old ones. Only humans flash their uniqueness with tales, opinions, and discoveries. Only humans feed the group IQ, the communal search engine, with such a steady stream of newly conceived or newly discovered novelties.

We feed our need to preen and to parade incessantly. And though it seems absurd, this itch drives our evolution in ways no bower bird or other flashy animal could conceive. What seems so private and so petty drives an engine far greater than you and me. It guns the evolutionary search engine. It powers the secular genesis machine. It fuels the rise of ideas and technology. It adds to the store of human capabilities.

27

WHY NEANDERTHALS COULDN'T CUT IT— THE CRUCIAL USE OF VANITY

What killed off the Neanderthal? Could it have been too little jewelry?

Modern *Homo sapiens*—our branch of the primate family tree—were not the only competitors for the niche now occupied by you and me. There was a hardier, more muscular people who were far better equipped by their biology to face the shocks of cold that came and stayed for periods so long that these periods are called ice ages. Tall, long-legged, skinny folks like our more human ancestors had huge areas of skin exposed to the cold. But our rivals, the Neanderthals, were sturdy, hulking, and muscular.[1] With their built-for-power bodies, the Neanderthals had less naked skin per pound of muscle and bone—less skin to chill, to shiver, to get goose bumps, and to be chewed by frostbite. Evolutionary expert Valerius Geist and many others believe that Neanderthals had the strength to wrestle wild animals to the ground—something we couldn't do.[2] Neanderthals' noses, Geist points out, were better equipped than ours to warm the chill out of ice age air before they inhaled it into their throat and lungs. And even Neanderthals' brains were bigger than ours.[3]

So why did we survive and Neanderthals disappear? It all has to do with vanity and with the attempt to fit into the crowd but still stand out, the ability to out-spangle the folks around you. The Neanderthals went down the tubes when a huge blast of frigid air swept across Asia and Europe 25,000 years ago and froze nearly everything in sight. At that point, according to one school of anthropologists, the ancestors of modern humans—the ancestors of you and me, *Homo sapiens*—had been indulging for over a quarter of a million years in luxuries that Neanderthals apparently disdained. We *Homo sapiens* had been coming up with new ways to show off. We'd been accessorizing. We'd been going superficial, indulging in trivial and useless vanities.

In the process, we'd gone way beyond makeup. We'd created another offshoot of the identity industry—the fashion biz. We'd made beads, bracelets, necklaces, bone needles, and a form of thread. We'd sewn clothes and had decorated them to show how many hundreds of beads we could afford to have stitched on just one shirt. Then we'd learned to sew mammoth hides together, to throw the hides over a taller-than-human frame of mammoth bones and tusks, and to make something new with which to outdo each other—homes. Well, in reality, tents. But very big tents. Tents big enough to house several families.[4]

When the chill winds blew and the glaciers crept into every neighborhood, we almost-modern humans had devised so many ways of primping, preening, and flaunting our stuff that we'd invented almost everything we needed to brave the cold.

The ascetic Neanderthals were great hunters. They crafted astonishingly aerodynamic spears. And they had the genes for cold-resistant bodies. But they couldn't hack the new conditions. Why? Says paleontologist Juan Luis Arsuaga, who codirected the dig at one of the biggest Neanderthal and prehuman sites ever found, the 400,000-year-old "Bone Pit" at Atapuerca in Spain, the key was superficiality. The key was vanity and the identity industry. Says Arsuaga: "Many paleoanthropologists attach considerable importance to the fact that the Neanderthals, for the most part, did not use personal ornamentation. . . . Not that scholars think that ornamentation itself offered some great advantage in combating a harsh environment; but rather they see it as a sign of a different mentality. Or to put it another way, compared with Cro-Magnons, Neanderthals were deep-seated realists, not so carried away by their imaginations."[5]

Imagination counts, as we'll see at every level of the history of the Western system.

* * *

Create what would delight you—no matter how frivolous it may seem—and your useless display of trinkets, toys, and treasures may come in handy in a future time. If not for you then for one of your great-great-grandkids far, far down the human line.

Stretch in your unique direction like a finger probing the loops of carpet for that missing contact lens. Spread, explore, and speculate. Then condense and structure-make. Those are the rules of the evolutionary learning machine. And they would pay off mightily for us human beings.

* * *

Who has decided what's trivial and what's not? A self-appointed judge. A half-blind blunderer and sometimes killer. It's that crucial newcomer to the human scene, reason. Reason is a powerful tool. But all good things in overdose are a poison. When reason isn't joined with intuition, it can make monumental mistakes. And in judging what's trivial, superficial, and vain, reason has made an arrogant error.

Reason works with tools just like hands do. But its scrapers, blades, and separators aren't made of stone. They're concepts. Concepts can be changed. Our concepts about things "economic" cry out for overhaul and upgrade.

When we get down to thinking, we often lean on unseen intellectual tools, some of the most powerful tools we've ever invented—clichés. Here's one example. Grammar school kids, college students, would-be homebuyers, and credit card abusers are taught to make up lists of needs versus wants.[6] The implication of the lesson? "Needs" are serious and "wants" are frivolous. Kids are taught that only three essentials count—food, clothing, and shelter. These same unspoken intellectual assumptions underlay the revolutions of the twentieth century: the upheaval led by Lenin in Russia and the overturn of ancient culture led by Mao in China. Mao, Lenin, and Lenin's successor, Stalin, were idealists. They put ideas ahead of all the rest but ironically claimed the opposite. They claimed to put "essentials" first. The ideas of Lenin and Mao accepted the assumption that man lives by food, clothing, and shelter and that all the rest is drivel or worse—

phony needs imposed by the slick and greedy, imposed by the destroyers of the soul, imposed by the capitalist, corporate machine.

In the name of just the basics and no frivolity—no makeup, no trinkets, no luxuries, and no religion—the socialist revolutions of Lenin, Mao, and Stalin killed more than 80 million human beings. This was the world's biggest experiment in economic theory, the world's biggest experiment in creating a society on the basis of sheer reason. And it failed miserably.

The mission of Lenin, Mao, Stalin, and of those who believed in them fervently was to break the chains of wage slavery and to liberate man and womankind. Lenin, Mao, and Stalin reached out for a higher good. But the ideas that they used were wrong. Their concepts were cockeyed. The result of their experiment was a stark and brutal truth: When your ideas and your clichés go awry they can mass-produce misery and worse, they can mass-produce sheer murder on a scale that boggles minds.

Our material goods can elevate our dreams. And our dreams can carve out new realities. That's a basic message of *The Genius of the Beast*. It's one of the secrets powering economies. It's at the very heart of putting soul in the capitalist machine. But not all dreams are equal. Some that purport to offer liberty and justice are killers in disguise. Wrong ideas can spill rivers of blood. So it's time to add more accurate ideas to the tool kit of the Western mind.

Let's start with the sterile notion of the marketplace—the notion of exchange and trade.

28

SWAPPING DROPS OF BLOOD

The Animal Roots of Trade

How bats invented credit and commerce.

Just so our heads won't swell with so much goggle-eyed pride that we can't squeeze our cheeks through the door, let's get something straight about trade, commerce, and exchange. They're at the heart of business, economics, and earning your daily bread and mine. But we humans didn't invent commerce, consumerism, and exchange. We didn't invent trading. Mother Nature did.

First off, Mother Nature invented marketing—gaudy displays and advertising. For proof, consult your nearest flower—a flashy billboard for the humble dust of pollen. One of the most powerful messages from a blossom is this: if you want to be all natural, then trade, seduce, display, broadcast, recruit, and spread your billboards left and right around the land. Do it as flagrantly as the first ropes of DNA. Do it as flamboyantly as orchids, snapdragons, and dandelions. That's what masses of fireflies do when they flash on cue like pixels on a downtown Tokyo video display. That's what moths broadcasting sexual perfumes for miles around, crickets making music in the grass, flowers, birds, and bees do. That's what even fish and lizards do. And I am **not** saying this to be cute.

A flower also engages in barter. Every blossom offers a deal to bees. It offers an exchange. It will pay nectar to any bee that will sell it transportation. To any bee that will carry its pollen far and wide. A flower also demonstrates nature's flagrant waste. Flowers consume precious resources, then are tossed away. Once their purpose has been served, they are casually dropped from their stem and left as trash and litter to shrivel and fade. Which brings us back to the subject at hand: the marketplace.

Commerce and exchange mean trade. Long-distance trade is unique to human beings. But it's less unique to us than it seems.

Some lady vampire bats set out from the highway underpasses or caves in which they live to find the food that's number one on their menu—blood. Other bats stay home to babysit the kids. When the hunters and seekers come home gorged with yummy gore, they pay their babysitters. How? They disgorge some of the day's blood into the mouth of their daycare providers. But that's not the end of the bats' commerce and exchange. Bats are generous. Those who've come home with a full tank of blood also share some of their food with the less fortunate—with bats whose search has not gone well, bats who've come home hungry.[1] And someday the bats that received this generosity will repay the favor. Apparently this system of trade and philanthropy between two thousand bats or more has rules of fairness and of gratitude built in. It has rules of who you should repay and how. This raises a question: Is the concept of fairness and gratitude built into the bats' genes and brains the way that language and its "universal grammar" are built into ours?[2] Or is fairness among bats cultural? Is it a pattern invented way back when, a pattern that animal parents teach their kids? Is it passed on from one generation to the next via learning? How is the measure of what's fair and of what's not handled by sheer gut feelings like gratitude, obligation, and justice?

Is fairness and gratitude built into our brains as well? Or is this strictly an invention that we've passed along from one generation to another via training and education? There's a clue in the word *gratitude*. Gratitude is an emotion. It's an emotion that rises when we're given something we didn't expect. It has a hormonal basis. When we give something away, our generosity is powered by a hormone—oxytocin, a hormone of warmth and bonding.[3] And when we receive something, we get a boost of guess what hormone? You got it. Oxytocin[4] all over again. Oxytocin is the hormone that courses through a woman's veins when she holds her newborn baby and puts its lips to her nipple for its first taste of her milk. Some women have described the experience as akin to orgasm—an addictive high. This is not surprising, since oxytocin levels rise during lovemaking, too.[5]

Oxytocin is the hormone of two things we often think of as opposites: warmth and commerce, warmth and exchange. So is commerce and exchange something we humans have invented? Or is it something we inherited? Is it an artificial aberration? Or is it built into our biology?

Bees do it. Bats do it. Blossoms do it. And I suspect our hormones have evolved to help us do it, too. No wonder gratitude nags us to repay a debt. No wonder indebtedness is an emotion that often sticks around like a Post-it note hung on a cupboard door in the pantry of our memory. Even if we cheat, something in us eats at us. Something often says it's wrong. I suspect that exchange and the rules of the marketplace churn our emotions for a reason. They're built into our biology.

The rules of the marketplace are built into our cells and our genes? Surely that's sloppy thinking, isn't it? No, it's not. The evidence fills books, but it begins with an amazing bit of research done with brown capuchin monkeys (which have much more gorgeous fur coats than you and I do) at Yerkes Primate Center in Atlanta, Georgia. These monkeys can be taught to use rocks as money and to trade stones in for stuff to eat—a prized piece of fruit or a yucky vegetable.[6] Female capuchins, says primate researcher Sarah Brosnan, who did this study, have a sense of "fairness." This lady monkey sense of what-I've-got-that-you-have-not looks an awful lot like pettiness and jealousy. But is that silly anthropomorphism? You be the judge.

First, put yourself in Brosnan's place. Here's how your experiment works. You train five female capuchins to realize that if they hand you a rock, you will give them a snack. In other words, they can buy snacks from you. And you'll accept stones as if they were ten-dollar bills. When the training is over, you put two of these bargain-hunting capuchin females together in one room so they can keep a wary eye on each other. When monkey number one hands in her rock, you give her something sweet and succulent—a grape. Monkey number two gets all excited. When she turns in her rock, she expects to get a grape too. But instead you give her a pathetic substitute, a cucumber. Is she "smart" enough to compare the "value" of the cuke she received to the value of the grape that monkey number one scooped up? Does she have the sort of social savvy (or emotional curse) that makes us view what others have as wealth while we see what we've received as a shabby pittance? Yes, monkey number two is just as blessed and damned as we are by the passions that power economies. She regards monkey number one's bonanza of sweetness as a rain of riches and her own bitter but vitamin-rich reward as a sign of penury.

How can we be sure she's miffed? We can't claim to read her mind. But here's the evidence. Here's how the monkeys behave.

Hold out your hand to encourage monkey number one to turn in her first rock, then give her a grape. Now turn to monkey number two. When she cashes in her rock, give her a cucumber. You'll see a look of consternation. Do it again and again and again, until monkey number two gets the message that you're a prejudiced seller. The rocks of monkey two are worth less to you than the stones of monkey number one. You'll soon see what we humans call outrage. Monkey number two will reject your monetary system. She'll turn up her nose at you and refuse the vegetable, despite the fact that it's good for her. She'll say in a monkey sort of way that she'd rather starve than be humiliated. Worse yet, she'll overturn the economic system. She'll refuse you when you hand her a purseful of rocks. And if you get pushy and continue this hideous distortion of economic justice, she's likely to use the rocks to gain another form of satisfaction. She'll start a private riot and hurl the stones at you. Not to mention the fact that she'll vehemently toss away her cuke.

So like us, these small-brained animals compare their lot with the fate of other monkeys in their spot. They see an "unequal distribution of wealth." And they insist on putting up a fuss about it. That's the primitive core of revolutions. It's also the primitive core of economies.

But the capuchin's fury flies in the face of today's economic and social theory. Economics and today's "neo-Darwinian" evolutionary psychology both use something called the *rational choice model*. Rational choice theory says that each of us in an office, a bedroom, a primate center's research lab, a grocery store, or at a dinner party calculate each move by going for what will get us the most. We are greedy gamesters totaling up our prizes.

Suppose a grape has a hundred calories and a slice of cucumber has twenty. You are monkey number two. I hand monkey number one a grape. I hand you a cucumber slice. I do this twenty-five times in a row, just as the folks in Atlanta did with their silky-furred brown monkeys. What does the rational choice model say you should do? It says you will be smart and take the cucumber. At the end of twenty-five rounds, you will have collected five hundred calories. You will be five hundred calories—over a quarter of a day's nutrition—ahead.[7] Says the rational choice model, there is no way that you are going to turn down those five hundred calories and the vitamins of those twenty-five veggie snacks.

But the rational choice model's got it wrong. Food means less to you than social standing. You don't merely calculate what those cukes are worth to you. Something more important is going on. Food means less than pride to you. It's all about identity. You just racked up five hundred unexpected calories. You should be delighted, shouldn't you?

Monkey number one is your only species mate in the room. She carries most of the same genes that you do. Theoretically, as your gene mate, she should be your chum. But that's not the way you see it. In twenty-five rounds monkey number one piled up twenty-five grapes. She piled up 2,500 calories. What does this have to do with you? You racked up only 500 calories. So you feel you're running a deficit. Your sense of worth is not in the food. It's in where you stand compared to monkey number one. She's got 2,500 calories. You've just got 500. So you are not up 500, you are down 2,000. That's why you refuse to play the game. That's why you refuse "perfectly good food." That's why you turn down rocks and toss out the system of exchange. And that's why you hurl your paltry pile of "wealth" directly at the damned experimenter.

Social standing is worth a lot. Food is just a commodity. Unless it's caviar. But what counts is not a satisfied stomach. What counts is your place in the pecking order. What counts is what lifts you on high. And the currency of pecking order lift is not the calorie. It's the attention, admiration, and envy you are able to command.

Why did humans invent makeup 240,000 years before they crafted such practical, food-getting things as fishing tackle? Because identity and social standing go hand in hand. Even grapes and cucumbers play a role in the identity industry. Or, to put it differently, style is everything. And style's not private. It's a social thing.

The same thing goes for humans in strange places who've kept their tribal ways. They, too, have their sense of pride. They, too, are not fooled by the math of practicality, the math of rational choice.

They, too, are ruled by the arithmetic of pride, the calculus of vanity. They're ruled by the calculating tool that totals up the score for the core we call identity. In the 1990s, eleven anthropologists and an economist coordinated by Joseph Henrich at the Institute for Advanced Study in Berlin searched the globe for cultures so out of the way that they had radically different approaches to dealing with each other and with the world around them. Then the scientists performed more than a hundred economic experiments spanning fifteen societies in twelve different countries.

How would the folks in these societies handle the task of bargaining? Would they do what economic theory says that rational choosers do? Would they go for the options that in the end would give them a guaranteed prize, no matter how lowly? Would they go for sheer practical self-interest? Or would they act on something else? Would they act on something silly and impractical? Something like pride and vanity?

Three of the societies that the researchers chose were hunters and gatherers. Six were primitive farmers who used the slash-and-burn technique. Four were animal herders who traveled with the seasons to the spots where the grass was greenest. And two were societies of farmers living in a permanent village. Some lived in Africa. Some lived in Asia. And some lived in South America. The values used to rank your standing in each society were different. But when these humans were offered the equivalent of a cucumber or a grape, they didn't behave according to practical "self-interest" and "rational choice." They didn't take whatever they were given and hoard it with great glee.

Like the capuchin monkeys, they turned down offers that were beneath contempt—they spurned gifts that would have upped their cash but lowered their dignity.[8] According to Heinrich and his sixteen coauthors, the rational choice "canonical selfishness-based model fails in all of the societies."[9] Heinrich is very emphatic. He declares that "the predictions of the textbook representation of *Homo economicus*" simply do not match reality. In fact, he says, the predictions of standard economics are dead wrong.

Money is more than practical stuff. Like makeup, it's a marker of pride, a marker of status, a marker of identity. Or, to put it differently, sometimes the things that pocket change will buy mean less than social standing. At the heart of trade and economics lies something we don't ordinarily see. No matter what field we think we're in, we're in the pride industry. We're artists in the field of social standing. We're in the biz that cares and feeds our hunger for attention, admiration, and envy. We're in the business that feeds our need for identity.

VI

THE INFRASTRUCTURE
OF FANTASY

29

THE CANNONBALL
TO THE MOON

How a nineteenth-century stockbroker's nutty notion
of firing men to the moon with an artillery piece
changed history.

One of the most astonishing slivers of brilliance in the genius of the
beast is built on the trivial and the superficial. It's built on using ideas
and dreams as badges of identity. It's built on what seems like an
impractical waste of time. Yet that source of genius utterly remakes
reality. It's one of the things that drove Abraham Lincoln to dream
feverishly of a transcontinental railroad. It's one of the things that distinguish human beings from bees and capuchin monkeys. It's one of
the things that we carry in our tool kit of concepts from our ancestors. It's the infrastructure of fantasy.

What's an infrastructure of fantasy? Once upon a time, a part-
time French stockbroker who loved science wrote a story about an
imaginary voyage of discovery, a voyage to the moon.

It was 1865. The American Civil War had just ended. The North
had built a most peculiar superweapon, a cannon that could heave a
projectile the size of a livery coach. The Frenchman told the fictional
tale of the members of an American gun club, a club of men who had
fought in the War between the States. The club members bet to see if
you could, indeed, build a supersized version of this already mam-

moth cannon, fit something like a coach into the artillery pieces' mouth, put people into this capsule, and aim it at the moon. The fantasy was called *From Earth to the Moon*. When it hit the bookstores, it did quite well, helping make a name for its author: the king of a new field, science fiction, Jules Verne.[1]

A new material object and a hateful one at that—the new cannon, the Columbiad—had led to new imaginings. And to a sense of a new destination awaiting all humanity.[2]

But that was by no means the end of things. Verne had laid a foundation for something new. For a collective vision. For a shared dream. For the kind of dream that hardens into a structure that elevates us. He'd laid a new foundation for an infrastructure of fantasy.

Far from Jules Verne's France, in Russia and Germany, two kids grew up reading Verne's *From Earth to the Moon* and imprinting, fixating, on Verne's fantasies. Each of these kids grew up to write a book on how to achieve Verne's goal in a very dangerous way. In a cannon, the explosives remain in the barrel. Once a theoretical passenger capsule is launched, the inhabitants are clear of the destructive force. But they also have no control over their movement. The two Verne fans—the Russian and the German—proposed putting the explosives in the rear of the capsule itself. Sounds like a good way to incinerate your passengers, right? But the idea was very old. The Chinese had invented cylinders filled with explosives that whooshed into the air, carrying their incendiary substances within them. Westerners had taken up their use in war. The line in the national anthem of the United States about "the rockets' red glare" describes the use of these explosive-packed, thirty-five-pound cylinders in the War of 1812 between Britain and the United States. They were called "Congreve rockets."[3]

The German and the Russian Jules Verne fans—Hermann Oberth and Konstantin Eduardovich Tsiolkovskii—wrote books proposing that we humans should aim to escape the planet and get into the territory of Galileo's and Newton's circling spheres, space.[4] The vehicle they recommended? The rocket. Oberth and Tsiolkovskii added a first floor to Jules Verne's basement and foundation. They added to the infrastructure of fantasy.

Meanwhile, a fresh batch of kids was growing up. These kids read Jules Verne, then they topped off their reading with the books of Oberth and Tsiolkovskii. They imprinted on the idea of shooting rockets into space. Among those kids was a young member of the German Rocket Club named Wernher von Braun.[5]

The rockets of von Braun's day were pathetic, skinny, amateur devices about as big around as your arm. Von Braun dreamed of rockets so big they could make it all the way to Mars. But turning a dream like that into reality would require a budget. A very big one.

Then the twenty-seven-year-old von Braun had a stroke of luck. War. The leader of his nation started a flat-out battle to take over the world for the blue-eyed, blond Aryan race. And that leader was intent on conquering England, on bringing the Brits to their knees. Rockets carrying walloping payloads of explosives, payloads big enough to level a city, seemed like a great way to achieve this supreme commander's goals. So he gave Wernher von Braun a budget, and von Braun developed the V-2 rocket, a rocket big enough to deliver a 2,200-pound warhead to London.

A rocket big enough to make it to the edge of space.

When Germany lost World War II and the leader who had funded von Braun, Adolf Hitler, committed suicide in his underground bunker below the Reich Chancellery in Berlin, von Braun told his brother to jump on a bicycle and pedal out to the front lines to find the Yankees. Both the Americans and the Russians were closing in on Berlin, and von Braun wanted to make sure that he would not have to live under the dangerous rule of Russia's murderous dictator, Joseph Stalin. Said von Braun's brother when he reached an antitank brigade private who looked like a citizen of the USA, "We are a group of rocket specialists up in the mountains. We want to see your commander and surrender to the Americans."[6] Then von Braun demanded a meeting with the leader of the Allied Forces, future president of the United States Dwight D. Eisenhower. He didn't get it. But he did get privileged treatment from an American Army eager to tap the brains behind the V-2 rocket.

Five years later, von Braun was firmly settled in America. There, he recruited a famous architect and Hollywood special effects artist who wanted more than anything else in life to paint space dreams. That artist was Chesley Bonestell, the man who had designed the art-deco façade of one of the most amazing skyscrapers of all time, Manhattan's Chrysler Building. But that's not all. Bonestell had also designed "the Plymouth Rock Memorial, the U.S. Supreme Court Building, the New York Central Building, Manhattan office and apartment buildings and several state capitols."[7] When von Braun brought Bonestell into the fold, the German rocket creator was building a second floor on the infrastructure of Verne's, Tsiolkovskii's, and Oberth's fantasy.

Bonestell's paintings were so startling that *Collier's Magazine* published them from 1952 through 1954 in a two-year series of splashy stories, some of which were cowritten by von Braun himself.[8] Meanwhile, a New York publisher—Viking—put Bonestell's pictures out in a series of twelve drop-dead gorgeous books.[9] And the articles, books, and pictures attracted fans. One of those fans had just landed a television deal with a brand-new TV network—ABC. He sent messages to von Braun, explaining that he now had a Sunday night show in prime time and asking if von Braun would host the "Man in Space" segments. That fan was Walt Disney. And von Braun's segments helped lay the groundwork for the building of Tomorrowlands in theme parks that did not yet exist—Disneylands.[10] Chalk up one more floor on the infrastructure of fantasy.

Bonestell's paintings and Disney's shows caught the attention of yet another generation of aficionados, building yet another level of fantasy into children's dreams. When a young president was looking for a vision that could unite America and score a victory in the cold war against the Soviet Union, he chose to adopt the goal laid out by Jules Verne in 1865—putting men on the moon. That president was John Fitzgerald Kennedy, who told us that we were shooting for the moon not because it was easy, but because it was hard.[11]

One of the key people in this "space program" was, you guessed it, Wernher von Braun. How did von Braun land the assignment? By building on the daydreams of Jules Verne, Tsiolkovskii, and Oberth. By building on the daydreams of Bonestell and Disney. By building on the peculiar achievements we're about to see—the achievements of men like Columbus, Magellan, and Marco Polo. By building on the cycle of exploration and digestion, on the cycle of search and consolidate. By building on the strategy of the evolutionary search engine, of the secular genesis machine. By building on the strategy behind boom and crash. By building on the strategy behind the genius of the beast. By building on the infrastructure of fantasy.

* * *

Who will dare to be the next Jules Verne?

30

INVENTING THE CITY

Even the Walls Tell Tales of Soul

How Stone Age dreamers in the Middle East came
up with a crazy idea involving boulders and invented
the first city.

Fossils don't let us peer into the infrastructure of fantasy 2.5 million years ago. But they do help us see into the heart of another mystery—the way in which material goods upshift our biology. Recent research reveals something startling: that stone tools were man's first accidental genetic engineering kit.[1]

How? With tools we could chop our foods or pound them to make them tender. Once we could smash and slice steaks and mash and dice vegetables, we could dispense with the super-strength jaws our ancestors had used for power-chewing. That allowed a radical downsizing of the massive, flaring temporal bones that had stuck out like hand grips on either sides of our skull. Why? Those huge flanges of bone had been anchors for the immense jaw muscles we'd needed to chew tough, hard, and tooth-resistant foods. Prechewing with stone blades and hammers opened the space for a huge expansion of a slightly higher part of our skull. It opened the space for a ballooning of the cranium, the semispherical hangar that houses our brain.

Stone tools indirectly deactivated one old gene—the maker of giant jaw muscles, MYH16.[2] And they opened the way for as-yet-unspecified genes that would upscale the brain case, including genes like FOXP2, a gene that helped add another girder to the infrastructure of fantasy—language.

Brains are expensive. Your brain and mine take up just 2 percent of our body mass, but they burn up as much as 25 percent of our energy. Stone hunting weapons and stone culinary instruments would open enormous new stores of nutrients and calories. Just as important, stone tools would open a highway for a gene that would dramatically increase our life span. Here's how.

With tools, our early hunting ancestors could eat far more meat than we do today, and that heavy meat diet cracked open a door for a gene that upgraded our metabolism. Specifically, a gene for a substance called apolipoprotein E3. Apolipoprotein E3 breaks down a very specific range of fats and makes their energy available. Those fats are called triglyceride-rich lipoproteins. Upgrade the apolipoprotein makers in the body and guess what? You double or quadruple the human life span.[3] Longer-living humans are longer-learning humans, humans who can accumulate wisdom. And longer-learning humans can pass their wisdom on. They can become the sages, the insightful elders, the ancestors we cite and worship. In other words, there are spiritual fruits—mind-expanding powers—to material things.

Stone tools were also arm-and-hand upgraders, world remakers, and openers of new frontiers of human mastery. They were material goods that changed the range of what we could envision and conceive. And, most important to a book re-visioning capitalism, stone tools were our first capital.

But there's more to capital than mere things.

Capital has traditionally meant machines, buildings, tools, shafts, hafts, instruments, plans, savings, and the training that we use to make things that others crave. The followers of Karl Marx called capital "stored labor."[4] And the Marxists were right. Capital is stored muscle work and stored sweat. But Marx picked up just one piece of the puzzle and left the others scattered on the floor. Breakthroughs come from more than just the work of those who carry out another's intention. Every piece of capital begins as a new invention.

It's time to rewrite Economics 101. Capital is stored imagination. Capital is stored stress, stored diligence to persist, and stored ability to inspire others to complete a task that seems impossible or frivolous.

Capital is stored risk! And, most important, capital is stored vision! Capital is stored fantasy!

The stone hand axe of 2.5 million years ago was used wherever prehumans traveled. It showed up in Africa, China, Malaysia, and 13,500 miles away in Boxwood, England. But I suspect the stone axe owed its existence to a mob of innovators and creators driven by odd-ball accidents and daydreams:

- the first man or woman insane enough to try to chip one stone with another
- the crazed obsessives who tried stone after stone after stone and discovered that some types held an edge far better than others
- and the gossipers, promoters, preachers, and teachers who spread the skill and made the strange behavior of the chippers universal.

In other words, I suspect that the hand axe owed its existence to an infrastructure of fantasy.

The first upgrade to the basic hand axe came a million years after the original. Called the Acheulian hand axe, it probably also owed its existence to some lunatic with a fantasy one and a half million years ago, the man who dreamed up a crazy notion—that you could flake not just one side of a blade but two—and could double your cutting power.

Capital is stored courage—the courage it takes to turn an off-the-wall new vision into a daily reality. And capital is stored persistence. Capital is based on one of the most stressful acts a human can undergo: having a wild-eyed notion, holding onto it despite self-doubts and mockery, infecting others with your vision, then persisting for as many years or decades as it takes to turn what seems like insanity into a new reality.

Flip the calendar forward to the days when the last ice age ended roughly 12,000 years ago. For 2 million years, glaciers had covered roughly 60 percent of the planet. Now they retreated north, leaving the Near East a paradise. The Near East's seas of grass were top heavy with seeds. Its meadows were grazed by armies of roastable and stew-able red deer and by herds of the nine-foot-high, bakeable wild bull, *Bos taurus*.[5] Nature had granted humans a new summertime, and the living was easy. But even in the laziest of days, humans thrive on challenge, on creating new opportunities, on testing out new ways of doing things. Emotional brain centers like the nucleus accumbens and the mossy fibers of the hippocampus force us to seek and to create the new, to seek and to create novelties.[6] These gnarls of neurons drive us. They play a key role in the bioplan of human needs. They are hunger makers in the fissures of the brain. They drive economies. And they drive the evolutionary search engine, the secular genesis engine.

A short walk from their homes in the Near East's caves, hunter-gatherer bands called the Natufians gathered the seeds of wild grass with a new invention, the sickle—a curved blade made of flint set in a handle made of bone.[7]

In the valleys below the Natufians' hills, Stone Age tribes of hunter-gatherers contrived an invention of yet another kind—a civilization maker, a culture-weaving forward leap that would satisfy the human need to meet, to greet, to clump, and to cluster. They contrived a new material breakthrough that would raise and slake the thirst for unheard-of amazements—from novelties and oddities to utterly new frivolities. They contrived a breakthrough that would accomplish these emotional feats with capital—with stored imagination and stored persuasion. A breakthrough that would lift humanity to new levels of the impossible, to what Dallas corporate development architect and public policy analyst Woody Buckner—who helped inspire this book—calls "unreasonable future outcomes."[8] Inconceivable utopian realities.

That new creation would be the very first city.

If you scrimped, saved, traded, swapped, and slaved, you could make a stone axe on your own. But cities would be the product of vast teamwork done with stone. The inspiration that gave birth to the first city—Jericho—11,000 years ago was the notion of shaping stones bigger than a giant's torso.[9]

Boulders were nature's castoffs, overgrown pebbles too big for any use. For a hundred thousand years, boulders had been obstacles men and women had tripped on, had walked around, had hidden behind, or had leaned against when it came time to sit. The first human who thought of employing them for a grander purpose was a madman, a prophetic leader, and a redeemer to the nth degree. Think of all the impossible steps he or she had to foresee:

- Leveraging a massive rock out of the ground or from the base of a nearby cliff.
- Doing it long before the discovery of metal and the invention of the crowbar.
- Chiseling its surface with mere stone tools and with the branches of trees.
- Hammering for weeks or months if that's what flattening its surface would take.
- Organizing teams to do the chiseling.
- Persuading others to take time out from hunting and gathering. To do what? A task that must have seemed worse than useless at the time.
- Getting those teams to lug each hulking hunk to a central place—again, for what? For no practical purpose anyone with common sense could see.
- Piling the stones atop each other and fitting them into each others' jigsaw shapes. For what? Just to make a heap? What in the world could a heap of boulders be good for? Who could tell? A boulder pile had never proven useful for a thing—not in the entire time this planet had hosted human beings.
- Extending the heap upward and outward until, years later, it finally made some sense. Aha, it was something formerly only made of wood—a palisade, a mega-fence.

The result was a masterpiece of capital—of stored fantasy, stored persistence, and stored leadership. It was a radically new way of housing humans in something better than a cave. It was a new way to gain control over where your homes were placed. It was a new way to protect yourself from more than cold and rain. It was a new way to defend yourself when your rivals came to raid. It was a new way to gather many tribes in one common place.

The new stone masterpiece would soon prove to be far, far more. It would radically upgrade the art of trade. And it would produce a new way to lead lives, a way in which you could pick and choose your calling, your career, your specialty, and even your identity.

This masterpiece of stored emotion, stored vision, and stored persuasion was a form of capital we mistakenly take for granted—the permanent high-tech defense, the spear-and-stone-axe-proof protective wall, the enduring building—and something else beyond belief, the choice of living in the big burgh, in the central spot where everything is happening, in the vivid center where the glittering crowds parade and strut.

The name of this miracle heap of stone? The city of Jericho.

Capital has become a dirty word, but it has the power to lift, to save, to reinvent, and to transform.

Like the earliest city builders, it's time for all of us who run corporations, small businesses, or who are self-employed, for those of us who work for a paycheck from a capitalist corporation, for those of us who hanker after promotions and higher salaries, it's time for all of us to wake up to our powers and to our obligations. It's time for us to realize we, too, have the power to transform. We have the power to help others soar. That power is hidden in our crazy visions. It's hidden in our lusts, in our convictions, and in our need to be part of something bigger than ourselves. The future of the human race is hidden in our fantasies.

31

TRY A LITTLE CRAZINESS

Why capital is stored courage.

Inventing the first city, Jericho, required seeing an absurd goal so intensely that you could take it from mere daydream into being.

The notion of building Jericho's stone wall—a vision of a thing that's never existed in the heavens or on earth before—must have felt insane even to the man or woman who first fantasized it.

We humans don't take kindly to insanities. Wild ideas scare us, they fill us with anxiety and doubt. They make us fear we're losing it, straying grotesquely from the beaten path, losing touch with the hard and fast, and losing our normalcy. Committing yourself to a crazy notion can set your body churning with a frenzy of self-destructive hormones—glucocorticoids.

To have an idea it'll take thirty years to complete, to stick with it, to preach it with such fervor that you make others see it too, to recruit a team, to teach them, to organize them, to evangelize them, to reaffirm the goal in their emotions and in their reason day after seemingly useless day and year after year seemingly useless year, to carry on with nothing to show for the sweat and pain—that is what corporate development architect Woody Buckner calls "leadership beyond reason, leading from the future," beckoning from a vision so vividly that you can make others taste a paradise they've never seen.

This is what leadership at its truest means—leading from the future toward unreasonable expectations, leading past the impossible to the point of victory.

In capitalism, it's the passion, stupid! Jericho was a treasure trove of emotionality. Its mortarless boulder walls provided a feeling for which the human soul cries out—security. Jericho's high-tech fortifications were six and a half feet thick and four times the height of a man. They were surrounded by a trench nine feet deep and twenty-seven feet wide and topped by the world's first lookout tower.

This was the Stone Age, a whopping eight thousand years before the heyday of ancient Rome. Hunter-gatherer tribes outside of Jericho's wall, tribes out on a raid, eager to slaughter other humans and to nab their victims' weapons, clothes, and jewelry, had mere spears, arrows, and bows. They must have looked at Jericho's defenses and despaired.

The creation of Jericho's walls had an unintended consequence—it led to the lifestyle breakthrough called city living. The hunter-gatherers who switched from traveling in a tiny band to hunkering down together in seven acres of round, one-room permanent homes circled by a single palisade of stone were probably the first humans ever to be freed from the narrow limitations of living in a tribe.[1] They could exult in strolling down the street to meet and greet the folks of other clans, swapping knowledge, skills, arts, crafts, beads, pottery, and, in all probability, stories, songs, and poetry. This was capitalism's gift—choice—taken to the nth degree.

Jericho looked for other dreams and found them. It was built on the site of an oasis, so it had a monopoly on the local water supply. Jericho turned itself into a rest-stop, a paradise on a trail that traders followed. The capitalists of Jericho invented inns and transformed their town into the grand hotelier of its time, offering new forms of relaxation and haven in the midst of travel.

The meals were a meat-eater's dream—fillet of wild gazelle, deer steak, rabbit stew, snails, a bit of beef from the huge wild bulls and cows called aurochs, and just a tad of goat to freshen the taste. But don't forget the fruit and vegetables—wild vetch, wild barley, wild einkorn wheat, and a salad of wild grasses. Then for the crowning treats—wild grapes, berries, pistachio nuts, acorns, and figs.[2]

Jericho saw the birth of many firsts:

- The first woodworking axes in the Middle East—heralding the arrival of the Levant's first lumber industry, one that probably specialized in building with oak.
- The first storage bins for extra food and extra water. Tuck something away today and keep tomorrow's hunger at bay.
- Raised doorsills to keep the floor of your house from being muddied by the rainy season muck outside.
- Plastered walls.
- Stone tools in your choice of colors—translucent, opaque, gray, brown, honey, or purple veined with pink.
- The first sophisticated arrowheads. (Earlier arrows had probably been tipped with random sharp stone flakes.)
- Obsidian imported from Turkey over 590 miles away.
- And the first mortars, pestles, and grinding stones for grain, which hints at the first flour and the first bread.

The mere existence of Jericho raised the ambitions of the human enterprise. There's a good chance that Jericho's presence inspired the traditional hunter-gatherer groups in its vicinity—the Natufians—to stop harvesting seeds at random and to deliberately plant them,[3] thus inventing farming. Agriculture fed more than the stomach—it satisfied the human need to know where your next meal was coming from.

Jericho literally put a roof over your head. It gave you a place to come back to at day's end, a place to call your own, a place you could call home. It did this for the first time in the history of humanity. Jericho raised the level of human powers. And it did so mightily.

We take the bounty given us by agriculture and by the town for granted. But we should never be blind to basic satisfactions. Filling them is one of capitalism's most critical commands.

Ten thousand years ago, when Jericho was founded, capital did what it does today—it raised the level of what we take for granted—the level of the mundane. And as we'll soon see, it raised the level of desire. It raised the level of daydreams. In other words, it raised the infrastructure of fantasy.

32

QUANTUM LEAPS OF FANTASY

How lumps of mud became the walls that gave families their first privacy.

Capital changes the nature of the human race. It raises the level of the ordinary and of what we sometimes call the mundane. It raises the level of what's right under our noses. It raises the level of the floor that elevates us, the level of our everyday empowerments, the level of the things we fail to see. And in the process, it raises the level of our aspirations—it raises the level of our fantasies.

New ways of seeing lead to new ways of being. First we dream new things, then we make those dreams come true. That's the infrastructure of fantasy. And the infrastructure of fantasy is vital to the evolutionary search engine and to the secular genesis machine. The infrastructure of fantasy is one of the instruments with which the cosmos feels out her possibilities.

This sounds like an old Walt Disney cliché: all you have to do is wish upon a star and your dreams will come true. But it's no such thing. It's as real as bricks and mortar, literally.

Within two thousand years after the invention of the first stone walls of the first city—Jericho—numerous other cities sprang up. One of the first and most important was Catal Huyuk, 1,500 miles from Jericho in present-day Turkey. Catal Huyuk arose in the Late Stone

Age, over five thousand years before the birth of Rome. Like Jericho itself, Catal Huyuk was based on an amazing leap of fantasy.

Take mud. Yes, mud, that irritating stuff that slows you down when you walk the fields in the rainy season, that goop that wells up to your ankles and leaves its tracks on the floor of your hut wherever you put your feet. The gunk that even makes its way into your bed at night. The gloop you simply cannot escape.

The inventors of Catal Huyuk scooped up mud, mixed the muck with straw, and used their hands or wooden molds to shape the sludge into rectangles of a standard size and shape. They created the first real-life Lego block. They pioneered the concept of modularity. They shaped the first modular construction units. Then they left these geometric lumps in the sun to dry or hardened them in a bonfire. Catal Huyuk's wild dreamers inspired many of their clan mates and acquaintances to do the same. Like the wall builders of Jericho, these city fathers (or mothers) preached, sold, promoted, advertised, marketed, and evangelized. They gave others a vision of new possibilities in their lives. They excited others with their flame.

When enough bricks were made, the visionaries fired up the passions of the masses that they'd gathered and promoted yet another new form of collaborative enterprise—piling these modular mud units in carefully planned straight lines.

Once the baked-mud rectangles had all been slid into place, the leaders and the teams they'd inspired must have looked with awe at what they'd made. They'd created the first perfectly straight walls, the first rectangular rooms, the first standardized, multiroom condominiums, and the first super-long, two-story-high apartment complexes. They'd pieced together thirty-five acres of housing with just seven key ingredients:

- imagination
- persistence
- passion
- persuasion
- organization
- wood
- straw
- and mud.

Emotion raised the city of Catal Huyuk, and Catal Huyuk raised the heights to which emotion could fly. Oh, how the place was made to satisfy. Each family had an apartment of three rooms—one for sleeping, one for storage, and one for cooking and eating. Every apartment came complete with a carefully crafted hole in the eating room floor—a built-in hearth and oven. This was the very first single-family kitchen.

Like the huts of Jericho, this first apartment development catered to basic feeling—to the need not just for security from marauders, but for a place to sleep, for a roof over your head, and for a place to call your own.

Catal Huyuk went beyond these new emotional fundamentals. For the first time ever, its single-family apartments guaranteed a nuclear family something unheard of. They guaranteed a breakthrough we call privacy.

Catal Huyuk's acres of interior walls gave more scope to creativity than anything humans or nature had previously seen. Almost every indoor wall of Catal Huyuk was decorated with wall-to-wall and floor-to-ceiling color paintings. The walls were alive with goddesses, with birds of prey, with lions, tigers, bulls, red deer, men on hunting parties wielding bows and arrows, dancers, landscapes, and geometric patterns as varied as those in the ornate Eastern carpets of today. In fact, it's been argued that the patterns of Eastern carpets were first conceived by the weavers and the painters of Catal Huyuk back in those early city days.[1]

Catal Huyuk's walls held roughly as much square acreage of artwork as the Louvre.

Catal Huyuk went beyond new stratospheres of art. It labored fiercely to sell its infrastructure of fantasy. How? The city plunged into the emotion business big-time. One out of every three three-room suites was a shrine. Each of these worship chapels created a wraparound, full-immersion experience of divinity. The paintings were startling—like those of goddesses with their legs spread wide giving birth while holding the necks of leopards on either side. The furniture and the 3-D wall decor could awe and terrify. Thrusting from the plaster on all four sides were the jabbing beaks of birds, the sculpted heads of bulls, the breastlike, erect-nippled plaster mounds, and the genuine fanged jaws. The rows of seating or standing room were lined with bull skulls and with sculpted bulls' heads with enormous, flaring sets of horns, sharp-pointed and aimed at the worshippers' chests and sides.

An entire neighborhood of wealthy priests manned this industry of chills and passion. In all probability, these priests catered to the human need for guidance in moments of crisis and indecision, for feelings of exaltation, for gratitude, for penance, for awe, for comfort, and for humiliation. It's also likely that the priests specialized in the forms of prayer that some hoped would bring fertility and a nonstop flow of the organic meals, the plants and animals, in the wild, plus a never-ending harvest of the vegetables, fruits, and beasts that man had tamed and learned to raise with the embryonic new techniques of a revolutionary skill—farming. The emphasis on wild bull skulls and wild bull horns jutting from the walls and the furniture hints at one basic the citizens of Catal Huyuk wanted with all their hearts and souls—meat.

What would justify so many shrines in just one city? Catal Huyuk hosted a full-scale, intercity spiritual trade. Some think worshippers came from hundreds of miles to bathe in the feelings roused by Catal Huyuk's apartments turned to holy caves.[2]

When we imagine gods, we imagine new powers. Then we seek those powers for ourselves. Religion lifts us high in imagination. Many abase themselves and grovel before these deities of infinite mastery. But for those of us who wish to emulate the gods and attain their powers, religion lifts the infrastructure of fantasy.

Catal Huyuk found other ways of upgrading the range of human choice and the scope for creativity. It had a lock on obsidian from the twin-peaked volcanoes of Hasan Dag and Karaca Dag to the east. And it was the center of a net of trade routes that gave it bargaining leverage with lands as far away as Russia in the East and Jericho to the South. But this leverage was emotional.

The merchant discussions, in all likelihood, went something like this:

"We'll trade you the enchantment of a jewelry-quality, glistening black stone, a stone with transparent veins that slices, dices, chops, and stabs . . . and that does it in aristocratic style.

"Now let's see what you've got that will astonish the folks we've left at home.

"How about that gleaming orange copper, that red carnelian, that pink quartz, that clear rock crystal, and that lapis lazuli of sky-blue?

"We'll trade you an obsidian dagger with hand-carved snakes encircling its grip for that necklace, that bracelet, and that armlet. For a limited time only, we'll offer you this rare, exotic boar tusk carved with geometric designs. If you act fast, we'll toss in—for free—a kitchen set of horn-and-bone cups, ladles, and spoons. All we ask of you is that lace-up belt with eyelets, three dozen of those shells, and a set of those bone makeup applicators to please our wives."

The mud bricks and stone walls of capital had upgraded the range of human delight. They had made the unreasonable available, then put it up on sale.

When humans upgrade their powers, they upgrade their species. Thanks to emotional exchange—thanks to the passion for obsidian blades, the lust for bone-handled daggers, and the thirst for worship—by eight thousand years ago, when Catal Huyuk's first brick was cast, humanity had outpaced biology and put itself through three radical upgrades. It had gone from *Homo sapiens*—man equipped by nature with a brain that could store and create new knowledge—to *Homo silex fabricans*—man the stone trader and manufacturer—to yet another incarnation—*Homo urbanis*—man reinvented by his own invention, man reinvented by the city.[3]

33

THE FLAWS IN THE CONCEPT OF CONSUMERISM AND THE HUNGERS IN THE FISSURES OF THE BRAIN

"Consumer" lusts aren't manufactured by marketing campaigns. They're built into the neurons of your brain.

Of every hundred products launched each year, only twenty survive. Despite floods of marketing and advertising dollars, eighty bite the dust. Which hints that marketers do not control us, we control them.

Yet we're told that a cabal of insidious capitalists secretly rule our minds and, more specifically, manipulate our desires, twisting us with Machiavellian marketing campaigns that force us into a frenzy of false needs. The fact is very much the opposite. It's impossible for even the most bloated marketing budget to convince us to buy something that doesn't strike our fancy.

In the early 1970s Elektra Records decided to prove for all time that a marketing campaign with a big enough budget, a campaign shaped by a sufficiently Napoleonic mind, could make any human with the talents of a housefly into a superstar. Elektra took an interesting but utterly anonymous singer named Jobriath, set aside a marketing budget of nearly $22 million (in 2007 dollars), recorded an album of the most commercial music they could concoct, then spread Jobriath's name on everything from posters that went the full-length of buses to subway ads, radio, and TV. The result? Jobriath went absolutely nowhere.

So Elektra was forced to return to the old music industry approach, commonly summarized in the biz by the following unpleasant-sounding phrase: "throw the shit up against the wall and see what sticks." Translated from the vernacular, what does that motto mean? The music moguls should offer you and me a plethora of choices. Then they should let us dictate what we want.

What's the message of this and of many other big-budget marketing campaigns that have flopped? You can't shove products down our throats and make us want them. Not with standard advertising campaigns. Not with standard marketing plans. Not even with subliminal messages on film and video screens. When we want things, we want them for good reasons, even if we haven't a clue about what those reasons may be.

We'll strip away more of the wrappings that hide those reasons—the reasons we hunger for seemingly trivial things—as we continue to retell and reperceive the history of Western civilization. But here's one fundamental key.

Our needs are always with us. They're built into the canyons of our brain. They're in organs like our nucleus accumbens, our ventral pallidum, our amygdala, and our ventral tegmentum.[1] Those strange corners of the brain don't lust for the basics we commonly recite—food, shelter, and clothing—or even for basic dignity. Frankly, the dignity our brain assemblies crave is sometimes outrageous—it's not just basic, it's often way, way over the top. And that over-the-topness is built into our biology. What's more, our delight in new gadgets, new throwaways, and new novelties upgrades our species. Gadget lust and novelty hunger plug us into the group IQ. They plug us into engines of transcendence. They make us vigorous participants in the evolutionary search engine and the secular genesis machine.

The trivial uplifts us. So does the display of vanities. Think for a minute. Where did Johannes Gutenberg get the idea for his great invention, movable type?[2] He was in the vanity and status symbol business. He was a cutter and polisher of precious stones—useless trinkets with which the super-rich could show their stuff. He was also a goldsmith, making coins and, it appears, jewelry.[3] From these arts he took the skills he used to create molds for individual letters of the alphabet. Gutenberg was also a maker of a brand-new high-tech gewgaw—the glass mirror. A mirror made by pouring glass into a frame, then pouring in lead to back the glass. Pouring lead (mixed with a bit of tin) would become part of the secret to casting the a's, the b's, and the c's of movable type.[4]

What were Gutenberg's mirrors used for? Self-indulgence. Vanity. Right? Yes, but mirrors were also identity tools. In fact, they were one of the most astonishing identity extenders ever to appear in human history.[5] Imagine what your sense of yourself would have been in the days before mirrors. You would have never seen yourself and would have had no idea of what you looked like. The invention of the mirror put the "image" into your "self-image." And into mine.

Then there was another frivolous bottom line to Gutenberg's work. Only the super-rich could afford books. In fact, the megawealthy flaunted their ability to own books by binding their volumes in leather adorned with gold, silver, and jewels.[6] So the very products Gutenberg was working to mass-produce—volumes of the Bible, Psalters (books of psalms), Latin grammars and lexicons, and copies of a book by Aelius Donatus on the eight parts of speech[7]—were status symbols—things you bought to show off your wealth and your refinement. Vanity, all is vanity.

Yet a noted German intellectual who was born just as Gutenberg was printing his first tomes, Jakob Wimfeling, called Gutenberg's invention of printing "almost a divine benefit to the world."[8] And Wimfeling was right. Gutenberg's invention was capitalism at its best. It was a material miracle. It was an act of secular genesis.

New symbols of high status like the book sometimes play a powerful role in advancing something profoundly human—instant evolution, the technological upgrade of our species.[9] The digital watch was introduced in 1970 on the *Tonight Show with Johnny Carson* as a status symbol, an expensive luxury with a gold case and ruby-red numbers.[10] The Hamilton Pulsar cost a whopping $2,100—that's $8,738.45 in 2007 dollars. The battle to produce cheaper, lighter, and more reliable digital watches led to the miniaturization of a nearly complete computer on a single chip, the 5810 CMOS (complementary metal-oxide-semiconductor) chip from an unknown company called Intel in 1976. By the 1980s, the lust of the rich for this new electronic jewelry had driven prices down to the point where even a delivery boy could own a black plastic digital watch, a price so low that a watch fanatic of modest means like me could have ten digital time displays in just one room, my bedroom.

More important, the heart of a digital watch was a radically new slice of silicon. It was—bear with me while I repeat—the first complete electronic system on a single chip—an SOC (System On a Chip), in computer lingo. Why was this important? Digital watch lust drove the development of the microprocessor and of the megascale integrated circuit that put millions of transistors and a host of disparate functions on just one chip. Digital watch lust gave us the cell phone, the personal computer, and the laptop. And those devices utterly transformed our lives.

The trivial, the vain, and the frivolous can guide us to what could be but doesn't yet exist. The ancestors of the Aztecs and of the Mayas invented toys with wheels for their kids around 100 BCE.[11] But it never occurred to them to use wheels to transport heavy loads. Aztec and Mayan kids were one step away from inventing the wheelbarrow and the wagon. There's a good chance they might have achieved this breakthrough if only the conquistadors hadn't cut their culture short in 1521.

"Frivolous wastes of time" can upgrade our species. "Pointless" status symbols can fuel the engine that transcends.

34

THE SPIRITUAL FRUITS
OF MATERIAL THINGS

How the Flock Became a Metaphor

Crass materialism can upshift the human spirit. How
owning animals gave us a new way to see.

What we call grubby, crass materialism can upgrade the human brain
and set the human spirit free in vast new mind terrains. In 8000 BCE
we invented the idea of domesticating animals. We tamed pigs, cows,
and most of all, sheep. This was crass materialism big-time. A man's
wealth was judged by the number of sheep he could acquire for his
flock or by the number of bulls and cows that he could amass in his
herd.

The first step in the domestication of goats and sheep may have
come when a few cunning gray wolves managed to domesticate
human beings over twelve thousand years ago.[1] Dogs domesticated
humans? Surely that is backward. Right? It all depends on how you
look at things.[2]

Wolves are animals with an aristocracy. Males compete to be the
leader of the pack.[3] Once the competition is over, powerful losers
submit utterly to their lord and master, the wolf who won. They give
up on their urge to reproduce and cheerfully babysit and uncle the
pups who come from the one winning wolf and from his mate, the
top-ranking female.[4] When the time for the hunt arrives, every wolf
has a role, but the lead of the top-ranking male is all important. He is

at the head of the chase, sometimes accompanied in leadership by his mate, the alpha female.[5]

Humans and wolves may well have met each other most frequently in the kill. Humans and wolves both pursued the same kinds of animals—herd animals like antelope, deer, wild cows, wild sheep, wild goats, and wild pigs. Humans and wolves both learned how to take advantage of the herd instincts of these sheepish beasts, using the herd animals' social conformity, rounding them up in a mass, then steering them into ambushes and traps.[6] For wolves, even the cleverest ambushes only brought down one big animal at a time. But that wasn't true for human beings. Driving a herd of animals over a cliff, using a woven net, or driving a herd into a dead-end canyon with no exit could kill far more animals than the humans could hack up with stone tools and carry away.[7]

For some wolves, it made sense to occasionally ignore hunting on your own and to follow the human beings. When the human carving and slicing was over, the wolves wise enough to trail behind those nice two-legged folks with stone tools and fingers could move in on the remains and feast on the meat and the marrow bones the humans left behind.

But to do this, the wolves intent on exploiting humans had to stay close to their chosen people. Why? Wolf packs compete.[8] If another wolf pack got to the humans first, it could claim the man-made leftovers. To be first in line, you had to keep the humans in easy sight and easy reach, and, if necessary, you had to defend your prerogative against wolf packs that wanted to poach on your passel of men.

Human males—men and boys—love to compete to see who can show off the slickest mastery of prediction and control. We improvise games. We bet. We gamble. We devise clever new prediction-and-control contests. We wager on our ability to pitch stones, our ability to predict which of two cockroaches will come out first in a race, and which of us can make his urinary stream go farthest. These frivolous "wastes of time and energy," these nonsensical entertainments, are sometimes probes into the impossible.

There's a good chance that men competed to see who could get closest to the lupine killers, the wolves. Not just who could get the shortest distance, but who could lure the wolves close enough to touch and who could achieve the impossible and feed the snarling wolves from his own fingertips, not to mention from the palm of his hand. And the wolf who took up this offer—the wolf who decided to grab the payoff of food in exchange for allowing the human to beckon him at will—would have opened a bonanza for the canine line.

There are somewhere in the neighborhood of a billion dogs in the world today. And there's a $43-billion-a-year industry in just one of the earth's 195 nations, a massive business dedicated to making special food, special medications, and cozy accommodations for dogs.[9] All the dogs pampered by this business are descended from the first gray wolves that persuaded humans to feed and house them over ten thousand years ago. The first who lured humans by taking advantage of our infernal lust for gambling and for playing dangerous games. The first who suckered humans into caring for and feeding them. The first wolves that established the economics of the human and dog exchange.

Meanwhile, the wolves that decided to stay in the wild are not making out well. The descendants of the gray wolves that were too wary to partner with human beings are on the endangered species list.[10] And there may be fewer than 200,000 wild wolves remaining in the entire world today.[11] That's a nearly invisible fraction of the wolves that conned us with their love, the wolves who decided to sit, roll over, and obey.

What does this have to do with sheep? Humans and wolves had a lot in common. Both were pack animals. Both ate meat. Both enjoyed having a warm place to sleep. And both had learned how to round up and direct the movement of a pack of sheep. Put humans and wolves together in the herding process and you had a radical upgrade in the quality of control you could exert over a herd of wooly lamb chops on the hoof.

The next trick was for the humans to do for sheep what they had done for wolves: offer a deal too good to resist. A deal in which both the sheep and the humans could win. Let humans compete to see who could persuade a sheep to approach him (or her) to eat a treat out of the human's hand. Then compete to see who can rear a captured lamb smack dab in the middle of the human clan. Lambs, like most social animals, have an imprinting stage—a stage early in life in which their brain opens a space in which to insert mommy. And, as Konrad Lorenz has shown in geese, if you're an animal raised by human beings, the individual your brain inserts into the "mommy" slot may well be a human being.[12] Lambs raised around human beings attach themselves to the person who has raised them. The person who has fed them by hand. That's why hand-reared lambs are great pets.

Like wolves and humans, sheep are social animals. And in the wild they use a version of the fission-fusion, search-then-consolidate strategy, the search strategy behind economic boom and crash. Their adult males fan out across the countryside hunting for good places to eat.[13] That's exploration. In the breeding season these roaming males, these explorers, these wandering rams, return to the flock and compete for top position in the ruling aristocracy.[14] And once the competition is over, the winners get sex. They get to mount the females and sire the next generation of the flock. That's consolidation.

When the males go back to their solitary ways, the top-ranking female sheep leads the females and their lambs.[15] She's usually the biggest and the oldest of the sheep. Those beneath her follow wherever she leads. That, too, is consolidation. Consolidation and primitive structure building. So if you control the top sheep, you control the whole herd. Better yet, if the herd thinks YOU are the top sheep, you've got the whole herd snookered.

Making human-tamed sheep—or even human-tamed goats—the leaders isn't hard. The sheep you feed are likely to be bigger and stronger than their wild competitors. And their lead is more certain to pay off with food and a warm place to sleep.

What's in the deal for the sheep? Imagine that you're a ewe. You've persuaded humans to give you all the food you need. You no longer have to hunt that food down and compete with other herds to hold onto it. You've persuaded humans to shield you from disease. You've persuaded humans to protect you from predators like wolves. And you've persuaded humans and dogs to open up a new niche for you that will allow your species to out-multiply competitors like deer and antelope, competitors that were not smart enough to con humans into adopting them.

What price do you pay? You give up your wool once a year or so, if your humans are in the clothing business. And if you're less fortunate, you stand a chance of being killed and eaten in your youth or in your early adult years. But your odds of carrying on to a ripe old age and of having many offspring that survive you is greatly multiplied. Meanwhile, what's happened to your nature-loving relatives, your conservative cousins who stuck to the tried and true traditions of their ancestors? What's happened to the four-horned antelope, the giant sable antelope, the hunter's antelope, the saiga antelope, and the Tibetan antelope? All are endangered species.[16] And you, the supposedly meek but secretly clever sheep, have managed to become a winning breed.

The payoffs of animal domestication for the human spirit were enormous. Let's switch you back to your identity as a *Homo sapiens*. Before the eon of your deal with sheep, you already knew where your next meal of carbohydrates was coming from. That was thanks to agriculture. But now you could count on your next dose of meat—your next stew of lamb or mutton. This increased your sense of security. The comfort of a steady source of food is so basic it was portrayed as one of "The Four Freedoms" in a series Norman Rockwell designed in 1943 to capture the key values of a democratic society.[17]

Domesticating animals gave us yet another new freedom—a sport. In the old days when you set off on a hunting party it was serious business. You were taking your life in your hands. And you came home empty-handed three days out of four.[18] Now that your animals were penned or herded at home, you could hunt red deer, rabbit, and fox for the sheer pleasure of it. You could hunt for sport. In hunting for sport you were as likely to come home empty-handed as you were when your next meal depended on your success. But the difference is this. In sport when you come home empty-handed you haven't starved your family. In fact, if you can afford the luxury of time for sport, you can use it as a status symbol. You can use even your failing expeditions to one-up your fellow human beings. What other values does sport present? Like all games, it ups our feeling of control. And control, in turn, up-tweaks our brain, our hormones, and our immune system. Control upshifts our physiology.

But there's more, and it's important. Every new invention upgrades the vocabulary with which we seek to understand reality. Every new invention upgrades the infrastructure of fantasy. From the invention of animal taming, we gained the metaphor of the shepherd and his flock. During the next ten thousand years, this new thinking tool would change the way we see society. It would lead to a basic message of the Bible and to a basic message of this book—capitalism is about caring for your flock.

35

ACCOUNTING AND THE BIRTH OF THE WRITTEN WORD

The Art of Finding Wealth in Toxic Waste

From bickering and feuding came a massive upgrade in the range of human powers.

Once we humans have possessions, we squabble over them. Men and women have slippery memories. Research hints that when we make deals—like the example we saw way back when you and I were swapping sheep for grain—our boastful memories exaggerate what we were owed and downplay what we promised in return. This often leads to nasty arguments, arguments that can end in murder.

There's a secret to capitalism that Mother Nature first invented. Turn trash into treasure. Turn disaster into opportunity. And turn garbage into gold. Heated disagreements were a form of garbage waiting to be annealed, waiting to be transformed.

From the bitterness of bickering and feuding came a new industry roughly five thousand years ago. This business led to a massive upgrade in the repertoire of human powers. The new industry was lawyering and accounting—being present when a deal is struck and keeping track of who owes what. Remember the scribes who witnessed agreements, then took tokens in the form of sheep and sheaves of wheat and put them in a clay envelope to literally seal the deal? And the scribe who got the idea of stamping the tokens onto the surface of the clay envelope so he wouldn't have to break the clay packet open every time you and your customer bickered crazily? That scribe invented the first alphabet—the cuneiform script.[1] From the need to referee over human greed came a massive upgrade in the repertoire of human powers—the world's first writing.

Bickering isn't pleasant. All things that happen are not good. But all things, even the bad ones, present an opportunity.

36

MEANING AND MARKETING

Moses and the Slogan

The seven slots of memory, the hungers of the soul,
and why we need both branding and the slogan.

When souls hunger, one of the first things they seek is a sense of
meaning. Meaning and a sense of higher purpose is something less
ethereal than we tend to believe. It's a sense that your group can
achieve great things, and that by dedicating yourself to its goals you
will lift your group's standing. That you will lift your group's stature
whether you live for the group or die for it. This sense of contributing
to the achievement of a higher goal is at the heart of meaning and
identity.

As Barack Obama put it at the Democratic National Convention
in August 2008, "Part of what has been lost these past eight years
can't just be measured by lost wages or bigger trade deficits. What has
also been lost is our sense of common purpose, our sense of higher
purpose. And that's what we have to restore."[1]

Meaning is a mind's way of mapping the terrain of the future.
And, silly as this may sound, a need for meaning is not just a human
matter. Remember the worker bee that went to yesterday's big flower
patch, found it nearly empty, and came home with next to nothing in
the carrying hairs on her thighs? When she arrived at the cargo dock
in the hive, the unloader bees ignored her. She became more and more

251

discouraged as she continued to do her equivalent of a job. She moved more and more slowly. And even her body temperature went down. Then she found a new source of direction in the bee dance competitions and underwent a conversion. She shifted her focus from the industry that no longer paid off for the hive to the new industry that fed the hive's needs of today perfectly. Once again when she came home to the hive—this time with her carrying hairs loaded with the pollen that the hive needed—the unloaders rushed over to her and gave her what seemed like all the attention in the world. Once more the worker bee had a sense of meaning. Once more her body temperature rose and she moved with alacrity.

How did the dancing bees give a sense of meaning? They gave a map. A map to something the hive valued. Something for which the hive had a craving. Something that would help the hive survive its next crisis, the coming of the next winter. Something that would keep the hive alive and growing. Among the bees, meaning came from a map of the future. A map of a destination. A map with physical and emotional payoffs. A map that promised two bonanzas—the next big nectar and pollen patch. And the excited attention you'd get when you brought back the goods.

Under the surface, it turned out that excitement and attention were more than just personal rewards. They were indicators. Indicators of a bee's contribution to the rapidly shifting needs of a growing and changing society.

Like anything good, like anything that can uplift humanity, a new meaning has to be sold, marketed, promoted, communicated, and conveyed in every way at hand and in several ways no one has previously conceived. Bees know that. It's why they dance like crazy. But among humans, those dance steps reshape destiny.

Moses was one of the greatest shapers of meaning in all of human history. His maps of meaning were so potent that a thousand years after the prophet's death on a mountaintop overlooking Canaan, his maps to the next resource laid the foundation for two of the most widespread religious movements on the planet—Islam and Christianity.

How did Moses shape a new culture and a new system of belief? How did he go beyond the human equivalent of a searcher bee's waggle dance? How did he make his sense of meaning stick? If you can believe the Bible and Sigmund Freud's brilliant analysis of Moses and of the basics of community building in his *Moses and Monotheism*, Moses invented the bumper-sticker catchphrase without the bumper or the sticker. Moses boiled all his convictions down to a simple motto: "Listen up, Israel. Our Lord is our God. Our Lord is one." (Standard translation: "Hear, Oh Israel. The Lord our God, the Lord is one.")

Then Moses demanded a never-ending saturation display and Simon-Says campaign. He insisted that you write his new religion's motto down. He commanded that you use those scraps of parchment you'd written to stamp the catchphrase into your neurons every day and night. "Thou shalt bind them for a sign upon thine hand," said Moses, "and they shall be as frontlets between thine eyes. And thou shalt write them upon the posts of thy house, and on thy gates."[2] In other words you were required to see the Moses motto a dozen times a day. You were commanded to obsess over it, winding leather thongs with a small box attached, a small box that contained the parchment with the motto, on your hand, your wrist, your arm, and your forehead. The ritual of winding those leather straps would be painful to learn and take great effort to execute. Thanks to the thongs around your head that positioned the box right above your eyes, the Moses catchphrase would literally be in your face.

Even Coca-Cola, one of the most successful phrase makers and logo spreaders in history, never convinced its drinkers to wear Coke sales phrases on their wrists and foreheads.

Don't imagine I'm being cynical when I use business terms to describe a figure like Moses. He believed so deeply in what he was doing that he gave over forty years of his life to it. He point-blank refused to die until he'd driven his new beliefs home.

Why? Because he believed. Because he tapped his passions. But Moses was also a marketer-par-excellence. Look at another of his super-simplified poster messages, the Ten Commandments. Short, sweet, and to the point:

> Thou shalt not kill.
> Thou shalt not commit adultery.
> Thou shalt not steal.
> Thou shalt not bear false witness.[3]

But those are not the first commandments. The first six paragraphs of the Ten Commandments are demands for brand loyalty. For brand loyalty or else! Said the Ten Commandments, "Do not have any other gods before me. . . . You shall not make for yourself an idol. . . . You shall not bow down to them or worship them; for I the Lord your God am a jealous God, punishing children for the iniquity of parents, to the third and the fourth generation of those who reject me."[4] Moses' fear tactic was execrable. But it worked.

Why? What was Moses really selling? The key ingredient of meaning. A destination. A vision of where his people were going and why. A vision of how his people's destination would move it up in the global pecking order. And a vision of how that move up would pay off for all humankind.

Moses offered a new promised land that turned out to be piss poor. It had very little milk and honey. But Moses' real contribution was to the infrastructure of fantasy. And to your sense of identity. Moses offered a map of the world we cannot see. He offered what seemed a clearer way to understand reality. He offered the sense that by cozying up to the hidden god, praising the heck out of him, brown-nosing and bargaining with him in the language he commanded of you, bowing, scraping, and lowering yourself in his presence, you could gain control over something slippery, your destiny. Yes, you could gain a sense of control. The sense that boosts your immune system and that brings the hormones of blessedness.

Moses also offered you a community that would accept you eagerly when you mouthed God's messages with passion and studied his words. Moses offered you a God you could talk to when humans turned their backs on you. Moses offered you a new cargo dock in which he promised eager unloading bees.

How does a religion like the one Moses marketed upgrade your standing, your stature, your dignity? Moses' belief system tells you that at the very top of the pecking order of heaven, there stands a god who puts all the other deities to shame. And only your tribe has direct access to that god. Only your tribe ascends on high by having the most powerful god in the sky.

But there's more. Belief in one god brings one of the prime pay-offs of branding. Why is branding so necessary to us human beings? Why do we need to have just a small Olympus of stars and leaders we can gossip about? Why do we focus on brands like Coke, Pepsi, and Dr. Pepper, but toss lesser-known brands aside? Why do we show interest in only two or three presidential primary candidates—Obama, McCain, and Hillary Clinton—much to the consternation of the other five or six? Because a little choice is freedom. Too much choice is agony.

We have only seven slots for short-term memory in the brain.[5] This limits the information we can handle. It limits the number of choices we can comprehend or tolerate. So to get through to us, you have to make it simple and you have to make it stick. You have to repeat it over and over again until we get it. Once we've gotten it, we can slide it from consciousness into the scaffold of habit. We can shuffle it from front of the brain, from what psychologists call explicit memory, to the automatic reflex area further back, to what psychologists call implicit memory. Once we've gotten it, once we've welded it into the scaffold of habit, we can concentrate on something else. "Hear, oh Israel, the Lord Our God is One" was one of the world's first slogans.

37

THE POSITIVE POWER OF NOVELTY LUST

The Phoenicians and Their Wonder Ships

How "trivial" desires led to intercontinental teams.

Emory University's Gregory Berns is one of the great fMRI brain divers of our time. Berns uses sophisticated brain-imaging equipment to find the pleasure centers of the brain and to determine exactly what they make us crave. What is the strangest item on the list of things the nucleus accumbens and the mossy fibers of the hippocampus thirst for? It's the secret fuel of what we call consumerism: novelty.[1]

This hunger for the seemingly-trivial-but-different hasn't undermined families, eroded brains, or brought down the pillars of civilization. It's done the opposite. It's empowered families in new ways. It's put brains on a path of nonstop upgrade. And it's built new floors of human culture on the roof of the social structure that came before. It's erected new towers on the infrastructure of fantasy.

* * *

How do material things upgrade the infrastructure of fantasy? Take the case of the Phoenicians—the great sailors of the days when Moses' story was being written up in the Bible—roughly 800 to 200 BCE. The Phoenicians steered their long, thin sailing ships from the cradle of civilization in the Near East to Greece, to Italy, to North Africa, and to Spain, a full 3,500 miles away. What for? To find new things, new novelties, new status symbols, new kinds of wine, a new metal—tin—new forms of cloth, and pottery with exotic new designs: all those little things we humans use to make our neighbors envy us.

What a petty goal, you might well say, trying to one-up the folks next door. And I agree. Petty it is.

But you should see what it's given us! One of the richest and fastest transcontinental data flows in the 3.85-billion-year history of life. New ideas, new technologies, and new improvements to the human condition have poured forth thanks to what the Phoenicians pioneered—swift long-distance trading, snooping, shopping, and swapping, prowling the planet for novelty.

In fact, with our novelty-craving brain centers—our nucleus accumbens and the mossy fibers of our hippocampus—our biology has sutured us humans into giant productivity-and-upgrade teams. Novelty lust and status games brought the tin miners of Cornwall, England, and of northern and western Spain[2] together with Celtic and Iberian overland tin transporters, with Phoenician sea-mastering merchant traders, with Iraqi jewelry makers, with Mesopotamian bronze weapon crafters,[3] and with Ukrainian wheat growers, a productivity team that stretched across 1,950 miles.

Did Mother Nature do good by us when she endowed our brains with novelty lust and with status-symbol cravings? She made us evolutionary sprinters in a world whose other species crawl. She made us fingertips of the evolutionary search engine and the secular genesis machine. Fingertips with which the cosmos stretches eagerly to feel out new possibilities.

38

RIGHTEOUS INDIGNATION— THE WESTERN SYSTEM'S PROTEST INDUSTRY

Isaiah's Swords to Plowshares

A dissident markets a hormonal drug . . . and creates a counterweight.

The prophet Isaiah. How did he get into a book on capitalism? Isaiah installed a vital new component in the evolutionary search engine—a new component in the secular genesis machine within which capitalism operates—a new component in the Western system.

In roughly 742 BCE, Isaiah got a call to tell truth to power.[1] He got a call to report on the dark side of the actions of a people who thought all of their moves sparkled with light. He got a call to tell the wealthy and the powerful the last things in the world that fat cats and power brokers want to hear. He got a call to deliver a stinging critique of the power players' evils. And he got a call to issue a demand for a different way of life. That call came in a dramatic way. Isaiah saw God. And God was not a happy camper.

Isaiah was in the temple—probably in Jerusalem—when he saw the Lord complete with dazzling special effects, God "upon a throne, high and lifted up, and his train filled the temple." But that's not all. Above the throne were magnificent angels with six wings apiece. With one pair of wings they covered their faces. With another pair of wings, they covered their feet. And with the remaining pair of wings, they flew. The seraphs shouted to each other a well-worn divine cheerleading slogan, "Holy, holy, holy is the Lord of hosts, for the whole earth is full of his glory." The words were God's usual self-promotion. But the special effects were not. Isaiah claims that "the posts of the door moved at the voice" of every angelic bellow, "and the house was filled with smoke."

God was about to ask for a volunteer to deliver a nasty but necessary message. And Isaiah did not feel up to the task. It wasn't the specter of unpopularity that put him off. It was the fact that in his view, he was "a man of unclean lips." No problem! The angels had an instant solution. One took a live coal off the altar with tongs, flew over to Isaiah, and put it to Isaiah's mouth. Problem solved. "Thy sin," said the angel, is "purged."

What was God's beef with his Chosen People? There was too much self-indulgence. Too much wealth concentrated at the top. Too much leisure. Too much drinking. And too much music. There was even too much worship. Too many holidays. Too many sacrifices. Said God, "I am full of the burnt offerings of rams, and the fat of fed beasts; and I delight not in the blood of bullocks, or of lambs, or of he goats." What's more, said the Lord, "incense is an abomination unto me," and "the new moons and Sabbaths, the calling of assemblies . . . , even the solemn meeting" just won't cut it anymore.

What did God want? A simple social program: "Cease to do evil; Learn to do well; seek judgment, relieve the oppressed, judge the fatherless, plead for the widow." And God was willing to be open-minded about this. "Come now and let us reason together, saith the LORD: though your sins be as scarlet, they shall be as white as snow."

What if no one wised up? Well, God would just have to remind the Hebrews of what happened when he withdrew his protective shield. "If ye refuse and rebel, ye shall be devoured with the sword," says Isaiah, reporting God's message. Isaiah adds, "Then said I, Lord, how long? And he answered, Until the cities be wasted without inhabitant, and the houses without man, and the land be utterly desolate."

And that's what happened. The Assyrians smashed the Hebrews. When the Jewish city of Samara—capital of the kingdom of Israel—refused to pay its tribute, the Assyrians besieged the place for three years, took it, and deported twenty-seven thousand Israelites to the border regions in the far north of the empire. The Assyrians scattered the kingdom of Israel's inhabitants within the Assyrian-occupied territories so thoroughly that ten of the twelve Hebrew tribes were "lost" forever, assimilating into the cities of the Medes and the lands around the river of Gozan.

Just what part did Isaiah play when he railed against the rich real estate promoters, the farmland consolidators, of Jerusalem? What upgrade did Isaiah make to the evolutionary search engine of the Western system? What did he add to the secular genesis machine? Isaiah and his fellow prophets sparked an industry that markets three key things:

- The hormonal drug of *righteous indignation.*
- Protest and rebellion.
- And identity for those who feel outside the mainstream.

Isaiah was a pioneer of the opposition biz. He was a founding father of an institution that makes the Western system unique: the protest industry. Isaiah's use of idealism and righteous indignation to prod the rich and powerful has provided one of the great counterweights that balance the Western system—including capitalism. Isaiah was a father of freedom of speech.

*   *   *

Isaiah and Moses both endowed us with something else whose value we seldom recognize. They were superstars of history. They gave us the poster power of their lives. They offered role models to people like you and me.

Isaiah yelled loudly—and in verse. That was a marketing technique. The message of Moses' and Isaiah's examples was this. If you believe in something, sell it. If you feel you know how to save your neighbor, persuade him of the value of what you're offering. If you fail to get your courage up, if you fail to speak with power, if you fail to promote and sell, you are sinning in a way that's inexcusable. You are letting a good idea, a needed technique, an upgrade in fairness and justice, or a necessary passion die. You are standing by and doing nothing while your neighbor—or someone thousands of miles away, or even twenty generations down the line—goes down, is defeated by ignorance, and emotionally dies.

39

THE MOOD-SHIFT INDUSTRY

David's Songs and Orpheus's Lyre

Why entertainment has the power of salvation.

The year? Roughly 1021 BCE. The place? The kingdom known as Israel. The first king of the land, King Saul, was going through a murderous depression, one so bad it crippled his ability to do his military and administrative job.[1]

God had ordered Saul to specialize in genocide, which may have helped his misery along, but that's another story. God, it seems, was punishing Saul for his kindness—and for his greed. God had ordered Saul to go to a neighboring Philistine city, level it, and eradicate it completely. That meant killing the men, women, children, and even the animals. But animals—oxen, asses, and sheep—were a form of wealth. They were the money in the bank of their time. So Saul followed orders, but only up to a point. He carried out the genocide but kept the best of the animals, "the best of the sheep and of the oxen and the fatlings and the lambs and all that was good."[2] But all that was good was not good at all. God isn't pleased when folks fail to follow orders. To get his revenge, God drove Saul mad.

What did King Saul do to soothe his psychic pain? He called in the leading antidepressant of the day—a musician. The young singer and instrumentalist, David, was then paid off with a kingdom. This was an early eruption of what some call show business. Perhaps we should view it differently.

Over in Greece a few hundred years earlier, Homer had done something similar. He sang for his supper. But he sang cliff-hangers, stories whose next episodes you couldn't wait to hear. Homer entertained folks over dinner for two, three, or four seasons in a row. If he managed to finish chanting the twenty-four books of the *Iliad* and you wanted more, he could always chant the *Odyssey*.

Orpheus—or those who made him up—had more of a handle than we often do on what these entertainers were achieving. "Music hath charms to soothe the savage beast" is one phrase that comes up when Orpheus's name is mentioned. "Music hath charms to soothe the savage breast" is another common variation. Music has the power to save us from ourselves. Like an ant who strokes her exploring sister and calms her nervousness, music cushions us from our corrosive brooding and our hidden insecurities.

Orpheus, David, and Homer were in the mood-shift industry. And mood shifting has the power of salvation. What do I mean? Research hints that we humans go through roughly seven major mood swings every day.[3] Roughly seven times a day we're deep fat-fried in the private fires of our personal hell. What saves us? Sometimes nothing, alas. But way up there on the list of things that free us from our interior torture chambers is something that "takes us out of ourselves," that yanks us from our private flames. Often it's a story or a song.

So the real business of the entertainment industry is to provide a mood shift, a small but critical act of secular salvation. And the story of the dancing bees hints that music and entertainment may be something more. They may be clues to the next target at which we have to aim. Clues to our next mission in life. Clues to where we belong. And clues to a daily but often overwhelming puzzle we shall get to shortly—the mystery of meaning.

But first . . .

VII

JACKING UP THE
SYMBOL STACK

40

HOW SYMBOLS EXPAND OUR POWERS— CROESUS INVENTS MONEY

How cash rewires the brain.

Symbols have the power to take the human species to new heights. Songs are strings of symbols. The writing invented by the early protolawyers who stopped the bickering in the Mesopotamian sheep industry was a string of symbols, too.

Here's a hypothesis about the hidden gifts of symbol making. A hypothesis about the hidden payoff for raising the symbol stack. The higher the level of abstraction, the broader the spectrum of cultures a symbol can stitch together. The higher the level of abstraction, the more powerful a symbol can be as a barrier breaker and a cross-culture alliance maker. The higher the level of the symbol, the higher the level at which the symbol can knit together long-distance productivity teams.

In Lydia in roughly 700 BCE, in the days of David and Saul, there ruled a king named Croesus. He was so good at cornering wealth that his name today is synonymous with swollen bank accounts. We still say, "That guy is rich as Croesus." Croesus and his hunger for treasure made a vital contribution to your life and mine. A vital contribution to the symbol stack.

The Phoenicians had knit together Spanish tin miners, Greek wine makers, and Babylonian signet ring creators, weaving them into a transnational productivity team.[1] But the going was a little rough when you had to carry a cargo of wine and trade it for whatever someone living on the Black Sea coast of the Ukraine had in hand. Supposing you'd arrived at the Greek Black Sea colony of Chersonesus, perched on the edge of the Ukrainian agricultural district. Suppose the winds had driven your ship there in the planting season, long before the harvest had come in. And suppose that you'd been unable to call ahead and see how things in Chersonesus were going. If the Chersonesian locals had no wheat in hand, how could they pay you for the things you'd hauled from France, Italy, Greece, Carthage, Egypt, and Babylon?

This is where King Croesus came in. He invented something that may sound grubby to idealists like you and me. But it was a symbol that worked wonders to boost the power of international productivity teams. It's called money.

If the Ukrainians couldn't pay for a load of Greek wine in grain, now they could pay for the bulging amphoras of alcohol in something new, an innovation we call cash.

Croesus created new symbols—gold and silver coins.[2] And new symbols have the power to rewire your brain and mine. How? You were born with twice as many brain cells as you needed. And those brain cells obeyed the rules of "to he who hath it shall be given, and from he who hath not, even what he hath shall be taken away." Neurons that came in handy stayed. They were nurtured in a tonic of neural growth hormones.[3] Neurons that found no use were forced to depart the scene. They were squeeze-played into apoptosis—into preprogrammed cell death.

What determined which of your brain cells hung in tight and which were forced to kill themselves off? Symbols. Yes, it takes a village to raise a child. And it takes a symbol stack, a scaffold of habit, an infrastructure of fantasy, and a technology. Your culture's symbol stack gave you your vocabulary. Your culture's scaffolding of habit gave you another tool kit of symbols—your body language. And according to one of the founding mothers of anthropology, Ruth Benedict, your culture's scaffolding of habit even mapped out the emotions you're allowed to display and the emotions you are forced to hide.[4]

The brain you have today was shaped by your early days with your dad, your mom, your family, your teachers, and your friends. What do all these people share in common? A common symbol stack, a common infrastructure of fantasy, a common scaffolding of habit, and a common technology. Or, to put it differently, a common culture. Culture dug the foundation of your group's symbol stack into your brain when it wired you for your culture's language. For the first six months of your life you were capable of hearing and repeating all the sounds of all the world's languages. Then your brain hardened itself around the neurons that helped you discriminate and imitate the sounds that you heard others say. In all probability, those were the sounds of English. And your brain wiped out the neurons that could have helped you hear and repeat !Kung San tongue clicks or Chinese sing-song prosody.

Your brain gave over 60 percent of your language neurons self-destruct commands.[5] Why? You weren't using those neurons. And neurons that aren't used are forced to commit suicide. By the age of five, you still had the capacity to pick up French, Tibetan, or Japanese as flawlessly as your native tongue.[6] Then that ability, too, disappeared. Why? Your brain kept the connections that helped you master your mother tongue but wiped out those that would have helped you gain a perfectly accented command of the language of "parlez-vous Français."

Then came years of education, and every lesson you sat through wired your brain to fit your culture and its symbols even more. You didn't need evolutionary changes in your genes to give symbols this brain-shaping power. Epigenetics handled the job very nicely, thank you very much. And what's epigenetics? The way your genes are flexed and bent by experience. What, pray tell, does more to color your experience than just about anything else around? Ummm, could it be symbols? As in all those lessons in how to boost your vocabulary, how to use grammar, how to craft polite phrases, and how to use money? How to balance a checkbook, how to make change, how to open a bank account, how to use a credit card, and how to spend your allowance?

To see the impact of symbols, try teaching the "candy game" to chimpanzees. The "candy game" was invented by Ohio State University psychology professor and researcher Sally Boysen.[7] Here's how it goes. Put two chimps in a room together. The goal is to see if the chimps can learn generosity. Offer one of the chimps a tray with just two candies on it and another with six. Which is she going to pick? She's a chimp, not a chump. And she loves sweets. She'll dive for the tray with half a dozen sugar-saturated confections.

Now try to teach her that if she demonstrates self-control and a charitable nature, she'll get a bonus. Show her that if she's generous, if she picks the tray with just two candies for herself and gives the tray overflowing with six to her temporary roommate, she will get a bonanza—ten. But show her that if she selfishly hogs the tray with six for herself and gives the tray with only two bonbons to her chimp companion, she will get only one candy. You're offering a big payoff for just a short instant of restraint. And the chimp knows it. But even after a hundred trials, she still can't bring herself to finger the tray with only two candies for herself.

It's not that she doesn't try, mind you. She seems to know that she is getting it wrong. Her face is twisted in a grimace. And when each round of the game ends, she slams her fist down on anything in sight. You can practically hear her saying deep inside herself the primate equivalent of "Damn. How could I be so stupid? I've muffed it again."

Now train your frustrated chimp to recognize symbols. Train her to use numbers on plastic chips. Get her to the point where, if she's given a plastic chip with the number six on it, she'll pull six candies out of a pile and if she's given a chip with the number three, she'll pull out only three candies. Now try the generosity experiment all over again. But this time with a token bearing the numeral two, representing two candies, and a token with the number six, representing six sweets. Now the chimp has an easy time of it. Freed of the sight of food, she can blithely pick the coin representing six candies as her companion's reward and the piece of plastic with the number two for herself.

Without symbols, the chimp can't control her impulse to grab the biggest pile of sugary lumps for herself. With the symbols, everything changes. Congratulations, you've just helped a chimpanzee demonstrate what neurobiologists call one of the "executive functions" of the brain—patience, delayed gratification, restraint. You've just demonstrated what Boysen calls the *symbol effect*. And you've just shown one of the powers of the symbol stack—the power to free the brain to do things it was never able to handle before the symbols came along.

Restraint is a product of inhibitory centers in the brain. In humans, the center of that sort of inhibition is the prefrontal cortex. When you introduce symbols you give inhibitory centers like the prefrontal cortex new power. In other words, symbols rewire the way you use your brain. And if you're raised with these symbols, the rewiring determines the neurons that go and the neurons that stay. The symbol stack changes the subtle details of the circuitry of your brain.

What does this have to do with the genius of the beast? What does it have to do with emotional capitalism? Think for a minute. What does money rely on? An emotion we call trust. Trust that when the Greek merchant sailors arrive again with their amphoras of wine—or, better yet, with scrolls of Greek philosophy—they'll accept the jingling gold coins you've stashed beneath the dirt floor of your home.

Let's be serious. Aside from turning screws (which didn't exist) with dimes (a variation on Croesus' coins), of what practical use are small gold and silver disks? They're nice status symbols. They're interesting jewelry. But that's about it. Or that's it before you slide the first layer on the symbol stack. Then, if you trust a traveling merchant and he trusts you, gold and silver are good for trade.

What Croesus kicked off was only the beginning of a symbol stack that compacted feelings—feelings of confidence, obligation, faith, and trust. There would be considerably more to come.

THE MIGHT, HEIGHT, RIGHT, AND GLORY BIZ

The Seven Wonders of the World and How They Got to Be That Way

Where the need for uplift comes from.

Back to the mystery of meaning. Meaning is one of the basics we humans need as much as we need tofu, bean sprouts, burgers, and potato chips. Meaning is all about aspiration. It's all about climbing to new heights. It's all about spirits soaring. Look at the words I just used. They're all about moving up.

This is a cue to a passionate need stitched into us by biology, the need to show that we can buck nature and her most fundamental force, her gravity. Nature rewards those who oppose her most. This fact is fundamental to the secular genesis engine. Bear with me while I repeat it. Mother Nature loves those who most successfully oppose her. But before I explain, bear with me again while I sidetrack for a moment to explore this odd and highly presumptuous proposition.

Which is the real nature, the nature of what was or the nature of what can be? Which is the real nature, the nature that demands that we preserve the past or the nature that commands us to create a radically new future? Before you make up your mind, take this into account. Nature builds a challenge into us. To grab her rules and twist them in utterly new ways. To be the tools of her creation, tools of her self-upgrade. How do we know she wants us to oppose her? How do we know she challenges us to seek her unseen possibilities? How do we know that challenge is why she fills us with impossible dreams? How do we know that this is a universe Googling her future through you and me? For an answer, go to the bacterium, the lizard, and the fighting fish.

Early bacteria opposed a natural order in which all atoms, molecules, dusts, waters, planets, moons, stars, and galaxies were lifeless. Early bacteria defiled the natural environment of air and sea and toiled in teams of trillions to reknit nature's inanimate elements into biomatter. The primal bacterial colonies twisted and tormented the virgin molecules of waters from the sea, chain-ganging them into polypeptides, protein atom-ropes, histones, and nucleotides.

But the rebellion of bacteria against the "natural order of things" was about to get far worse. Roughly 1.75 billion years after life began, bacterial colonies came frighteningly close to extinction. The time was 2 billion years ago, and bacterial colonies polluted the planet's methanated, carbon-monoxided, and carbon-dioxided gaseous mantle with a toxic poison, a life killer, oxygen. That oxygen led to a mass die-off that wiped out most of the species in existence at the time. But the Oxygen Atrocity also led to a great lurch forward. It led to the sort of cells that would someday build multicellular beasts. It led to cells with a walled-off inner core housing something new—a highly ordered nucleus of DNA. It led to cells with oxygen-eating internal power packs, mitochondria. It led to cells that would someday be able to stick together in communities of hundreds of millions to make fish, lizards, fleas, and you and me.

Had conservationists been present, they would have decried the Great Oxygen Crime as an act of environmental destruction that reached the level of the obscene. And you and I would have sprung into action to stop Mother Nature's war crime—her act of mass murder. But Mother Nature rewarded those who changed her most— those who turned her into biomass. She gave her bacterial desecrators outrageous longevity. Her sinful bacterial children have survived three and a half billion years.

Nature used the sins of her offspring to turn catastrophe into creativity. She turned oxygen pollution into a challenge. Mother Nature showed the greatest love to those who had opposed her most. Why? Because her mutineers and her order-overturners do her work. Her rebels help her repurpose herself. Her revolutionaries help her upgrade. Her mutineers are re-creators. They are the makers of secular genesis. They are the tools with which matter transcends itself.

Three hundred million years ago, earthworms labored to violate and deform the landscape, leveling hills and shaming nature's naked rock by clothing it with soil.[1] Another act of desecration. Another act of creativity. Another act of secular genesis. Another way the cosmos Googled her future through lowly beasts who profaned her.

Trees and grass dared stab their roots into the coverings that the worms had left in their tracks. These outrageously arrogant new plants perverted nature's mantle of gases as microbes had done before, sucking in the atmosphere's virgin carbon dioxide and turning out more of that searing, burning substance, oxygen.

Termites challenged the hardness of nature's ground and dug mounds six feet deep—432 times their height. Then they topped these deep wounds off with ragged scars—peaks twelve feet high, peaks that once again desecrated nature's sky. In the hidden chambers of their towers, termites distorted the composition of nature's air, tweaking it with moisture or with carbon dioxide.

Earthworms had the audacity to snub the globe of stone that nature gave and to remake it as bioterrain. So did corals, stromatolite-building microbes, beavers, flowers, and bees.

The lizard that wins shows he's special by breaking one of nature's most primal laws—by defying gravity. The raven who craves a mate defies nature by soaring where no animal should go—into the clouds of nature's sky.

A winning Thai fighting fish shows off his victory by trapping bubbles beneath the surface of the sea and gluing them together, creating a bubble palace and defying nature's buoyancy. He not only challenges nature, he advertises the act. His palace blasts the message of his power to break the rules, the power of his might. And his palace lets Mother Nature know that she's been bested in her game.

We humans have had the audacity to build our own mountains, our real-life towers of Babel—ziggurats and pyramids. We've terraformed our cities and built monuments that fight that basic law of nature, gravity. We've done it with defiance. We've done it with showbiz facades and spike-like building tops. We've scraped and gouged the sky with steel and concrete hives of office space.

Will nature reward us as she has the others who have tortured and reworked her? Are we inadvertently doing what bacteria, worms, fighting fish, and trees have done before? Are we building the outrageous—new niches, new eco-pockets, vast new opportunities for life? Are we, too, helping nature Google her future? Are we helping her feel out her possibilities? Is that what the evolutionary search engine is all about? Is that a key to the secular genesis machine? And is the proposition that nature loves those who oppose her most a central key to understanding an economy?

How willing are we to impress nature by reshaping her in the ways she favors most—ways filled with hubris and audacity? Will she give us permanence as she has with beasts of single cells, with termites, and with trees? How sinfully defiant does the nature-who-rewards-her-wreckers require us to be? We shall have to see.

* * *

Like lizards, termites, and ravens, we have a biologically built-in height fetish. Tied to our obsession with defying gravity is our sense of just how high our group has climbed on the totem pole of families, tribes, or nations. Yes, we're back to status again, a built-in need that winkled its way into the brains of fish, lizards, and human beings over 250 million years ago.

The status of our group means far more than we generally perceive. In fact, working for a rise in our group's position binds us together in idealism—in the feeling that we're laboring not just for our selfish interests, but for (here comes height again) a higher purpose, for something bigger than ourselves. When our efforts pay off and our group moves up, we have a tendency to go euphoric. Look at the way we go crazy when our team wins the Super Bowl, the World Series, or the World Cup. And look at the way the business sector feeds our indispensable need for group competition and group victory by giving us the sports industry.

Men and women enhance themselves with status symbols like jewelry, horses, chariots, and cars to show how high they've climbed. Groups use status symbols like the pyramids, the Hanging Gardens of Babylon, the Cathedral of Notre Dame, the Petronas Towers, the Sydney Opera House, the skyscrapers of Dubai, and the nearly half-mile-high statue of Christ the Redeemer (*O Cristo Redentor*) on a peak overlooking Rio de Janeiro. The folks in one seaport 2,400 years ago advertised their city's might by using a nude statue of a man so high that he straddled the entrance to the harbor, standing with one of his feet planted on one side of the harbor's entrance and the other foot planted on the opposite bank. This was the Colossus of Rhodes. Once upon a time, America used the World Trade Center as a group status symbol. And once upon a time, Osama bin Laden used it, too.

Cheops, the inventor of the first pyramid, was the founder of this group-euphoria industry. He fed our need for heights, our need to climb high. Architects, builders, and developers are in the same business today. But there's a more serious aspect of the need for meaning, one that transcends naked profits. Meaning can come at the price of blood. Or it can come through the productivity of teams and through individual inspiration and creativity. It can lower other humans. Or it can lift us all. We can feed our need to "rise" above each other, our need for competition, with violence or with commerce and creativity. When we compete with gadgetry, status symbols, services, and games, we keep the violence at bay.

Which brings us to yet another basic of a re-visioned capitalism, another basic of a reperceived and reinvented capitalism, and another basic of your emotions and mine, a basic at the seat of your passions. As with Cheops, your mission, should you choose to accept it, is this: to find the needs you never knew you had. To do it so selfishly that your new dreams take hold of you. And to make your fantasies come true. When you do the insane-but-fantasy-driven thing, like building the first pyramid, you have a shot at making a contribution to more than just yourself. You have a shot at making a contribution to all humanity. Why? You raise our visions, our aspirations, and our dreams. You add towering new spires to the infrastructure of fantasy. And you help the cosmos explore her future possibilities.

What's more, the voices of your most intense private passions often echo other silent voices, the voices trying helplessly to speak in your fellow human beings. This is one of the secret gifts of tuned empathy.

Mother Nature loves us most when we defy her gravity.

42

THIS DOLLAR IS MY BODY AND MY BLOOD

Banking and Cicero's Family

How you and I became long-distance cablers.

Rome had banks and bankers.[1] It had its masters of the symbol stack. Cicero, the orator, author, and enemy of Julius Caesar, had the leisure to speak eloquently, to write, and to snipe at his friends because of his investments in the loan industry.[2] Cicero was in the symbol business on two fronts, the realm of ideas and the business of banking.

Just what is the banking business? Some twentieth-century banks called themselves "trust companies." Some used the word "assurance" in their names. Banking is an emotion-industry. It takes what Croesus started and raises his emotional token—money—to another level of abstraction. It puts a second layer on the symbol stack. If you give me your money and I call myself a banker, you trust that I will give it back to you when you show up demanding it.

What's the result of this emotional industry—this trust business? It drives the transnational productivity team into higher gear. You give my bank one hundred gold aureuses—the hundred-dollar coin of Cicero's day. My bank keeps ten, just in case you come back looking for grocery money. Then it lends ninety out to ship owners about to sail to Egypt to purchase grain.[3] The steady flow of cargo vessels to the Roman port of Ostia from Egypt's Alexandria makes grain plentiful and cheap.[4] The poor of Rome come to expect—and get—a reg-

279

ular diet of bread and circuses (we'll get further into circuses later).[5] You're assured that your money is safe with me. And every aureus you deposit magically turns into ten that feed, clothe, and upgrade both of us with inexpensive imports—and with a few expensive ones, like that Chinese miracle fabric, silk, a fabric super-rich Roman women used to strut their stuff and show just how much richer than their friends they really were.[6] A fabric with which they topped each other, to use another metaphor that comes from breaking the rules of Mother Nature's gravity.

Bankers are in the emotion business. If my bank crashes and you lose what you've deposited, you plunge into suicidal depression. You feel the pangs of apoptosis. You are swiped by your self-destruct mechanisms. You are attacked by your own biology.

In a system so heavily based on emotion, how can anyone who expects to make a contribution, who wants to do something worthy of his salary, who lusts after a big-money position, and who hungers to do something that advances humanity, how can anyone go to work under the illusion that raw rationality will be the key to his success? Look at how your heart sinks when a huge new bill arrives and when you know you've reached your credit limit. Look at how your heart leaps when you get a whoppingly big and unexpected tax refund. Or a bonus you didn't anticipate.

Even your weekly savings deposit or your monthly credit card balance carries a cargo of your hopes and of your feelings of well-being. Even a banking statement carries a freight of human feelings. Even the Federal Deposit Insurance that guarantees your savings carries a payload of comfort and belief.

When CEOs, VPs, and you and I shun the emotional core of our labors, we plunge daggers into our eyes. It's time to see with clarity, not blindness. It's time we zero in on our role as caretakers, launchers, and long-distance cablers of passions, as re-perceivers of the value of emotion to humanity.

43

DECISION PANIC AND THE ANTI-ANXIETY TRADE

The Roman Dream Book Industry

A little choice is freedom. Too much choice is agony.

We say we want freedom, but when we get too much of it, it drives us nuts. Humans (and our animal cousins) cannot stand what science calls "ambiguity." Making choices often is an agony.

Why do some decisions come so hard? Below the surface we know that our choice of a girlfriend, a husband, a wife, a job, a new pair of shoes, or even a weekend sweater and jeans will tell the world just who we are and who we want to be. We go into a tailspin when we have to make a choice that seals how others see us—that determines whether they accept us or reject us, whether they will look upon us and despise us, or will look upon us with admiring eyes. Some choices are crises of identity.

Then there's the sort of problem we have when we get into a struggle with a colleague or have a battle with our boyfriend or our wife. The torture of our inner sensations sends us scuttling to others for interpretation. The self on its own is insecure about the quivers inside of us. We need others to reassure us and to give a name to the strange things our self has sensed pulsing in our personal core.

Fortunately, we clever business-making humans have created an incredible list of anti-anxiety industries. Following our intuition and our instincts, we've invented many an aid-to-choice and many an identity-boosting biz.

The Babylonians came up with astrology and sold decision-making guidance and horoscopes that told you who you were. Two thousand and six hundred years later, many of us can't wait to get a glimpse of the daily horoscope page and read the words that seem to shine a spotlight on us—the words in which a media figure—an author—talks about us, flatters us, says soothing words about our weaknesses, and gives us the equivalent of that boost beyond all boosts, a caring and admiring gaze. The astrologer seems to focus on us and only us through the symbol stack of the written page. In Babylon, you had to pay an astrologer to give you that magic attention for a quarter of an hour.[1] You had to pay an astrologer to settle your decision panic, your anxieties, and to point you in a direction for the year, for the month, or for the day. Daily personal consultations were only available to the rich and to the super-rich, to the folks who could fork over symbols of silver and gold.

Then came the Greeks, with their Delphic Oracle—a decision-making helper for the very rich and powerful. Imagine that you're a troubled landowner in the Roman Empire's slice of Britain. You have a problem that gnaws at your vitals. A woman has fallen in love with you. You have a chance to marry. But in your eyes this woman is plain and not that bright. If you marry her, you will be perpetually dissatisfied. But no other woman has shown interest in you in a long, long time. Should you marry the available woman or not? Should you consign yourself to a fate in which you'll always be hounded by regret, in which your eyes will constantly be measuring other, prettier, smarter women for their mating potential?

You don't want to discuss this with your friends. You don't want to make yourself look pathetic in their eyes.

How do you blunt the teeth of the uncertainty gnawing you? If you've had many years of good harvests and you're flush with silver denarii, you can arrange a trip to the great answerer of all tricky questions, the Delphic Oracle—the prophetess who channels the opinions of the god Apollo in her smoky cave in Greece.[2] But it will cost you a fortune. And it will require months of your time. Months to make arrangements for a 1,500-mile trip. Months of expensive stops in inns for food and shelter, including food and shelter for your horse. Not to mention food and shelter for your slave. And it may also take months or years on the oracle's waiting list for consultations. After all, emperors, kings, senators, territorial governors, and the ranks of the famous take priority over the likes of you (and over the likes of riffraff like me).[3]

The Romans found a way to drive down the price of advice from the gods and from the stars, to mass-produce it, and to bring the guidance of the oracle and the canned attention of the horoscope to the masses. They started the dream book publishing biz.[4] If you couldn't afford a trip to Greece or Babylon, if you didn't have the gold coins or the time for a visit to your local astrologer, if you were embarrassed by superstition and wanted to retain what Plato's books and Lucretius's poetry told you that you had to display—your rationality—you could buy an inexpensive, hand-copied dream book, one you could stash at home in your *domus* or your *insula*, where no one could see.

Then you could wake up each morning, look up the meaning of your latest dream, read about yourself on a page handwritten by another human being, get an identity boost, and figure out which girl to marry, which line of Numidian goods to carry, which toga to buy, and what to say when you stepped out in the Forum to give a speech later in the day.

Is it valid to help others with identity crises and with an inexpensive sense of recognition, a sense that, hey, those words on that scroll, they're me? Is it worthwhile to provide others with the "trash" that helps them make up their minds in critical (or trivial) decision-panic times?

Yes. As rational intellectuals, we may despise these aids. But as emotional capitalists, we have to care for others, not look down upon their needs. We have to go further. We have to admit that we, too, feel these "shabby" cravings.

In fact, emotional capitalism urges us to use our intellects and our emotional insights to create more accurate aids for those in identity crises, for those in the throes of decision panic—for all of us who have trouble making up our minds.

44

TURNING GARBAGE
INTO GOLD

The Romans Invent Concrete

The secret in the sludge.

"They make a desert and they call it peace," said a tribal leader, Calgacus of the Caledonii, on the night before a battle with the Roman legions in 83 CE. But the real knack of the Romans was the opposite—taking the sand and gravel that piled in useless dunes deep in the desert, mixing it with pebbles and water, and turning the sludge into astonishments:

- an aqueduct that would bring water to a city ninety miles away,
- a coliseum in which ordinary citizens could afford to watch spectacles and plays put together for the edification of the man in that ringside box seat way down below—the emperor,
- building public baths with heated floors and heated pools,
- building amphitheaters in Roman Empire towns, from England and France to Syria and Egypt,
- and creating the best transcontinental highway system the Western world would see until the 1800s.[1]

The Romans were masters of turning trash into treasure and garbage into gold. With their invention of concrete—the sand and pebble sludge—they gave new powers to the ordinary woman and man. This upgrade in human abilities is microempowerment, giving normal humans powers it would take biological evolution 300 million years or more to achieve. Microempowerment is one of the finest fruits of stored vision, stored fantasy, and stored persistence. It's one of the most astonishing fruits of capital.

Microempowerment is also one of the most important upshifters in the evolutionary search engine and in the secular genesis machine. Microempowerment is material-miracle-making gone big-time. It's an act of a universe Googling her future and wrestling the impossible into reality through tools like you and me.

45

CHOICE PRODUCTION

Meet Me at the Medieval Fair

The nightmare of the Dark Ages and the dawn of new
emotion tools.

In 407 CE Rome fell to the German Visigoth Alaric and his invaders. In the following years Rome was invaded over and over again. By 600 CE, indigenous peoples across the face of Europe who had formerly cursed Rome learned the hard way what Rome's constant capital improvements had wrought.

As a battered Rome crumbled, the aqueducts that watered the towns broke down. The highway system was diced and chopped by bandits. The baths and amphitheaters were ripped apart to provide stone for something cities hadn't needed under Rome—walls that locked invaders out but that penned and caged the citizens in.

The flow of cargo shipped from one end of the Mediterranean to the other was stopped by pirates. The cheap grain of Egypt no longer made it to the Roman port of Ostia to be baked into free bread. Wheat no longer reached the seven water-powered grinding mills of Barbegal in France, where it had been formerly turned into flour. The result was a catastrophe. Half of the population of Europe died of starvation or of plague. And the Western world went into the nose-dive of a long Dark Age.

The average European's biology shifted. It went into free fall, the sort of plummet that comes with a self-destructive slide in wet-ware, in software, in hormones, and in neural receptors.[1] How in the world do we know? The visions in Europe's poetry, statuary, and religious fantasies changed profoundly. They switched from delight in the new to a dark foreboding about anything out of the norm. They switched from visions of forces men could comprehend and control to visions of demons who laid in wait to torture the human soul. Europe's dreams switched from the delights of life on earth to the agonies of a shatteringly painful afterlife in hell. The carvings on the facades of medieval churches featured gargoyles and the frying pans of the inferno. Sacred decor went from exultation to nightmare fixed in stone.

The Dark Age version of Christianity was no picnic. It was a religion that feared knowledge. A religion of self-denial. A religion that warned you against eating and sexuality. A religion that made gluttony its number-one sin. Yes, gluttony. In the view of Dark Age Christianity, overeating was a greater sin than murder.

Just as there had been a dream book industry in ancient Rome, there was now a travel literature of the afterlife, a travel literature focused on just one destination: hell. *The Vision of St. Paul* was a document that first appeared in Greek in the third century CE and gained an immense circulation in Latin translation after Rome fell to Alaric the Visigoth. In the *Vision*, St. Paul had been given a trip to see the hereafter. He'd visited both heaven and hell. But says Carol Zaleski, the Dark Age editors of the *Vision* were not interested in Paul's trip to heaven. They were single-minded in their fixation. All they wanted was Satan's torture zone. Or, as Zaleski puts it:

> Heaven is conspicuously absent from these abridgements, but the pains of hell are described with great relish. Sinners swing by their ears from flaming trees, revolve like Ixion on a fiery wheel, and stand immersed in an infernal river where their flesh is nibbled by monstrous creatures; those beyond hope suffer confinement in the dark pit "sealed with seven seals," which is opened momentarily for Paul so that he can savor its stench. In case all this is not impressive enough, Paul is told . . . that "there are 144,000 pains in hell, and if there were 100 men speaking from the beginning of the world, each one of whom had 104 tongues, they could not number the pains of hell."[2]

A perceptual system that consistently sees the dark side is not manic. It's depressive. It's the mind-set of those who see a cloud in every silver lining. It's the pattern of thought of those who see catastrophe in every opportunity. It's the perceptual predisposition of a period of crash.

When Rome fell, Europe plunged into an ignorance so profound that in heroic poetry composed in Middle English in 800 CE, even the memory of the West's history had been wiped away. The ruins of Roman cities in the provinces, the poetry singer sang, were the remains of giants whose real nature no one knew. The biggest buildings the singers and their patrons could conceive were drinking halls made of wood. Yes, drinking halls very much like the longhouses of the big men of New Guinea.[3] And that's what the hall builders were, primitive big men who humbled others by throwing feasts and by giving meat, mead, and golden rings away.

Who were these big men of the West? These pygmies who knew no history? They were primitive sea raiders. Vikings, Angles, and Saxons. The creators of our language. The killers even Thomas Jefferson admired and claimed were the forefathers of our democracy.[4]

Then, in the 1100s, the continent-spanning trade hookups that had once given life richness began to snap together again. The pulverized remains of the Roman roads, for all their devastation, were still the best that Europe had. The bandits were on the run. And merchants dared to trudge out again, carrying goods from Italy to France, England, and Germany. The capitalists were back. The entrepreneurs had returned to bring light to Dark Age life. And the evolutionary search engine roared back to life.

The result was the return of emotion expanders that had been forbidden and starved for five hundred years:

- **choice producers**—Traveling merchants gave you the chance to buy a glass vase from Byzantium or a steel knife from Spain. Like any good thing, choice in overdose can be a poison. But in moderate amounts, choice gives you a sense of control. And a sense of control ups the power of your immune system, boosts alertness in your brain, and stimulates new brain cells to grow.[5]
- **microempowerers**—Your old iron eating knife from a local foundry forced you to bludgeon the food on your plate. But your steel blade from Toledo, Spain, allowed you to slice, sliver,

julienne, and, yes, stab in whole new ways. The blade of steel upgraded the power of your hand in stunning ways.

- **identity-boosters**—Up until now you wore a tunic your wife put together at home. But think of the difference a tunic from Italy will make. The old tunic makes you just another peasant in the crowd. The Italian tunic sets you apart and makes you the focus of admiring eyes. Or so you hope.
- **mood shifters**—Like the songs that David sang to Saul. With the rise of fairs came new kinds of entertainers, troubadours, musical storytellers who ditched the old "heroic" poems about wars and gore and replaced them with tales of love and romance.
- and **novelties**—Things from places far away—from China, Syria, India, and England. Eye-boggling things you'd never seen before.

But the most important gift of the cultural rebirth of the 1100s may well have been frivolity. The trivial and the useless. Stuff we use to show off and display. The paintings of Giotto, the poetry of Dante, the ribald tales of Boccaccio's *Decameron* and of Chaucer's *Canterbury Tales*, and later the paintings of Leonardo da Vinci and Raphael—things of no earthly use at all. Things that brought no food, clothing, or shelter. Things that fed the spirit and the spirit only. Things that elevated the level of imagination. Things that raised higher struts and girders for the infrastructure of fantasy. Things that lifted the passions we call a soul.

The evolutionary search engine flared with life after six hundred years of neglect. Local fairs connected peasants to Venice, Padua, India, China, Africa, or simply to a village a hundred miles away. How? Through the exchange of material things. Meanwhile, a pope— Urban II—preached a new vision to the killers who got their kicks from committing war crimes in Europe. He preached of making a crusade in the land of the birth of Christ. In the process he brought Europe's idealism back to life and gave the warriors someplace else to fight. And the traveling singers warbling tales of love and of adventure reinvented romance, and brought back a long-lost, forbidden thing, fantasy's delight.

In France, the abbé Suger invented a challenger to the pyramid.[6]

But this new sky-penetrator achieved its miracles of height not just with stone but with light. This first real effort to touch the sky in over six hundred years was the form of capital and status symbol for which every big community would soon clamor—the Gothic cathedral. And the cathedral was far more than a material thing. It was an emotion expander, an attempt to defy the burdens of the earth in order to lift the spirits of a people on high.

Abbé Suger apparently felt that the Christian God shared Mother Nature's appetite for defiance of the law of gravity. And Mother Nature did her usual trick—she rewarded the man who dared oppose her most. The abbé increased his influence over history. He helped two kings—Louis VI and Louis VII—reform the French government. He reshaped your notion of a religious building and mine. He redefined the self-image of his nation. And, perhaps most important of all, he brought the group identity biz back to life.

Stripped of the Western system, stripped of its businessmen, its bankers, its long-distance traders, its entrepreneurs, and its freedoms, Europe had been shackled in a cave, sunken in ignorance, in poverty, in mean-spiritedness, in self-hatred, in self-punishment, and in self-denial. Now Europe was ready to rise once again.

46

SECURITY IS AN EMOTION, CREDIT IS A FEELING CALLED BELIEF

Venice and the Resurrection of Banking and Accounting

Three secrets in your checkbook and how they landed there.

In the centuries after 1100 CE, there was a radical turnaround in the trades that care for and feed emotions. That turnaround went hand in hand with the resurrection of long-distance productivity teams, the resurrection of the sort of webs of humans that had been pulled apart when ancient Rome went down.

Traveling merchants and fairs turned villages thousands of miles apart into spokes in a wheel of trade, letting a talented leather tooler in Spain focus on his craft, become a virtuoso, then trade the leather saddle he'd made for a bronze harness bell from India and a wheel of cheese from France.

Pushing this process from low gear to high was the resurrection of the banking industry and of a new layer of Venetian symbols that turbocharged the trust and security business. One was the letter of credit. Named for an emotion. Credit comes from the Latin *credere*, to believe, to trust. Trust and belief are emotions churned up in the emotional brain. Trust and belief spring from "Brodmann's area ten," a bit of brain directly behind your forehead. Trust and belief come from your thalamus buried deep in the emotional pit of your brain. And trust and belief come from bursts of the hormone of trust, oxytocin.[1]

Say you are a clothing designer in Florence, a master of your craft. You love to trim the gowns and the men's jackets you design with fur.[2] I'm your banker. You give me a thousand florins and you trust that I, your banker, will make sure that your thousand florins go to a Hanseatic merchant in Lübeck, on the coast of the Baltic Sea. I keep your thousand florins but send a piece of paper to a banker I work with in Lübeck. It asks him to trust that I will repay him with a profit if he gives a thousand Florins to a Baltic fur trader who knows precisely the shade of dark gray with a base of white that you are looking for.

The fur trader, who loves the fancy prices you pay, then scouts the docks of Lübeck for new shipments of gray fox fur coming in from the port of Riga, on the coast of the deep-forested Slavic lands.

The letter of credit is a symbol of a symbol. It's a symbol of gold. And gold is a symbol of furs. The letter of credit is a second-order symbol on the symbol stack. But there's more. That piece of paper, that letter of credit I sent, is a stand-in for emotions. Emotions that pin us together across vast stretches of land and sea. Remember, in Latin, a letter of credit literally means a letter of belief. Belief is what holds you together with me, with my banker friend in Lübeck, with the Lübeck fur merchant, with the fur merchants he deals with in Riga, and with the Slavic tribesmen deep in the Northern forests whom clever foxes have learned to fear. Ultimately emotions—and an emotional symbol, the letter of credit—tie you and me together with the king of England, who trusts in your creativity and in your taste and is your most important customer.

Meanwhile, I, your Venetian banker, and my fellow guild members have also invented a new way to keep track of our trades— double-entry bookkeeping.[3] True, we distrust those new-fangled things called Arabic numerals. We refuse to include them in our scaffolding of habit. We block the migration of Arabic numbers like "1," "2," and "3" into our symbol stack. Why? We suspect that they are sneaky innovations, snake oil designed to help embezzlers steal and cheaters cheat. So we keep track of our debits and our credits, our double entries, with the tried and true, with Roman numerals—with "i," "ii," and "iii"—numbers that make sophisticated math almost impossible.

Nonetheless, like most new inventions, double-entry bookkeeping does more than merely give new powers to me. It upscales *your* vocabulary. It adds new metaphors to your infrastructure of fantasy. Now, when you go to church, you're told that God is keeping an account book on your soul, complete with debits and credits. Yes, thanks to my accounting system, you can now keep track of your balance sheet with heaven. You can total up the wages of your sins. You can say your prayers, go to confession, give money to the church, and try to run up a positive balance with God and with the Holy Trinity.

New symbols on the stack upgrade your powers and mine to reach out beyond the confines of our towns. They upgrade your ability to create and to be paid. And they upgrade the tools with which you and I think, the tools with which we go for insights in our daily lives. New symbols like the cross, the words of the Qur'an, or the theories of Darwin give you and me new insights into our dealings with what we believe is divine, and new insights into the nature of the daily dealings between the plants, the animals, and the human beings of our time. New insights into the deal we make with celery—I'll give you all the food you want and will protect you from nibbling rats and rabbits. In exchange, you will let me eat you when you hit your peak. The same deal we make with chickens, cows, and pigs. Symbols like the word "ecology" give us new ways to see our integration with nearly everything on the planet.

Where do our symbols come from? Many arise from what some call "grubby, squalid, materialist consumerism." Bookkeeping, for example, gives you and me a mind-and-soul tool of enormous powers— a new metaphor, a whole new way to see. Not to mention a whole new way to dream. And new dreams someday shape new realities.

That's how new metaphors erect new spires on the infrastructure of fantasy.

VIII
THE TRANSCENDENCE
ENGINE

47

QUANTUM SHIFTS IN THE SCOPE OF DREAMS

Marco Polo, Author

A jailbird plants a seed that changes the course of history.

Marco Polo changed the world by turning his woes into opportunities. He put more soul into the capitalist machine than he would ever get to see. He changed the nature of reality for folks like you and me.

The Western system depends on a balance between four groups:

1. businesspeople;
2. the protest industry;
3. government; and
4. explorers.

Of these four, the explorers are the most unique. Countries of the East seldom nourished a culture of exploration. The West encouraged it mightily. That's one reason that from 1600 CE until the year 2000, the Western system grabbed more rules of nature, twisted them together in more new ways, and added more to the evolutionary search engine and the secular genesis machine than any civilization that had ever been. But in the twenty-first century, if we're not vigorous in the pursuit of fantasy, that balance between East and West will soon change.

Explorers may never make profits for themselves, but they ultimately carve the path to your affluence and to mine. In the mid-thirteenth century the Mongols conquered nearly all of Asia and united it in the largest empire—and the largest free-trade zone—the world had ever known. That's when one of the first men to establish the Western exploring tradition entered the scene.

Marco Polo set off in 1271 CE on a voyage meant to slake the hunger of Europe's rich for things so rare and expensive that their wealthy friends and neighbors, their wealthy show-off competitors, would despair. That lust for one-upmanship is the root of the discovery impulse. The discovery impulse motivates human societies to stretch their scope and to trade with civilizations, towns, or tribal villages thousands of miles away. It thrusts us into the cycle of exploration and consolidation, into the fission-fusion strategy, into the basic algorithm—the fundamental rule—of the evolutionary search engine, of the secular genesis machine.

In 1271 Marco Polo's dad and uncle had just come back from an earlier trip to China. They'd gone off in search of trade goods—consumer luxuries and status symbols—they could sell for outrageous prices back in Europe. They'd been after things only the Chinese knew how to make—silk and porcelain. Instead they'd caught the eye of the Mongol emperor of China, Kublai Khan.

Khan distrusted the Chinese people that his family—led by Genghis Khan—had conquered at the cost of roughly 25 million lives. Kublai preferred to hire foreigners, like the Polos. So he tapped the Polos for their knowledge of siege machinery—the catapults called mangonels. And he sent them back home to set up a new long-distance exploratory tendril, an ambassadorial connection with the pope in Rome. The pope gave the Polo brothers a handful of letters and a vial of holy oil from the lamp that burned at the Sacred Sepulchre in Jerusalem—in other words, material goods—to deliver to the Great Khan in Shangdu.

Yes, Shangdu was the place that Samuel Taylor Coleridge called Xanadu when he wrote a poem triggered by Marco Polo's legacy (and by another product of the far, far east—opium).[1] Samuel Taylor Coleridge's poem "Kubla Khan" was one of the spiritual fruits of Polo's materialist zeal.[2] A spiritual fruit of the Polo family's and Kublai Khan's greed. It read:

In Xanadu did Kubla Khan
A stately pleasure-dome decree:
Where Alph, the sacred river, ran
Through caverns measureless to man
Down to a sunless sea.

Yet another contribution to the infrastructure of dreams, to the infrastructure of fantasy.

But I'm getting ahead of myself. Marco Polo, along with his father and his uncles, set off on the dangerous three-year trip from Genoa to China to deliver the pope's presents (minus the hundred wise men that Kublai the Curious had asked for). When they reached Shangdu, Kublai took a liking to young Marco and gave him a series of assignments. The emperor sent the Italian twenty-something on a series of fact-finding missions. Then Khan reportedly gave the young whippersnapper the task of ruling the city of Yangzhou for three years. And he made Polo a tax collector and a settler of disputes. Knowing that Polo was homesick for Italy, the Khan finally assigned the kid a job that would take him West toward Europe—accompanying a Mongol princess across many a land to the Persian leader with whom Kublai had arranged a marriage that would sustain the empire's peace.

It wasn't the merchandise with which Polo returned home to Italy in 1295 that really set us free. Polo had barely settled into his old digs again when his patriotism got the better of him. Venice was in a status contest, a battle of the big men, an identity maker or identity breaker, a war with a rival trading town, Genoa. Polo joined the navy. In a clash between battle galleys, his ship lost. He was taken prisoner and jailed by the Genoese.

The printing press would not be invented for another two hundred years, but the publishing industry was already going into high gear. Rooms of scribes worked feverishly to mass-produce the best sellers of the day—ballads, narrative poetry, annals that told tales of local history, Albertano da Brescia's *Moral Treatise*, Dante's *De Vulgari Eloquentia*, in which the Italian poet asserted that the vulgar language of daily life was more eloquent than Latin and championed the employment of the local Tuscan tongue among intellectuals and aristocrats,[3] and Chaucer's *Parson's Tale*, which Chaucer, a good Englishman, originally wrote in Latin in about 1250 and which was translated into Italian in 1268.[4] And folks bought a new high-tech gadget called spectacles to see the written words on these handwritten pages.

Polo's prison roommate was a professional of a new kind—a freelance writer. When Polo told his story, the writer—a now-forgotten author named Rustichello—was wowed. So the two collaborated and wrote down the tales of Marco Polo's adventures in Asia. The result was a material product that owed its existence to a binding process invented by the Coptic Christians of Egypt, a binding process first mass-produced by the monks of Byblos in today's Lebanon. It was a book—*The Travels of Marco Polo*.

The events of the next three hundred years would show that the most important thing you can leave to others, your most important capital, is often not the attainment of the goal you worked to reach. It's the tale of the achievements you racked up trying to arrive at that goal. And it's the string of how-to secrets you applied along the way. This is a message Plato didn't understand. Your most important legacy, should you choose to live heroically, just may be the story of your life.

48

VISIONEERING

Lead with Your Fantasies— Prince Henry the Navigator

The passions behind the NASA of the fifteenth century.

The East Indies were rich in spices, rich in cottons, and rich in silk. These were things that Europeans, filled with novelty lust and status-symbol hunger, wanted badly. By 1350 CE, the megarich of Europe could afford these luxuries, thanks to the growth of long-distance productivity teams, thanks to the growth of commerce, thanks to the growth of the symbol stack, and thanks to trade.

But rarities and treasures did more than titillate kings, queens, and aristocrats. Those who couldn't scrape together the cash to buy such things received gifts anyway. They had new substances and new furnishings to dream about. What they couldn't possess in reality enriched something more important in the evolution of economies and cultures—the scope of a culture engine, an economy driver, an insight maker, and a history changer. That changer, driver, and upgrader was, of all things, fantasy.

Those without large sums of money acquired new riches for the princes and princesses in their fairy tales. They had fresh amazements—brand-new aspirations—to drive them in their daydreams and to wow their children in their bedtime stories. They had new imaginary heights to scale thanks to the infrastructure of fantasy.

Isn't this just a way of cheating and exploiting the masses by giving them the opium of false dreams? Look at the evidence with fresh eyes.

To see the impact of new fantasies on the daily life of the poor and of the middle class, let's dive into what fresh obsessions gave to the life of one royal dreamer—and what his obsessive fantasies gave to you and me. One of the readers who grew up on Marco Polo's stories of the riches of the East was Prince Henry of Portugal.[1] Not exactly a poor man, but a man who would lift the poor many generations down the line. And Marco Polo's adventures set a bonfire going in Prince Henry's dreams.[2]

Henry set his sights on getting to the wonders of Marco Polo's glittering East by approaching them in a whole new way. Asian goods were making their way into Europe at prices beyond belief. Why? Because the empire of Islam created a 2,700-mile-wide no-go zone, a 2,700-mile-wide wall that sliced through the land and sea routes from China and India to Europe.[3] And only Muslims were allowed to transport and sell the goods that crossed this barrier. Needless to say, the Islamic merchants wholesaled the goods to Europeans at a staggering markup.

Henry had killed many an Islamic citizen in his personal crusade to take and to subjugate the rich North African trading city of Ceuta. No wonder Christians were not welcome in the Islamic world. If they were caught in Muslim territory, they could expect a not-so-painless death.

Only the Venetians had been able to work out a deal with the Arabs of the Levant. From the Muslim point of view it went like this: We Arabs will send our three-masted sailing ships—our dhows—to India, China, and the spice islands of Indonesia and Malaysia. We'll bring back the riches of these lands to Oman and ship them across the desert in camel caravans of the sort Muhammad organized before he saw the light and was prophetized. We'll sell them to you Venetians. And you Venetians will be able to sell them to your fellow Europeans at a price that will delight you.

Henry dreamed of a way of getting around the Venetians, their Arab partners, and the Arab-Venetian monopoly. His dreams were so inflamed with Marco Polo fever that he invented a new form of ocean-going ship, the caravel. He also created a new way of using ships and sailors. He conceived a new way to upgrade the probing end of the speculate and consolidate, fission-fusion search strategy. It was called "exploration." Prince Henry sent his sailors out on a sixty-seven-year-long NASA-style reconnoitering mission. First his expeditions mapped the northeastern shores of Africa. Then, when Africa took a sharp turn to the left and seemed to disappear, Henry sent his ships farther out on the waters of the mid-Atlantic than any European had ever gone—searching for a current of wind that would carry his ships across the gulf under the zagging African coast. Henry's ships next probed the terrible reality below the belly of the earth, below the earth's equator. Beyond that line scholars and the superstitious said you might fall off the planet's face. Or, if you were more fortunate, you might find yourself sailing upside down. Who knew? It was even possible that you might vaporize instantaneously.

The expeditions Henry launched were told to map, to probe, and each year to go just fifty miles farther into the unknown. In other words, Henry's expeditions were unknowingly more than what they seemed. They were multicontinental upgrades of an evolutionary search machine.

Finally, after Henry died, his mission paid off big-time. One of Henry's explorers, Vasco da Gama, found that Africa had a tip. Sail around it and you could head back north, all the way to the Arab coast. The sailing was a breeze, quite literally, thanks to the Arab Sinbads who had discovered how to harness a disaster, the monsoon winds—winds that once a year blew your sailing ship from the Arab coast to India, then six months later blew your ship back to Arabia once again. When he reached the Islamic port of Malindi in Kenya, Vasco da Gama had a stroke of luck. He picked up an Arab passenger. That passenger was reportedly Shihab al-Din Ahmad ibn Majid, the greatest expert in the Arab world on the tricks of the winds that could carry you lickety-split to the coast of India.[4] Between the doubling around the tip of Africa strategy and the Arab monsoon trick, da Gama had discovered a new direct route to the treasures of India and of China. The riches of the East were now ablaze with possibility. Their price to the common man and woman would soon plunge. So would their availability.

Marco Polo's grubby battle against foot sores, fleas, and local disease—his adventures—had inflamed Prince Henry's dreams. Then

Henry had turned his dreams into realities. And what Henry achieved, in turn, became the source of yet new human fantasies.

Chalk up one more victory for the search strategy that defies nature in the way she loves the most. Chalk up one more victory for the way nature Googles her potential through people like you and me. Chalk up one more triumph for the infrastructure of fantasy.

* * *

Economics is an emotion flow. The most important capital is passion. Capital starts as fantasy. Whole new ways of living would soon come to be based on the words of Marco Polo's book. Whole new ways of living would come to be based on Polo's high-risk travels and on Prince Henry the Navigator's Marco Polo obsession. Based on Prince Henry's Polo-induced dreams.

49

CHANGE THE WORLD

Promote—Christopher Columbus, Mass-Market Pamphleteer

How a mere adventure book gave us a New World.

The word "selling" sounds smarmy. Use it anywhere near the folks who dictate our vocabulary, the folks who tell us which ideas to love and which to loathe, and you'll get a look of utter contempt.

But, to repeat, if you believe deeply in something that you feel could upgrade the quality of all our lives (or could aid just a few) and if you fail to sell it, you're robbing humanity. You're also undercutting your own life—and its meaning.

Can ideas, stories, entertainments, and philosophies really make a difference? Marco Polo's did. And Polo's book erected an infrastructure of fantasy for far more than just one determined prince in Portugal. In Genoa, a boy prone to dreaming also grew up with the visions of Polo's adventures dancing in his head. He read Polo's book, scribbled notes in the margins, and thought of Polo so obsessively that he came up with a wild scheme for a shortcut to Polo's Chinese wonder-cities, an express sea-lane that would make Prince Henry the Navigator's still-incomplete new route seem silly.

Following childhood passions is one key to a vivid life—and to a life that upgrades the destiny of others. When we whisked through the tricks of the world's first shepherds many pages ago, we peeked at how the brains of lambs open to insert a moving object they'll follow

307

for the rest of their lives, how the lambs' brains open to insert the sheep—or the human—they'll identify as "mommy." That's called imprinting. Whorls of our brains are literally shaped by these imprinting points. Our brains, like those of sheep, open at a key point in our childhood and youth and seek a role model or a formative experience to guide us like a compass for the rest of our lives.

Konrad Lorenz's life is a study in imprinting.[1] Lorenz was born November 7, 1903, in Vienna, Austria. His father was an internationally famous orthopedic surgeon, a man with enough money to buy a house in the country near the Danube River and to move his family into it—a huge house. Near the house was a wood famous in German folklore as the "Fairy Tale Forest"—the forest where the dark scenes of many a children's story had taken place. As a child, Lorenz loved animals, and in the spacious Altenberg house he was allowed to go hog wild with them. He kept dogs, fish, ducklings, and the big, black cousins of crows and ravens called jackdaws. Konrad lured the jackdaws into his attic and encouraged them to make a home there. When Lorenz hit his late teens, his father wanted him to become a doctor and sent him to a pre-med program at Columbia University in New York City.

But medicine didn't interest Lorenz. What did? The animals he'd kept in his family's attic. He wrote his first published paper on jackdaws. And many years later, when he won the backing of the Max Planck Institute, he turned his old family home in Altenberg—the home where he'd grown up—into a research facility, a field station. Lorenz had faithfully followed his childhood passions. And in the tried and true tradition of evolutionary search strategies, they'd led him into a new territory.

Lorenz was one of the founders of a new field called ethology. Ethology involved observing animals in their own environment and seeking out the signals that triggered automatic behavior, the signals that set off basic instincts, preprogrammed reflexes, inborn infrastructures of habit. Says Lorenz about his family home as an animal behavior field station and research facility:

> Altenberg is a real "naturalist's paradise." Protected against civilization and agriculture by the yearly inundations of Mother Danube, dense willow forests, impenetrable scrub, reed grown marshes and

drowsy backwaters stretch over many square miles; an island of utter wildness in the middle of Lower Austria; an oasis of virgin nature, in which red and roe deer, herons and cormorants have survived the vicissitudes of even the last terrible war.[2]

Altenberg had ducks, geese, and wild birds like the Shama thrushes that nested in Konrad's room. But it was the geese outside in the huge yard who helped Konrad Lorenz win his Nobel Prize.

Have you ever seen fluffy goslings or ducklings just a wee bit bigger than your thumb walking in perfect single file behind their mother? Their instinctual regimentation is astonishing. One day Konrad Lorenz peddled up to his farmhouse on his bicycle and walked toward the back door, passing a mother goose's nest on the ground. As he marched past the nest, the goslings tumbled out, lined up in single file, and followed him into the kitchen. Their brains had opened up a slot for an object moving at a certain speed, a slot that would lock on to that moving target permanently.[3] In the goslings' brains, Konrad Lorenz had just become "mommy."

The result? This batch of roughly eight goslings followed Lorenz every day from that point on. Eventually they grew. And they hit the sexual flowering of adolescence. Now, like you and me at that stage of life, they were horny. What or whom did they see as the ideal lover? With what or whom did they try to mate? You guessed it. Konrad Lorenz. Or they courted humans who looked very much like him. Were these pubescent birds sexually interested in other geese? Not a bit. Lorenz called this "sexual imprinting."[4] Just how deep did the birds' cross-species crush go? A jackdaw Lorenz had hand-raised courted him so assiduously that it brought him fresh worms every day and even tried to poke the worms into his ear hole.[5]

You've seen how geese fly in a perfect V pattern when they're migrating. In Konrad Lorenz's books, there are photos of the great ethologist riding his bicycle down the road on the outskirts of his research farm. Flying behind Lorenz's head a mere five feet off the ground is a perfect V of geese. Magnificent, full-grown geese. And at the center of their V is Konrad Lorenz's head.

That's imprinting. And it doesn't just happen to geese. It happens to you and me. It forges the imprinting points that anchor and fuel our passions for the rest of our lives, our passion points.

As a youth, Christopher Columbus had imprinted on Marco Polo. The Genoese lad's Polo mania was so strong that he did the unthinkable. He traveled Europe from one country to another for fifteen years, wangling introductions to kings and queens. Though his background was lowly he had the advantage of a commanding presence. He "was tall rather than of middling height," said the historian Bartolomé de Las Casas in 1527.[6] In May of 1486, Columbus finally found someone with the guts to back his scheme—not one of Europe's ballsy male leaders, but a queen.

Columbus's sense of earth science was, alas, a bit off base. His calculations of the size of the globe seriously missed the mark. He figured the earth was only eighteen thousand miles around. Queen Isabella put together a royal commission of world-renowned geographers to evaluate Columbus's scheme. They turned thumbs down on Columbus's enterprise. Why? They reckoned the earth's circumference was twenty-eight thousand miles—a difference the width of the entire Eurasian continent. Which meant that any ship that set sail to the West in search of a direct route to China would literally rot out from under its sailors before it could reach the Asian coast, its planks eaten by toredo worms.[7] While it was rotting, its crew would run out of food and starve.

The geographers were closer to the real figure than our Italian dreamer. But Christopher Columbus found land anyway. Yes, it was land that had been found before. But the previous discoverers, the Vikings, hadn't sold it, hadn't promoted it, and hadn't publicized it. They'd failed on one end of the evolutionary search strategy—expand and compress, explore and digest, speculate and consolidate. The Vikings had explored but had failed to consolidate their gains.[8] They'd failed to turn their finds into the tenth-century equivalent of headlines. They'd been like ants that trip across a cheesecake in the grass but go back to the colony and don't bother to advertise their find. The Vikings had broken the rules of the evolutionary search engine. In the world of ants and bees, that would have been an unspeakable crime. That could have condemned the colony or the hive.

But the Genoese lunatic—Christopher Columbus—did what insects do. He flashed. He flaunted. He danced. To be more precise, he promoted. He marketed. He advertised. When Columbus returned to Europe, he took advantage of a new invention—the printing press.

He pioneered the use of a new mass-communications tool—the pamphlet. He flooded Europe with leaflets about his new discovery and he set the imaginations (and the greed) of millions of Europeans ablaze.

Columbus's pamphlets made adventuring and exploration permanent parts of the Western way of life. And his pamphlets produced horrors in the Americas. In the sixteenth century, Catholic friars in Mesoamerica mounted an Inquisition and tortured, flogged, and burned alive the natives they felt were guilty of "idolatry and superstition." These ministers of Christ worked hard to increase the pain of their punishments, forcing water down the gullets of Aztecs and Mayans until their bellies swelled as if they were pregnant with triplets. Then the Christian torturers allegedly jumped on the distended bellies until their victims' intestines exploded.[9] The Inquisitors created a hell on earth. All in the name of saving souls from hell in an imaginary eternity.

But Columbus's flyers extended the exploratory tip of Europe's search-and-digest engine, the risk-taking end of the speculate-and-consolidate mechanism, the seek-and-you-shall-find end of the evolutionary search engine. Columbus's pamphlets built another tower on the infrastructure of fantasy. And while they were at it, they sparked a revolution in the way that we in the Western system would see nearly everything around us, from the place of man in the universe to the nature of the human soul. Columbus's pamphlets revolutionized the Western infrastructure of fantasy.

No, Columbus hadn't found his way to China, and he didn't know it. But it didn't matter. The world changed when Christopher Columbus promoted, sold, persuaded, and mentally upgraded not just our ancestors, but you and me.

* * *

Do mere symbols scribbled or stamped on paper change the world? Can impassioned salespersonship shift the course of history? Did the book Marco Polo wrote in a Genoese jail cell make any difference? Can a mere story do more than jewels and treasures? Should we consider Columbus's sales and marketing to be predatory media manipulation? Should we view it as the cheap act of a commercial promoter and exploiter perpetrating a scam? Or should we see it as a contribution to human uplift, to human powers, and to human history? Do the dreams of those whose curiosity is voracious or the fantasies of those motivated by material greed sometimes change the nature of reality? You tell me.

50

MESSIANIC ACCIDENTS

The Spread of the Chili Pepper

The day the ancient Mexicans revised Chinese cuisine.

Columbus's travels didn't just lift lives in Europe. They were a global choice producer. They increased the range of foods you could choose from Dublin to the mountains of New Guinea and the banks of the Yangtze River. But in the big-picture view, Columbus's trip and his publicity campaign did more than merely change Asia's and Europe's menus.

Every religion promises to raise the poor and the oppressed. Every religion—including Marxism—promises to feed the hungry and to uplift the downtrodden. No religion that I know of has ever paid off on its promise. But a nonreligion, a pluralist system—the Western system—has.

Does this sound like tripe and hogwash? Go down to your local Hunan restaurant. What makes the food so special? Hot peppers. In fact, the use of chili peppers in Hunan is an identity tool—a device with which the Hunanese flaunt their difference and their superiority to the citizens of other Chinese territories.[1] But where did their hot peppers come from? They weren't cultivated from wild plants in China. They were perfected by the indigenous "Indians" of Central America.

The Irish, the Belgians, and the Russians took up farming roughly seven thousand years ago.[2] From that time on they were both blessed and cursed by their bounty. When the harvests failed, these Europeans were killed off by famines. Then came the potato, which fed them so well that the number of kids per family shot sky-high and produced a population explosion. The potato lifted Ireland from a population of a million in 1700 to 7.5 million in 1843. Two years later a fungus, *Phytophthora infestans*, started a four-year killing spree. This microorganism starved its victims by spoiling their potato crops. The fungus demonstrated just how much the potato had become a microempowerer, a vital life extender. Without potatoes, over a million people died.[3]

Did the Europeans genetically engineer the wild tubers from which potatoes were perfected? No. These, too, were gifts from the natives of South America.

The indigenous peoples of Malaysia and Indonesia lived for centuries on yams. Did they breed these yams from wild plants themselves? No. They were yet more gifts from the agricultural plant tinkerers—those who dared defy Nature by upgrading her—the Native Americans of Mesoamerica. The pepper, the potato, and the tomato upscaled the lives of humans in Asia, Europe, and even Africa, thanks to the expansion of the evolutionary search engine, the spread of international productivity teams, and most of all, thanks to Marco Polo's stories.[4]

You can guess—or already know—where the corn that feeds the world today originated. China exports it. So does the United States. But the Native Americans of Mexico genetically engineered it. That is, they bred it from a native grass. Today the world is fed using Mesoamerican agrotechnology.

Columbus opened the Americas to a reign of conquest and disease that, as we said, may have killed as many as 70 million of the new continent's native population. This was an atrocity.

But Columbus's discovery brought far more than 700 million new lives into being. It fed the poor and the oppressed of lands we think were totally unspoiled by Western civilization. Facts are facts. Many a "native people," an indigenous tribe in New Guinea or Africa, owe their lives and their full stomachs to Columbus's wild chase of a maniacal dream, one that Marco Polo's book had planted in a Genoese child's fantasies.

* * *

Capital is more than just stored labor. It's stored vision, stored courage, stored obsession, stored persuasion, stored organization, and stored persistence. Capital is stored fantasy. Sales campaigns for seemingly selfish things can feed the poor. Sales crusades for the seemingly useless can play a massive role in the advance of the evolutionary search engine, in the advance of the secular genesis machine. And sales crusades powered by "the truth at any price including the price of your life" can set the spirit free.

IX

EMOPOWER

The Lift of Generous Selfishness

HE WHO FEELS WILL LEAD

The Power of Self-Revelation—
Martin Luther

How to use the mirror in your soul.

After Columbus, nothing was the same. The shape of Europe's vision and of its reality had changed.

Italy was no longer the navel of the world. There were new horizons opened up, new frontiers, new mysteries. Attention swiveled north and west, to those European cities on the Atlantic fringe that could live off of trade with the Americas.

Rome's spell—and the spell of the Catholic Church—was broken. The Americas didn't circle around the city of the seven hills, the city of Romulus and Remus. They didn't orbit the dead Latin empire that lived on vividly in Europe's memory.

The Catholic Church used the memory of Rome to maintain its power. For example, the church still used the old Roman organizational system. At its top was the Pontifex Maximus, the Pope. The title "Pontifex Maximus" in pagan Rome meant the head priest of the Roman Empire, the head of the Pontifical College, the head of the college of very, very pagan priests.[1] Despite its idolatrous origins, the popes took over the title and gave it to themselves. Why? Because the term Pontifex Maximus was like capital—it carried the stored power of 2,300 years of tradition.

In ancient pagan Rome, the emperor had ruled through "vicars" who administered massive territories called "dioceses." The Catholic Church took over these titles, too, using the word diocese to define the territory ruled by a bishop and a vicar for a priest who works on behalf of a priest above him in rank.² In the church, the Roman Empire remained alive. And that gave the church heft. It gave the church *gravitas*.

At least it gave the church *gravitas* as long as the center of gravity of the known world was Rome. But Columbus's discovery of the Americas shifted Europe's center of gravity to the West.

If Rome was no longer Europe's center, why should folks in Germany, Holland, and England have to pay the pope in Rome his due? Why did they have to cough up funds to build a marble church complex the size of a small town, St. Peter's, complete with chapel ceilings decorated by Michelangelo?

A German son of a brutal miner who believed that sparing the rod spoils the child took his childhood traumas seriously. When his father sent him off to law school, he traded his coach tickets in and went instead to a monastery and eventually to Rome. In a church ruled by a Holy Father, he let his emotions go and finally rebelled against his holy dad—the pope.

Martin Luther knew a rule that I made my clients in the music business follow—you owe your audience more than just your songs. You owe your audience your life. Never sell a formula. You are selling your audience your soul!

Why? Luther bared his agonies and others heard his words with gratitude. The pains that drove him they felt too. Until Luther, those were pains without words, torturing insanities, pains without recognition, pains without public ritual, and pains devoid of dignity.

Luther offered a direct connection to God through a radical software upgrade, a new symbol on the symbol stack, a new upgrade of the infrastructure of fantasy. And a new technology. The Bible had been walled off by inaccessible languages——Hebrew, Aramaic, Latin, and Greek—for over 2,200 years. Didn't know Latin, Greek, or Hebrew? You couldn't read it. And you couldn't afford it. Bibles were hand-copied and cost a mint. In fact, Bibles were so rare that it's said in 1353 CE three students came from Ireland to England to study theology at Oxford University. But "not a copy of the Bible was to be found at Oxford."³ So they were forced to turn around and go home.

Without God's book, how could you find your path to heaven and avoid the barbarous flames of hell? You depended on a vast bureaucracy to open God's message to you so you could follow the painful route to the pearly gates. Then came the device that had made all the difference in the world for Christopher Columbus, the printing press. And translators appeared who were willing to dedicate a huge slice of their lives to giving you the Bible in your mother tongue, in the language you spoke every day. Now you could be a search engine testing God's word about the invisible world on your own. You could read an inexpensive printed Bible in your very own home. You could follow the example of the great discoverers and sail the seas of God's words on your own.

But the church said no. God was only available through the antique hierarchy of priests, bishops, and a pope.

Reading the Bible, heck, reading at all, rewired your brain.[4] Dramatically. It gave an edge to entirely new neural assemblies when you were three or four. Way back then, your oversupply of neurons was still deciding which half of your brain cells should stay and which should go. If you grew up reading, your grasp of words on a page gave a competitive edge to the cells that connected your left frontal cortex, your languaging and speaking brain, to your right pattern-recognizing brain. Reading gave a competitive boost to the cables that connected your forebrain to the back rooms of your visual centers and to the motor strip across your brain's roof. Reading boosted the mesh between forebrain, hindbrain, and the motor neurons that control your tongue. All of these networks now had a whole new role. A role that called for whole new interconnects. A role that called for a whole new grand alliance, a whole new form of neural productivity team.

But there was more. Going to God directly paralleled a new secular reality. Ordinary folks were about to discover that they could now grow rich without a hierarchy of landed aristocrats holding them down. They could grow rich by trading with the Indies of Asia, with the Indies of the Caribbean, and with North and South America. They could make it on their own.

But no one spoke for the feelings this new freedom engendered. No one spoke to and for the emotions of those who had grown up with the unfamiliar spirit of a very new age shaping their brains when they were kids. No one until Martin Luther came along.

We humans can't endure pains that remain nameless. Martin Luther revealed his deepest pains and his deepest rage and in the process set free the souls of millions. How? He sold, sold, sold, sold. He followed Christopher Columbus's course and pamphleteered like crazy.

When a musician, a poet, a maker of practical products, a maker of films, or a creator of TV shows gives a name to a phantom pleasure or a phantom pain, she offers secular salvation. Her tool is her inner core. Her tool is self-revelation. Which means you can't sell what's dead to your fellow humans. You have to sell your soul!

Martin Luther's pain had come from his father's beatings. And his mother's. They came from his imprinting experiences, from his passion points. Says Luther, his mom beat him "until the blood came out." For stealing one nut.[5] Against his memories of a rigid father he needed to cut loose. But most of those in his generation had suffered from brutal parents, too. Brutality was the norm in fathering and mothering in 1483, the year of Martin Luther's birth.[6] So when Luther spoke his rage, others felt released from their emotional cage.

The printing press and the passionate belief that makes a salesperson remarkable made Martin Luther a superstar. The opening of the sores that cut his heart sold like crazy. Martin Luther didn't know the first two rules of science, but he followed them with all his energy. Rule one, "The truth at any price including the price of your life." Rule two: "Look at things right under your nose as if you've never seen them before, then proceed from there."

Luther gave expression to the feelings of millions of Europeans born into a world that had been changed dramatically in the very years when they'd first emerged from the womb. He gave expression to the emotions of a generation that ached to hear its voice and know its mind. Feelings without words are agonies. Luther gave chaotic emotions a shape and a validity.

Validation is one of the most important products of the Western system. It's at the core of pop culture and of elite art. It's a product that liberates the individual and that advances a thirty-five-thousand-year-old joint enterprise: human self-understanding. Validation advances the evolutionary search engine. And it's vital to identity.

Martin Luther's baring of his private wounds changed history. Most of Northern Europe broke ties with the Vatican and stopped navel gazing at the Mediterranean. All in Martin Luther's name and in the name of his radically resculpted religion—Lutheranism.

Luther gave his fellow Europeans a radically reperceived God and a radically reperceived path to God's heaven. Martin Luther wrote hymns that changed ritual.[7] And he put us on the path that led to daily Bible reading at home, opening a new avenue to power by rebuilding the scaffold of habit.[8] Like Columbus, Martin Luther upgraded the evolutionary search engine. He added new uses of the brain to the search engine of a cosmos Googling her possibilities. He added new roles for man-made microempowerers that were just catching on with the lower ranks of society—books. And when Luther spoke of God, he accomplished something ironic. He upgraded the operations of a *secular* miracle maker, the secular genesis machine.

Luther gave the Western system something else new. He was intolerant as hell. When he hated you, he hated you profoundly. Jews were high on his hate list. And I'm a Jew. But despite the flaws of a founding figure, the results can be bigger and better than the man himself. Martin Luther lashed out at those he loathed. But the base he laid provided a foundation on which, two hundred years later, would rise tolerance, pluralism, and ultimately freedom of speech. Freedom to propose new ways of looking at the world. Freedom to promote new dreams. Like Isaiah, Martin Luther helped build the infrastructure of fantasy and the scaffolding of habit that would lead to democratic government in Europe and to the Constitution of the United States.

52

THE ROLE OF
SEX AND VIOLENCE

Benvenuto Cellini and Will Shakespeare

> Never look down on a human need. Even what
> seems seedy can upscale the power of dreams.

Never snub a human need. If it's a need to do harm, muzzle it and let it play itself out in a harmless realm, the world of fantasy. But what does playing out a human need harmlessly mean?

Evolutionary biologist David Barash tells a tale he calls "The Strange Case of the Plucked Ocelot."[1] The Seattle Zoo managed to acquire an ocelot. Ocelots are gorgeous animals. They have what the Zoological Society of San Diego calls "one of the most beautiful coats of any animal in the world."[2] So the zookeepers in Seattle expected their new ocelot to dazzle one and all. But that didn't happen. Why? Because every day the ocelot chewed at its skin, yanked out its fur, and opened bloody sores. And no one could stop it.

Giving the ocelot a better cage didn't do a thing. Changing his diet didn't stop the self-destruction. No remedy seemed to work. Then someone had a bright idea. Ocelots hunt birds. But ocelots have a problem when they manage to bring down a flying bit of poultry. That problem is the bird's packaging. Feathers are inedible. And they're irritating to the mouth, the nose, and the digestive tract. So an ocelot has a built-in circuit, a genetically prewired behavioral loop, a necessary but very demanding instinct—feather plucking. If you let the ocelot pluck a chicken a day, the plucking instinct will be satisfied. If you don't give the cat something to pluck, it will pluck itself. It will turn its gorgeous coat into a tattered and bloody mat of fur.

The Seattle zookeepers learned their lesson. Every day they provided the ocelot with things to pluck. Then they watched as the cat's coat healed and grew glorious. The Seattle zookeepers had learned to exercise the animals within.

We, too, come prewired with instincts that have helped us survive. Among them are instincts we rein in, ban, restrict, hide, and sometimes loathe. In some cases the loathing is absurd. And in some cases it's on target. The two most important of these prewired instincts are sex and violence.

What's the lesson of the Case of the Plucked Ocelot for you and me? Our instincts have to be exercised. They have to be exercised where they will not harm others or tear a hole in our coat. One good way to provide that exercise is fantasy.

Here's how Benvenuto Cellini and William Shakespeare showed us the way in the 1500s. But first, a message from your instincts. Let's face it, boys and girls. We humans need sex. Thanks to sex, there have been 125,000 generations of us toolmaking hominids. Without sex, there would be none. So sex is built bone deep into our biology. And sex is built bone deep into our passions. Why? Because sex is an indispensable survival device. One of the most important survival devices of them all.

There's another prewired emotion that's almost as powerful as sexual hunger. It's the urge that comes to the surface whenever we're motivated to mutter, "I wish I could kill that bastard." Or "I wish I could kill that bitch." It's the urge that boils to the top a lot more often than we'd like to think, surfacing when we're driving a car in traffic, trying to wade through government red tape, or battling insurance company bureaucracy. Yes, we humans sometimes boil with hate and with a lust for violence. We even simmer with the urge to kill. And this planet's mob of more than six billion potential killers includes you and me.

The desire for sex is endless. The supply is very small. And sexual hunger is one of the tortures men endure in silence. It's a pain beyond belief, a pain that society doesn't dignify but tries its best to demean and hide. Meanwhile, our violent undertows are even more explosive. And even more difficult to restrain.

How do you handle these problems without rape and massacre? And how do you stop the capture of "slave girls" and the abuse of prostitutes? How do you establish an emotion industry that gets too little respect, the professional sex and violence fantasy trade?

You take a tip from the masters. And among those masters are William Shakespeare and Benvenuto Cellini. In 1373, Benvenuto Cellini, a maker of metal fantasies in goblets, water vessels, silver boxes, salt-dispensing table centerpieces, and statuary, came up with a solution that the Greeks and Romans, too, had often used.[3] Indulge your sex and violence fantasies by casting them in gleaming gold and silver. Then sell them to the wealthy. If you sell them to the poor, it's called pornography. But if you sell them to the rich, it's called art.[4]

Cellini isn't known as a sleaze peddler. He's thought of as one of the greatest artists of his time—the Renaissance. Others who learned Cellini's way of dressing up the animal passions in the brain would someday include the twentieth century's porn king and multimillionaire, Hugh Hefner (who sold his *Playboy* centerfolds as highbrow reading by surrounding them with interviews with elite thinkers like Jean-Paul Sartre, CBS's William Paley, and Pablo Picasso).

Cellini sold his erotica to the rich. But to prevent rape and violence, the arts that exercise our passions have to be available to the masses. Which is where little Willie Shakespeare comes in.

* * *

William Shakespeare was born on April 26, 1564, in Stratford-upon-Avon, a town that was small and sleepy way back then.[5] And a town that remains small and sleepy today.[6] Shakespeare's father was active in the town's politics, first as burgess of Stratford's borough, then as alderman, and, finally, as bailiff. In essence, he was Stratford's mayor. And Shakespeare's mother came from minor aristocracy. So little Willie Shakespeare grew up with privilege and with a keyhole view of power.

In Stratford, schooling was free and the teachers taught Latin. Then they plunged their pupils into the works of Roman historians and poets, ancient Roman writers from whom Shakespeare would later draw material. Shakespeare was a libidinous lad. And sex played a powerful part in his plays and in his life. Like most late teenagers, when he was eighteen Shakespeare had his lusts. But he was luckier than some. Or was he?

Will managed to wangle his way into the bed of a twenty-six-year-old woman, Anne Hathaway. Sounds good, right? Unfortunately, Will's sexual bliss was not to last. Anne became pregnant and Willie had to marry her. The proof? Shakespeare's first daughter was born six months after the marriage. Which means Will began to sleep with Anne at least three months before the ceremony.

Later, Anne bore Will twins, a boy and a girl. The boy, Hamnet, died at the age of eleven. But at that point it appears that Shakespeare was no longer living at home in Stratford with Anne.

For eight years William Shakespeare disappears from the historical records. When he reappears, he is in London, the big-time, the town where men and women literally risked their lives to experience excitement, a city where everything was happening and where you could make a permanent mark if you tried hard enough. And if you lived long enough. Yes, the life expectancy in London was lower than in the countryside.[7] So living in a city of stench, poor sewage, insects, plagues, fires, the smoke-spewing chimneys of glass and iron works, plus the feces of transport animals like horses and mules, the offal of food animals like sheep and cows that were butchered in the street before your eyes for their meat, and the excrement of pigs and dogs munching the town's garbage in the gutters, involved a gamble of years of life expectancy.

Meanwhile, Anne and the kids were still back home in Stratford, fifty miles—a full day's carriage ride—away. For all practical purposes, Shakespeare was single.

Folk tales claim that William Shakespeare got to London by watching over the horses of theatergoers. But when he first reappears in handwritten or printed records, Shakespeare is a threatening young turk, a twenty-eight-year-old invader of the London entertainment business, an upstart whose ambition threatens those at the top of the theater heap. Wild Bill Shakespeare first pops up in London in a pamphlet penned by another playwright on his deathbed. That dying playwright, Robert Greene, tells us, "There is an upstart crow, beautified with our feathers, that with his Tygers heart wrapt in a Players hide supposes he is as well able to bombast out a blank verse as the best of you, and, being an absolute Johannes Factotum, is in his own conceit the only Shake-scene in a country."8 Before the pamphlet could be published, a friend of Greene's wrote a preface that apologized to Will and flattered him. This hints that Shakespeare's high aspirations were resented and mocked by those who had already established themselves as authoritative figures in the theatrical community. And it suggests that Shakespeare was also winning over influential friends.

But Shakespeare's most serious opposition came not from his fellow dramatists but from London's city fathers, who had the same fears about entertainment that would-be censors have today—the fear that pop culture was going to ruin the minds and morals of London's kids. An angry preacher, John Northbrooke, explained just how savagely the plays of Shakespeare and his competitors could maul the minds of young and old alike. Go to plays, he said, and "you will learn how to be false and deceive your husbands, or husbands their wives, how to play the harlots to obtain one's love, how to ravish, how to beguile, how to betray, to flatter, lie, swear, forswear, how to allure to whoredom, how to murder, how to poison, how to disobey and rebel against princes, to consume treasures prodigally, to move to lusts, to ransack and spoil cities and towns, to be idol, to blaspheme, to sing filthy songs of love, to speak filthily, [and] to be proud."9 And Northbrooke was right. His catalog was a valid summary of the contents of Shakespeare's plays. But was Shakespeare's theater and that of his competitors and colleagues a savager of the mind? Did it reduce adults and children to swinish barbarians? Did it consign their souls to hell? Or did it exercise the ocelots in the brain? More about that in a minute.

Greene's words pegging Shakespeare as "the upstart crow . . . [who] in his own conceit [is] the only Shake-scene in a country" hint that Shakespeare had big dreams. But Will was going to have to work against self-doubt and hang tough in the face of attacks to turn those dreams into realities. How do we know Shakespeare had self-doubts? He tells us so in his sonnets, like one of his best, Sonnet 29.

Sometimes, Shakespeare says, he feels despised by all around him. He feels "in disgrace with fortune and men's eyes." In moments like these, Shakespeare loses hope of ever achieving a thing. He says he

> Look[s] upon myself and curse my fate,
> Wishing me like to one more rich in hope.

He wishes he were better looking, he tells us. He wishes he had more friends. He wishes he had more talent. And he wishes he was not so damnably limited in his abilities. He wishes he had "this man's art and that man's scope."

Shakespeare may have been making all of this up. He was capable of using empathy to put himself in the shoes of just about any human on this planet, even in the slippers of Moors, Jews, and murderers. But it's doubtful that this sonnet revealed only fictional moments of insecurity.

What did Shakespeare do in the face of his apparent crises of confidence? How did he overcome his moments of hopelessness and humiliation? Shakespeare persisted. He wrote 37 plays and 154 sonnets. In his *This Is Your Brain on Music*, Daniel Levitin points out two vital facts about persistence. The difference between a virtuoso and a good but ordinary mathematician, musician, baseball player, or writer is not the talent he or she shows as a child. It's ten thousand hours of practice. And the men and women who experience the greatest success are those who have the greatest number of failures.[10] Why? Because they make the greatest number of tries. In the words of Winston Churchill, they "never give up."

Dean Keith Simonton, vice chair of the Psychology Department at the University of California at Davis, surveys the lives of the men and women who've had the greatest impact on Western history and comes to the same conclusion.[11] Persistence is the key to turning daydreams into realities. Persistence is the key to turning the infrastructure of fantasy into new material fact. And to turning new material fact into brand-new struts of fantasy.

Despite Shakespeare's occasional envy of others who had more friends or more contacts in high places, once he was up and running in theater, Will was in a position to acquire acquaintances on the highest levels of power. The Puritans were on the rise, especially among the middle class. And those with a Puritan mentality hated the theater. But the nobles did not. In fact, they hung around with the actors and producers, upping the potential influence of folks like Will. Shakespeare was particularly anxious to court the support of a young lord, Henry Wriothesly, the third duke of Southampton. He dedicated his two earliest poems, "Venus and Adonis" and "The Rape of Lucrece," to the duke.

Meanwhile, back home in Stratford, Shakespeare's dad was rising in the ranks too. He was granted a coat of arms in 1596, when Shakespeare was thirty-two years old. The *Encyclopedia Britannica* speculates that Will paid for this honor to raise his own image. Is there any clue that this may be true? Yes. The record of the granting of the Shakespeare coat of arms is not in Stratford, Will's hometown. It's in the College of Arms in London—the town where Will hung out.

Will lodged in London with a French Protestant family—a Huguenot family, the Montjoys, a family who had fled France's genocidal attacks on its Protestants. So Shakespeare knew that big-scale violence was more than fantasy. It was real. He'd made enough money by 1597, when he was just thirty-three years old, to buy a bigger house for his family in Stratford, a house he didn't live in. In other words, Will had enough to invest in real estate. He would later buy more real estate in Stratford and in the place where real estate investments could pay off the most—London. The rising poet also invested in a money market instrument of his day—he bought a big share of the Stratford church's tithes.[12]

Like the keepers of Seattle's ocelot, Shakespeare exercised the animals in the brain—the animals of sex and violence. And his ability to take those creatures out for a stroll—plus his empathic powers—were making Shakespeare rich.

In 1594, Shakespeare became a key figure in the top theatrical company in England, the Lord Chamberlain's Company. Says the *Encyclopedia Britannica* of the Lord Chamberlain's Company, "They had the best actor, Richard Burbage, they had the best theater, the Globe . . . , [and] they had the best dramatist, Shakespeare."[13]

For the next twenty years, Shakespeare, a man in the fantasy industry, wrote his heart out, pumping forth over a million words of brilliance. Over a million words of catchphrases to guide the scaffold of habit. Shakespeare was one of the greatest manufacturers of clichés in the English language.

What are clichés? They are some of our most powerful tools. They are automatic sayings that guide our perceptions, our decisions, and the ways in which we behave. They are cross-braces in the scaffold of habit.

But that's not all Shakespeare's million words gave us. His characters, his situations, and even speeches like Hamlet's "To be or not to be," Polonius's "This above all to thine own self be true," and Romeo and Juliet's balcony scene gave us new braces and columns for the infrastructure of fantasy.

What was the role of sex and violence in Shakespeare's work? It was the pumping, thumping heart. In *Titus Andronicus*, for example, Titus's daughter Lavinia elopes.[14] But her new husband is killed and she is raped on top of her dead husband's body. Her tongue is cut out to stop her cries, and her hands are hacked off so she can't write the names of her attackers.[15] Eventually she writes the names in the dirt with a stick in her teeth. But by that time, nearly half the cast has killed the other half off in a tangle of mistaken and real revenges.

That's just the beginning of Shakespeare's violence. Hamlet murders his mother's new husband, his Uncle Claudius. Othello kills his wife, Desdemona, then himself. Macbeth kills his king, the Scottish ruler Duncan. Romeo kills a rival, Paris, and takes poison. Juliet uses Romeo's dagger to kill herself. *Richard II* comes complete with deaths by the thousand—a war in Ireland, a military invasion of the North Coast of England, and the murder of the protagonist, Richard II. We won't even touch the remaining seven of Shakespeare's history plays. You get the general idea.

Why all this carnage? Seneca the Younger invented a new form of drama in the first century CE in Rome. It was called the revenge tragedy. And it was more than just a hit. It opened a permanent niche in our culture.[16] *Star Wars* is a perfect example of a revenge play. In the beginning, we see Luke Skywalker's adopted family, his Uncle Owen and his Aunt Beru, their home and the warmth of their domestic team. We bond with Luke's family. We identify with them. Then Luke goes into town and the faceless enemies in white arrive, the troopers of the Empire. They kill Luke's uncle and aunt brutally and destroy their stone-domed dwelling. When Luke comes home, all he sees is the burned and blackened bone of his uncle's arm sticking from the rubble, imploring Luke. And imploring you and me.

Now we are hooked. Now we are angry. Now you and I, the audience, want revenge. Now we do what we accuse the villains of doing. We dehumanize the enemy and want to see the bad guys wiped off the face of the cosmos. Savagely and cruelly. It's that motivation, that deep hunger for so-called justice that drives a revenge play.

Why did revenge plays succeed? Because of the need for hatred in the human heart. We either exercise that hatred harmlessly or we exercise it in blood. We exercise it harmlessly when we loathe a murderous fictional rapist, a bad guy, a fantasy enemy on the stage or on a screen. We hate Aaron the Moor in *Titus Andronicus*, the man who has Titus's daughter raped and dismembered, his sons beheaded, two others murdered, and who tricks Titus into having his own hand lopped off. We hate Darth Vader in *Star Wars*. Or we exercise that hatred in reality and destroy real lives. Shakespeare gave us the option of fantasy.

* * *

The officials of London didn't see it that way. They attacked Shakespeare and London's entire theater community for over forty years, trying to shut London's theater world down.

The itch to make entertainments that outrage parents and authorities, and the demand to ban it, are as alive in the present as they were in Shakespeare's day. And they do something astonishing. They upgrade the evolutionary search engine and the secular genesis machine. Sounds like an absurd claim, right? It's not.

Video games first appeared in 1971. By 2007 the video game business was a ten-billion-dollar-a-year industry, competing with film to be the biggest revenue producer in entertainment. But did video games destroy kids' morals and their brains? Or did they, in some mysterious way, build kids' minds?

In 1997 a Scottish company, DMA Design (later known as Rockstar North), introduced a video game called *Grand Theft Auto*. *Grand Theft Auto* encouraged you to hijack cars, to splat pedestrians with your vehicle, to get a nice, comfy job working for a crime boss, to kill off members of rival gangs, to pick up prostitutes, and to save yourself some loose change by killing the call girls and taking your money back.[17] In short, *Grand Theft Auto* was utterly despicable.

But did it generate real-world violence? Here are the bottom lines. Three of them. After thirty-one years of video gaming, the number of juvenile homicides in 2002 was 44 percent below the peak year of 1993 and at its lowest level since the 1970s. In essence, the thirty-one-year rise of violent video games hadn't increased, or decreased, the long-term murder rate.[18] And murder rates had gone *down* dramatically in the five years since *Grand Theft Auto* had first appeared.

Here's the second bottom line. Since roughly 1950, when parents were trying to outlaw another sex-and-violence youth-culture entertainment form, the violent comic book, a strange thing has happened. It's called the Flynn effect.[19] IQ scores have risen. They've risen by as much as twenty-five points in a single generation.[20] And they've risen worldwide. But they've been accelerating the fastest in the countries of the developed world—the countries that indulge in video games.

At least one author, Steven Johnson, believes he knows why. In a brilliant book, *Everything Bad Is Good for You*, Johnson analyzes the evolution of plot structures in television shows, films, and pop culture and comes to a simple conclusion.[21] Since the 1950s, pop culture has been growing in complexity. The most intricately structured TV show in the 1950s had one main plot and at most one subplot. But some TV shows in the early twenty-first century had as many as ten plots tying together the lives of twenty-four characters.[22] And many shows introduced those subplots in such subtle ways that you had to watch every episode of the series over and over to pick up the hidden stories' traces and to figure them out.

The bottom line is that people in the entertainment industry succeed only if they can titillate, tantalize, and excite your brain. They have to go beyond the ordinary to the extraordinary. They have to find the limits of the familiar and break them. They have to tickle the novelty-seeking centers—the nucleus accumbens, the striatum, and the mossy fibers of the hippocampus—in your brain. Only if they achieve this do they make money. Only if they achieve this do they succeed.

I know. Remember, I did twenty years of fieldwork in the backstage dressing rooms and executive offices of the entertainment industry. I helped build stars like Prince, Joan Jett, and Billy Idol. And I helped sustain the careers of icons like Michael Jackson, Bette Midler, and Billy Joel. One of my jobs, and one of the key jobs of pop culture, was to stretch the envelope of what your brain can handle. To stretch the envelope of what you, I, and the group IQ can perceive. To stretch the envelope of what the evolutionary search engine and the secular genesis machine can conceive. My superstars and I needed to astonish, surprise, tease, treat, and overwhelm you.

Napoleon Hill, one of the most penetrating writers ever on making money by changing history, says that anything you conceive and you believe, you can achieve.[23] New ways of perceiving lead to new realities. Or, to put it in slightly catchier words, new ways of seeing lead to new ways of being. From the Flynn effect, the dramatic rise of IQs since the 1950s, it appears that pop culture vastly upgrades the level of what we can perceive and conceive. We may not know how, but pop culture's outrages help lay the groundwork for new parapets in the infrastructure of fantasy.

* * *

Back to the man with a "Tygers heart wrapt in a Players hide," the would-be "only Shake-scene in a country"—William Shakespeare. The outcry against Shakespeare and theater was best expressed by the sixteenth-century Anglican pamphleteer Philip Stubbes, who fumed that "the arguments of tragedies is anger, wrath, immunity [from the law], cruelty, injury, incest, murder, and such like, the persons or actors are gods, goddesses, furies, fiends, hags, kings, queens, or potentates; of comedies the matter and ground is love, bawdray, corsenage [cheating], flattery, whoredome, adultery; the persons or agents, whores, queans [prostitutes], bawds, scullions, knaves, courtesans, lecherous old men, amorous young men, with such like of infinite variety."[24]

And Stubbes was right! That is the beauty of entertainment. It turns garbage into gold. And in the process it exercises more than just the animals in the brain. It elevates the human soul.

Elevates the human soul? Surely that's an exaggeration. And yet we know it's true. The proof? We force-feed Shakespeare to the young today. We try everything in our power—including Shakespeare manga[25]—to shoehorn the very plays that once were said to corrupt the young into the brains of guess who? Kids! Innocent children! Why? We are convinced that if our children can connect with the messages in Shakespeare, they will mount to a far-loftier plane. Are we right? If we are, does this mean that mounting on high demands footsteps on the solid rock of sex and violence? Does it mean that the stone and steel of the towers we build to reach the skies rest on the bedrock of our animal drives?

We know that Voltaire was motivated by groupies.[26] And he wrote *Candide*. Jean-Paul Sartre and Bertrand Russell were groupie relishers. And they reshaped our philosophies. Is greatness built on the platform of our baser drives turned into stepping stones? Does sex motivate you and me from hour to hour and day to day? I strongly suspect that the answer is yes.

The moral of this tale? Remember "The Case of the Plucked Ocelot." Exercise the animals in the brain. But by all means keep them chained.

53

NEW DEEDS LEAD TO
NEW DREAMS...
AND TO VIRTUAL REALITIES

Robinson Crusoe

Building new planets of imagination.

In 1486, one of Prince Henry the Navigator's ship captains, Bartholomew Diaz, reached the southern tip of Africa and solidified the first leg of what would turn out to be a new route to Asia. But no one knew that Asia was now within reach. And Prince Henry himself had been dead for twenty-six years. So Henry's sixty-six-year-long investment of money and of his nation's energies still looked like a madman's dream.

But when Columbus reached America and Vasco da Gama reached Asia by two radically different routes in the same year, 1492, Prince Henry's loony fantasy no longer looked insane. In the years from 1486 to 1700, over twenty others raised the funds to purchase ships, crew them with men who knew that their chance of ever returning home again was a meager 25 percent, and set off as something the West had never known before—as explorers.

If you think that only the rich would benefit from this Age of Discovery, think again. Every story of adventure brought home by Abel Tasman, William Dampier, James Cook, Vitus Bering, or George Vancouver multiplied like a virus in tens of millions of minds. Every tale enriched the collective perceptions of the European masses. Every tale advanced the process of exploration and consolidation.

Every tale upgraded the evolutionary search engine. And every tale helped lay the base for breakthroughs in the secular genesis machine.

One secular miracle was a new form of virtual reality that went beyond what humans of average means had ever experienced before. A virtual world that wraps you up and carries you away when you read a book. A world so much more compelling than the everyday that when you're called to dinner or to bed, there's no way in hell you want to leave the expanse of feeling and imagination the book has opened in your head. Thus, the novel was born. New realities upgrade our fantasies. And new fantasies drive us into making new realities. That's the escalator of complexity at work. And that's a key to the infrastructure of fantasy.

Daniel Defoe, the son of a butcher, invented a form of freelance writing that vastly surpassed anything Marco Polo's ghostwriter could have imagined. He wrote for twenty-seven different publications—many of which owed their birth to two things: the printing press and the voyages of discovery. Defoe edited one of these new-fangled periodicals—the *Review*.[1] The newspaper and the periodical had been invented in part to serve the men who invested in sailing ships and who sent them off to find new riches. Sorry. I'm getting ahead of our story. We'll see the birth of magazines a few chapters down the line when we explore the tale of coffee.

There was a serious problem with the writers of the days of Defoe. Defoe, like many journalists in his time, did not feel strictly wedded to the truth. At the age of sixty Defoe tried his hand at a new kind of lie. A minor hoax. A bogus journal from an ocean adventurer, a discoverer who had never been. The result was *Robinson Crusoe*—which many consider the first novel. But Defoe did not package this as fiction. He pretended it was the real thing.

Robinson Crusoe, Defoe alleged, was a real English adventurer and plantation owner living in Brazil who grows restless and joins a ship about to embark for Africa to import slaves. The fictitious ship sets sail on September 30, 1659 (details are important when you are pulling off a hoax). It leaves from the mouth of the Orinoco River in Brazil, but a mere forty miles out to sea, it's seized in the furious fist of a storm and wrecked on an island. Crusoe is apparently the only survivor. He slowly adapts to living on his own and learns how to build himself many of the comforts of modern civilization from raw materials he finds in the forests, on the beach, and in the wreck of the ship before it finally sinks.

The scam of a phony travel journal worked. The public bought it. *Robinson Crusoe* opened new worlds of long-form fiction and new skies of escapades in which imaginations for the next three hundred years or more would glide. Novels would vastly expand hundreds of millions of Western minds, setting them astir with wild new ambitions, new fixations, new passion points, new imprinting moments, new plans, new inspirations, and new fantasies. And *Robinson Crusoe* would inspire nineteen films, eight television series, and even the hit reality series *Survivor*.[2]

Robinson Crusoe has been a hit for four hundred years for a reason. New frontiers of fantasy feed a vital hunger of the human mind. Like the desires that drive the makeup and the trivia industry, the hunger behind Crusoe's success has a name that's synonymous with the unimportant. Yet that hunger is as potent as a thousand heavens and hells. It's a vital driver of the evolutionary search engine and of the secular genesis machine. It's a radical expander of the infrastructure of fantasy. Its name? Novelty.

54

CASH IS MASSED ATTENTION, COIN IS EMOTIONAL NEED

The Tulip Craze

Don't let economists fool you. Demand is not an equation, it's a passion.

Flash is seldom trivial. Frivolity makes things happen. So does novelty. Ever since Charles Mackay's brilliant *Extraordinary Popular Delusions and the Madness of Crowds* in 1841, those who've wanted to understand the dips and flips of markets have pondered an amazing tale, the story of the Tulip Craze.[1]

In the 1600s, the Dutch of Amsterdam were growing wealthy off the post-Columbus, Age of Discovery, spice and fabric from Asia trade. Shop owners of all kinds had more money than they could spend. Why did many need to spend it? They were driven by the bioplan of human needs. In this case they were propelled by the need for status. When status-symbol needs kick in, it doesn't matter what object you use to one-up the neighbors on your block. All that matters is that it's impressive, rare, and expensive, and that it makes others swivel their eyes your way with astonishment and envy. You're not buying a mere material good. You're buying admiration. You're purchasing attention. You're purchasing an upgrade in your identity. Which is where novelty comes in. Novelty is a head-turner.

At first glance the demand for flashy goods that will rivet the gaze

341

of friends and strangers—the drive for status symbols—seems wasteful, ostentatious, and appallingly trivial. But is it?

Take another look. The things the rich use to flaunt their wealth often cement a connection between distant places and far-flung cultures. They build long-distance productivity teams.

In 1700, the Turks had just bred a new form of flower—the tulip. A flower named for what it resembled, a Turkish turban—in Turkish, a *tülbent*.[2] Anything from Turkey was exotic. It was scarce and hard to get—which means it was extravagantly expensive. One of the leading social psychologists of our time, Robert Cialdini, has outlined what he calls the "scarcity principle."[3] The harder it is to get something, the more we want it. And the more we feel that *other* people want it, the more we lust to get our hands on it, too. Attention breeds attention. The object at the center of an attention storm becomes nearly irresistible.

Many of us dream of diving into the spotlight, where the eyes of others focus. We dream of scooping up the attention of the mob that's looking on. We dream of being the center of admiration and of jealousy. We need others to notice us, to fasten their eyes and their emotions on us. We sometimes need this emotion-charged attention more than we need life itself.

Attention hunger and its product, the status symbol, is a key driver of the Western system and of its productivity. It's a driver powered by the cycle of explore and digest, by the cycle of speculate and consolidate, by the cycles that drive the evolutionary search engine. Attention hunger is a key to the genius of the beast. That's why in Holland in 1700, men and women vied with huge sums to get their hands on one-of-a-kind tulip bulbs. One bulb sold for the money it would cost to buy a carriage, four horses, a cottage, and a small farm. Another bulb was traded for an extraordinarily high-value business, a brewery. Even the prices grabbed attention.

One Dutch shopkeeper put his life savings into a bulb that others lusted for, but he made the mistake of leaving it on his counter when a sailor walked in to make a purchase. The shopkeeper went to the back of his store searching for the item the sailor wanted. When he came back, the bulb was gone and the sailor was munching a sandwich. In a state of shock the tradesman frantically searched his shelves and floor looking for the lost bulb. The sailor had mistaken it for an onion and had added it to the sardines between his slices of bread.

By the time the tulip bulb–crazed merchant and the sailor figured out what had happened, the bulb had been thoroughly chewed and was on its way down the sailor's esophagus. Explore and digest indeed. What had the merchant lost? A plant? A mere flower? No, a magnet of one of the things that you and I need the most—attention.

Meanwhile, the wave of contact with Istanbul that the Tulip Craze accelerated led to an increased flow of new ideas. In 1717, the wife of the British ambassador to Istanbul, Lady Mary Wortley Montagu, sent letters home to England praising a Turkish medical innovation—inoculation against smallpox.[4] What's more, she put her money where her mouth was. She'd had smallpox shortly after marrying Montagu, and it had left permanent scars on her face. What's more, some of her closest friends had died of the disease. She didn't want her kids to get it. So she made the embassy's doctor learn the Turkish technique and had her own son inoculated. Then, when she returned to England, she had her five-year-old daughter inoculated while the physician who'd tended her during her bout with smallpox watched. That physician was at the top of his field and was about to rise even higher—becoming physician to the royal family and president of the Royal Society. Mary Wortley Montagu's gutsy move, says a Boston doctor writing a short history of smallpox in the *American Journal of the Medical Sciences* in 1846, was "the first step toward the general intro-duction of the practice" of smallpox inoculation in England.

Lady Mary Wortley Montagu had acted as a search antenna. And she had played intellectual politics to make sure her news made it to a relatively new information consolidator—the aforementioned Royal Society—one of the key hubs in the new spoke-and-hub network of a field that still called itself "natural philosophy." Today we call natural philosophy's new scaffold of habit and fantasy "science."

The product of Mary Wortley Montagu's trip to a novel place, Turkey, would eventually save millions of lives and make smallpox a killer of the past.

But that was by no means the only fruit of the Turkish connection. It was not the only payoff from what the Tulip Craze had nurtured—the Turkey trade. Others returned from Turkey with a new form of furniture—the divan.[5] They returned with the Turkish word by which we'd name a Western upgrade of the divan—the sofa. They returned with the women's clothing outfit called the caftan. They returned with the words for new delicacies—caviar, yoghurt, and shish kebab.[6] And they returned with new military words—horde and janissary. Big deal, right? But there was something far more powerful. A social fastener and quickener, a potion with the power to turbocharge the evolutionary search engine—coffee and the place where you enjoy it. A fantasy factory called the café.[7]

The pursuit of material novelty ups the level of fantasy. And fantasy ups the level of material reality. That's the secret formula of the infrastructure of fantasy.

55

THE BIRTH OF TEA AND THE RISE OF THE CUP AND SAUCER

Mindmaps of the Day

How China gave England a social landmark with which to map the day. And how rituals like teatime keep us sane.

In September 2008, I was onstage in San Diego appearing on a panel with Peter Norvig, head of research and development for Google, Prabhakar Raghavan, head of research and development for Yahoo, and Jon Udell, an "evangelist" from Microsoft. Our topic was the distant future of the Internet and of the World Wide Web. Our host was panel head Nova Spivack, founder of Radar Networks and of twine.com. And our audience was two hundred Silicon Valley innovators—venture capitalists and entrepreneurs.

Nova Spivack is *the* leader in the development of something new in the information-access industry, semantic webs. He is so much the leader that he's made it to page one of the *New York Times* with his semantic-web pioneering. But I could never get a handle on what semantic webs are. And believe me, I researched it. Every brain has its limitations, and in tackling the subject of semantic webs, I'd apparently hit one of mine.

The one thing I did understand is that to make an effective semantic web, you need a "taxonomy of knowledge." A family tree of information. And on that panel, I disagreed about the taxonomy of knowledge. To my limited brain a taxonomy of knowledge was not what we needed most to power the next material miracle in the secular genesis machine. It wasn't what we needed most to energize our daily labors or to restart the motor of a dying economy.

What was needed? A taxonomy of emotion. A taxonomy of a very specific emotion: a taxonomy of desire. A taxonomy of that living, breathing, wriggling, constantly shape-shifting, half-spiritual and half-material beast that economists call "demand." Why? Desire is what makes an economy tick. It's what powers the relationship between you and me. Desire is what keeps me typing this sentence on my laptop in the darkness of the Tea Lounge in Park Slope, Brooklyn, and what impels you to read my ponderous and peculiar syllables. Desire.

No, money isn't my primary objective. And it is probably not yours. I want to do something worthy of your attention. Something that tweaks and delights your brain. Something that in ways big or small changes your life by changing the way you see. We both know that I may or may not succeed. But I will try for all I'm worth.

And what drives you? The need for some new way to get a feeling of control over the jumbled hurricane of your life? Some new way to derive insight? Some new way to derive delight? Some new way of fascinating shapely people of the opposite sex? Some new way of moving up a bit on the totem pole of status? Some new way to know who and what you are? Some new way to feed, tickle, and please your feelings? Some new way to solidify and upgrade your identity? And, again, some new insight? When needs like these are kind enough to reveal themselves, they show up as desires.

Desire is the force behind every exchange, behind every bit of commerce between you and me. Behind every exchange of money. And behind every exchange of information. Demand is not a number. It's a feeling. We demand because we want, we're in pain, we're bored, and we need relief. We demand because we emote, and we emote because we need. When we desire things we can't articulate, we ache even for the words that will express our needs.

Desire is the force behind supply and demand. And, again, desire is not a number, it's an emotion. Coin is massed attention. Cash is emotional need. The taxonomy that can move us forward is not cold and rational. It's a taxonomy of passion. It's a family tree of desire. It's a bioplan of human needs.

* * *

The bioplan of human needs, the taxonomy of desire, is spelled out in the neurons of the brain. It's in the hypothalamus, the hippocampus, the striatum, the nucleus accumbens, the ventral pallidum, the amygdala, and the ventral tegmentum. Our basic shopping list of cravings includes eleven things we are desperate to achieve: control, status, attention, belonging, identity, love, sex, meaning, structure, uplift, and novelty. If we want to make a living, those are needs we have to feed.

Rituals that bring us together and that help us map out the patterns of our days are far higher on that taxonomy than you'd think. Without mundane temporal milestones, time-markers like breakfast, lunch, dinner, weekends, a yearly vacation, and a periodic raise, we can go crazy. Those who suffer from structure deprivation fill the emptiness of chaotic hours with alcohol, gambling, compulsive shopping, compulsive eating, and even with compulsive picking at every microhillock of skin their restless fingers can find and try to pry it loose.

The opening of the sea-lanes to the East gave Europe and England a host of brand-new things. The Chinese were exquisite masters of porcelain manufacture. From the ports of China, explorers and merchants brought home three extremely queer inventions—three new sources of novelty—the cup, the saucer, and a pouring vessel—the teapot. The world scourers also brought home that strange new beverage, tea. And, most important, they hauled back a thing without substance, a ritual, the tea ceremony.

In England that ceremony became a landmark in the map with which we structure our day—tea in the afternoon. Teatime gave us the kind of structure we all so badly need. Just as important, tea was a group thing—you used it as an excuse to get together with friends and family. When we are not in each others' presence we shrink—we lose our sense of solidity. We are like the bee whose temperature goes down when she doesn't attract enthusiastic attention, when she doesn't get her hugs and rubs. Tea enlarged the social web with which we humans comfort ourselves and with which we boost our confidence, our connections, and our powers. It boosted a potent power, the *group IQ*, the mass intellect we generate when, like bees, we pool what we know. The evolutionary search engine we generate when our bodies follow the rules of enthusiasm and dejection, the rules of attention, the rules of the cycle of insecurity. But let's get back to tea.

Until roughly 1690, the Brits and the French had gotten together around pints of alcohol—a brew that slowed their brains. Europeans in the pre-tea days even fed their babies beer and wine. Now in 1700 Englishwomen and Englishmen congregated with friends over a beverage with caffeine, a pick-me-up that sped the brain.[1]

But high tea wasn't the only social fastener and structure maker that came from the rakish adventures of those who went out on sailing ships. Let's switch over to that sludge the Turks passed on along with their tulips—the beverage made from coffee beans.

56

LIGHTING UP THE GROUP IQ

Here Comes Your Cup of Coffee

The tale of the Turkish hangout that turbocharged the
British brain.

The next imported novelty came from Yemen via that ever-so-conve-
nient conduit (and enemy), the empire of the Turks. The Turks took
advantage of China's cups, but filled them with a brew made from the
nuts of a tree that grew on the eastern edges of the Arabian Desert.
Yes, that's Yemen. Then the Turks set up comfortable rooms where
men could congregate, sit, tell tales, swap rumors, exchange information, and sip the caffeinated stuff that the Turks brewed as a thick and
bitter mud.

Who cared about the taste? This drink made even the sleepiest
come awake. And it made the already bright-eyed positively hyper.
Talk about mood-shift industries!

When the idea of the coffeehouse caught on in England, men got
together over steaming cups and gossiped about the ships in whose
voyages they'd invested. With their brains hopped up on coffee and
their needs for warmth and belonging satisfied—their needs for company, connections, and friendship—the British coffeehouse customers
came up with a plethora of new inventions, new ways of getting status
and attention—the magazine, the business newsletter, the newspaper,
the company, the stock exchange, and the insurance industry. All of

these innovations turbocharged the powers of long-distance productivity teams, spreading the web of interchange from Bristol and London to Bangalore, Bermuda, and Boston.

Consumerism and materialism can lift the spirit to new heights. And rising spirits reinvent material reality. Coffee and tea lit up the group IQ. And the IQ of the group is where the genius of the Western system lies.

57

THE BLESSINGS
(AND THE CURSES)
OF OBSESSION

Inventing the Plantation

Feed your obsessions and they'll feed you. The birth
of Britain's breeding fixation.

Let's step back for a minute from 1700, when the first coffeehouses got their start, to roughly 1509.[1]

Henry VIII, king of England, had a bright idea.[2] His nation was a relative nothing on the outskirts of Europe, a little kid who tried and tried but never seemed to make the grade in the grown-up club of nation-states. In those days a navy was a bunch of long, lean, vicious war machines—galleys. Galleys were great in the Mediterranean, where most of the military action took place. When you were in a close encounter, you could lower your sails, whip your slaves or conscripts into action at the oars, jackrabbit forward, and sink another galley by ramming it in half with the metal galley-splinterer on your prow.

The Turks, who had fought a five-hundred-year-long naval jihad with Christian Europe for control over the Mediterranean Sea, picked up a new accessory from the Chinese (who had far more than cups and saucers up their sleeves). It was a long metal barrel, a batch of gun-powder, a fuse, and something heavy you wanted to hurl at high speed at your enemy. In a stroke of genius, the Turks put these cannons (from the Italian word for an empty tube of sugar cane) on their vast arrays of galleys and made them even more formidable than before.

Galleys were fine on the calm and sheltered waters of the Mediterranean Sea. But thanks to trade with the Americas, the action was shifting westward, to lands where the seas were by no means as peaceful. Galleys wouldn't cut it on the choppy English Channel or out in the stormy wastes of the Atlantic Ocean. So Henry VIII had a brainstorm. Why not base your fighting ships on the huge, round-bellied three- or four-masted vessels favored by yet another Henry, Portugal's Prince Henry the Navigator.[3] Those ships—called *caracks*—had been adapted for exploration and were outfitted to survive the storms of hell. They had big bellies and carried men and cargo comfortably.[4] What's more, a galley could at best carry seven cannons.[5] But a cargo ship built to brave the battering of the ocean's storms could carry a minimum of forty artillery pieces. And it could go where galleys disintegrated—so far over the horizon that the land disappeared from sight. Thus was the modern warship born.[6]

However, Henry had a problem with this plan. Ever since there'd been a London (London had been around by then for 1,466 years), the English had used the trees of their island's forests to heat their homes and to fuel the furnaces of their iron makers and glassblowers.[7] There weren't enough trees left to build and maintain the ships that would make a navy.[8]

Henry cleverly followed Martin Luther's example. He broke his ties with the pope. The traditional explanation for this split was Henry's need for a divorce. Henry was having horrible luck on the reproductive front. Every time he managed to sire a child, it came out a girl. And in the opinion of the received wisdom of the day, girls were not tough enough to guarantee that Henry's family would reign over England once he passed on. When Henry applied for divorce number eight so he could speculate with his sperm once again, so he could gamble his seed on another womb, the pope turned Henry down. Luther had just flipped the pope the bird, and the idea was infectious. King Henry, too, did the spiritually unthinkable, said good-bye to the Catholic Church and set up his own divorce granter—the archbishop of a strictly English church. But was this the only reason Henry said adieu to the holy prelate? Or was Henry really after real estate? Was he after the loyalty that real estate could buy? And was he after—lumber?

The Vatican had owned a third of England's land. Henry tossed out the monks and the nuns, then handed the bonanza of former monastery acreage to his friends, many of them very clever fellows. Thus he bought himself the gut-deep loyalty of a new class later known as the "squirearchy"—the men whose wealth would come from lands that Henry had stolen from the pope.

Wood, Henry told these new landholders, I want wood.[9] Which triggered a new industry based on obsession. The new landholders surveyed their formerly holy territories, drained their swamps, figured out what kind of wood would grow best on which kind of soil, tossed out any peasants who were in the way, and focused on raising just one crop on each huge swatch of property. Then they went hog wild over an addictive new hobby—breeding—crossing plants to get the straightest oak for masts, and the fastest-growing trees to make the planking of ships' hulls.[10]

Once you get the hang of breeding, why stop at trees? Lords and squires spent their days and nights figuring out new schemes to tweak the genes of horses to make them strong and heavy or light and fast, new ways to tweak the genes of dogs to make them useful for the hunt, and new tricks to tweak the genes of cows and pigs to make the best possible meat.[11]

What good came from this manic, aristocratic hobby of genetic shuffling? The specialized super mass-production of one crop on a big swatch of land was called the "plantation." Put a plantation on the tropical islands Columbus had discovered and you could raise huge quantities of sugar cane (yes, the stuff from which cannons got their name). You could also raise two other microempowering luxuries: coffee, or that rare import from India, cotton.

We all know what horrors of slavery this discovery led to. Death, rape, torture, and chains. Destruction of the nuclear family and poverty. The capture of between eight and fifteen million human beings[12] and the death of up to two million of them in the passage across the Atlantic. In short, atrocities. Capitalism can be creative and uplifting, or it can be criminal and degrading. In this case it was both. And the negatives were appalling. But mass-produced sugar fueled the poor and the oppressed of Europe. It gave the sweetness of "snacks" to folks who formerly couldn't afford anything tastier than gruel. It sweetened the lives—and the coffee and tea—of the middle and upper classes. Sugar helped the quickness of caffeine kick in.

Sugar is more than a junk food or an indulgence. It's one of the fuels your body welcomes with the greatest alacrity. It's the raw material your body finds it easiest to convert into the fuel your cells burn—glucose.[13] So when you crave a sweet and when you indulge that desire in moderation, you are doing your metabolism a favor. You are boosting your biochemical efficiency. And if you are a peasant or an urban serf in the England of the eighteenth century, you will be among the first humans on the planet to have this luxurious superfuel available daily.

Exploration and consolidation, the fission-fusion strategy, generated material miracles in the lives of an entire continent of humans—the Europeans. The deeds of Christopher Columbus the explorer and of the monocroppers—some of them good, and some of them morally repulsive—gunned the evolutionary search engine and upped the torque of the secular genesis machine. For hundreds of millions of humans, exploration and consolidation literally made life sweet.

But that's not all. The horses bred by Henry VIII's squirearchy changed the face of Europe. Horses bred for strength and bred in quantity relieved workmen of many a horrid chore and literally horse-powered the rise of a new British economy. And thanks to obsessive genetic tinkering, new meatier breeds of cattle and pigs upped the protein in the average Englishman's meals. Then there was the realm of metaphor. Obsessive bovine genetic tweaking produced the unofficial English symbol, the roast beef.

* * *

Roast beef, too—like cups of coffee and of tea—was more than it may have seemed. It was a civilization, mood, and mind advancer. Beef is loaded with two key psychoactive chemicals: the cognitive enhancer choline and the friendship maker and alliance creator cholecystokinin.

Horses, beef rumps, coffee, sugar, and tea—along with magazines, newspapers, and the leisure that came from getting rich on breeding and monocropping—gave the grandsons and great-granddaughters of Britain's plantation owners a terrific opportunity: to invent the Western system's protest biz. These kids with silver plantation spoons in their mouths founded a vigorous movement to abolish slavery. John Newton, the son of a trade ship captain, made his fortune captaining a slave ship and carting human prey from Sierra Leone to the New World.[14] When his ship seemed on the verge of being ripped apart by a storm off the African coast, he got religion, returned home, wrote a song called "Amazing Grace," and helped found the antislavery movement. The progeny of plantation-owning families joined him, raised their voices high, used the new mass-communication technologies—magazines, newspapers, and an old networker that Christopher Columbus and Martin Luther had employed, pamphlets—and for the first time on this earth outlawed slavery.

Four hundred and fifty years down the line, the plantation system's legacy of industrial crop production would do something ironic. It would put the cloth of kings—cotton t-shirts—on the backs (and fronts) of even the poorest Africans, the very people who'd been left behind when their neighbors had been kidnapped as slaves.

* * *

Remember the *Caulobacter* bacteria that were born with propulsive tails? Remember how they rebelled against their parents and developed a distaste for the delicacies on which their mothers fed? Remember how those young tail-snappers raced away from home and staked out a brand-new territory of their own? Freud says we humans all eat our parents. We set ourselves apart from them. We build a barrier. We leave a gulf, a generation gap, a trench. This kind of space making is *lateral inhibition*. And lateral inhibition, space making, is an underlying pattern of the fission-fusion strategy. Could this gulf generation, this space making, help explain the protest industry? I suspect the answer is yes.

But lateral inhibition doesn't make protest industries inevitable. In 1592, the Muslim emperor Akbar tried to start a free speech movement in India. He promoted what he called *Din-i Ilahi*, a religion of tolerance toward Hindus, Jains, Parsis, Buddhists, and Christians. He also promoted *sulh-i kull*, "universal peace."[15] Despite his wealth and power, Akbar attracted only nineteen supporters to his movement. And when Akbar died, Orthodox Muslims called his movement heretical and crushed it utterly.[16]

The truth is that only one civilization has made its protestors a permanent fixture, a full-fledged industry. Just one civilization has made the protest industry a multigenerational institution. Just one civilization has given the protest industry the tools of mass media and mass marketing. Just one has made the protest industry a permanent key to the genius of the beast. And that civilization is the civilization of the West.[17]

58

TRANSUBSTANTIATION

Making Spirit Flesh—
The Tale of the Piano

How a daydream and a Medici built a soul extender.

Daydreams, fantasies, wild ideas, imaginary hungers waiting to be filled—these are the raw stuff of the Western way of life—they are secular paths to making spirit flesh, to bringing dreams from darkness into the light, to making wishes (corny as this may sound) literally come true. Fantasies and daydreams are the tools with which we make genies in a bottle in our time.

After the mythical Orpheus and the slightly less mythical David strummed their instruments and played their songs, more and more of the multitudes wished that they, too, could strum and sing along. Many a human had new tunes going through her head but no way to take those tunes and play them for her friends, much less to awe an audience of strangers or an entire world with them.

Lutes and harps are difficult things to play. They tear the skin of those who try to pluck their strings and leave calluses the size of lima beans. But in 1709, in the days of the great plantations, in the days of the first coffee shops, and in the days of the early journalism of Daniel Defoe, those who peddled novelties had learned how to make things work with gears and springs—mechanical dolls that danced and clocks that paraded small armies of figurines. These were useless delights, consumerism at its height. Or were they?

Italy had lost its chokehold over trade with Asia. Its wealth was slowly going down the tubes. But the Italians hadn't lost their imaginations. And super-rich Italians hadn't lost their knack for piling up the lira.[1]

Bartolomeo Cristofori, a musical instrument maker, moved from Padua to Florence to pursue a ridiculously indulgent and seemingly time-wasting idea he'd dreamed up with Prince Ferdinando de' Medici, a musician and high-tech mechanical gizmo collector from one of Europe's richest families. Cristofori and de' Medici imagined an instrument that would use a keyboard and a clever system of levers to ding a hammer on the strings of a full-sized harp hidden in a curvaceous wooden box. With this absurd invention, Cristofori the instrument maker and de' Medici the rich patron made playing the tunes in your head a breeze for millions (though not for clumsy folks like me). They created the piano.[2]

A century later, the piano infected the dreams of Mozart and Beethoven, moving the use of piano chords to whole new levels of lusciousness, passion, and intricacy. Not to mention giving birth to opera, the sonata, and the symphony.

The nineteenth-century German philosopher Georg Hegel wrote in his nearly incomprehensible *Philosophy of History* that history is a struggle of spirit to become flesh.[3] And in a sense he's right. History is a struggle of fantasy to become reality. It's a struggle of what's imaginable to become material. It's a struggle of the implicit to become explicit. It's a struggle of vision's wine and wafer to become the real world's blood and flesh. It's an evolutionary struggle for a secular equivalent of what the Catholic Church calls transubstantiation.

Inventing the piano in the seventeenth century was transubstantiation in one of its most amazing forms. Music lovers had dreamed only in the harmonies of chorused human voices or in the tinny chords of instruments like the lute. Then the piano came along and gave them chords that rumbled, thundered, tumbled, and soared.[4] Those chords were what led to the dreams of a five-year-old Mozart. Beethoven would never have had fields, storms, and the anger of the heavens and earth rolling in rich harmonies through his head without the chords of Mozart and something more, without the invention of the orchestra by the Italian opera composer Monteverdi and without the orchestra's radical upgrade as a "symphonic" proposition complete with woodwind, horn, percussion, and string sections by Johann Stamitz in eighteenth-century Germany.

The piano triggered two hundred years of cultural and musical innovation that turned the keyboard into a tool of transformation for mere mortals with clever fingertips. The piano went from the precious instrument of a few aristocrats and their court musicians to an instrument of the masses. The piano made it possible for an African American bordello entertainer in New Orleans named Jelly Roll Morton to play a form of music that danced through his head to a very different beat than others had known. A syncopated rhythm that was named for the disreputable red-light neighborhood, the neighborhood of despised sex workers, in which it had been born. The new music of Jelly Roll Morton's rhythm would be named with the slang term for the forbidden stuff with which van Leeuwenhoek had helped start modern science—sperm. The slang term was "jizz." And the music was called jazz.

The invention of the piano opened new horizons of sound for another Afro-American kid, this one from Pittsburgh, Errol Garner, for another black kid from Red Bank, New Jersey, William Basie (who later dubbed himself a count), for a white Jew from LA, Dave Brubeck, for Keith Jarrett, Irving Berlin, George Gershwin, and for one of my friends in high school, a hood, a gangster with greased black hair and a black leather jacket, a social reject among his middle-class schoolmates. The invention of the piano allowed these disadvantaged kids to play jazz improvisations—the music of the angels rolling itself together on the spot spontaneously in their minds.

The piano took what would have boiled silently in their spirit as a vapor and gave it presence in the hard world of sound and air and ears, in the world of friends sitting next to them on the piano bench, and of folks seated on couches in the living room. The piano eventually gave the rippling sounds in their souls presence in the solid world of audiences that often mounted to the tens of millions. The piano carried the thrill of creation from one mind to another. It freed spirit bursting to be real. It carried the shiver of the soul, like an Olympic torch through shimmying air from mind to mind. The piano carried spirit on vinyl, radio waves, CDs, and mp3s from continent to continent, from one generation to the next, on so on down the line.

The piano generated household miracles for those of little means.

Basie and Brubeck were sons of musical families. Dave Brubeck's grandmother, father, uncles, and three brothers were professional musicians. Basie's father was a trumpeter and Basie was taught to play piano by his grandmother. But Basie's family was not rich in gold and silver. It was only rich in melody. Jazz pianist Errol Garner taught himself to play piano at the age of three and never learned to read music but was a melodic genius. He, too, came from a family of modest means. And Dave Brubeck was playing at the age of seven. Largely because he had a piano in his living room to play.[5] These were poor kids uplifted by a toy a rich man had invented to indulge his fantasies. These were kids whose parents had only modest paychecks. Yet those parents played instruments that most of the generations of humans on this planet couldn't even conceive. The powers of the piano were beyond our ability to dream for our first 2.5 million years or so on this planet. Yet the modern equivalent of peasants had these musical magic makers—trumpets and pianos. And the sons and daughters of the poor made music that raised the level of imagining for hundreds of millions of other human beings.

Many a social critic feels that mass production and industrialism has given us just one thing—the monstrous waste called consumerism. It's time to apply the second law of science: look at things right under your nose as if you've never seen them before, then proceed from there. Music is not materialism. It's spirit on the fly.

* * *

Even the piano was just one step on the escalator of complexity, one new level on the infrastructure of fantasy. Until 1985 or so, kids who wanted to make music had to slave over a piano, a violin, or a guitar for years to learn a bunch of finger skills—chords, melody, walking bass—their "chops." At his adopted home in the valley over the Hollywood Hills from Los Angeles, Rick Davies, co-leader of the British band Supertramp, told me about the seventeen years it had taken him to master the piano's keys. And he agonized over the fact that a new technology had just made it possible for a new band, Simple Minds, to replace his group as the new superstars getting all the attention on his record company's Hollywood lot. Why?

While Davies was learning his piano chops in Swindon, England, there were other kids with good musical imaginations who heard new tunes in their heads but had no way to share them. I was one of those kids back in Buffalo, New York, in the 1950s, walking the two miles to my piano teacher's house with new jazz riffs running through my brain but no way to play them. The piano teacher loved to discuss philosophy with me, but winced every time my fingertips stumbled over the keys. At the end of the summer he confessed that in his opinion, my hands would never obey me in the ways that led to music making.

But in 1985 or so, something astounding happened. Samplers, synthesizers, and small-sized MIDI-equipped computers materialized at affordable prices in local music stores in Japan, Europe, England, and the United States. Imagination was liberated. Suddenly kids could leap beyond the handicaps of their fingertips and focus on the power of their fantasies, on the power of their emotions to cook up new musical treats. And one of the groups that took advantage of the new technology was Glasgow's Simple Minds, the group that had snatched the center of the attention storm from Supertramp on the A&M Records lot in Hollywood.

The mind should never be restrained by muscular clumsiness. The spirit should never be shackled by the awkwardness of fingers and of vocal chords. The materialization of inexpensive electronic music machines was one more step in the evolution Hegel described in his *Philosophy of History*—the escalating entry of Spirit into the realm of possibility, the manifestation of imagination in the material cosmos and in the alteration of reality. But there are many steps left to go.

* * *

Raising the level of fantasy is one key to the Western system. Dreaming strange new dreams is one of the by-products of what seems like a foolish waste of money on novelty and trivial things. From new dreams come new realities. New facts, new gadgets, new social tools, new catchphrases, new clichés, new poetry, new plays, new Nobel Prize–winning theories. The material products of yesterday's dreams ratchet up the level of today's spiritual hankerings. From new lusts come new peaks of the impossible turned to easy walking for you and me.

What's the moral of the saga of the piano? If you want to make money and to earn it, too, if you want to contribute to humanity, dream your ass off, sell your visions, then make your fantasies come true. You will radically upgrade the dreams of those who come after you.

59

HARNESSING THE MASS IQ

Offering an Ego-Stake—
Linnaeus and His Viral Meme

Starting the science craze. The profits of sharing the credit.

In a system driven by emotion, money isn't the biggest motivator. Ego is. And ego in moderation is not the negative we're told it is. It's a driver of social evolution, a hormone of social growth. It's a flotation device that keeps us moving toward our aspirations. It's a way of making what we're striving for a part of our identity. So when you want to motivate, offer folks an ego-stake.

Here's one way to do it. African American kids in the inner city during the late twentieth century were often threatened with ridicule and pummeled if they tried to get good grades. Their friends hounded them for being traitors to their race.

So imagine that you've come up with a slam-bang idea—a campaign to give a status boost to slum-dwelling kids who are willing to take the risk and try for good grades. You've sold the notion to a superstar—let's say Lionel Richie (who it was, in my case). Now you have to sell it to a bunch of folks you've never met before—the executives at Coca-Cola, whose money you'll need to pull off the plan. What does Coke need you for, you have to ask yourself. To let the black community know that Coke does more than take profits out of the ghetto. That Coke tries to give something back.

When you're alone in your office or are driving home, lay out your step-by-step game plan for the education campaign. Set up a meeting with Coke. Fly to Atlanta and get to the Coca-Cola conference room before anyone else arrives. Have your pen and pad or TRS-101, your prehistoric laptop, handy.

Introduce yourself to each Coke person as he or she comes through the door. Then write down his or her name. Remember, much of capitalism hinges on identity needs. Names count.

Deliver your basic idea, then shut up. Let the Coke VP chairing the meeting go around the room to hear each executive's point of view. Keep notes on which opinion belongs to whom and on the overlap between that opinion and your detailed strategy. Once everyone has been heard, an eerie silence will descend upon the room. Each person has staked out his turf, his emotional real estate, but no one is quite sure where to go next. Now's the time for you to break the awkward pall.

Start with one of the ideas that fits your game plan's steps. But give the credit to Heather, who presented a fair semblance of it. Then paraphrase the things that Derek said, showing how his suggestions build the base for your game plan's step two. Give Derek the credit for fathering this clever addition to the blueprint. Keep building your plan step by step, giving credit generously. Don't mangle what others said or misrepresent them. The truth at any price, including the price of your life. But do give credit to each person who has presented a part of your master plan. Wrap it all up in one big bundle—a simplified summary of the next steps to take—before you finish speaking, and hand it as a gift to each person whose notions dovetailed with the plan.

If you hog all the credit for your brainstorm, others will resent you and shoot you down. Give others the ego-boost and the ego-food. Then each will have an ego-stake in making the plan succeed. The educational initiative with Coke, by the way, was called the Lionel Richie SuperStudent program. It reached roughly a million kids. We did another with Pepsi and Kool and the Gang called It's Kool to Stay in School. This one was designed to reward kids with good attendance records. It did its job too, in roughly thirty-two cities. Both these crusades were executed by the Howard Bloom Organization, Ltd., the PR firm I founded in the entertainment industry as a science project. As an expedition into mass behavior.

Giving away an ego-stake has an illustrious pedigree. In 1732, a most unlikely man, the son of a Swedish pastor, used the principle of the ego-stake to stoke the mass IQ of a new worldwide community. Carolus Linnaeus set off from Sweden to Lapland to study a freshly fashionable idea, a concept that would have made many a begonia blush—the notion that flowers were sexual organs, clues to the bawdy lives of plants. While finding a hundred new species—all of them very flirtatious—Linnaeus invented a new scheme for naming plants and animals—a new taxonomy.

How do you get your fellow humans excited about one of the most yawn-producing projects of all time—laying out plants and animals in a new family tree? You let each person who discovers a new plant give it two Latin names. Plus a third that makes the finder's name a part of the plant from here until eternity. For example, if your name is Michel Begon and you fund two scientists to travel to the West Indies just to catalog new species of plants, one of those new plants may be named the *begon*ia.

With this simple ego-stake—this viral marketing technique—Linnaeus joined specimen gathering with the care and feeding of identity. And he gave a huge boost to the evolutionary search engine, to the secular genesis machine. Tens of thousands of gentlemen from a brand-new subculture—the middle class—threw their Sundays and vacations into hunting down new plants. Each wanted to immortalize his (or her) name. Each wanted a piece of Linnaeus's clever ego-bait.

One of the new enthusiasts for nature was a Lichfield, England, country doctor who not only spent his weekends rummaging the hills, the dales, and the woods for new specimens to bear his name, but who also noticed a pattern emerging from Linnaeus's categories, and from its connection to an avalanche of new data and new theory tumbling from the study of the earth's rocks, its layers, its folds, and its outcrops—geology.

The nature lover was Erasmus Darwin. The pattern he spotted and wrote a book about in 1795 was called evolution. Erasmus Darwin's grandson Charles would take the notion further sixty years down the line and would ride it to the heights of fame, subsidizing his efforts with money made from reverse-engineering the cups and saucers first encountered in the China trade. Charles Darwin's wife was from England's greatest Chinese porcelain retro-engineering family—she was a Wedgwood.

Linnaeus and his generosity in giving ego-stakes away helped boost a one-hundred-year-old new enterprise that would prove vital to the Western system—science. Harnessing the middle-class mass mind to the scientific enterprise would pay off for commerce and for the Western system big-time in the nineteenth century and the twentieth—giving birth to the electrical industry, to new medicines, to chemical fertilizers that would more than quadruple plant yields,[1] to new materials like aluminum and plastic, and to vast improvements in the Western way of life.

Is giving ego-stakes away a form of manipulation? Yes. Every time you try to influence another human being, you're trying to change his mind. I'm trying to influence yours right now. Someday you may well try to change mine. That's manipulation. When is manipulation good and when is it bad? Any good thing in overdose is a poison. That's true for ego. It's also true for influence. If you're trying to scam and steal, changing someone else's mind can be despicable. But if you're trying to advance something you know is right and true, then ego-stakes are vital. Even if you're wrong—which you will be a good slice of the time—you have to give it a try. Mistakes are a risk of courage. But work as hard as you can to avoid leading others astray.

The giveaway of ego-stakes in the seventeenth and eighteenth century went big-time in a different realm than that of intellect alone. While Carolus Linnaeus was hunting plant specimens in Lapland, ego-stakes were building something radically new in business—the corporation.

60

CREATIVE CAPITALISM VS. CRIMINAL CAPITALISM

The Rise of Stocks and Bonds

It's 1720 and selling shares is a hot new notion. But when overhype leads to ruin, will the Western system punish its abusers?

There's a potent ethical commandment hidden in the depths and folds of the capitalist system. Every dollar that you bring in comes courtesy of another human being. Every dollar represents an obligation to a person whom you serve. If you want to bring in millions, then commit your passions to uplifting, upgrading, consoling, delighting, and caring for the bodies and the souls of millions. If billions is what you seek, it's billions of humans you must serve.

If you fail to care for those who sustain you, if you fail to benefit and nurture not just bosses and shareholders but the masses who actually pay you, then the capitalist system may get its revenge. It may well punish you.

Go to your workplace every day carrying those you serve within you. Feel their needs and champion them in every meeting you attend. Why? Because the feel of working for something larger than yourself will sustain you. The knowledge that others need you will maintain and lift you.

Remember when you were sixteen years old and wanted to work with other people so you could make a difference in their lives?

Remember when you were idealistic and wanted to find something bigger than yourself that you could commit to? Every day at work is a day of opportunity. Every day at your desk demands that you see beyond the numbers, the spreadsheets, the PowerPoints and the e-mails. It demands that you see the people far outside your building and that you please them, empower them, or raise them. Even when you don't see it, you are what you wanted to be—committed to something higher than yourself—committed to making a difference in the lives of far more fellow humans than you ever imagined.

Don't let the symbols of stock values and profit margins fool you. Croesus created a wireless connector when he minted a new symbol and gave us money. That symbol was a long-distance synapser between humans with feelings, humans with emotions and humans with crude body needs just like yours and mine. You have to realize a bottom line—no matter what business you're in, you're in the business of nurturing souls. Even if you sell toilet paper, imagine a world without toilet tissue and you'll realize that you're in the business of giving new powers to your fellow human beings.

If you're lucky, like Bartolomeo Cristofori, the maker of the first piano, you'll give other humans brand-new powers. You'll turn soul stuff, wishes, and desires into realities. You are the genie in the bottle. See what you can do to please.

If you fail to heed this capitalist imperative, the system may well punish you. In 1710, overseas trade was raging. And the bright men of the coffeehouses found a way to give the average citizen an ego-stake. Housewives, coachmen, and shopkeepers put their savings into *shares* in joint-stock companies like John Law's Mississippi Company in Paris and the South Sea Company in England. Both ventures looked promising. Both tried hard to deliver the riches that they promised when they enticed frenzied crowds from all over Europe to come and plonk their money down.

Both failed. John Law, head of the Parisian-Mississippi venture, fled France on a false passport and felt lucky to escape with his life. The heads of the South Sea Company—some of the most august gentlemen in England—were sent to the Tower of London. Law and the South Sea officers were deprived of more than just their freedoms and their funds. They were deprived of their dignity, their identity, their status, and their sense of meaning. This kind of shame can torture your emotions to the point of suicide. From the days of the first trading companies in the 1600s to the self-inflicted death of Enron's vice chairman J. Clifford Baxter during the Enron scandal in 2002[1]— suicide is the way in which some of the formerly high and mighty have escaped torture on the punishment racks of the capitalist system.

But here's the problem. In the South Sea Bubble of 1720 and in many a later boom, fraudulent traders like 2009's seventy-billion-dollar Ponzi schemer Bernie Madoff took advantage of the sizzle and sold stock in companies that didn't exist, then pocketed the money.[2] And some got away with it. The Western system punishes only its super-high-profile abusers. What should be done about the rest? And what is abuse in a system that nurtures dreamers?

Speculators and entrepreneurs are not criminals. They are like sperm. They are packets of capital with propulsive tails. They transport money and energy to niches they hope will pay off big. But only one in a billion sperm succeeds in hitting pay dirt—the egg. Speculators and entrepreneurs are society's gambles. And it takes many a failing bet to win a game. Some fantasies that the speculators and entrepreneurs chase succeed in touching a nerve. Some fantasies fail to connect, or even fail to materialize.

But isn't every honest guess worth a gamble? Isn't every would-be transubstantiater a benefactor even if she fails? Wasn't she trying to open a genuine new opportunity, a genuine new good or service that would augment you and me? What's the difference between users and abusers?

Any good thing in overdose is a poison. Those who take your money with no intention of creating more than an illusion are thieves. Theft and deception are crimes no matter where and how they happen. They are crimes when they take the form of muggings. They are crimes in the halls of corporations. They are crimes against an obligation—the ethical imperative of capitalism, the messianic imperative—the demand that you use the best in you, your passions and your aspirations, to rise above the daily grind, to see and feel your audience, your market, your multitude whose souls and imaginations you are trying to feed, and who, if you listen carefully, are calling to you.

61

SELF-REVELATION AND SECULAR SALVATION

Rousseau Goes to the Bone

A Frenchman's dive in the darkness of mind reveals
a bit of what we really sell.

This is a story I used to tell my clients who wanted to establish enduring careers in the entertainment industry. It helped some of them find their way to superstardom. It gave them something vital to offer, something vital that their audience would always need. It may help you understand what you really have to offer, too.

In the 1700s, as the publishing industry roared, as literacy soared, and as the contagious new addiction to the virtual reality of books took hold, there was a huge demand for stories of the lives of the great.

People like to pay attention to what other humans are paying attention to. Greatness is a wave of mass attention carried from one generation to the next.

In the midst of this fever for biography, a grubby little man in France with a tongue so savage it could sever his relationships even to his dearest friends, a man who had taken each of the five babies he had sired by his common-law wife and had consigned them to death in an orphanage, told those who would still listen that he was planning to pen a biography. What great man did he have in mind portraying? his friends wanted to know. They were appalled to hear the answer: me.

You're not great, they said. Scarcely anyone has heard of you. Why would anyone bother to buy the biography of an unknown? Because, said the grubby, obnoxious little man, anything I find in me that's never been expressed before, any darkness, any light, I'll find on behalf of the multitudes, I'll find on behalf of humanity. When I find words for feelings that have never been expressed before, I'll find feelings deep in everyone and set those feelings free.

So this nasty excuse for a human looked deep inside himself, found angers, hopes, woes, and new words for emotions others recognized in their souls. And the public loved it. Why? Because of deep-identity needs. The literate masses saw in the paragraphs of this man's biography the very feelings they had felt for ages but had never known how to say. They received validation of the feelings they thought that they alone experienced, the ones that made them suspect that they were borderline insane.

This bitter little man had told his readers that they weren't crazed isolates filled with feelings no human should ever have. They were no longer alone, they were in good company. In fact, they were a movement. We call that movement the Age of Reason, the Age of Light, the Enlightenment. And we call it the rise of personal emotions, the rise of Romanticism.[1]

By baring his soul, Jean-Jacques Rousseau gave all of our souls room to breathe. He also produced a book—*The Confessions*—that is still in print roughly 250 years after it was written.[2] Rousseau's book sold because it gave its readers a sense of belonging and self-expression. It expanded their sense of understanding. It added to their feeling of identity.[3] This is emotional capitalism. This is the recognition of something crucial and profoundly human—we live in an identity economy. We pay and are paid in the hidden currency of attention. We buy not just to feed, clothe, and shelter. We buy to show that we belong. And we buy to get others' eyes to swivel our way. We buy to move up on the social ladder. We buy to attract admiration. And we buy to get a sense of control. We buy to build our sense of identity. Identity is the need that Rousseau fed mightily.

Try Rousseau's approach and you may find the same thing works for you. Take your emotions to work with you. Dig for the feelings that no one dares express. Then make a product or a service that satisfies your silent desires. You may well make a fortune.

62

WORDS REMAKE REALITY

Adam Smith Sparks Economics

The power of a theory that gets it wrong.

New ways of seeing lead to new ways of being. Words are our lenses, our looking glasses, and our tools. They can refashion more than the way we see. Like so many of the tools of emotional capitalism, words can reshape reality.

The year of words that would change the Western world was 1776. Men and women had been upgrading themselves via capital since the introduction of the first stone tool roughly 2.5 million years ago. Europeans had been building civilizations, watching with despair as they fell, then building new ones in their places since the days of the Trojan War in roughly 1193 BCE.[1] Europeans had also invented step by step new forms of intercontinental trade since Vasco da Gama's first voyage to India in 1492.

Westerners had been trading shares in commercial ventures since their grandfathers' and grandmothers' days in roughly 1710. And something new was putting in its first hint of an appearance—mass production. In 1776 the first automatic looms were up and running. Early steam engines were pumping water from mines. And in England there arose one of the firsts of its kind—a factory.

Rousseau had found new words for human misery and triumph, but few had found a way of putting in words what traders, stock speculators, manufacturers, and business empire makers do. Then came a mass infusion of new words.

A professor of moral philosophy at the University of Glasgow had toured Europe and become fascinated with a new form of business, a futuristic way of manufacturing—a pin factory. Another Englishman was obsessed with history books in Greek and Latin. He'd toured Europe and had trained his obsessions on Rome. And a group of amateur philosophers in Britain's North American colonies had gathered in Philadelphia to try something that had not been done since roughly 600 BCE. They'd attempted to invent a new form of government.

In 1776 Adam Smith, the Scottish moral philosophy professor published *The Wealth of Nations*, a book that kicked off a new discipline, economics. Smith's book gave dignity and an identity boost to trade and industry. It proposed a new concept Smith had seen at work in the pin factory—the division of labor. And Smith's *Wealth of Nations* endowed us with a new word, "capital."[2]

Meanwhile in 1776, the English bibliomaniac with the history obsession—Edward Gibbon—gave us *The Decline and Fall of the Roman Empire*, a three-book series whose title would forever shake our sense of the solidity of nations. Behind every rise, it made us foresee a fall. And in 1776 the amateur philosophers in the British colonies of North America gave us a Declaration of Independence that redefined what it meant to be human. "All Men are created equal," said this short, bold document, "they are endowed by their Creator with certain unalienable Rights." And "among these are Life, Liberty and the Pursuit of Happiness."[3]

Words have power. The wealth and business practices of the West had reshaped the Western way of thinking. Now new thinkers looked at what the Western system had achieved and used the publishing industry to give us all a new sense of a future and a new sense of identity.

It was a brilliant start at helping us see what we were, what we are, and what we must become. But it was by no means the end.

We still haven't found or given words to most of what we do in the Western system. Or we've used words that have misled us: "capitalism is theft," "lean and mean," "corporate greed," "the superstar CEO," "exploitation of workers," and even "consumerism." We've looked with scorn at the miracles we've made.

What's worse, some CEOs *have* perverted the system by

exploiting others—by becoming new robber barons without making the contributions the real nineteenth-century robber barons made. They've followed the motto "greed is good." In the fall of 2008, while the US government was spending seven trillion dollars to bail out the nation's faltering financial giants, the CEOs of those failing companies gave themselves a total bonus package of forty billion dollars.[4] That's enough money to buy modest houses for 160,000 people, including you and me. It's enough money to buy every house in Kansas City. Forty billion dollars to reward CEOs for failure.

Words are power. Osama bin Laden knows that. He has words for murder, words that give it dignity and meaning. But his world—the Arab world—is suffering. Says the United Nations Development Programme's *Arab Human Development Report*, "Arab countries have not developed as quickly as comparable nations in other regions. Indeed, more than half of Arab women are illiterate; the region's infant mortality rate is twice as high as in Latin America and the Caribbean. Over the past 20 years, income growth per capita has also been extremely low."[5] The Arab world has lost its commercial zest. It's lost the power of entrepreneurial enterprise that gave Muhammad—the husband of a fabulously wealthy businesswoman in the transport trade—the luxury of communing with his God in a cave and emerging with "the one true message" of divinity to mankind.

Capitalism needs what Adam Smith, Jean-Jacques Rousseau, and Martin Luther gave to you and me. It needs new words as its mirror. It needs new words to find its identity. It needs new words as elevators, goal makers, and guides. It needs new words to steer it toward its future. It needs new words with which to see its destiny.

X

AN EXTRA TWENTY YEARS
OF LIFE?

63

THE SOAP REVOLUTION, MASS MARKETING, AND THE RISE OF ADVERTISING

Messianic Capitalism

How bathing and laundering boosted your life span and mine.

Roast the meat of your choice outdoors over an open flame and let the fat soak into the ashes. If the rain comes the next day and seeps this mixture into the ground, a month or a year down the line you may dig down and find, well, to tell you the truth, nobody quite knew what.

Some thought the waxy residue might be good for whatever ailed you and sold it as expensive medicine. Others learned how to make translucent nuggets of the stuff, hung them from gold pendants, and sold them as jewels.

Then came three unlikely breakthroughs: the invention of the plantation, Richard Arkwright's creation of a top-secret British economic weapon, the mechanized weaving machine (anyone who tried to smuggle plans for the mechanized loom out of England was clapped in jail), and the production of steam engines that could turn the mass-loom's gears. The result was what seemed like an infinite bolt of the cloth of kings, that hideously expensive miracle fabric that formerly came from only India—cotton. The price of cotton goods went from astronomical to affordable in a mere thirty years.

The citizens of India, who'd supplied the world's cotton rarities ever since the heyday of ancient Rome, now waited to buy cotton goods until British vessels sailed—or later steamed—into port with the latest shipment. British cotton was cheaper in Bombay than the handmade goods from the weavers down the road. The miracle of Richard Arkwright's factories and of Henry VIII's squires' monocropping had driven the luxury fabric's price down, down, down.

Which meant that Euro-citizens who had worn wool-based felt that couldn't be laundered, who had taken baths only twice a year,[1] and who had kept close company with the insects living in their clothes could now afford a change of shirts, pants, hosiery, and dresses. Among other things, clean clothes meant you could dip into a tub more often and bathe your dirt-encrusted skin.

But what would these bathers use to wash off the grime? And what means aside from soaking, boiling, beating, stirring, pounding, and paddling would they employ to launder their new extra drawerfuls of cotton garments?

Two French chemists—Nicholas Leblanc and Michel Eugene Chevreul—perfected a process for making inexpensive artificial ash, soda ash, in 1804.[2] Then they combined the ash with vegetable fats. New industrialists harnessed steam engines to duplicate this task and began the mass manufacture of inexpensive soap. But having made it, they needed to sell it.[3]

First came celebrity endorsements. The empress Josephine, Napoleon's first wife, bucked the tide of dirt in 1800 and bathed daily, using something new and exotic, manufactured soap.[4] Fourteen years later, England's biggest male superstar chimed in and backed the notion of a bath a day. What's more, he took one himself. That superstar was the Duke of Wellington, the man who had defeated Josephine's by-then-ex-husband Napoleon at Waterloo.[5] In future generations, Thomas J. Barratt of Pears' Soap in England would sign up the biggest female superstar of the century, Queen Victoria, and her husband, Prince Albert, as well, getting the firm of A&F Pears' appointed the official supplier of toilet soap to the king and queen.[6] But in 1825, long before Barratt appeared on the scene, the aristocracy was already imitating its celebrities. Ladies and gentlemen showed how different they were from the "barbarians" of the lower class by washing, bathing, and taking liberal advantage of the new rituals associated with "soap and water."[7]

Next came face-to-face salesmanship.[8] The new industrialized soap companies sold their goods through a small army of what the law called "commercial travelers," "drummers," "salesmen," and "solicitors of trade."[9] The sales process was called "talking soap." Here's how it worked. If you were a drummer, you'd buy a big cake of soap from one of the new mass producers. You'd whittle it into bars, put on your own label, and sell the bars for twenty-five cents each.

Ann Anderson, the author of *Snake Oil, Hustlers and Hambones: The American Medicine Show*, tells the tale of a soap drummer named Charlie White, "who sold White's White Wonder Soap." White, says Anderson, "found himself broke and stranded in Omaha. All he had were his white broadcloth suit, his hat, a gross of soap, and ten dollars."[10] How did White squeeze out of this pickle? He explained his technique like this:

> I paid three dollars to get the suit cleaned and the hat blocked. I paid two dollars for a license. I hired a white horse, hitched to a cream colored buck-board, paying three dollars in advance. I drove to a street corner and gave a boy the last two dollars to get me a pitcher of water—and the 'flash' of that two dollars for a simple errand sold over three gross of that soap, at twenty-five cents each, in two hours. That night I ordered another two gross of soap.[11]

White had pulled in a total of $108 in an afternoon. That's $2,464.75 in 2007 dollars.

What did White mean by the phrase "the 'flash' of that two dollars?" Whipping out two dollars and spending it on a two-penny bit of gofering made White look like a rich man on a splurge. It was the equivalent of ostentatiously tipping someone with a thousand-dollar bill today. White knew the power of the Matthew effect—"To he who hath it shall be given."

In the 1880s and 1890s, soap went high-tech. It plunged into the mass media. Thanks to coffeehouses and steam-driven rotary printing presses, magazines and newspapers were flourishing.[12] So the makers of soap bought space on the printed page and almost single-handedly invented the advertising industry.[13]

The phrase "soap opera" gives an idea of how effectively they spread their efforts to promote the use of what they cranked out. The soap makers pounded away with advertising, marketing, and promotion year after year after year. What you hear once, you usually forget. What you hear twenty times or more sticks in your memory. The promotional campaign for soap stuck in the public mind. It stuck so successfully that it changed the West's perceptions and, more important, the West's daily routine. By the mid-nineteenth century, when the soap marketing campaign was roughly forty years old, it was commonly said that you could measure the advancement of a civilization by the number of times its citizens washed per day. Converting heathens to Western ways was now called cleansing "the great unwashed."[14]

Everyone ignored the fact that even Western aristocrats had been encrusted in dirt just a generation or two ago. They forgot that a daring noble at the court of Louis XIV in France had been seated next to a great beauty, had noticed dirt under her nails, and had indelicately mentioned it. The gorgeous noblewoman was reported to have said, "If you think that's bad, you should see my feet."[15]

Did advertising bleed the poor and force an addled citizenry to addict itself to phony needs? Did the consumerism pushed by the capitalists of soap pervert the Western soul and cripple its critical faculties?

No. In fact, there was a sudden spurt in rates of health and in the length of life.[16] Folks could look forward to an extra twenty years before their meeting with the grim reaper. This massive boost in wellness and longevity just happened to coincide with the cotton revolution and the promotionally aided craze for washing regularly.[17] Was cotton and soap this longevity breakthrough's cause? Along with improvements in the quality of the water supply, the odds are good that the answer is yes.

A system worth living and dying for has to uplift the poor and the oppressed. That's what capitalism does best. That's exactly what cotton, soap, and advertising—three tools in the kit of the Western system—did in the nineteenth century. But keep one thing in mind. A tool can be used to elevate or it can be used to kill. A hammer can be used to build a house or it can be used to bludgeon another human being. And any good thing in overdose can be a poison. Both use and abuse would be the fate of promotion and advertising.

64

A BOURGEOIS LUXURY

Rebellion—Karl Marx and His Manifesto

How soap helped the son of a German lawyer hang
a poisoned portrait in the gallery of mass mind.

Back to the Western system's counterbalance—the protest industry
that Isaiah started—the business that sold:

- rebellion
- identity for those who feel outside the mainstream
- critiques of the system's failings
- and the hormonal drug of righteous indignation—the crack and
  cocaine of the intellectual elite.

Karl Marx was the son of a wealthy lawyer in Germany. But Marx,
like many a kid, was a misfit with zero social competence who got his
sense of identity via complaint.

On a trip through England, Marx caught a glimpse of the
"brickies"—child and teenage laborers who toiled in pits, digging out
clay and turning it into the Mesopotamian mud invention—bricks.
These kids were dirty as could be. Marx, on the other hand, was a child
of the promotional campaign of the soap industry. Without realizing it,
he had come to equate cleanliness with dignity. And without realizing
it, Marx was imposing his middle-class views on everyone around him.

That included the unwashed workers in the brickyards and the mills of Birmingham. Marx thought these laborers were being degraded. Would he have felt that way two generations earlier when he, like most others, would have seldom washed his face?

Marx took Adam Smith's term, "capital," and distorted it. Adam Smith said "capital" was all the extra stuff you and I make and store so we can trade it with each other someday.[1] Marx said capital was something far more specialized. It consisted of a single ingredient—stored labor. There was only one ingredient worth paying for in soap, in a cotton shirt, in a wagon, in a barge, in a canal, or in a monumental building like the British Library, where Marx did most of his research and his writing. That was the hard labor that the proletarians, the muscle workers, put in.

Would Marx have said that only the printers, binders, and papermakers contribute to the value of a book?[2] And that authors and thinkers like Marx contribute nothing? If Marx stuck with his labor theory of value, the answer would almost certainly have been yes.[3] Here's the closest Marx comes to a definitive statement on the economic value of brainwork: "Skilled labour counts only as simple labour intensified . . . for simplicity's sake, we shall henceforth account every kind of labour to be unskilled, simple labour."[4] So much for labor's nature as stored vision and stored persistence. To Marx, stored vision and stored persistence literally had no "value."

More important, Marx's theory said unequivocally that greed would always drive capitalists to suck the blood from the working class. Capitalists could only prosper, said Marx, if they kept wages so low that the weekly trickle of cash barely covered the cost of food, clothing, and housing. Others said there was a serious flaw in Marx's theory that only sweat labor, only muscular labor, makes a product valuable. But the real disproof came not from a critic but from reality. From Marx's day until 2008, the pay a low-wage London laborer received in a year went from the equivalent of $5,112.12 in 2007 dollars to $38,750.84.[5] And that wage covered far more than just food, clothes, and shelter. It bought cars, TVs, cell phones, and designer jeans. It bought the gifts of the identity business. And if you were lucky, it bought the products of the health industry. But this mushrooming of the average paycheck wouldn't happen until after Marx had been long gone. Meanwhile, Marx stuck to his labor theory of value until his death.

Karl Marx deceived us. He left out the meat and fed us artificial sweets. Capital is stored vision, stored courage, stored persistence, and stored persuasion. Capital is stored imagination, stored daring, stored promotion, stored advertising, and stored social organization. Capital *is* stored fantasy. Capital is even, brace yourself, stored ego. Without those elements Karl Marx would not have had the soap that gave him the privilege of a bourgeois status symbol—a clean face. Without the vigorous promotion of soap, Marx might never have struggled for the dignity of those with dirty hands and dirty foreheads, chins, and cheeks.

With his self-published pamphlets, Marx was a small-time entrepreneur. With his visions, with his freelance work for the *New York Herald*, and with his cantankerous self-promotion, Karl Marx was the ultimate bourgeois, the ultimate middle-class kid, the fearless small-scale capitalist.

Marx left us a hideous legacy. He left us new ideas and new ways of perceiving things. All that is positive. But he promoted the notion that capitalists are vampires driven by greed. Meanwhile, no one produced a countercreed. No one—not even Adam Smith—told capitalists the obligations of their state—to uplift, console, empower, and delight. To give identity and validate. To elevate their fellow human beings. No one told capitalists that profits come from prophetic leadership. No one told them that their task is messianic.

* * *

Marx's notion that capitalism equals greed and its update in the iconic 1987 movie *Wall Street* as a simple slogan—"greed is good"[6]—went hog wild in the CEO culture of the early twenty-first century. The average CEO of a Standard and Poor's Five Hundred company gave himself a compensation package worth a hefty $14.2 million a year in 2007.[7] That's not much if you're buying Rolls Royces. It will get you only 30 Rolls Royce Phantoms. But it's enough to buy 645 Toyota Priuses. And that's just the *average* top five hundred CEOs. Angelo Mozilo, chairman and CEO of Countrywide Financial Corp., gave himself a hefty $48 million a year.[8] For what? For running a company widely blamed for the great mortgage crisis of 2008. More specifically, for running that company, Countrywide Financial, into the ground. Other masters of greed also gave themselves monstrous salaries for deep-sixing their companies. James E. Cayne, the chairman and CEO at the helm of Bear Stearns when it sank, gave himself $40,004,315.[9] Kerry Killinger, the chief executive officer of Washington Mutual, was far more modest. He gave himself a mere $14,364,883 for collapsing his company.[10] Then there was John J. Mack, CEO and chairman of Morgan Stanley, a company that miraculously stayed afloat. But in 2007, Morgan Stanley experienced its first loss in seventy-two years under Mack's reign. What did Mack pay himself for what appeared to be some whopping errors in judgment? $41,790,854.[11]

Some in the capitalist system have been encouraged to believe that bleeding a company to build personal wealth is a part of the capitalist creed. It's not. It's the very opposite of the capitalist imperative. You get paid for what you build. You get paid by those you save.

65

WHAT SEDUCTION
WAS MARX SELLING?

How the "workers' movement" of Marx fills three
middle-class needs.

Marx used words, research, and reason to justify an extreme of emotion—a need to distance himself from his lawyer father. A need to get attention and identity by battling against the others in his niche, the middle class. A need to kick loose from the normal path to success. A need to rebel against those who find a human yearning and fill it. A need to kick in the teeth of the ambitious, achieving, and contributing bourgeoisie. A need to stretch into the emptiness of possibility and to set himself apart. A need kindled by an evolutionary search strategy, the fission-fusion strategy—stretch out, explore, then consolidate, digest.

But what began as Marx's noble attempt to reform society ended as a social sickness, a cultural pathology. In the long run, Marx and his followers' promotional skills would kill forty million people in the Soviet Union[1] and another forty million in Mao Zedong's China.[2]

In the long run, Marx's idealistic words and fantasies would kill almost as many as soap and cotton saved.

What made Marx's misleading doctrines so magnetic? Here's a guess. Marx felt his audience in his chest—a capitalist necessity. He resonated to the frequency of a brand-new generation—a cadre of kids given their freedoms by the cotton revolution, the soap invasion, magazines, newspapers, and steam-driven mass production. A cadre of kids whose brains were subtly shaped by technologies no human had previously seen. Marx gave meaning and identity to middle-class kids from Asia, Europe, and the Americas, kids who needed to establish their identity and to get attention by rebelling. Kids who needed rebellion, differentiation, and validation as much as Marx did.

By leading with his passions, Marx struck a responsive chord in generation after generation. He liberated those driven by a need they can't explain, driven to battle the "establishment" of their day, driven to topple the culture of their parents' generation. The Marxist experiments of the twenty-first century should have ended Marxism. To repeat, they killed over eighty million citizens. They tormented the poor, they did not uplift them.

But Marx's message sells and sells. Marxist rebels are fighting today in Colombia, Mexico, the Philippines, and Sri Lanka.[3] In Nepal the Maoist Marxist party put down its weapons, swept the country's elections in 2008, and dropped the Maoist label in 2009.[4] And in Cyprus, the Marxist "Akel" party won the island's presidential election in February 2008.[5] Meanwhile, London has an active Stalin Society.[6] Sweden has a communist party—the Kommunistika Partiet—that runs candidates in elections and occasionally wins. And in Russia many an intellectual wants Stalin to return from the dead. Marx is, alas, alive and kicking in the twenty-first century.

Marx was one of the most successful self-promoters, idea sellers, and identity merchandisers the Industrial Revolution has ever produced. His vision was stupendous. His persistence was amazing. He stuck with the promotion of his concepts for over forty years. And his message had that essential of all good services and products—a powerfully passionate core.

What was Marx's secret? Going with his feelings. Selling his emotions. And being tuned—not to the masses—but to the kids of the middle class.

Marxism has been discredited by the atrocities of Stalin, Pol Pot, and Mao. So why does it still continue to sell? Because it's a status symbol, a badge of identity, a source of warmth, a source of group belonging, and a source of camaraderie.

Marxism fits the bioplan of human needs. It fits the taxonomy of desire. Marxism says to kids who feel alienated, who fear that they can't make it in their parents' competitive world, that they are high above all others. They are the leaders of the poor. They are the saviors of the workers. They are the vanguard—the elite commanders—of a people they actually dislike.

We all need to be saviors. But Marxism is a murderous invention. It represents the worst that marketing can achieve. It is an irony of ironies. Marxism is based on tuned empathy—empathy tuned to an audience of the well-to-do. But Marxism is manipulative . . . it claims it's tuned to the problems of the poor. It's not! Marxism is based on mass promotion, mass media, and the tools of the capitalist system. Marxism feeds in the niche of the protest industry. Marxism provides identity, a feeling of solidarity, a feeling of community, and a deep sense of meaning. It also provides a means of self-deception. Marxism is the ultimate commercial product of the capitalism of passion. But not all capitalism is messianic. Some of it is criminal, even when it's well intentioned. Some capitalism robs, steals, cheats, intimidates, and even murders.

Marxism is ironically what it claims to hate the most. Marxism is criminal capitalism in disguise. Marxism has proven that it has the power to crush hundreds of millions of human lives.

66

THE HEART HAS REASONS
REASON NEVER KNOWS

Saturated Intuition and the
Culture Lift of P. T. Barnum

What Marx got wrong and Barnum got right.

Who was the real savior, Karl Marx or P. T. Barnum? Who sold bunkum and who sold liberation?

From 1836 to 1891, P. T. Barnum was the most flamboyant impresario of his age.[1] He almost single-handedly created modern pop culture. He was the mass promoter of the circus, the creator of the mass-media sideshow, the man who invented the modern transport-based touring entertainment industry, and the man who created the phrase "show business."[2] What, if anything, did this mere showman contribute to the evolutionary search engine and to the secular genesis machine?

P. T. Barnum was born July 5, 1810, in Bethel, Connecticut, at a time when you had to make the trip from Connecticut into Manhattan by sailing vessel, a trip that could take five days if the winds were against you.[3] Today that trip is an easy morning commute.

Barnum's family was in the shopkeeping business, and young Phineas T. was fascinated by the shrewdness of the farmers and the peddlers who came to the store and bargained to sell their goods, putting up one perceptual front after another to ratchet up the price of what they were selling or to drive down the cost of what they were buying. This was the New England "Yankee shrewdness" that became infamous throughout the still-young United States.

As a boy Phineas T. Barnum was also impressed by another bit of perceptual flimflam, the practical joke. He was particularly impressed by a practical joke his parents and his grandfather played on him from the time he was old enough to understand English. His grandfather, father, and mother told him year after year that when he attained his majority, Phineas would inherit a wondrous piece of real estate, a paradise on earth that would make him rich—Ivy Island. When he was ten, Phineas T. Barnum decided to go out and see this marvelous piece of land for himself. As he approached his destination, he was forced to wade. He was stung by wasps, and, floundering through the bog, became covered with mud. Finally he crossed over a stream using a felled tree "to the centre of my domain." What did he discover? "I saw nothing," he writes in one of his many autobiographies, "but a few stunted ivies and straggling trees. The truth flashed upon me. I had been the laughing stock of the family and neighborhood for years. My valuable 'Ivy Island' was an almost inaccessible, worthless bit of barren land."

Not only that, but the few inhabitants of the place did not exactly welcome him. "While I stood deploring my sudden downfall, a huge black snake (one of my tenants) approached me with an upraised head. I gave one shriek and rushed for the bridge."[4]

One other insight made an impression: the fact that sharp haggling and practical jokes were among the few forms of amusement available thanks to the Blue Laws of Connecticut's churchmen, its Calvinists, who frowned upon earthly pleasures. Or, to put it in Barnum's words, "the old Puritans had laws so rigid that it was said, 'they fined a man for kissing his wife on Sunday.'"[5] These lessons in perception were Phineas T. Barnum's imprinting moments, his passion points. And they would determine the course of his life.

When Barnum was fifteen years old, his father died and the job of supporting his mother and five sisters fell on his shoulders. He ran a store, followed in his grandfather's footsteps by starting a state-wide lottery, and became the publisher of a weekly newspaper, the *Herald of Freedom*, in nearby Danbury, Connecticut. There he was jailed twice for uncovering the hypocrisy of the local church fathers.

When lotteries—one of Barnum's main income producers—were banned in Connecticut, Barnum moved to New York and went into the very field the church fathers of Bethel, Connecticut, had frowned on most—entertainment.

When he first reached New York, Phineas T. was confused. "The business for which I was destined, and, I believe, made," he writes in his autobiography, "had not yet come to me; or rather I had not found that I was to cater for that insatiate want of human nature—the love of amusement; that I was to make a sensation."[6] However, he wrote, "I had long fancied that I could succeed if I could only get my hold of a public exhibition."[7] And get his hold of a public exhibition he did.

The year was 1835. Slavery was still alive and kicking. So was the form of black entertainment for white audiences called "minstrelsy."[8] A Kentucky gentleman with very little talent for showmanship had tried to make money by touring a pipe-smoking elderly black woman who was blind and almost entirely paralyzed. His hook? This shrunken, forty-nine-pound "living mummy" with unclipped, claw-like fingernails claimed that she'd been George Washington's nanny and that she was 161 years old. That made her a double-whammy, both George Washington's nurse and the oldest woman in the world. This angle, true or not (and it wasn't) wasn't making the novice promoter money. So he sold his ownership and rights to display the woman to Barnum.[9] Barnum arranged to debut Joice Heth with a two-and-a-half-week engagement smack dab in the middle of the mass-media capital of America, at New York's fashionable Niblo's Garden. Barnum then had a lawyer with a literary flair put together a pamphlet on Heth, a pamphlet that sold for six cents. And in his own words, Barnum "flooded the city with 'posters.'"[10] Then he set up one of the world's first press briefings. He arranged a private interview between Heth and New York's key newspaper editors.[11] An interview at which "Aunt Joice" told how she'd been an African princess, how she'd been captured and sold as a slave, how she'd been converted to Christianity, and how she'd raised the apple of her eye, little George Washington. The result was a storm of newspaper coverage. And the age-stiffened and wrinkled woman was a smash.[12]

Then Barnum took Heth out on the road for seven months. Despite her paralysis and her wizened appearance, she was a nonstop talker, spurting stories of "Little George" and of the Redcoats.[13] And when she didn't talk, she sang. Not familiar tunes, but hymns so obscure that only preachers seemed to know them. Barnum says that the Niblo's Gardens engagement alone paid fifteen hundred dollars a week. That's almost thirty thousand dollars a week in 2007 money.

Joice Heth—the oldest woman on the planet—died a year after Barnum acquired the right to work with her. Barnum had her autopsied to prove her age. But the examination proved that she was probably a mere eighty years old. How did Barnum recover? For one thing, he stopped flitting from one business to another. He stuck with "exhibitions." He said many years later, "Engage in one kind of business only, and stick to it faithfully until you succeed, or until you conclude to abandon it. A constant hammering on one nail will generally drive it home at last, so that it can be clinched."[14] Barnum was learning the value of persistence. So he put a variety act, "Barnum's Grand Scientific and Musical Theater," on the road. Then came the crash of 1837 and three years of hard times. Until Barnum bought a failing museum on Broadway and Ann Street in Lower Manhattan.

How did P. T. Barnum take Scudder's American Museum out of its nosedive? By redefining the "cabinet of curiosities" business. By attracting attention. By startling passersby. By revolutionizing three new things—advertising, promotion, and publicity. And by putting the dazzle in razzle-dazzle. Barnum hired a brass band to play on the American Museum's balcony. He installed a red, yellow, and blue spinning light high on the museum's building to light the sky and earth alike at night. And, on the American Museum building's crown, he set up the first Drummond Lights New York had ever seen, nexttech limelights, lighthouse-style superbeacons that could be seen for fifty miles.[15] Barnum decorated the building with roughly thirty flags, festooned the place in bunting and put new-tech illuminated "transparencies" seven feet high and two feet wide on the facade—the first of these transparencies New Yorkers had ever seen.[16] These colorful see-through illustrations pictured, in Barnum's words,

> The largest man in the world, Mr. Hale, being eight feet high, and weighing five hundred and eight pounds; Miss Eliza Simpson, the giantess, also eight feet high and weighing three hundred and thirty-seven pounds, the fairy queen 'Titania,' twenty four inches in height.

And much, much more. Barnum installed a garden for strollers on the roof, scheduled daily hot-air balloon flights from the roof garden, and added "'curiosities', including albinos, giants, midgets, 'fat boys', jugglers, magicians, 'exotic women', detailed models of cities and famous battles, and eventually a menagerie of animals."[17] Barnum renamed the place the American Museum, and, crash or not, the American Museum took off.

In 1842 Barnum went further in his invention of two new things: the techniques of modern publicity and a new kind of superstardom. He got word of an astonishingly undersized four-year-old—a boy who was a mere two feet one inch tall and weighed a stunningly low fifteen pounds.[18] This seriously abbreviated little lad was Charles Stratton, and he lived in Barnum's stomping grounds, Bridgeport, Connecticut. Barnum met Stratton and his parents, was impressed with the child's talents, upped his attention-grabbing capacity by renaming him General Tom Thumb, concocted an exotic biography far stranger than the real thing, and taught Stratton to sing, dance, and do imitations of the famous. Barnum also taught Stratton the manners with which to hobnob with the rich and famous. Like Joice Heth, Charles Stratton was physically challenged but he had a magical ability. He could entertain.

Then Barnum used the press briefing once again. He set up meetings between General Tom Thumb and the editors of New York's leading newspapers, all six of them, and set General Tom Thumb on the path to fame.[19] General Tom Thumb would go on to perform for Queen Victoria in England, to tour the world, to accumulate a not-so-small fortune, and to become one of P. T. Barnum's closest friends.

Barnum had set a pattern. Find the bounds of the normal and exceed them. Give people the tallest, the shortest, the fattest, the thinnest, the fastest, and the slowest. Feed the human need for oddity. Fill the human need for novelty.

Steven Johnson and James Flynn contend that pop culture boosts the IQ of the masses. Johnson and Flynn argue that pop culture expands perceptions by steadily climbing the escalator of complexity. If Johnson and Flynn are right, P. T. Barnum did more to grow the mass perception–stretching capacity of pop culture than any single human in history.

In the next forty-nine years, Barnum would bring to North America and Europe: the world's tallest woman, Anna Swan, who he said was eight feet tall but was, in fact, a mere seven feet five and a half inches. George Washington Morrison "Commodore" Nutt, the world's shortest man, who made the minuscule General Tom Thumb look like a giant. "The Missing Link," also known as "Zip the Pin-head"—William Henry Johnson—an American Barnum claimed came from Africa and whom he dressed up in a monkey suit. And Jumbo the elephant, the first elephant most Americans had ever seen.

Jumbo the elephant toured like a president in his own custom-built railroad car and eventually died trying to save a baby elephant that had wandered onto the railroad tracks adjacent to the seventeen acres surrounding Barnum's deliberately peculiar home in Bridgeport, Connecticut—Iranistan.[20] What was an elephant doing on Barnum's personal property? The railroad track near Barnum's home went from New Haven to New York City and carried a horde of potential customers. So Barnum grabbed the attention of the railroad commuters and put excitement in their day. He built his home in Persian style and had elephants pulling plows on a portion of its grounds. Said Barnum, "Newspaper reporters came from far and near, and wrote glowing accounts of the elephantine performances."[21]

Barnum had done it once again. He'd "blown your mind." And that explosion of the mind would contribute more to the group IQ than Barnum could conceive. But that's not all. Barnum also pioneered one of America's most profitable exports, entertainment. Writes University of Michigan historian James W. Cook, "During the early 1870s, Barnum had acts in Cuba, Egypt, Hawaii, Australia, New Zealand, Malaysia, Japan, China, and the East Indies." But this was a two-way street. Says Cook, "By the 1880s, his circus agent sent back animals, peoples, and artifacts from virtually every corner of the globe."[22] Barnum had become an antenna of the evolutionary search engine.

But even this was by no means the end of the emotional products Barnum created. In the days before the Civil War, the public's lust for novelty was restrained, repressed, chained up, and disdained. All entertainment had to be "moral." All had to pass the standards set by a tyrannical mass of hellfire-breathing clergy. What's worse, those who put on shows looked down their noses at the average citizen, the riffraff in the street. They didn't want "the lower half million" anywhere near their strictly for aristocrats theaters.[23]

Barnum got a kick out of tickling the tastes and pleasures of that "lower half million."[24] He gave them the Fejee Mermaid (half woman, half fish); a Wild Buffalo Hunt a mere hop across the Hudson River from Manhattan in Hoboken, New Jersey; ostriches, elands, zebras, reindeer; a hippodrome with chariot races and steeple chases; and the Siamese twins Chang and Eng.[25] He sent a super-modern transport device, a steamship, to Africa to bring home the biggest menagerie of exotic animals North Americans had ever seen. His goal was to create amazement—something he did by tapping his own ability to be amazed. Commentator after commentator saw that Barnum was doing something important—he was making theater democratic. But he was doing more—he was performing a strange form of education, a broadening of horizons.

Barnum delivered mood elevation and secular salvation—a lift out of the troubles of the everyday. He provided entertainment to rural folk who had been isolated in their farms and cabins. The touring circuit he pioneered opened the way to the Chautauqua lectures, the touring events in which great thinkers, reformers, and politicians like William Jennings Bryant and Maud Ballington Booth, the "Little Mother of Prisons," carried their messages to the nooks and crannies of the United States.[26] Barnum's autobiography—all eleven rewrites and updates—became the Bible of the new advertising business.[27] His ingenious use of a trainload of freight cars to transport a bigger-than-life, put-it-together-on-the-spot extravaganza changed military strategy. His dioramas, georamas, and cycloramas showed city dwellers and country farmers huge scenes of places like the Rocky Mountains and the Grand Canyon, exotic locations they'd never be able to visit in their lives. And his American concert tour of the Swedish super-songstress Jenny Lind sent lower- and middle-class audiences into raptures over music by classical masters like Rossini.

Finally, Barnum created "The Greatest Show On Earth," the modern circus. He premiered what he at first called the "Great Traveling World's Fair" in Brooklyn in 1871 to a crowd of ten thousand. Then, in 1873, he gave the spectacle a more ambitious name, "P. T. Barnum's Great Traveling World's Fair Consisting of Museum, Menagerie, Caravan, Hippodrome, Gallery of Statuary and Fine Arts, Polytechnic Institute, Zoological Garden, and 100,000 Curiosities, Combined with Dan Costello's, Sig. Sebastian's and Mr. D'Atelie's Grand Triple Equestrian and Hippodromatic Exposition."[28] Why this mind-blasting title? Because Barnum put the extravaganza on the road in what eventually became seventy railroad cars, expanded it from one ring to three, and gave us the cliché "a three-ring circus." Eventually Barnum slimmed down the title to "P. T. Barnum's New and Greatest Show on Earth."

The result? P. T. Barnum erected a landmark on the mindmap of the year. He made the arrival of the circus one of the two most-awaited days in America. The other was Christmas.[29] That may be why President James A. Garfield called P. T. Barnum "the Kris Kringle of America."[30] Barnum brought an entire society the gift of surprise.

Along the way, Barnum invented the beauty contest and the baby contest. And he pioneered the use of posters, display ads, classified ads, and window signs to raise the level of excitement. Says author James Trager, eighty-two million people came to Barnum's American Museum in Lower Manhattan in just sixteen years.[31] Eighty-two million at a time when the entire population of the United States was only thirty-one million.[32]

* * *

Like Marx, Barnum wanted social change. As a showman, he fought to free the slaves, putting performances of the abolition-promoting play *Uncle Tom's Cabin* on the road. *Uncle Tom's Cabin* and another Barnum production on race issues, *The Octoroon*,[33] helped motivate the North and symbolized what the Union forces stood for in the Civil War. In fact, Barnum did so much to promote the Northern cause in the Civil War that when a group of Southern saboteurs came to New York intent on fire-bombing the city, the only amusement house they targeted (and succeeded in burning to the ground) was Barnum's American Museum.

What other contributions did this mere showman produce? Says the *Readers' Companion to American History*, "Barnum laid claim to delivering his compatriots from the 'thrall' of puritanism and in so doing became a cultural hero of the first importance."[34]

And Barnum encouraged disbelief. He wanted people to see through the Yankee shrewdness that had flummoxed him as a kid in his father's store and that had sent him on a wild goose chase to "Ivy Island" when his grandfather had tricked him with a practical joke. He wanted Americans to see through what he called the "humbugs," the preachers who used religion to choke others' lives.

The best services to humanity are often those that stretch the boundaries of what we know, feel, desire, and perceive in ways we can't express with words. Marx was a master of words. In fact, he was so good at their use that he could employ persuasive words to mislead. He suffered from an overdose of reason. Barnum was a master of intuition and gut feeling—of desires for which words are utterly lacking. He was a virtuoso at feeling out the bounds of current perception and inventing ways to go just beyond their limits. That ability is what leads to surprise, astonishment, and awe. Surprise, astonishment, and awe, three emotions that could lift you as if you were a discouraged worker bee.

Barnum had a very different handle on the human condition than did Marx. Barnum and Marx both used their own emotions to see inside the hearts of others. But Barnum's goal was to delight the masses, not to incite them. Barnum and Marx were both masters of tuned empathy. But Marx's empathy was for his peers. For other kids of the middle class. Marx gave the children of the bourgeoisie a false veneer with which to claim power over the underclasses.

Barnum did something very different. He actually loved the masses. And he did more than Marx to open "the democratic audience's" critical faculties. Barnum not only warned you against sharp traders—he told you he was one of them. Then he winked an eye and left you guessing. He helped you see how much the "truth" deceived, how much what you felt was right might be wrong, even though it was what you wanted to believe.

P. T. Barnum's most famous epigram was, "There's a sucker born every minute." There's just one hitch. Barnum never said it.[35] In fact, his attitude was the opposite. He said, "Every man's occupation should be beneficial to his fellow-man as well as profitable to himself. All else is vanity and folly." "We cannot all see alike," he wrote, "but we can all do good."[36] The suckers weren't the people who bought tickets to see Barnum's extremes of the human—and animal—condition; they were the folks who swallowed the idea that Barnum had ever called his audience suckers. Among the biggest suckers of all were the folks who bought into the bloodbath-producing, militant interpretation of Karl Marx's "Workers, throw off your chains."

Barnum offered things of solid emotional value. He simply couldn't explain in slick and easy words just what those feelings were and why they counted, despite the fact that Barnum wrote thirteen books. Barnum left a legacy of wonder, fantasy, and excitement. A hundred years after Barnum's escapades, children still dreamed of running away to join the circus and of living a free life among the lions and the clowns.[37] Upgrade the level of fantasy, and somewhere down the line you upgrade the level of reality.

The public paid Barnum with both gratitude and money, money it felt he had richly earned. One newspaper said, "It is universally conceded that . . . Barnum is the greatest man . . . in the world."[38] As for cash and profit, Barnum's insistence on championing the rights of Marx's proletariat to "the pursuit of happiness" grossed him $712,161 for just one of his projects—his national tour of "the Swedish nightingale," the aforementioned singing wonder Jenny Lind. That's over a quarter of a billion dollars in today's money.

In two new fields, positive psychology and behavioral economics, there's a word for what Barnum did.[39] It's a core term in the work of Nobel Prize winner in Economics and Princeton University psychologist Daniel Kahneman. The magic word? *Hedonics*—the science of generating happiness.[40]

Why did the American public pay hefty sums to Barnum and pay them happily? Barnum fed the most difficult thing to feed in us—the quality of wonder. He fed the emotions that evade all rationality. The emotions beyond the power of words to express. He legitimized fun and play—unseen sharpeners of instincts, of intuition, and of minds. And he added a new emotion to the palette of human feelings. "Fun" was a word that only assumed its modern meaning after Barnum came along.

The early twentieth-century British intellectual G. K. Chesterton said that American humor, the sort of humor P. T. Barnum specialized in, was "wild, [and] sky-breaking." That's what P. T. Barnum's challenges to reason, to the emotions, and to the boundaries of the possible achieved. Sky-breaking exercise for the infrastructure of habit. Sky-breaking challenges to the imagination. Sky-breaking contributions to the infrastructure of fantasy.

And when Barnum stretched the boundaries of wonder, he did something more. He acted as an antenna of the evolutionary search engine. He proved that wonder, astonishment, novelty, terror, and delight are some of the most important expanders of mass mind. He hauled new realms of the possible into focus by straining the limits of credulity and breaking the laws of impossibility. And there's a very good chance that Barnum kicked off the Flynn effect in the nineteenth century—upping the IQ of the average man and woman in the street. And upping the group IQ of Western society.

Where did Barnum stand on the first law of science, the truth at any price, including the price of your life? His commitment was to an emotional truth. Said author and Congregationalist theologian Lyman T. Abbott, who was a child when Barnum was doing his sky-breaking, "If from any entertainment which he provided the spectators had gone away disappointed, he would have regarded the entertainment as a failure, no matter what money it brought him."[41] That's messianic capitalism.

* * *

Which contributes more to the human enterprise—amazement, joy, and fascination, or the bloodbath of revolutions and the rise of new tyrannies? Which was the ultimate sucker master, P. T. Barnum or Karl Marx?

To which would you rather give power over your destiny?

THE ART OF FINDING WEALTH IN TOXIC WASTE PART II

The Kitchen Sink, Indoor Plumbing, and the Crapper

How the Western system's wonder team—government, business, explorers, and the protest industry—stopped the waves of mass deaths in the cities.

> Out of clutter, find simplicity.
> From discord, find harmony.
> In the middle of difficulty, lies opportunity.
> —Albert Einstein[1]

Evolution favors those who turn garbage and catastrophe into uplift and opportunity. So does the Western system.

Follow the threads of your disgust. Look at what's under your nose as if you've never seen it before, then proceed from there. Don't turn your nose up at the offensive unless it robs, assaults, or destroys your fellow human beings. If a need sends others away shuddering, it's a mark of their blindness to a necessary facet of their own humanity. It's a lack of their compassion and of their curiosity. And it's a challenge to your creativity.

Be messianic. Where others see disaster, see a chance to save your fellow humans. Where others see a toxic waste, find opportunity.

The Western system's wonder team—government, the protest industry, explorers, and business—stopped the waves of mass death in the cities. In 1835 New York was hit by a fire. Five hundred and thirty buildings were destroyed. The public water supply wasn't equipped to put out the flames.

So New Yorkers corrected this problem by building one of the first public water systems to take advantage of underground piping, massive reservoirs, and the pumping power of steam engines. But New York overlooked the problem of sewage. So did the town fathers of virtually every other city on earth.

If urban myth has got it right, at roughly nine o'clock on a Sunday evening, October 8, 1871, Mrs. O'Leary's cow kicked over a lantern in her barn in Chicago. Myth or not, the fact remains that the city of Chicago literally went up in flames. Citizens were helpless to fight the fire because—despite a highly publicized new twin-tunnel water system—they, like the New Yorkers thirty-six years earlier, lacked the water needed to drown the inferno's rage.

In 1885 Chicago was hit by yet another disaster—a massive rainstorm, a storm so torrential that the waters of Lake Michigan (where the city dumped its sewage) backed up for miles. The floods spread behind the town and spilled fecal material—raw shit—into its water supplies. The result? Ninety thousand people, over ten percent of Chicago's population, died of cholera and of other water-borne disease.[2] Fate, it seemed, was trying to teach the city on the lake a crazy lesson.

Until then, major cities had taken only partial steps to invent and put in place modern water supply and drainage systems. Taking the next big leap and offering every social class running water, flushing toilets, private bathrooms, and sinks was way beyond the realm of possibility. Plumbing, in fact, wasn't even recognized as a specialized trade.

All that changed thanks to the great disasters in New York and Chicago. From toilets, faucets, municipal sewage systems, and water supply systems, many a fortune would eventually be made. The new water systems would also supply the water that would up the availability of "soap and water" to all.

But that was not the end of fortunes and small miracles built from toxic waste. Thomas Crapper was an Englishman who had remarkable success in marketing a new invention to the British public.[3] Did Crapper invent the crapper? Probably not. But whether he created it or merely popularized it, the fact remains that his name continues to reign. Why? Because doughboys—American soldiers—came home from Europe after World War I having seen Crapper's name on British toilet tanks every time they flushed. Most of these fine young American lads had been accustomed to relieving themselves in holes in the ground in outhouses back in the United States. To these soldiers, the flush toilet was a miraculous new luxury.

From indoor plumbing and the mass merchandising of the toilet comes my ability to type these words to you for hours at a time without being forced to leave the Brooklyn Tea Lounge in which I labor over my laptop. From indoor plumbing comes the fact that I do not have to trek to an outhouse to relieve myself. From indoor plumbing, you, too have achieved the luxury of reading these words without concern about putting on your coat and trudging out through the winter snow to find a quiet place to urinate and defecate. Plumbing has changed my human capabilities—and yours. It's given us the luxury to concentrate.

Plumbing has also become one of the most lucrative small-business industries in the Western world.

We view too many attributes of our humanity as disgusting, debasing, and taboo, as things we simply should not talk about or see. But when humans have a lust, an embarrassment, an excrescence, an obstacle, or a fantasy, it's crucial that we open our eyes and take heed.

* * *

Running water was just the beginning. There was many a Western miracle yet to come. For an example, look right under your nose, this time at the contents of your breakfast bowl.

68

WHEN SELFISHNESS
IS A BLESSING

Kellogg and His Flakes

Use your feelings. Use your needs. How a personal
obsession and a kitchen accident changed America's
morning meal.

Your best guide to the needs of others is your own desires. Get out
among your customers—or among those you'd like to serve
who've never patronized your company. Feel out their needs by
finding the cravings inside of you, the desires that you share with
them. Pay attention to your obsessions. That's where you'll find
your guide to the next transformation or minor gift that you can
bring to others' lives.

John Harvey Kellogg and his brother, Will Keith, grew up in the
rural Michigan of the 1850s and 1860s in a family riddled with health
problems.[1] But their biggest health problem seemed to be conventional medicine. When John Harvey was a toddler, his eyes became so
badly inflamed that he was nearly blind. The family called in the local
doctor, who applied a "fly blister" to John Harvey's neck. The result
was what's called an iatrogenic malady, a "fearful sore." What's *iatrogenic* mean? An illness caused by your doctor. But the neighborhood
doctor did not give up on John Harvey. When the fly blister didn't
work, he tried another approach, megadosing the three-year-old with
calomel. Another iatrogenic blunder. In the words of one of John

Harvey's biographers, the calomel "caused John's tongue to swell until it protruded from his mouth."[2] Not a pretty sight.

Meanwhile, John Harvey's mother had come down with coughing spells and soon was coughing blood. The local doctor came to the rescue once again, advising two remedies. Sprinkling resin over hot coals and inhaling the fumes. And bleeding. The coughing went on for four years. When John Harvey was only three, his mother died of a massive lung hemorrhage. But medical matters didn't get any better when John Harvey Kellogg's father remarried. John Harvey's new stepmother, Ann, gave birth to a baby girl who came down with breathing problems. Enter the local doctor once again. Ann felt that the medical miracle worker should treat her sick daughter's lungs. Instead, the doctor explained that the baby had worms and gave her antiworm treatments. The result? The baby died.

Ann was heartbroken and furious. She had an autopsy performed on the infant in front of her eyes. The dissection showed no worms anywhere in sight. But it did reveal something else—badly inflamed lungs. That was it. The Kellogg family had had it with conventional medicine. Instead, the family subscribed to a publication on water cures, the *Water Cure Journal*, and converted to a religion that insisted on exercise, natural remedies, sanitation, and a healthy diet— Seventh-Day Adventism.[3] And the Kelloggs went further. They moved from Jackson, Michigan, to Battle Creek—a town of Seventh-Day Adventist health and religion fetishists—to protect the remaining family members from the Grim Reaper. That's where Will Keith Kellogg was born. In the coming years, John Harvey Kellogg and Will Keith Kellogg's parents would help make Battle Creek a capital of Seventh-Day Adventism.

The upshot of all these medical blunders and wanderings? The Kellogg brothers were obsessed with health. John Harvey signed up with two founders of Battle Creek's flourishing Seventh-Day Adventist movement, James and Ellen White, because the Whites promised that through diet and strict practices they could drive the devil of disease away. The Whites sent John Harvey Kellogg to medical school then put John Harvey and Will Keith to work in their Health Reform Institute. The Kelloggs renamed the place the Battle Creek Sanitarium and turned it into a high-priced health spa for the rich and famous of an entire nation.[4]

The Kellogg brothers and the Whites believed fervently that by eating temperately you could overcome not only death but you could banish something more immediate—the stomachache—or, as physicians to the rich called it, dyspepsia. Temperate eating meant no alcohol, no caffeine, no meat, and lots of something Michigan had in abundance—grain.

The problem was this—how do you make three meals of grain a day without driving the taste buds of your high-end guests nuts? The Kelloggs crushed grains, milled them, boiled them, put them through rollers, toasted them, roasted them, and tried more tricks than you can shake a sickle at. In the process, they invented peanut butter and granola. But that didn't satisfy them. And it didn't stop their edible experiments.

One day the Kellogg boys grew careless. They left a batch of boiled wheat dough out in their kitchen/lab overnight. The next morning it was still edible, but theoretically not worth baking. It was stale. The better part of creativity comes from turning trash into treasure—from seeing the potential value in what others would throw away. The brothers ran the day-old dough through rollers, toasted the thin sheet that emerged, and discovered that the wheat crinkled and broke apart in flakes. Eventually they tried the same trick with corn dough, thus creating Kellogg's Corn Flakes. Chalk up one small victory for the way the taste buds drive us to try new things. Chalk up one nano-victory for the evolutionary search engine and the secular genesis machine.

The Kelloggs had made a new product to satisfy their own obsessions—their need to defend against their family's personal nemesis—their need to erect a dietary fortress against an unjust and early death. By zeroing in on their emotional needs, John Harvey and Will Keith Kellogg served the needs of others by the hundreds of millions. This is one secret to tuned empathy. This is one secret to using your own emotions to understand the emotional needs and delights of your fellow human beings.

You have to tune your personal passions to those of the people you serve. That means stepping out of your private plane, out of your limo, or out of your office and getting to know the people you need to please. The Kelloggs learned instantly that the flakes they'd made were tasty. They were the first to taste them. Testing to see if their taste mirrored the taste of others wasn't difficult. They had a captive audience—the clients in their sanitariums' dining rooms—eaters who spooned in the new flakes with great delight. What's more, it is said that the sanitarium's guests frequently wrote back asking for packets of the flakes to eat at home.

But here's where the fine line between following your passions and tuning to the needs of others comes in.

John Kellogg, the doctor, was a rigid health dogmatist. He refused to add any ingredients that didn't fit his dietetic philosophy. Will Keith was less of a zealot. He wanted to make a cereal that would pleasure the palate of nonbelievers, too. So Will added a forbidden ingredient: sugar. John wouldn't hear of such heresy. The two brothers split. Each started his own company. Lateral inhibition turned one gamble-on-the-new into two. The firm of the brother who followed his passions but who had mercy on the taste buds of his customers—Will Kellogg—is the one that brings us Kellogg's Corn Flakes.

What happened to John Harvey Kellogg's more rigidly health-oriented approach? It also found a market, but in a very different subculture. It became the cornerstone for much of today's health and organic food industry. After the brothers split, John Harvey's four companies created or pioneered the modern vegetarian diet, vegetarian meat substitutes, soy milk, soybean flour, soy biscuits for diabetics, yoghurt, acidophilus, soy acidophilus cheese, soy gluten bread, and even the health food magazine.[5] Add in writing more than twenty-six popular books about illness, health, nutrition, exercise, massage, and more, and you have quite a legacy.

Each Kellogg brother found that his taste resonated to the frequency of a different buyer in a different niche. By separating to follow their own instincts, the two Kellogg brothers pleased two different publics at one time.

* * *

Follow your passions, but go out among the multitudes so you can tune your own obsessions to their frequency. This is one secret to tuned empathy.

XI

IS GOSSIP GOOD
FOR YOUR HEALTH?

69

HOW ROCKEFELLER
LIT THE NIGHT

How a brutal capitalist added six years to the average life.

John David Rockefeller pulled off a minor miracle at the end of the nineteenth century. There were more than fifteen hundred land-owners, entrepreneurs, and speculators duking it out for their pieces of turf in the production and sales of a strange black goop that welled from the ground in distant corners of Pennsylvania.[1] The stuff was primarily employed for medicine (in the form we know of as petro-leum jelly, Vaseline) and for paving floors and steps (in slabs of asphalt). But all that was about to change.

J. D. Rockefeller's father was a con man who'd abandoned his strict Baptist wife, then showed up for an occasional visit every year or two.[2] What's worse, Rockefeller's dad had married another woman twenty-five years younger than he and had become a bigamist when young John David was only six.[3]

Imprinting moments—passion points—generally hit around the age of five. They are moments that make an indelible stamp on your personality, your goals, and your dreams. Literally an indelible stamp on the neural setup of your brain.[4] Remember how when J. H. Kellogg was only three, death took his mother? And remember how escaping the Grim Reaper became a lifelong focus of Kellogg's emotions—and of his working life. When J. D. Rockefeller was six, he, too, was socked by imprinting points. But in his case, poverty, piousness, and abandonment placed their imprints in the wrinkles of his brain. The result? Rockefeller was determined to work his way out of a penniless state and never to go back to it again. So any opportunity to make a profit that fit into his strict Baptist principles seemed worthwhile.

Rockefeller went to work as a professional bookkeeper at the age of sixteen—turning penny-pinching into a high art. At twenty he started a wholesale hay, grain, meat, fruit and vegetable business in his hometown, Cleveland. And at twenty-four, he moved into a speculative new field that would change his life. And the lives of hundreds of millions of his fellow human beings.

When Rockefeller was young, the average human went to bed as darkness struck, wishing she could stay up late like the rich folks in the mansion on the hill or in the magnificent townhouses of the city. Why could the wealthy afford to dance, play cards, or engage in witty repartee until the wee hours? Why did the poor have to crawl beneath a blanket when dusk fell and escape in sleep?

If you were poor, you took a candle of a new, inexpensive high-tech material, paraffin wax (discovered in 1846 when John David Rockefeller was only seven years old), to bed, said your prayers, and waited to wake up at dawn.[5] If you were rich, you could afford to have forty servants spend two hours putting three thousand candles in one hundred and twenty-five chandeliers—and you could pay enough maids and coachmen to replace every one of those candles when the night's first batch burned down.[6] Which meant that you could throw balls or invite guests to bright-eyed, late-night sessions of elegant banter or fashionable card games.

Then came lamps that gave ten candles' worth of light.[7] But there was a hitch. The best lamps of the nineteenth century burned oil squeezed from the fat of sperm whales. Sperm oil lanterns cast a light of gorgeous white. But whale oil sold for eighty cents a gallon, the 2007 equivalent of $17.61 a gallon.[8]

The year that Rockefeller turned twenty, a highly speculative new business was in the making, one that aimed to offer a new form of lighting. In England James Young, a former assistant to the pioneering physicist Michael Faraday, distilled a multipurpose lubricant from a brown shale near Bathgate. In Canada, a geologist named Abraham

Gesner extracted a similar liquid from asphalt rock, purified it with sulfuric acid and lime, and sold it to the public along with an inexpensive type of lamp in the hope of competing with sperm oil. And in the Ukraine, a pharmacist named Ignacy Łukasiewicz worked with the drugstore owner who employed him and another pharmaceutical assistant to distill a lighting fluid from a tarry goo that seeped from the soil of the countryside nearby. Łukasiewicz invented a lamp that would burn the stuff, lit up the drugstore with his new contraption, then one night took the lamps from the store to the local hospital when an emergency appendectomy was being performed. Łukasiewicz brightened the surgical chamber in a manner that astonished the doctors. So he was asked to light the entire hospital with his new lamps, lamps fueled by the liquid he'd distilled from ooze.

The oil for these experiments came primarily from accidental seepages. It trickled from rocks, so it was called "rock oil." Then, in 1859, when Rockefeller was twenty, Edwin Drake, a farmer's son and railroad worker from the agricultural plains of New York State, hooked a steam engine up to a salt well drill and tried drilling straight down for the stuff.[9] His place of choice was Pennsylvania, and Drake became the first man to "hit a gusher" and "strike oil."

Four years later, the twenty-four-year-old J. D. Rockefeller and his meat-hay-fruit-and-vegetable partners took a chance and bought a toehold in the risky new endeavor—they purchased their first oil refinery.

Lamps became more powerful—they went up in candle power. And kerosene—the liquid Łukasiewicz, Young, and Gesner had all invented independently—soon demonstrated that it could do as well as sperm oil at a fraction of the price. Oil products promised to light the night for the middle classes and for the poor.

Under the Western system, boosting the powers of your fellow humans can bring profit. However, hundreds of wildcatters, barrel makers, drillers, and drill makers vied for a place in the rapidly blossoming oil industry. The result was a mess. Oil prices rocketed, oil producers got rich, then the market slumped so deeply that tycoons became paupers overnight. The public couldn't predict the price it would pay for kerosene from day to day. It couldn't depend on a steady supply. And it couldn't depend on consistent quality.

Shifts in the quality of your kerosene could have unpleasant consequences. If you bought a jug of kerosene on Tuesday, used it up by Thursday, bought another jug on Friday, failed to compensate accurately for the changes in the new jug's composition, and kept the settings of your oil lamp the same, when you lit the wick, your lamp could easily blow up in your face.[10]

Rockefeller set out to "standardize" the oil business—to give the public a steady supply at a low price with a consistent high quality you could rely on.[11] To do it, he bullied, twisted arms, and cajoled others to sell him their companies.

Rockefeller was also determined to make sure his oil got through to the public. Like the oil business, the railroads were suffering the wild ups and downs that came from a menagerie of companies undercutting each other. Oil gluts and oil famines were so unpredictable that the railroad companies couldn't justify the expense of building a large fleet of a new transport invention—tank cars. But Rockefeller gave the railroad barons that justification. He guaranteed a steady stream of shipping—and of revenues—if the railroads would provide a tank car fleet. In the process, Rockefeller connived and colluded with the railroads to get his cans of kerosene shipped at special rates—and to make sure that despite the hitches in the transport system, his kerosene would get where it was going and would arrive on time.

Rockefeller ruthlessly drove down costs. When a firm refused to cave in to him, he squeezed it out of business, often sickening his victim with stress in the process. He also was so tight about money that he made sure that his employees used a minimum of such basic goods as pencils.

The result for the average consumer? Remember the price of sperm oil? It sold for eighty cents a gallon in 1842.[12] But by 1895, kerosene would sell for less than a tenth that price. Six point nine cents a gallon, to be precise.[13]

Meanwhile, J. D. Rockefeller also put the poverty and insecurity of his father's legacy behind him. He made a fortune. Then he satisfied his Baptist sense of stewardship and obligation by founding charities to tackle new social goals and by giving much of what he'd made away.

For all his evils—his ruthless treatment of his competitors, his monopolistic practices, and the allegation by his critics that he "never played fair"[14]—J. D. Rockefeller was a messianic capitalist. As an ad for an oil burner company in 1919 put it, Rockefeller was "the great genius" who "developed light." He gave the poor from Peoria to Peking five extra hours in their lives each day—hours formerly swallowed up by night.

In fact, if you do the math, you realize that John David Rockefeller gave the average human being roughly 58,400 extra waking hours in her life—more than 6.5 extra years. That's a staggering figure. It's on par with the medical miracles of the nineteenth century—pasteurization, inoculation, antiseptics, and anesthesia.

What's the moral of the story? All of us dream of being part of something greater than ourselves. All of us want to make a contribution. The greatest contribution you make isn't in the money you give to charities. It isn't in the nonprofit foundations you establish. And it isn't in the work you do as a volunteer. Your greatest contribution to something greater, to the lives of others, comes in what you do from nine to five.

70

THE INVENTION
OF MUCKRAKING

The Ironies of Stirring Up Dirt

Who were Ida Tarbell and John McClure? Or, how the
instincts of a goose gave us investigative journalism.

One brilliance of the Western system lies in its ability to satisfy identity needs even when those needs are for rebellion. The Western
system balances its mainstreamers with its nonconformists and its
outsiders. It gives room to its creators, to its adventurers, to its innovators, to its organizers, to its connectors, to its critics, and to its protestors. The Western system at its best harnesses personal passions in
a play of checks and balances that tweak, tune, and sometimes reinvent the whole of which they are parts. Even those who level harsh
critiques play a role in the fission-fusion strategy of the West's evolutionary search engine and of the West's secular genesis machine.

Obsession, passion, and imprinting points—passion points—have
been keys to more than business success. They've also been keys to
success in the Western system's balancer—its protest industry.

Ida Tarbell was the daughter of an oilman who'd headed his own
company and had raised his family within thirty miles of America's first
oil well. Tarbell's dad was one of those oilmen who'd been viciously
elbowed out of business and bankrupted by J. D. Rockefeller.

Yet Tarbell was not a poverty-stricken victim. She was one of the
few women in the United States during the 1890s to possess both a

bachelor's and a master's degree. What's more, she was a capitalist, one of the two minority stockholders in a rip-roaringly successful magazine—*McClure's*.[1] The publication was awash in ads from the new mass-manufacturing companies whose goods were being spread from one end of the continent to the other by the railroads that J. P. Morgan was yanking out of chaos and tying into a national system.[2]

Magazines—like the ochre and hematite rouges used in the makeup industry three hundred thousand years ago—have been badges of identity for their buyers since they first landed on the coffeehouse tables and tea trays of the English in 1682.[3]

McClure's originally provided a mark of belonging to the rising middle class, the folks who couldn't identify with thirty-five-cent highbrow publications like the *Atlantic Monthly*, *Scribner's*, the *Century*, and *Harper's*.[4] *McClure's* sold for fifteen cents. It contained stories on art and history, but its heart was its focus on men who'd made successes of themselves, men whose path to success you, the reader, could follow, too.

Using this formula, *McClure's* began far behind its competitors when its first issue emerged in 1893. In fact, because of that year's financial panic, *McClure's* nearly died a premature death. But by 1898, *McClure's* was at the top of the heap, attracting more advertising than any of its rivals.

In 1901 the magazine was on the prowl for story ideas. S. S. McClure, the magazine's founder, was seldom in his office. He practiced something rare in his time, something whose value we'll soon explore for the twenty-first century—management by walking outside. McClure spent his days traveling, moving from the West Coast to the cities of the East and Europe, sniffing like a bloodhound for the whiff of new scoops.

McClure had a gut feeling that a series about the massive industrial consolidations like those of Rockefeller in oil, Carnegie in steel, and Morgan in railroads would sell copies and would give his audience meat to chew on. Exposés were not what he had in mind. He wanted stories that would explain how these massive new monopolies worked. He wanted intelligent, insightful tales with a take-home message:

- stories that explained the miracles industrial consolidation had wrought,

- tales of how the consolidators had pulled these miracles off,
- and wrap-ups that gave a glimpse of how you could do something like this, too.

One staff member took the train to California and proposed a story on the oil business taking root on the newly developing West Coast. Ida Tarbell—the minority stakeholder/editor of *McClure's*—at first opposed the notion. This was strange, considering what Tarbell had staked out as her mandate. Ida Minerva Tarbell said that in her form of journalism, she wanted to ballyhoo "the great industrial developments of the country." Why? Tarbell said she wanted to "show clearly not only the magnitude of the industries and commercial developments . . . , but something that will make clear the great principles by which industrial leaders are combining and controlling these resources."[5] When she said she wanted to illuminate "the great principles," she made it clear that she wanted to do positive journalism.

Tarbell wanted to shed a light on "the great principles" in every field but one—oil. Why? Tarbell had grown up in oil country and, frankly, she couldn't see anything great about it.

Then her childhood imprinting experiences, her passion points, rose to the surface. Tarbell's mother had written to her eight years earlier that, "Monopolies are fearful evils—and growing in their devilish power all over the country. . . . [They present] a terrible problem . . . to be solved; peaceably if possible—by force if it must be."

Tarbell's interest in the oil story slowly rose, especially when she researched the history of her father's enemy—J. D. Rockefeller and his company, Standard Oil. When Ida Tarbell finally wrote the first in her series of eighteen stories on Standard Oil, she did so with emotions new to the pages of *McClure's*: righteous indignation, outrage, and disgust, the emotions of a daughter whose father Standard Oil had once disgraced. Emotions sell magazines, and those of righteous fury proved addictive. The new emotional tone and the new facts that supported Tarbell's cascade of denunciation produced a tornado of sales and of publicity.

McClure was excited by this new reader frenzy and ordered his staff to produce an entire issue dedicated to scandal and denunciation. He thought that one issue would be the end of this approach and he'd move on. McClure had no idea of how deeply the public needs to make new heroes and to tear old heroes down. He didn't sense how deeply we need to feel superior to those on top. He didn't see himself as a drug dealer, and he had no research that would help him understand how addictive the surge of the hormones of hierarchy, the hormones of self-righteousness—serotonin, dopamine, endorphin, and testosterone—can be.[6]

Within months *Collier's*, *Cosmopolitan*, *Munsey's*, *Everybody's*, and numerous other magazines adopted the "new journalism of exposure."[7]

Teddy Roosevelt, one of the great crusaders against the criminal excesses into which capitalists can stray, was utterly dismayed. He called the new approach a form of dredging for rot at the bottom of a pleasant, useful pond. Wrote Roosevelt, "In Bunyan's 'Pilgrim's Progress' you may recall the description of the Man with the Muck-rake, the man who could look no way but downward, with the muck-rake in his hand; who was offered a celestial crown for his muck-rake, but who would neither look up nor regard the crown he was offered, but continued to rake to himself the filth of the floor."[8] Roosevelt felt the muckraker was so intent on the slime he pulled from the bottom of a pond, so intent "on the vile and debasing," that he never looked up to see "aught that is lofty," never looked up to see the sun.[9]

But the formula was set. To turbocharge the cash flow of your magazine, all you had to do was demonstrate that industrialism was the source of all corruption and, as Roosevelt put it in a letter to McClure that pleaded for balance, "to encourage people to believe that all crimes are connected with business."[10]

Just as the taming of sheep in the Middle East eight thousand years ago changed the way we see by giving us the metaphor of the shepherd and his flock, Marx's condemnation and Tarbell's new journalistic invention changed perceptions. When *McClure's* was founded, its mission was to portray the positive in the modern and to show its readers ways to create positives of their own. The profit formula of the muckrakers exposed many a misdeed and put a check on the excesses of the "robber barons," men who dominated entire industries and were accused of milking ordinary citizens to make outrageous profits.[11] But cultivating a culture of business hatred among some journalists was—remember this—a good way to make money for capitalists like McClure, a man whose commitment to quality and whose tuning to the emotional needs of his audience was great, but also a man who was driven by profits as powerfully as Rockefeller had been.

The journalism of complaint was also a source of wealth and fame for poseurs who pretended to loathe business and who genuinely did, but who also loved the money that came from their own business enterprise, their writing. The new clique of crusading journalists loved the perks their stories brought them, including money. Look how well they were paid for disseminating their hatred of the nineteenth century's new breed of retailers, wholesalers, and industrialists! Some of these men and women of moderate new wealth—investigative reporters like Ida Tarbell's co-worker at *McClure's*, muckraking journalist Lincoln Steffens—were socialists who wanted to see the capitalist system torn down and banished from the earth.[12] Yet it was the capitalist system that made Steffens a highly privileged man. And it was the capitalist system that gave his voice a place.

In 1919, nineteen years after Tarbell broke her first exposé on Rockefeller, Russia's fledgling capitalist system was torn apart by the Bolshevik Revolution. Lincoln Steffens traveled to Russia—a privilege only a small number of the wealthy could afford—and came back crowing the famous phrase, "I have seen the future and it works."[13] Had Steffens tried his muckraking in Moscow, he most probably would have been shot. Remember, even a mere statistician and numbers theorist like the Kondratiev wave's creator, Nikolai Kondratiev, was condemned to death for merely implying a minor deviation from the party line. Not a good way to run an evolutionary search engine.

But we in the Western system need something better. Give us honesty, intelligence, and independent thinking. Dig deep into the hidden seams of things that count but are outside the boundaries set by media fads. Take us beyond prejudices and stereotypes.

Open up our eyes. Amaze us with unexpected facts, not with clichéd fallacies. Follow your quirks and your obsessions into important corners others haven't reached. Be an explorer. Break out of your pack. Reveal what you are not supposed to say. Remember, we, your audience, lust for more than novelty. We lust for the grasp of things that comes from insight. We lust for the facts and the independent thinking that you hide. We lust for truth. And we lust not for complaint, but for meaning.

71

DON'T LET ENVY GET YOU

What Hath J. P. Morgan Wrought?

The contribution of another robber baron, and the
lesson of the curses in his blessings.

By 1911 J. D. Rockefeller had been dragged through what seemed like
a never-ending courtroom drama and had been forced to break up
and sell off Standard Oil of Ohio. The kerosene light he'd given to the
world was about to disappear in favor of a power source developed
by other creative capitalists: Edison, Westinghouse, and the genius
behind Westinghouse, the Serbian-American inventor and visionary
Nikola Tesla.

But Rockefeller's legacy—inexpensive petroleum products of consistent quality—would soon give us new mobility. It would give us a
machine—the automobile—that opened our horizons and totally
remade our lives. It would give us a new form of home heating in the
1920s. And it would give us petroleum side products like plastic and
nylon in the 1930s.

The Morgan family, like J. D. Rockefeller, would also be run
through the ringer of the muckraking and trust-busting machinery. In
the process, its messianic contribution would disappear from the
pages of history. J. P. Morgan had stepped in during the late nineteenth century when the railroad system was in turmoil. Those like
Leland Stanford, who'd been brave enough to build the first transcon-

tinental railroad in 1868, had risked their health and their fortunes on the enterprise. But once their years of torment were over and the line between the coasts was up and running, they'd made the equivalent of today's billions. In the years that followed, owning a railroad seemed like a good way to get rich quick. Enterprising entrepreneurs built new lines that connected to nowhere, founded new companies that flickered into bankruptcy, and operated trains with passenger cars whose riders were literally torn apart when a railroad track curved in the heat and ripped through the carriage floor like a giant's cutlass. These slashing, vicious accidents happened every week.

Massive American train disasters were so frequent that they became a cliché—"a train wreck."

Morgan, like Rockefeller, had bullied and blustered. And he'd sometimes been underhanded. But he'd also taught many a business owner how to make a go of his venture. More important, he'd pulled the railroads into a nearly seamless system that allowed you to travel without being disemboweled by a curled piece of iron track. Morgan's system allowed you to mail-order the delivery of everything from shirts and blouses to ready-to-build houses from the catalog of a company like Chicago's Sears & Roebuck. It was Morgan's railroad miracle that made it possible for titans like Rockefeller to offer necessities like kerosene to ordinary farmers in the nooks and crannies of the wilderness, and that made it easy for those farmers to sell their wheat to gigantic new food-processing companies like Pillsbury and Nabisco in the North American East or to bakers and grocers in Europe.

Morgan, like Rockefeller, made a fortune. And Morgan, like Rockefeller, was humiliated in court and in the press by crusading journalists whose stories made capitalists like Hearst and Pulitzer—newspaper publishers—rich.

You and I would have been greedy to read the tales of the capitalist scandals that rocked these industry giants. We'd have been after more than just raw facts. We'd have been after outrageous revelations of disgrace, something that satisfies our need to bring those in high position to their knees. Let's face it, it's galling to know that others have more money than we do. It's a hierarchical thing—an offense to our sense of achievement and of identity. It offends the animal in us. It tweaks a lust for vengeance in an area that a new discipline, neuroeconomics, is probing: our bioplan of human needs.[1] When a high-ranking chimpanzee tries to have sex, lower-ranking members crowd around and try to stop him. They don't want him to turn the tribe into a mechanism that gathers food and defends against threats just for the sake of raising the boss's progeny. Just for the sake of the high and mighty aristocrat's genes.

Envy and *schadenfreude* come from our nature as pecking order beasts. What's *schadenfreude*? A German word for our joy in the pain of others, especially our joy in the pain of those above us, others we no longer feel we need.

The self-correcting system of the protest industry is based on this primal motivation. But there's another fact we have to look squarely in the face. We, the people, want the inexpensive goods that come from the Rockefellers of the planet. When prices go up on a basic commodity like power, lighting, or food, who riots and complains? Who throws the bums out and sometimes makes revolutions? We do.

In the days of the robber barons—from 1860 to 1913—the income of the average American more than doubled.[2] Much of that increased income went to the readers of *McClure's* and to the buyers of Hearst and Pulitzer newspapers. It went to people like you and me.

From 1750 to 2006, the Western income per person (including babies, children, and the unemployed) rocketed from $182 per year to $4,970.[3] To put it differently, if the average Western income per person in 1750 were the size of a baseball, the average income in 2006 would be more than twice as tall as, well, of you or me. Taller than your head would be even if you stood on my shoulders.

So by all means, let's remain on the lookout. Let's protect those who are crushed or who have their pockets picked and their savings plundered. Let's prevent government handouts to those who've inherited fortunes but have never made a contribution. Let's make sure we're not giving massive government welfare checks to men and women with $100 million golden parachutes. Let's purge the political system in which the super-rich get back six dollars' worth of favors and special breaks for every dollar they invest in a political campaign. And let's lessen the distance between the super-rich, the poor, and you and me.

But let's not throw out the innovators. Let's not throw out the quality makers. Let's not throw out the price-lowering and consistency-raising consolidators. Let's not toss out the good with the bad simply because we can't stand it when someone else gets rich.

72

THE SECRET OF
TUNED EMPATHY

Why Reason Is Insane[1]

Alfred P. Sloan, the founder of modern corporate
management, demanded that executives be rational
and "objective." But there's a hitch. Science shows
that reason sometimes has less power than it thinks.

Alfred P. Sloan, the founder of modern corporate management, told
us from the 1920s to the 1950s that if you're in business, you have to
leave your emotions at the breakfast table when you head out to the
office. Sloan set the following example. "It is the duty of the Chief
Executive Officer," he wrote, "to be objective and impartial. He must
be absolutely tolerant and pay no attention to how a man does his
work, let alone whether he likes the man or not. The only criteria
must be performance and character. And that is incompatible with
friendship and social relations. . . . Loneliness, distance, and formality
. . . are his [the CEO's] duty."[2]

All of us—from venture capitalists, VPs, mailroom clerks, students, college professors, and scientific researchers, to oil painters,
Web site designers, computer programmers, and poets—are in business. In business, said Sloan, you have to be rational, not personal.
You have to be objective. You have to ditch the quirks of personality.[3]

That advice served very well for the era of corporate "rational-
ization" from the early 1920s to the 1950s. But it's very bad advice

for the twenty-first century.[4] Why? It's time to repeat a simple refrain. Reason is powerful stuff. But any good thing in overdose is a poison. Reason is like iron. A sword made only of iron is hideously heavy and brittle. But a sword of iron laced with just the right amount of carbon is light and flexible. In fact, it's a blade of steel.

What's the carbon to reason's iron? Intuition. But not just any intuition. Saturated intuition. Intuition rich in knowledge. Intuition rich in experience.

Mountains of scientific evidence indicate that your rational brain is sometimes a know-nothing, a backseat driver that pretends to be at the wheel.[5] Intuition and nonrational brain centers do better at tricky games with fast or unpredictable flukes. And this is a fluky, unpredictable world.

The heart has reasons reason never knows, said the French philosopher Blaise Pascal. And Pascal was right. One of the first laboratory hints that reason is nowhere near as powerful as it thinks came from an experiment in the University of Iowa labs of Antonio Damasio.[6] Formally it's called the "Iowa Gambling Task."[7] Another good name might be the Puzzle of the Poisoned Piles. Two groups of six subjects were given stacks of play money and four piles of cards. The card piles seemed random. But they weren't. Two of the piles were subtly stacked so they would make you money. And two of the piles were ever-so-slightly stacked with cards that would force you to lose, relieving you of your phony cash.

Six of the experimental subjects had brain damage and six did not. The subjects with normal brains got the fact that the decks were stacked and shied away from the losing piles. The experimental subjects with brain damage got the idea too. But they didn't learn from their insight. They could tell which card stacks would lose them cash, but they kept on picking cards from the poisoned piles.

Why? Because the brain-damaged and the non-brain-damaged subjects understood the problem of the poisoned card piles with different parts of the brain. The winning normal subjects grasped things with their intuition. They figured out the problem with their gut instinct. The losing, brain-damaged subjects only understood with reason.

In fact, the normal subjects began to grasp the problem intuitively long before they grabbed hold of it with their consciousness, with their sense of reason. But the brain-damaged patients never understood the poisoning of the piles with their gut sense. Instead, they only got it with their rational minds. And their rational brains were not strong enough to stop them from betting on the toxic stacks.

How could Damasio be so sure of who grasped the problem with reason and who got it with intuition? He measured the galvanic skin response—the subtle level of sweat—in his subjects. When your intuition senses a problem, it increases your level of perspiration ever so subtly. The normal subjects in Damasio's experiment showed heightened levels of this intuition indicator—galvanic skin response—when they put their hands over the cards in the poisoned decks. And they showed those heightened levels long before their reason figured out that the polluted decks were loaded with toxic cards. In other words, the subjects who won the most money triumphed because of their gut instincts. Because their intuition figured out the problem.

The brain-damaged subjects were hobbled by reason. They eventually understood the problem of the poison decks consciously and could articulate it. They could say it out loud. But they still pulled cards from the polluted stacks. Their difficulty? Head but no heart. Reason but no gut instinct. No intuition. Literally, no sweat. Or, as *Science News*'s Bruce Bower put it, "an ounce of intuition trumps a pound of pondering."

The moral of the story? Reason without intuition is a cripple. But when intuition and reason work together, they form a powerful team.[8]

As for games of strategy and of "the brain," games like chess, even here reason may flunk the test.[9] A research team at the University of Minnesota used functional magnetic resonance imaging to peer into the brains of inexperienced chess players while they played the game of rooks, pawns, and kings. The researchers expected to see heavy activity in the "general intelligence" parts of the brain—the brain areas that produce the thinking measured by IQ tests. But that's not what they witnessed. The left lateral frontal lobe—the seat of our reason, the seat of our talking, conscious self, the area behind your left forehead—was silent.[10] The newbies at chess were using areas on the sides and in the back of the brain, areas that were associated with a "feel" of things. The University of Minnesota researchers speculated that the job of mastering chess was being handled by the spatial powers of the occipital lobes, the parietal lobes, and the hippocampus, areas that register where things are in relationship to each other, areas that do not use reason.

To earn your daily keep you must feed the needs of others. That is the moral imperative of capitalism. You have an instrument with which to sense what others are panting for but don't yet know they want. It isn't market research and focus groups. It's your feelings. Your emotions are analog computers, masters of social calculus. They are tuned to mirror the needs of others. You actually have "mirror neurons" prepared to take on this task.

In the late 1980s a neurobiological researcher at the University of Parma in Italy, Giacomo Rizzolatti, discovered something strange.[11] He wired up the brain of a macaque monkey to see which parts of the brain lit up when the monkey reached for food. He expected to see activity in the motor cortex, the ear-to-ear strip across the top of the brain that tells the muscles of your arms and legs when and how to move. Indeed, activity in the motor strip was what Rizzolatti got. But he got it too soon. The monkey's ventral premotor cortex fired before the beast was even offered food to pick up. Why?

It took Rizzolatti time to puzzle it out. Then he realized that he and his fellow researchers took their snacks and coffee into the room that housed the monkey. They picked up their food a few minutes before they gave the monkey the opportunity to pick up some food for himself. The motor neurons in the monkey fired when the monkey saw an experimenter pick up a cup of coffee or a pastry. And they fired exactly as if the monkey were picking up that cup or that bakery treat himself. The monkey had a primal form of empathy with his researchers. His brain put him in the researchers' shoes—or at least in the researchers' hands and arms.

Rizzolatti called the neurons that aped the actions of others, the neurons that modeled the actions of others and that reflected them internally, "mirror neurons." You, too, have motor neurons rehearsing things you see others do as if you were doing those things yourself. So do I. They're in our premotor cortex and inferior parietal lobe. They are our scopes into the emotions of others. They are our imagers of others' hearts and minds. They are our lenses of empathy.

But to use these scopes and imagers, you have to feel the ripples of the inexpressible within you. You have to know your hidden wishes, your passions, pains, frustrations, and even your insecurities.

You have to ask yourself, "If I could have anything in the world I wanted, anything at all, what would it be? If I could have a gizmo that would help me pole-vault over the irritations of the day, a gadget that's sexy and exciting, a dream gadget that turns the unendurable into fun, what would I crave? If I could call on armies of others to help me, what help would I really love to receive?"

Remember the second rule of science: look at things right under your nose, then proceed from there. Look at things that you and everyone you know take for granted, then act on what you see.

To use your motor neurons, to use your instruments of empathy, you have to find the emotions within you that are tuned to the frequency of the people you want to serve. You have to break out of the boundaries of your normal group of friends and immerse yourself in the world of those you want to win over, those whom you want as your audience, your customers. You have to saturate yourself with their daily grind, their daily feelings, and their daily flights of fancy. In doing so you will achieve something paradoxical—you will expand yourself. You will come to feel your audience—your customers—in your chest and gut. You may even learn to care about them deeply. This is what I call "tuned empathy."[12]

Empathy, says Daniel Goleman, the psychologist who introduced the term EQ—emotional quotient—is "the fundamental competence of emotional awareness."[13] Empathy, he implies, is the ultimate tool in business. Empathy, he hints, is the ultimate tool in life. And Goleman may well be right.

In the early twentieth century, empathy in business was in very short supply. Here's the reason why.

* * *

Reason is a good guide to serving others when it's fortified with every emotion and every bit of tuned empathy you and I can bring into focus and express. Reason is a necessary partner to passion. But the twentieth century gave us seventy years in which passion, emotion, and that potent combination of intuition, obsession, and everything-we-know that puts soul into your work and mine were all too often shoved aside.

In 1874, Frederick Taylor, the obsessive-compulsive son of an aristocratic New Hampshire family, graduated first in his class at one of the most august, elite prep schools in America—Phillips Exeter Academy. He went on to Harvard then was forced to drop out. His problem wasn't too little study; it was too much. Long nights hitting the books had damaged his eyesight.

Taylor's father had been an attorney, but young Frederick made a strange move—a move of lateral inhibition—and fled his father's footsteps. Now that he could no longer go to school, he opted for the new world of industry. Taylor apprenticed himself as a machinist and patternmaker at the Enterprise Hydraulic Works in Philadelphia, then worked his way up from common machine shop worker to chief engineer at the Midvale Steel Company.

All this was admirable. But there was more to come. In 1881 Taylor was only twenty-five years old, but he did something only a brilliant obsessive-compulsive would think of. He studied men and women at work, clocked their movements with a stopwatch, and figured out how to make a laborer accomplish the most with the least amount of effort and lost time.

Then Taylor promoted an insidious notion—that there was just one best way of doing anything. Taylor called his tool of analysis "time-motion studies" and his list of one best ways "scientific management." Taylor's stopwatch-studied manner of doing every task lowered costs, upgraded the level of what the ordinary citizen could afford to buy, and played a major role in streamlining mass production. But it treated factory laborers like robots, improving the movement of their hands but muzzling their emotions and their minds.

Henry Ford used Taylor's new techniques to make a middle-class toy out of a luxury that only the super-rich could previously afford to buy—the automobile. Employing Taylorism, Ford made cars reliable and astonishingly cheap—a mere $290 for a Model T. But there was a hitch. You could buy one of his internal combustion buggies in any color you wanted, bragged Ford, as long as you bought it in black.

Commodification is a term that crops up when economists or social critics are chatting. It is *not* a high abstraction. It's a term that disguises emotional facts. A commodity is something so profoundly reliable that you can afford to ignore it. Like meat, wheat, and the floorboards beneath your feet. When Ford made the first inexpensive autos, they were potent tools of empowerment. They made it possible for a middle-class family to go out into the country on a Sunday drive. They made it possible to visit relatives far from the nearest railroad line.

But cars were also badges of identity. They made a statement—I can afford what only rich men could bring home just five or six years ago. Riding into your town square with your brand-new Ford got you everyone's attention. And attention is the hidden currency of emotional capitalism.

Twenty years later, when nearly everybody owned a car, the novelty value wore off and the attention bonanza disappeared. When you drove up in your brand-new shiny Ford, people hardly noticed. In fact, some folks joked, "Why is the Model T like a bathtub? Because nobody wants to be seen in one."[14] Cars had gone from a luxury to an everyday necessity. They'd become something middle-class folks could take for granted.

Taking things for granted yet relying deeply on their availability is commodification. A thing becomes a commodity when it's lost its sizzle, when you rely on its presence in your driveway or garage but when it's no longer an identity tool—when it no longer sends a signal to your neighbors, friends, and co-workers, "Hey, look what I've got that you've never been able to get your hands on. It's time to focus your eyes on me."

William Durant took another approach to the auto, one that fit the emotions that successful capitalists must serve. There were often five or six auto companies in a major city, each one turning out a different style of car but doing it by hand. Durant bought the best of these companies, converted them to mass production, and tied them up in a single corporate bundle. Then he realized he'd created an organizational monster. Running a gaggle of companies was far more than he could handle.

So he brought in an expert from an old industrial family—one that had made its fortune in explosives. And he hoped that this master of corporate structure could turn his swarm of companies into something manageable. The man with the magic powers was Pierre DuPont of the DuPont chemical family. Magic comes from spotting talents and from building teams. And DuPont spotted a talent. He promoted a twenty-six-year-old electrical engineer from Brooklyn who was running Durant's auto parts operations. This whiz-kid had grown up knowing both machinery and the business of buying and selling. He'd graduated from MIT as the youngest member of his class. And his father had been a machinist who'd started a tea and coffee import business. (Yes, tea and coffee—those great stimulators of the eighteenth century—were still business catalysts.)

Alfred Pritchard Sloan—the son of the tea and coffee merchant— would be the savior and the Satan of twentieth-century business. He followed Durant's path and encouraged Durant's clutch of companies— General Motors—to turn out cars in a variety of colors and styles. This was exactly what the public hungered for without quite knowing it— cars that once again tweaked your novelty lust and satisfied your identity and attention needs. If your car was brown or blue, if it was a coupe or a sedan, once again you had an impressive novelty that could win you envy and swivel the eyeballs of your friends.

Sloan satisfied another identity hunger. He made cars that announced how you wanted to be seen and that proclaimed which group you wanted to belong to. A Chevrolet said that you were working class and proud of it. A Pontiac said that you were working class but wanted to be seen as adventurous. An Oldsmobile announced that you were middle class and satisfied to remain that way. A Buick said that you were middle class with upwardly mobile goals. And a Cadillac shouted that you were an aristocrat, that you'd made a bundle of money, or both.

Here's the irony. General Motors' success was based on the emotions of identity. But Alfred Sloan ripped the emotional guts out of everything he touched. He announced proudly that a company is "an objective organization, as distinguished from the type that get lost in the subjectivity of personalities."[15] He took the passion out of what Durant's stylings and color choices had done to liberate the needs of individuals. He gave an impersonal name to Durant's legacy: "market segmentation." He also popularized another new term, one that often demeans creativity and human feeling—*management*.

Sloan's system of "decentralization with coordinated control" was a huge success. From 1923 to 1929, General Motors doubled its share of the auto market. And Sloan had an overwhelming influence on American industry. Says one of the world's premier business magazines, Britain's *Economist*, Sloan's example "became the template for virtually every corporate entity for the rest of the [twentieth] century."[16] But three generations of executives followed what Sloan *said* he'd accomplished rather than his real deeds. They ignored what Sloan could not put into words—Durant's success at sensing human feelings and caring for emotional needs.

General Electric, United States Rubber, Standard Oil, US Steel, DuPont, and many others switched to Sloan's invention—management—and to its attendant techniques. All these firms put decision making into the hands of a small cadre of professional smart guys—people trained by business schools to do things in the Sloanist way. All of these companies took the Taylorist time-motion studies attitude toward their workers, turning them into robots. This approach was best expressed way back when Henry Ford complained that every time he hired a pair of hands, he was cursed by being forced to hire the hand's transporters, a human being.

America would soon gain from Sloan's and Taylor's insights. And America would soon suffer for Sloan's and Taylor's mistakes.

73

THE FALL OF THE AMERICAN AUTO INDUSTRY

Breaking the Commodity Contract

Economics is an emotion flow, not a number stream.
How the number chase blinded a giant.

By the 1950s, Sloanism had run amok. The factories of the other great manufacturing powers—Germany, England, and Japan—had been flattened by the bombs of World War II. America was the dominant supplier of goods like autos to the world.

The American automobile industry came to take its preeminence for granted. It callously pushed identity peddling to the fore and forgot the emotional meaning—the emotional contract—of commodity. A commodity is something you and I can count on, something we need but that we take for granted, something that gives us a solid and legitimate sense of security. That's the implicit compact, the unspoken promise, that a commodity provider makes to you and me. J. D. Rockefeller kept this commodity contract in mind in the nineteenth century when he made kerosene a commodity. He lowered the price. He made the buying easy. Standard Oil cans were the same whether the kerosene was sold in Boston, Berlin, or Beijing.[1] More important, so was the kerosene's quality.

Any good thing in overdose is a poison. America's automakers invented a new term in the 1950s, *planned obsolescence*. They worked hard to create new design changes and to announce them

439

with great fanfare every year. But they took callous advantage of identity hungers and of novelty lust. They made it unchic, unhip, uncool, and ever-so-terribly downscale to own a car that was last year's model or, God forbid, that was more than three years old.

General Motors, Chrysler, Ford, and American Motors tossed aside the emotional contract of commodity. They invented tail fins and new chrome grills, but they let the quality of the workmanship slide. Americans bought new cars to "keep up with the Joneses." But when they drove their huge new purchases home to show their families, often the handles that raised the windows fell off. The engine pinged unnervingly. And the car was filled with rattles and strange knocks from loose parts in the transmission or the trunk.

Meanwhile, the Japanese had studied Alfred Sloan's management approach and found it wanting. When they rebuilt their bombed-out auto companies, they searched for better gurus. They studied the Austrian American Peter Drucker, whose books said that the brains of workers were a company's greatest assets. And the Japanese imported an innovative thinker from Wyoming who no business in America would hire. His name was W. Edwards Deming. Deming repeated Drucker's message—go beyond your elite corps of managers, those who were trained in business school to execute the "objective" theories of Alfred Sloan. Use the brains of your workers.

There was more to Deming's message. Engage the passions of your laborers in "quality circles"—brainstorming groups empowered to conceive improvements—empowered to propose new ideas to upgrade the manufacturing process, empowered to propose new ideas to upgrade the cars, and empowered to propose new ideas to upgrade the company. Take advantage of the fact that not all pay comes in the form of money. Humans need to be listened to. They need to know their ideas count. And they need to put emotion into anything they do. They need the pecking-order pride of knowing that what they make is the best. They need to know that someone wants and needs what they create. Laborers want identity. They need attention. And they need Linnaeus's secret motivator, an ego-stake.

In the early 1960s, Americans and Europeans were offered an inexpensive way to skirt the high-style, low-quality cars of America's Big Four. The Germans presented two low-priced alternatives: the Volkswagen Beetle and the Volkswagen Van.

Planned or not, these cars catered to the identity need of a new community, of a new subculture, of a new group that needed to parade its sense both of belonging and of standing out. The subculture hungry for a car that screamed nonconformity was the hippie generation, the counterculture. What better way to thumb your nose at American capitalism, at "The System," than by buying an auto from a former enemy, an auto that looked more like a ladybug than a tail-finned aircraft about to take off. What better way to let your friends know that like millions of other simpaticos spread across the North American continent, you were a nonconformist.

A few years later, another option appeared. This next wave bore cars that weren't fancy. Like the Volkswagen, they didn't change in style from year to year. They didn't embarrass you if they were five years old or more. They were low in price. They had improved engines that saved you money on gasoline. They came complete with options you had to bargain for if you were buying an American auto—radios and air-conditioning. And, most important, nothing fell apart. The handles worked. There were no knocks and pings.

These bargain cars filled the commodity contract. They worked with uncanny reliability. They continued working for fifteen years or more. They gave you a feeling of security. They were the autos from Toyota, Honda, and Nissan, the autos of the Japanese.

Colorless as these cars were, Americans and Europeans had sated their novelty hunger and their identity needs. The craving of the moment was for a sense that the workers who made your auto cared, and a sense that they'd care for you in years to come when repairs would be inevitable. The Japanese sold emotion and attention. They sold commitment to their labor. They sold commitment to their customer—to you.

By the time 1973 rolled around, the Sloanist, "objective," emotionless managers of GM, Ford, and Chrysler were in trouble. A formerly rock-solid company, American Motors, was on the verge of collapse (its remains were bought by Chrysler in 1987). The Japanese share of the American auto market was growing steadily. That's putting it in the dehumanized terms of Sloan. More and more Americans wanted to escape from Michigan carmakers who put no passion into what they built. More and more felt safe in the hands of the Japanese.

Meanwhile, entire industries like electronics slid into the hands of the folks from Tokyo. There were big questions on the minds of those who watched as American companies floundered. Would American businesses and jobs survive? Would the United States figure out the Japanese secret and learn to compete with the Far Easterners at this new economic game?

As of 1980, America's odds of making a comeback looked very dicey. Very dicey, indeed. How would the American economy be saved?

* * *

American automakers surveyed the Japanese factories and came to an objective, rational, Taylorist and Sloanist conclusion.

The United States had invented the industrial robot, but American automakers hadn't bothered to use it. The Japanese, on the other hand, had built new plants in which robots reigned supreme. So the auto manufacturers of Detroit went whole-hog into robotization. American automakers installed giant, robotic swinging arms that painted cars without human intervention. It didn't help.

Then came a flood of books on the secrets of Japanese management techniques. In these books were eye-opening descriptions of procedures like quality circles and just-in-time delivery. More important, the books on Japan Inc. hinted at an underlying truth. The answer wasn't in the machines. It was in the emotions and the hearts of human beings.

Tom Peters, of the management-consulting firm McKenzie and Company, caught the essence of the Japanese approach in a 1981 book called *In Search of Excellence*. Every worker, said Peters, comes to work with a beef. Every worker shows up at his job knowing there's a better way to do it. And every worker knows that no Alfred Sloan–style manager will listen to him.

If only 170 smart guys—executives with MBAs—make all the decisions, and if those 170 smart guys treat their 35,000 employees as time-motion-study robots, that means only 340 pairs of eyes and ears are trying to fathom an operation that snakes and winds through tens of thousands of strange corners and that ties itself in thousands of unforeseen knots. But if the 170 smart guys open their ears and let their 35,000 time-motion-shackled workers open their mouths:

- the number of eyes looking for waste goes up to 70,340;
- the number of fingers unraveling snags goes up to 351,700;
- and the number of brain cells on the job rockets to more than 3.5 quadrillion.

Get out of your office, Peters told us. Spend time with your workers. Listen to their beefs. They see the creases and crevasses in your operation every day. Let them make the rough run smoother. Let them put their identity into your products. Let them take responsibility. Let them add the output of their brains. Let them solve the problems that bug them the most.

Peters was pleading for managers to give their workers an ego-stake—an investment that means more than money, an investment born of attention, influence, and pride. Peters called the new partnership with workers "management by walking around." But the next step in emotional capitalism must go beyond Peters's insights: it's "management by walking outside."

74

THE BRILLIANT DEMISE
OF CBS

The Perils of Management
by Walking Inside

William Paley's CBS did everything right, or that's the
way it seemed.

Books on management and leadership have been misleading us. Here's
what they've led to. According to urban studies pioneer Jane Jacobs:
"Many . . . workplaces . . . have become self-involved to the point of
becoming introverted. They have also become . . . narcissistic."[1]
Many modern firms have shut out the most important contributors to
what they do, the folks who pay their salaries. They've shut out their
customers. And they've done something worse.

No company is an island. Management by walking around has its
limitations. Walking inside is not enough. In fact, in the last decades
of the twentieth century and the opening decade of the twenty-first, it
wasn't the solution, it was part of a brand-new problem.

Allan Ginsberg, the best-known Beat poet of the 1950s and a
leader of the protest industry of his day, wrote a classic poem called
"Howl" in 1956. In its opening lines, Ginsberg wrote that he'd seen
"the best minds of my generation destroyed by madness, starving hys-
terical naked, dragging themselves through the negro streets at dawn
looking for an angry fix."

In my fieldwork in the corporate world from 1968 to 1988, I saw
the best minds of my generation, and they were not crawling on the

rooftops of the ghettoes in search of heroin. They were in the conference rooms and the boardrooms of America's biggest corporations looking for an angry fix of another sort of drug entirely. Like all of us, they were driven by an identity need, a need to show that they belonged, and a need to show that they stood out.

All of us have the hunger for belonging and the lust for attention, the need to seem special. But any good thing in excess is a poison. Our identity needs can be powerful lenses of insight or they can utterly blind us. Identity needs can put out the eyes of those whose mandate is to serve millions of others. I saw the best minds of my generation blunting their intellects, amputating their independence, and sealing up their passions in what seemed like a nonstop stage show—posturing for their peers.

The CEOs, VPs, and managers I knew, from LA and Nashville to New York, London, and Germany were high on cliquishness, high on the drug of false superiority, high on the drug of feeling like an elite.

Despite this, some of their companies had what looked from a distance like amazing track records. From the early 1970s until the 1990s, two companies dominated the music industry. One was CBS. The other was Warner Brothers. Each had 33 percent of the total music pie. CBS and Warners held on to this massive market share year after year after year. They had something magnificent in their social and corporate structure. I wanted to know what it was.

I dissected these companies for nearly two decades, using every tool of analysis that I could borrow or adapt to get a handle on what these companies were doing right. In the process I found more than I'd bargained for. I discovered not only the secrets to their success, but the secrets that would lead to their decline.

CBS and Warners shared something critical—each tapped the brains of its top employees. Each brought those brains to life. And each did it in a different way. CBS periodically sent its vice presidents to woodsy resorts for management-refinement retreats. The manual used in these sessions changed from year to year, but it was NOT supposed to be shared with those outside the company. Meanwhile, I visited the conference rooms at CBS constantly, working with the company's VPs and managers on joint projects. I lunched with CBS executives. I fed them potential employees (including a young writer named Ed Naha—who would later go on to write *Honey, I Shrunk the Kids* and turn it into a franchise). And eventually CBS made a practice of stealing employees from me—taking as many as six in a single year. One CBS Records senior VP reportedly told promising job applicants who had little experience in the entertainment industry, "Work for Howard Bloom for two years. He'll give you the best training you can get. Then come back to me."

Meanwhile, another CBS VP set up a swap. We'd meet for lunch every few months. She'd pick my brain on whatever subjects she liked. In exchange, I could pick hers on what she knew fascinated me—the secret to CBS's consistency, its year-after-year stability and success. One year she was sent to a week-long management retreat. She returned with an overstuffed three-ring binder that no one outside of CBS was supposed to see. She passed it to me under the table of an Italian restaurant on Manhattan's West 55th Street as a birthday present.

What was CBS's secret? What did this manual preach? One of its messages would have pleased Tom Peters enormously: grow the people under you. Look for their talents, foresee their promise, and nurture their achievements. Teach them everything you know. Train them to replace you. Why? Because once you've groomed a person to occupy the office you possess, we—the top management—will promote you to the job of your dreams. If you're in books and you've always wanted to be in TV, we'll let you switch to the television division. If you're in TV and you'd love to go into music, we'll shift you to our music operation. If you've been in toys but want to go into books, we'll give you a job in publishing.

This helped explain why CBS's music operation changed presidents periodically, lost brilliant top executives like the Man with the Golden Ear, Clive Davis, and yet steadily held its market share. CBS was an elite community. It hired the best minds, then groomed them from the inside, sometimes growing their abilities for over twenty years.

But not everything in the CBS manual looked so promising. CBS had picked up a technique called *management by objectives*—an insidious practice invented, ironically, by Peter Drucker, the man who had tried unsuccessfully to tell Alfred Sloan that your biggest untapped asset is the mind power of your workers and whose message had been tossed aside by GM but had been picked up by the Japanese.

There was something soberingly mechanical about management by objectives, something that seemed to miss the point of the capitalist imperative. Management by objectives as preached in the secret CBS manual deadened the emotions and the soul. The management by objectives materials told you to sit down with your superior every quarter. Lay out the profit figure your division aimed to hit in three months' time. Review your progress toward that target profit at frequent meetings. Then adjust your strategy to hit your mark. If you were undershooting your goal, lower the manufacturing cost of your goods. Lower the budget for recording-studio time. Find cheaper cardboard for album covers. Lower the quality of the vinyl in your LPs.

CBS VPs were being trained to answer to accountants, not to care about us music lovers.

This was the very opposite of the CBS tradition. From 1928 to 1990, CBS's founder, William Paley, had stood for excellence. CBS's radio and early TV broadcasts had made an implicit quality contract with listeners like my parents in the 1940s and 1950s. Paley and his company sent Edward R. Murrow to London in World War II to cover the Blitz—the German saturation bombing campaign targeted at London and designed to break the British spirit.[2] In those years, CBS established a mark of excellence in broadcast journalism that's never been surpassed.

CBS-TV trumpeted its quality again in the 1950s and 1960s with superb shows on Sunday evenings and mornings—shows that seemed to exude a subtle elegance.

But CBS VPs were being trained to answer to bean counters. And to shareholders. Not to customers. Not to people like you and me.

Management by objectives taught a very un-Paley message. If your department is not hitting its quarterly profit target, take action immediately. How? Cut costs. Even if cutting those costs also cut quality.

What's the problem with this approach? A vice president who fails to represent us, who fails to feel your needs and mine, is going to betray us. And when she does, we will abandon her. We won't even know why.

It's not enough to walk around inside your company. It's not enough to grow your own employees, to harness their ideas, and to fuel their passions and their souls. You have to represent us, your buyers, us, your audience, us, your flock. You have to know the needs we can't express. When you are in that conference room you cannot desert us. There is a capitalist imperative. You are our champion and our savior, our leader in the wilderness.

Would CBS be saved from this subtle poison? This lack of tuned empathy? Stay tuned. We're about to see.

* * *

But first, let's dig down to one the biggest and least visible mistakes that those of us in companies make—posturing for our peers.

A division of CBS Records hired me in 1979 to work with a band that every executive in the company despised—the Illinois group REO Speedwagon. CBS was the Harvard of the entertainment industry. It paid the highest wages, offered the best benefits, carried the most prestige, and attracted executives with the highest IQs.

But the CBS executives I knew and worked with used most of their energy trying to impress each other, not trying to serve people like you and me. There was no sense of love for music lovers in the corridors of Black Rock—CBS's solid-black skyscraper on New York City's Avenue of the Americas. CBS execs worked on the projects that would give them status among their peers—the projects that were stylish among their equals and their superiors. They worked on the projects that were chic in the social cliques of their industry.

Many a project was considered the antithesis of style. Admit to liking it in the least and you were shunned and ridiculed. Admit to *hating* it and you won your ten minutes of fame for the day—an extra ten minutes of acceptance, or, better yet, ten minutes in the spotlight as you cleverly mouthed a contempt that pulled your clique together, that helped it sense its warmth, its solidarity—and its sense of being an elite far above the masses, far above the people it should care for the most, its customers.

One day I was hailing a cab from a record industry luncheon party at 65th Street and Second Avenue in New York, roughly a mile away from my office and from CBS's headquarters. Just as a cab pulled up to me, three CBS executives emerged from the restaurant where the party was held and asked if they could share a ride. One of them was a product manager I had trained for two years. By now, this threesome knew I'd seen something genuine in REO Speedwagon, something worth fighting for, the cry of a Midwestern subculture vying for a right to its identity, a cry backed by extremely hard work, by a sense of humor that overrode all obstacles, and by a gift of melody. The CBS VPs and managers also knew I'd made the band a personal crusade.

The three CBSers spent the twenty minutes of our super-slow cab ride south through midday Manhattan traffic ridiculing the band among themselves. This made them look clever, hip, and socially adept in each other's eyes. And it made me furious.

Their jibes showed that they despised more than just the band. It showed that they looked down on the band's fans. Worse, it showed that they sneered at all those who might someday wake up and realize that this was a band with something personal to say to them, something that might save them from a moment of insecurity, that might console them when they were in a darkened state, something that might just plain delight them. The CBS staffers despised the bulk of their customers. And if we liked a song like REO Speedwagon's "Can't Fight This Feeling," that meant they despised you and me.

The same thing was true throughout the entertainment industry. I saw it at Warner Brothers when I was working with Prince. I saw it at ABC Records when I was working with Chaka Khan. I saw it at Paramount Pictures when I was working with Irwin Yablans. To show that he belonged to an elite, to an aristocracy, executive after executive looked down on the audience he served and displayed that contempt as a badge of rank, using it to win acceptance and attention from his peers.

In 1981, a year after the cab ride with the contemptuous anti-REO Speedwagon executives from CBS, the worldwide music industry went down the tubes, dragged into the plumbing by the worst twentieth-century economic recession since the Great Depression of the 1930s. Thousands of layoffs hit music industry veterans who'd been sure their jobs were secure. The joke of the moment was that you'd press a million copies of a record and ship it to the stores. A month later, the stores would send *two* million unsold copies of that record back for a refund.

But not a soul was pink-slipped at CBS in that year of economic plague, that year of mass job death. All three of the executives I'd shared a cab with were safe. Why? Because in the very year when it was said that you couldn't give away a record for free, much less sell one for money, REO Speedwagon sold fifteen million copies of their newest album and an uncounted number of copies of their previous LPs.

Fifteen million people needed the mood-controlling, mood-consoling power of music—the power that the mythical Orpheus and the very real David had pioneered. Fifteen million people needed it in spite of, and possibly because of, the whiplash of recession. Fifteen million people heard a value that the intellectual aristocrats at CBS had failed to hear or see. And those fifteen million made REO Speedwagon the biggest-selling band anywhere on the planet, if only for a year.

REO Speedwagon, the band the CBS executives despised, brought in the cash that paid these execs' salaries and saved their jobs! How many potential REO Speedwagons were destroyed by the contempt of the people hired to nurture their careers and to bring them to a hungry public? From my fifteen years in the music industry, I'd guess hundreds.

Ten years later, CBS hit meltdown. Its mistaken manuals of leadership came back to haunt and to dismember what had been a magnificent company. CBS was punished by the Western system and by the capitalist imperative. It was condemned for its failure to hear the cries and whispers of its constituents outside the company, condemned for its failure to sense the silent voices of those whose emotions and souls it served, condemned for its failure to care about ordinary outsiders like you and me.

CBS Records was sold off to Sony and plummeted in market share. CBS television was swallowed by Westinghouse, another company in search of its soul and unable to find it. The Black Rock of guaranteed quality William Paley had built disappeared almost entirely.

The executives at CBS had missed more than just the importance of one band. They'd failed to see the very essence of capitalism and of the Western imperative. Capitalism isn't about making yourself look good to the folks with offices on your floor and on the floors above you. It's not about preening fashionably for the folks at the water cooler, for the folks in the conference room, or for the folks at the next industry party, black-tie dinner, or softball game. It's about the people you never see. It's about the people you serve. It's about the people who will save you if there's catastrophe.

They will save you because you continue to feel their needs and serve them. Their gratitude or their disgust will appear as it did for CBS—on the long-term bottom line.

XII

THE ROCKET FUEL
OF EMPATHY

75

THE EMPATHY
DEEP INSIDE OF YOU

More Management by Walking Outside

How I, a Mozart lover and a scientist, accidentally became the editor of a rock 'n' roll magazine and doubled its sales.

When you enter a new social group, a new company, or a new industry, you look for a niche, some corner or some centerstage you can occupy, a place where you'll be needed and where you'll stand out. You do it whether you're conscious of what you're up to or not. It's one of those instincts that turns you into a probe in a social search engine, a fingertip of a universe feeling out her possibilities. It's an emotional need dictated by lateral inhibition and by the fission-fusion search strategy.

I stumbled into business by accident. And I found a niche few others seemed to want. It was a niche without a name, the slot of empathy specialist—the person who cared for the passions of creators on the inside of the team and for the feelings of customers on the outside. Ironically, this was the niche where the greatest cash flow was dammed up.

Way back in this book, I tossed you the tale of how science had snagged me when I was ten years old. A book had told the story of Galileo, had exaggerated his courage, then had explained that all science is based on the two rules that have cropped up many times in these pages:

1. The truth at any price, including the price of your life.
2. And look at things right under your nose as if you've never seen them before. Look at things you and everyone around you take for granted as if you've never seen them before. Follow your amazement. And track down answers to the questions your wonder throws your way.

That was it. Science. And I was hooked. What's more, those first two rules of science are the rules of a search strategy with a familiar twist. "The truth at any price including the price of your life" is a rule of consolidation. It means do everything in your power to reinforce something you believe in. "Look at things right under your nose" says the opposite. It urges you and me to spread out and explore—to look at ordinary things in radically different ways. To re-view. To reperceive. Then to come back to the center to consolidate by championing the truths we see. It's the fission-fusion strategy.

Yes, the first two rules of science are the rules of an evolutionary search engine. They are the rules of a universe scoping out her potential then making the impossible a reality. The first two rules of science are the rules of a secular genesis machine. They're rules of the genius of the beast. But back to the story.

The first two rules of science utterly converted me. I was too socially clumsy to make friends on planet Earth. But I felt that there may have been a home for me in space. At eleven years old, I put an engineering chart of the rocket speeds necessary to escape Earth's gravity on my bedroom wall, and I kept an old brass-barreled medical microscope on my bedroom desk, a professional instrument that I used to peeping-tom the single-celled animalcules growing in the five-gallon jar of pond water I'd stashed in the back of my bedroom closet.[1] So where, you ask, is business in this picture? Hang on tight.

By the age of twelve I'd built my first Boolean algebra machine and had co-conceived a computer that won a regional science prize. At thirteen I was doing what the book on science had told me, looking at things right under my nose as if they were brand new to me. Then something hit me. The stuff that we take for granted most isn't what's underneath our noses. The stuff we overlook is what's *behind* our noses—the gods and devils, the heavens and hells, the mystic raptures, the sense of play, the uncertainties, the shames, the insecurities, the lusts, the inanities, the pains, the rage for sports teams, and the bone-deep passion for the political dogmas of the Left or of the Right. This became my mission—to find the gods and the beasts deep inside of us, deep inside of you and me.

A poem by Edna St. Vincent Millay—"Renascence"—was an indispensable guide. It said that to see the infinite in every grain of sand, you have to feel all the pains, the pleasures, the extremes, and the day-to-day emotions of every conceivable sort of person sharing this planet with you, of every living human being.[2] You have to expand your empathy.

At sixteen, I spent a summer as a lab assistant at the largest cancer research institute in the world, the Roswell Park Cancer Institute. It was an eye-opener. The biochemist in charge of keeping me from breaking too many photo spectrometers, scintillation counters, and pipettes had spent the previous three years trying to synthesize one molecule. He had four huge piles of books in German on his desk—books he needed to plow through so he could finish making his molecule. He figured completing the task would take at least another two years.

This was not the kind of science I had in mind. I was an ambitious little sod. I wanted to fly over the terrain of all the sciences and use them to understand the mysteries of religion, poetry, the emotions, and something we science geeks seldom manage to experience—just plain everyday life. I wanted to piece together the big picture. Still doesn't sound like capitalism, does it? Hang on, that's coming.

Here's where my training in the hidden imperatives of the Western system began. I dropped out of Reed College in Portland, Oregon, in search of a mystic passion, the Zen Buddhist form of enlightenment, satori. I did my best to imitate Jack Kerouac—hitchhiking and illegally catching rides on freight trains for a year, shuttling from Seattle to San Diego and from San Francisco to Salt Lake City, pulling the life stories out of folks kind enough to give a very strange-looking kid with long, curly hair and bare feet either a lift or a tip about how to ride a freight train without being killed. My benefactors behind the steering wheels and in the freight yards included a carnival barker, a drug enforcement agent, several insurance salesmen, a lot of truck drivers, an alcoholic migrant fruit picker who feared for my soul and pleaded with me to go back home and visit my mother, and three murderers on their way from Vancouver to San Francisco to find heroin who tried to explain that, "You can't go on like this; you need a sense of meaning in your life." Not to mention a prairie state Bible college graduate who'd spent most of his adulthood trying to evade three groups that had placed radio transmitters in his teeth—the CIA, the FBI, and a Martian intelligence agency. Each of the people I ran across was fascinating and was someone whose story I could relate to. Strangely, this was an early lesson in management by walking outside. It was a lesson in what Edna St. Vincent Millay had preached. Tuned empathy.

By 1963 I was still isolated and socially incompetent. But I designed and implemented research on Skinnerian programmed learning at Rutgers University's Graduate School of Education, wrote and edited material for Sol Gordon, the psychologist and author of 30 books, at the facility he headed, the Middlesex County Mental Health Clinic in New Brunswick, New Jersey, and finally went back to restart college as a freshman at NYU.

Four years later, in the summer after my senior year at NYU, I was on my way to what felt like a scientific prison camp. I'd received four fellowships in clinical psychology and had accepted one from Columbia University. Columbia even caved in to my terms. I wanted to study the physiology behind the psyche. For that, Columbia agreed to let me take courses at its medical school.

But would it really be possible to explore the depths of human passion by designing paper-and-pencil tests and administering them to a few hundred college students in a classroom or a lab? I had the feeling that the answer was an extremely emphatic no. So how in hell was I going to plumb the depths of the human soul? How in the world was I going to find the place inside of you and me where the gods rage? How was I going to touch the infinite? How was I going to find the secular roots of the feelings we call "divine"?

The answer came from an accident. In my senior year at NYU, I'd been forced by the poet in residence, Robert Hazel, to edit and art-direct NYU's literary magazine, the *Washington Square Review*.[3] Why forced? I didn't want to do it. I hated literary magazines. They were ugly and boring. Hazel told me point blank that I was the editor no matter what I did to avoid the task. He played on my sense of duty. So I turned the publication into an experimental graphics and literary affair. The result? The *Washington Square Review* won two National

Academy of Poets Prizes while I was at the helm and caused a stir
among the art directors of three national magazines of the day, *Look*,
Evergreen Review, and, of all things, *Boys' Life*, the official magazine
of the Boy Scouts of America. (I'd been tossed out of the Boy Scouts
at the age of twelve for incompetence at Morse Code.)

The artists who'd helped staff the radically re-visioned *Washington Square Review* gave me an out, an escape chute from the
antiemotional Auschwitz of Columbia's ivory tower. My team of
artists unwittingly offered a voyage of the *Beagle* to the Galapagos
Islands of reality—to the lost continent of things we look at every day
and never see, to the submerged archipelago of gods, demons, passions, and frustrations—to the hidden heart of Western culture—to
the core of business, commerce, and industry, to the dark underbelly
of the secular genesis machine.

One day in the summer of 1968, I walked over to the Lower East
Side slum apartment of the most talented artist in the crew, a wiry,
energetic genius with a long, pointed mustache. I knocked on the door
and discovered the artist, his wife, and his two-year-old son sitting on
the carpet in a furnitureless room, crying in dismal harmony. Their
furniture had been repossessed. They were about to be evicted from
their apartment. The electricity bill was long overdue. And so was the
bill from the phone company.

This was outrageous. I hadn't planned the summer. I hadn't gotten
a job yet. But I knew that if I could take this bloody genius's portfolio
to the right people—whomever they might be—I'd get him work, he'd
be able to pay his rent, and all would be well. So he and some of the
other artists in the crew from the magazine I'd edited and art-directed
put together a portfolio of their work. I sat down with the Yellow
Pages, listed every sort of business that seemed it might need art, and
set up a routine—call twenty or more art directors every morning, set
up appointments, then visit five art directors every afternoon.

For the next three years I spent my afternoons in the offices of
America's top ad agencies, book publishers, record companies, magazines, and TV and radio networks, learning their needs. Cloud Studio
became one of the leading avant-garde art studios on the East Coast.
Forty years later, you can still see some of its work with a quick
Google on the Internet. We did animation for NBC-TV, all of the
advertising for ABC's seven FM radio stations, the art direction for a

new magazine—the *National Lampoon*—book covers, and illustrations for magazines of all kinds (the one that intrigued me most was Adam Smith's *Institutional Investor*). And we developed several new graphic styles still used in magazines today. ABC asked if we'd found an ad agency to handle their FM radio chain. I didn't want to learn how to buy ad space, so we passed. But I, a science nerd, was featured on the cover of *Art Direction Magazine*. Either this was utter madness—or this was management by walking outside.

I called Columbia University and told them I wouldn't be coming to grad school. Cloud Studio provided an accidental gift, a periscope position from which to inch toward the underbelly of the beast—toward the heart of mass emotion—toward our culture's myth-making machine. Cloud Studio was a transport vehicle, a deep sea submersible in the long-term mission to find the gods, the devils, the heavens, the hells, the ecstasies, the insecurities, and the ordinary feelings deep inside of you and me.

Once upon a time, Albert Einstein wrote a book on his theory of relativity, a short, sharp book aimed at a mass audience.[4] It implanted an important lesson in me when I was twelve. In his introduction to the volume, Einstein said that to be a genius it was not enough to come up with a theory so gorgeously complex that only seven men on the planet could understand it. It was not enough to come up with a theory of relativity. To be a genius, Einstein wrote, you had to be able to write that theory so simply and deliciously that anyone with a high school education and a reasonable intelligence could understand it. To be a genius you had to be a good, clear writer. I couldn't play baseball or football. And I didn't know how to hang out or date. So being a genius sounded like a good slot for me. And Einstein said that meant being a writer.

So at six a.m. in the morning I got up and wrote until it was time to go to the studio. I arrived at Cloud Studio's second-floor East Village commercial loft with nearly floor-to-ceiling, fifty-four-year-old display windows overlooking a seedy but yeasty part of Manhattan's Second Avenue, made phone calls, picked up the latest Cloud Studio portfolio, and headed from Fourth Street up to Madison Avenue, Rockefeller Center, and the Avenue of the Americas, where our clients were ensconced in luxury. Then I came home to my apartment in Brooklyn's Cobble Hill at seven p.m. and wrote until it was time to go to bed. But I couldn't figure out how to get my stuff published.

Two underground magazines I visited with our Cloud Studio port-folio saved the day. They asked if I'd write for them. Hell, yes. Albert Einstein himself had told me that writing was a scientific necessity. So both the magazines made me a contributing editor. And in addition to the art studio duties, I visited shops all over New York reviewing their offerings or interviewed folks on the lunatic fringes of science.

Meanwhile, *Esquire* magazine asked if I'd look into drugs and sex among teenagers in the suburbs. On weekends I'd sling the strap of a bulky new gadget over my shoulder, a cassette recorder, don my knap-sack stuffed with notebooks, and spend a day with thirteen-, fourteen-, fifteen-, and sixteen-year-olds in Connecticut, getting a feel for their lives. This was not just journalism, it was anthropology. It was another lesson in management by walking outside. Go among those you serve. Tune your empathy to their emotions. Come to know them in your heart. Follow Edna St. Vincent Millay's prescription for seeing the infinite in the ordinary. Try to feel all the emotions humans undergo in your heart. Try to sense the emotions of others in the mirror neurons of your brain, the neurons that have evolved a highly specialized task, helping you feel the emotions and the movements of others. Tune your empathy.

Then, at a conference I was covering on telenormal happenings, someone I didn't know walked up to me and asked if I wanted to edit a magazine. Yes, yes, and yes. The studio didn't really want me now that the *National Lampoon* sent a big check each month. No one was starving. And writing was something I needed to perfect. A magazine, any magazine, would let me write during the day, not at six a.m. in the morning and eleven p.m. at night.

I didn't ask what the magazine was about. It didn't matter. With good research and a kamikaze sense of concern for the folks who read your words, you could master any subject. I'd learned that lesson when I'd had a summer job writing for the Boy Scouts of America. Yes, let me repeat, I'd been tossed out of the Boy Scouts when I was a kid for incompetence at Morse Code. But for the Boy Scouts I put together booklets on stalking, tracking, camouflage, and *Ten Steps to Organize a Boy Scout Troop*—the basic booklet on how to organize a Boy Scout troop from scratch. I researched these subjects fero-ciously. Yes, it was true that I could hardly find my way into a forest, much less out of one. But I wanted the people who read what I wrote to reach the goal they were trying to achieve. This was an opportunity to stretch out and feel the hearts of people who could do the things I was incompetent at—a chance to carry out Edna St. Vincent Millay's directive of coming to know the feelings of every conceivable sort of human being. It was also another lesson in management by walking outside.

So I went uptown to Number One United Nations Plaza to meet the publisher of the magazine I'd been so strangely asked to edit, a monthly called *Circus*. It had nothing to do with clowns. Its subject was rock 'n' roll music—an art form I had very seldom listened to. But the publisher—Gerald Rothberg—must have been desperate. He hired me anyway. Then he showed me my office—a windowless, converted storage closet. I was horrified. But I signed on for the adventure.

When I settled in, my publisher tossed three magazines at me that he thought I might learn from:

- *Bravo*—a German entertainment magazine for teenagers that sold a million copies per issue in a country a fifth the size of the United States. (The biggest-selling rock publication in America—*Rolling Stone*—sold a measly 250,000 copies. Proportionally speaking, *Rolling Stone* had only one-twentieth of *Bravo*'s market penetration.)
- *Salut Les Copains*—a similar magazine with sales of a million copies per issue in France.
- And a magazine I'd grown up reading from cover to cover, *Time*.

Here was the business challenge of a lifetime. Master a subject you do not know. Get a gut feel for your audience. Learn the basics and the high-level tricks of magazine editing. If the tricks don't exist, invent them.

The real secret was this—get to know your audience. The real secret was saturated intuition, management by walking outside, and tuned empathy. Find that part of you that resonates to your audience's frequency.

The secret to *Salut Les Copains* was a simple audience-empowerment tool—a top-ten record chart compiled from ballots sent in by the magazine's readers. This gave readers an ego-stake. If they wanted to see their favorite singers go higher on the charts, they could buy the next issue, send in their ballots, and vote. The voting system also gave the staff at *Salut Les Copains* daily feedback on what their audience liked.

Bravo did something similar. It sent staff members out on the street to interview a few hundred kids at random every week. Then it took the opinions of those kids into account when it made its editorial decisions.

But, you may well say, my company already does that. We do marketing surveys. We run focus groups. When you say "we" do marketing surveys, who do you mean by "we," kemo sabe? Do you go out and do them? If you don't, you're likely to miss the boat. Here's something I learned the hard way at *Circus*: focus groups do not work. The minute you single out people and bring them into your space, you change them. Think of it as the Heisenberg uncertainty principle of marketing. In quantum physics, the Heisenberg uncertainty principle says that when you try to measure the motion of an elementary particle, you end up changing that motion. In trying to measure something, you can mess it up so badly that you can't get an accurate handle on it. The uncertainty principle's effect is massive when you assemble a focus group.

In my first year at *Circus*, I organized a focus group based on what seemed like a very clever scheme. We gave the kids who read us an ego-stake. We ran a contest asking kids to vote for their five favorite groups and to write a paragraph about why they liked music. We offered prizes and told the respondents that we'd choose a group of advisers from among them. We designed a simple mathematical technique to determine which twenty kids' tastes reflected the average opinion of our audience most accurately. Then we picked the ten high-typicality quotient readers who'd written the most articulate answers on the essay portion of our contest form and made them our advisory board.

The minute we put these highly typical kids into a group with influence over our decisions, our typical kids changed dramatically. Instead of giving us opinions that reflected the masses, they realized their positions of influence, picked groups that were way, way off the beaten path, then used their new position as insiders to try to make those groups happen. Why? Because if they could make a quirky unknown group succeed through their personal advocacy, they could demonstrate their power, they could increase their ego payoff exponentially.

Ego-stake is a very good thing. But all good things in excess can be toxic.

So we abandoned our focus group and realized that to get the opinions of our readers we'd have to do what *Bravo* did, reach out to new kids every issue. We stole *Salut Les Copain*'s approach and put a ballot in the magazine inviting our readers to push their favorite acts up to number one on a monthly music chart. Then we tabulated the results. New ballots came in every day, and I kept abreast of the tally. Now I had a way to tune my tastes to what my readers found delicious. I had a tool for championing my masses and a tool for tuning my mirror neurons, for tuning my empathy.

Equally important were the six months of weekends I'd spent among kids in Connecticut, exploring drugs and sex in the world of teens and tuning my empathy to the adolescent frequency at *Esquire*'s request. Then came a spare-time assignment while I was at *Circus*—another six months of work with teenagers in the swanky private schools of New York City, scoping out the sexual and drug activities of teenagers on behalf of *New York* magazine.

Sixty kids helped me go behind their parents' backs, slipping me into the secret community that kids hide from adults. I loved these kids. They helped bring out a part of me—the teenager—that, as a science nerd, I'd never been. Which is one secret to tuned empathy and to management by walking outside. Find the part of you that resonates to your audience's frequency. Carry your consumers in your heart. Crusade on their behalf. Don't posture for your peers. Fight for your audience. Fight for your customers. And for the creators in your company.

Another technique tuned me in to my kids emotionally. I ran more contests to get my audience's gut feel. One asked the readers to pick their favorite paragraph in the magazine. I read the letters that came in and had the results tabulated. The paragraphs the readers loved were vivid anecdotes, mini-stories that roused the emotions, especially emotions tinged with hints of sex and rebellion. Here's where it's critical to recognize a distinction. If you're cynical and keep your audience at a distance, little of what you learn about their wants is likely to help. Care about your audience, find the piece of them inside of you and find the piece of you inside of them. Use tuned empathy and the Force will be with you—the Force of emotional truth.

For the next two years I was a teenager at heart, fighting against the elitists of the rock-crit establishment, a self-appointed aristocracy that postured for its peers and despised its audience. This small group of rock rulers reviewed music for the *New York Times*, edited the music section of the *Village Voice*,⁵ edited rival monthly music magazines, and wrote for *Rolling Stone* and a rock magazine that was considered the ultimate in "gonzo journalism," *Creem*. The rock-crit clique clotted together at lunches and parties and gloried in its superiority. Which meant it got its kicks—like the folks at CBS—from hating the things its audience liked. Its members deliberately shoved oddball, snooty, groupthink choices down the audience's throat, determined to "educate" their readers, determined to "teach" and lead the masses.

Like the product managers and publicists at CBS, the rock-crit establishment postured for its peers but loathed the lowly proles it served, the flock that gave it its paycheck.

I did just the opposite. Emotion was at the core of what I did to create a new approach for *Circus*. But rigorous analysis played its part, too. This is where tuned empathy and saturated intuition meet. It's where emotion and reason combine in something far more potent than either on its own. It's knowing your field—knowing those you serve—in every breath, in every pulse, and in every bone. I retroengineered *Bravo*, *Salut Les Copains*, and *Time*, teasing out the fibers of their anatomies from paragraph structure to tricks of cover design and to the frequency with which they covered a celebrity. I listened to rock music obsessively and studied the stories of rock's stars as if I were a Talmudic scholar. I bought the first model of a revolutionary headset-radio Sony had just unveiled—a pair of hulking silver earcups with a bulky, rectangular black package of electronic circuitry perched like space-helmet equipment on the top of the head strap and with a pair of two-foot-long extendible antennae poking up from the earcups at just the right angle to be bizarre. Those antennae made you look like an oversized Martian ant. I wore it everywhere, listening to as much rock music as could fit into only two eardrums. At the price of looking utterly idiotic, I was saturating my intuition.

I challenged myself to identify songs on the radio after just hearing the first bar. I convinced the record companies to divulge their production schedules for upcoming albums and developed methods for predicting which albums would be in the top ten on the charts four months in advance. I persuaded my publisher to stop hiding the sales figures and to let me use them so I could design correlational techniques to determine which aspects of the magazine had the greatest impact on sales rises and sales dips.

And I read the history of the entertainment business, taking it back not just to Elvis and the 1950s, but to the birth of radio in 1922, to the Jazz Age, and to Irving Berlin in the 1890s when he was a waiter in the Bowery, a gang-ridden Tammany neighborhood in downtown New York.[6] I read the history of teen culture and adult outrage all the way back to Plato and Shakespeare. Then I spent a month tracing cyclic patterns and subcultural currents in *Billboard*'s music charts from 1911 to 1971. This was more than brain food, it was saturated intuition on an eating binge.

After a year of fourteen-hour days, seven days a week, I came to my publisher with a plan. It broke all the rules he'd laid down for the magazine in the past. But I guaranteed him it would work.

I wasn't kidding or using slick salesmanship when I made that guarantee. I *knew* sales would increase. It was a case of saturated intuition, of what P. T. Barnum had used to put wonder into the sourdough of American culture. I knew what my audience lusted for. I knew what we could offer them. I'd completed phase one of management by walking outside. Saturated intuition, tuned empathy, hard work, analysis, an ability to isolate and measure variables, and a love of your audience can give you something that seems very unscientific but is the key to business success—a vision, a vivid picture of a future waiting to be made. Visions are central to the Western system. They are the keys to capital creation. Visions drove the folks who planned the first stone wall and invented the brick. And visions drove the inventors of the weaving machine and the steam engine, the inventors of the Industrial Revolution. Ultimately vision can drive you and me, too.

Circus magazine's circulation rose steadily each month after we applied the new approach. Distributors vied to handle our publication. They offered ever larger amounts of money. Our publisher, Gerald Rothberg, went from renting an apartment overlooking Second Avenue on Manhattan's Upper East Side to owning a posh apartment the size of an aircraft hanger with a many-windowed, corner view of New York's East River.

In twelve months our circulation soared 211 percent. We became the biggest-selling music monthly in America.

Meanwhile, Gulf & Western heard the legend of a kid spinning straw into gold in a windowless, closet-sized office near the UN and asked if I'd establish a public and artist relations department for its fourteen record companies—at a hefty increase in salary. And they promised me an office with windows—three of them!

After I'd moved over to Gulf & Western's skyscraper perched on Columbus Circle and had settled into my office overlooking the southwest corner of Central Park, the publishers of rival magazines asked for the secret to *Circus*'s success. At first I wouldn't give it to them. Then *Circus* abandoned the techniques I'd mapped out in a fifty-six-page booklet before leaving. My ego was bruised. Capital is stored fantasy, stored persistence, and stored *ego*! So I gave my *Circus* strategies away to those who called, those who dropped into my office, those who asked for lunch meetings, and those who seemed to want the formula.

One magazine that applied the techniques found an editor who had an enthusiasm for his audience. His application of the *Circus* secrets succeeded mightily. Another applied the techniques with less love of its audience and a bit more of the old critical arrogance and increased its sales more modestly. Meanwhile, *Circus* learned the mistake it had made by straying from a formula based on constant contact with its readers. It went into chapter eleven bankruptcy for a year. Then *Circus* readopted the approach that I'd evolved. And it came back from near death as North America's number-one music monthly.

When a founding *Rolling Stone* editor, Chet Flippo, wrote a master's thesis on the history of rock journalism, it included six pages on someone the thesis said had invented a new magazine genre, the heavy metal magazine. Yes, it shocked me too, but that someone was a Rachmaninoff lover—me.

This adventure in commerce was a wild, rough, risky, and joyous ride, a strenuous power glide on the updrafts of tuned empathy. It was a live-or-die soar into the stratosphere of saturated intuition—saturation billowing with something that went far beyond mere scholarship. It was the hang glide path to management by walking outside.

76

WHAT HATH OCHRE TAUGHT? THE CARE AND FEEDING OF IDENTITY

One More Way to Manage by Walking Outside

Crusading for your customers—how one firm pulled it off.

The cosmetics industry, the identity business that first showed up in the human emotional tool kit three hundred thousand years ago, was growing at a double-digit rate in the 1980s.

Management by walking outside was one of the secrets to this boom.

The year was 1982. By then I had founded and was CEO of the biggest publicity firm in the music industry, the Howard Bloom Organization, Ltd. We'd taken bands, singers, and entire musical styles that the rock-critic elite and/or the folks at their own record companies often despised—like REO Speedwagon, John Cougar Mellencamp, Joan Jett (who'd been turned down by twenty-three record companies), Billy Idol, the disco movement, black crossover, country crossover, punk, and rap—to the top. We'd had the highest-selling album of the year three years in a row. We'd won four awards as PR firm of the year from *Performance Magazine*. We'd publicized films for Disney, New Line Cinema, and Warner Brothers. We'd helped Sony launch its first software beachhead in the United States, Sony Video. Delta Airlines' in-flight magazine had called us "one of the top pop PR firms in the world." *New York* magazine had said we were the most thorough and efficient firm in our business. And the leading text-book on music publicity, *Billboard's Guide to Music Industry Pub-licity*, had devoted twenty pages to me and to the development of the technique I called *perceptual engineering*, a method for getting a group that was unified in its condemnation of something to turn around and see that something's true value.

We'd had a few failures, too. Failures that still make me grit my teeth in shame. Failures whose lessons I'm still trying to extract to this day.

One midweek lunchtime I nipped into a hair emporium for Japanese executives below my two-story office on 55th Street and Lexington Avenue, in the heart of one of Manhattan's choicest busi-ness districts, for a quick haircut. Why a Japanese salon? It was the nearest I could find and I didn't have time to go on a haircut hunt. What's more, the Japanese business invasion was in full-court press, and Japanese managers needed a place that understood their lan-guage, and their tresses.

In that era haircuts weren't quick. First there was the rinse, then the shampoo, then the scissoring, and finally a tedious wait under the hairdryer.

Next to me in one of those chairs that flatten you out and put you under the total control of the Japanese woman who tends to your locks was a blond American woman who apparently also knew the secret of this place and was willing, as I was, to have her hair nipped and tucked by stylists who didn't speak English.

We had ninety minutes side by side while the lathering and the scissoring went on, so, just as in my hitch-hiking days, I was eager to hear the story of her life. Here's the key.

She was a product manager for a major cosmetics company. Her job had a yearly migratory cycle. She'd pick a major city almost arbi-trarily—Minneapolis one year, Seattle or Tucson the next. She'd find the biggest department store in town. She'd get a job at the cosmetics counter. And for six months she would minister to the needs of thou-sands of women who used the products made by her company and by its competitors.

This may sound very pedestrian, but it's not. Making decisions about emotional tools that will tell people who you are and who you want to be is one of the most difficult things on earth for us lowly human beings. It hits us with all the nagging uncertainty that once drove folks to the Delphic oracle. It intimidates us by challenging us to create, to choose, or to totally blow our statement of identity. It generates decision panic.

The woman next to me knew this experience well. She went through it every morning when she put on her own makeup. Her morning ritual was the secret to her powers, her touch point with her customers, the hot spot of tuned empathy.

A makeup counter salesperson is not just a retail clerk. She is an artist. She has to use everything she feels and knows, all of her creativity and her intuition, to help a customer through a crisis. A woman steps up to the counter. Sometimes she knows exactly what she wants to buy. More often, she doesn't have a clue. She wants a new look. Something not too radical. Something that feels just right. Her social calculator is raging at full speed, but it is wobbling crazily like a computer on the verge of a crash. There are thousands of permutations and combinations of color spread out below the glass of the counter. Which will make the masterpiece she craves? Which will tell her friends that they should accept her? Which will make her friends admire her, too? Which will catch the admiring gaze of men? Which will make her look like an utter fool?

Which will advertise that she belongs? Which will show that she's not beneath her friends but not too high above them, either? Which will also help her grab the attention of the higher-ranking groups that she aspires to join?

Which will make her look like the models and the actresses currently in vogue? Which will produce just the right combination of the looks of Raquel Welch, Mary Tyler Moore, Farrah Fawcett Majors, and Kate Jackson (remember, this was the 1980s)? The combination that will say, "It's me. But I'm new and improved and for heaven's sake, please admire me"?

These needs flicker through our minds at levels we can barely see. They hit us when we're in identity turmoil and decision panic, something the sales manuals of the 1940s and 1950s pinpointed more accurately than any studies done by marketing science during the last few decades.

Using her intuition and her own emotions, the makeup product manager from the big and sometimes aloof city of New York had to be a coach, a therapist, a mind reader, a shaman, a soul seeker, and a soul enhancer. She had to be an artist of identity in the way that Van Gogh was an artist of oil paint, canvas, landscape, sky, emotion, movement, sun, stars, and light. She had to do this act of soul surgery sixty times a day. She had to be a virtuoso of tuned empathy.

After six months behind the cosmetics counter, the product manager who told this tale knew deep in her heart what the women of Minneapolis wanted. She knew not only what they needed from the glass case of the makeup counter. She also had a sense of what these women hungered for but could not find. She had a sense of the things her customers had never seen but that the emotional core of these women cried out for.

When she flew back to New York, she went directly to the research and development department. There, a crew of scientists—most of them male—were inventing new colors, new shades, new textures, new glosses, new waxy or chalky sticks, new powders, new applicators, and new packaging. Shades of the stone-grinding makeup creators of 270,000 years ago.

Fresh from her immersion in the minds and hearts of her customers, the product executive looked over the new offerings, and if she was lucky or creative, she spotted many of the things her flock craved but had never imagined. She took a powder from one workbench, a color from another, thought of a way to use a newly invented applicator to end run old frustrations, and asked the scientific crew to make up a new combination so she could test it against the need she sensed so clearly in her gut and in her mind.

She was an advocate, a saint, and a champion for the thousands of women she had met. She was, in her own small way, a savior for the millions whose desires were reflected in the needs of the women she'd been nurturing.

Saving humans in ways that may seem petty is never small. Identity is the heart of who we are. And the woman telling her story in the next chair in the hair salon was an identity empowerer.[1]

This is carrying your customers in your heart. This is tending to your flock. This is more than just tapping the brains inside your company. It embraces the minds and feelings of the people you serve. This is the height of empathic tuning. It is an upping of group IQ. And it follows the second rule of science: "Look at things right under your nose as if you've never seen them before, then proceed from there."

It is a small example of messianic capitalism—capitalism that respects the dignity of needs we rational, intelligent people all too often deride.

This is management by walking outside.

77

YOU OWE YOUR AUDIENCE YOUR LIFE

The Curse of Losing Touch

A tale of two clients. One made *Lord of the Rings*.
The other lost his name.

"You owe your audience more than your music," I used to tell my rock 'n' roll clients, "you owe your audience your life." I wasn't exactly sure what I meant. But I knew with all my blood and marrow it was true. Now that I've been back in the science of mass behavior for twenty years, I have a clearer idea of why.

Your fans will put your poster on their walls. They'll read feature stories on you. They'll read your personal history. They'll read the story of your passions and of how you found them. They'll read the tales of how you went from nowhere—from where your fans are now—to fame. In you your fans will find a piece of what they want to be. They'll find in you a mirror of the selves they thought were crazy, the selves they had to hide until you gave them dignity. You give them a mirror they need to survive. A soul that is not validated by friends and heroes dies.

Use your passions in your work, I told my clients. Now I'm telling that to you. Stay true to your visions. Be aware as you grow older of how your passions change. Use those new passions in your work. Your audience is going through those changes too. Your audience needs the change in you.

Do not lose touch with the people you serve, even as you pursue visions that may seem utterly absurd. Capital is stored vision, stored courage, stored persistence, and stored persuasion. Capital is stored fantasy, stored daring, stored promotion, stored advertising, and stored social organization. Capital is stored ego. (Keep the ego hidden, but don't be ashamed of the fact that it's there.)

Be true to yourself and you'll serve others. Be true to yourself but keep the people you want to reach deep in your heart.

Prince pulled this off brilliantly from 1981, when I first began working with him, to 1987. He was only nineteen years old when I first met him, but he had a vision unlike those of any around him. Prince's passion welled continuously. He composed and made new music nearly every day. And that music expressed the feelings he couldn't say. That music told the tale of what he was, of where he'd been, of what he craved, of what he felt, of what he dreamed, and of what he wanted the world to be.

In 1987, Prince stayed true to his vision, but it failed him. Why? He cut his ties to his audience. His personal passions moved him in directions many of his fans couldn't follow. In his second movie, a film called *Under the Cherry Moon*, he seemed to kill the Prince he'd been and to show that he wanted to become someone new. I suspected that he stopped being Prince and tried to become his father—a jazz musician. Or, as he saw it, he made his music not for himself but for his God. And God was not as melodic as Prince had been.

Was Prince true to his obsessions? Absolutely. But without an empathic feel for his audience—without tuned empathy—his popularity plummeted. It showed. Prince renamed himself "the artist-formerly-known-as-Prince." (We'll poke into how Prince resurrected his career in a minute.)

Another of my clients from the late 1980s stayed in touch with his passions AND with those of his audience. When I first met him, his obsession with sci-fi and fantasy appeared on every shelf and horizontal surface of his Lower Manhattan office. His collection of futuristic toys made me want to drop my briefcase, forget the meeting, and let my inner kid go crazy. Seventeen years later, Bob Shaye took the credibility he'd earned with the successes of his company, New Line Cinema, wangled three hundred million dollars in funding, and laid it all down on the ultimate sci-fi/fantasy toy, a film trilogy called *The*

Lord of the Rings.[1] How did this trio of films do at the box office? By Reuters' calculations, it grossed over three billion dollars worldwide.[2]

What do Prince and Bob Shaye have to do with the jobs that you and I do every day?

This is no longer the age of mass production. Making things is now done by the Chinese. This is not the information age either. Information is stale and dry.

Lifelessness is not what you and I buy. We buy commodities, practical things that fill our basic needs. And we buy emotion: we buy passion, uplift, consolation, validation, new powers, and identity. We hunger to buy meaning, but that is in short supply.

This is the end of the age of objectivity. This is the age that wrings the meanness of "lean and mean" out of its system. This is the age that will finally couple reason to our passions. If we're to go to the next level in business, in the economy, in society, and in our personal lives, this will be the age of immersion in the feelings of those you serve. This will be the age of self-revelation. This will be the age of saturated intuition—knowing everything you can and taking the implications of your knowledge to the max. This will be the age of prophetic leadership, leadership that dares take on the tasks of supporting, consoling, empowering, and invigorating each of those you serve.

For business, this is the age that asks of you what only artists and saints have formerly been required to achieve. This is the age of secular salvation. This is the age of empathy. This is the age of epiphanies and vision. This is the age of the messianic. This is the age of goals and purpose. This is the age of identity. And, if we all work hard enough, this will be a turning point for Western civilization. This will be the age when a capitalism of the soul finally makes its imperatives explicit. This will be the age when our culture understands what it has achieved, eliminates its old mistakes, and attains new visions of its future missions. This will be the age of dreams turned swiftly into solid things. This will be the age of meaning. This will be an age of radical upgrade for the evolutionary search engine and for the secular genesis machine.

* * *

In the mid-1990s Prince found a new way to stay in tune with his audience, a new way to bring his customers inside his team. He started a Web site—npgonlineltd.com, the NPG, the New Power Generation—that allowed him to interact directly with his fans. By 2007, Prince was back on top again, selling 120,000 tickets to a London show at the Millennium Dome in twenty minutes and making headlines with his halftime appearance at the Super Bowl. Prince had returned to tuned empathy.

Others that caught the drift of bringing your customers inside your team include amazon.com, which enticed its Web site visitors into becoming its content providers, writing reviews of its books and other products and rating Amazon's offerings. And it includes Wikipedia, which gets all of its content, all of its encyclopedia articles, from its Web site viewers. Amazon and Wikipedia are remarkable organizations, new forms of consolidation and structure creation that many have tried to copy. Why do they succeed? They give their visitors an ego-stake. And they give their employees a remarkable tool with which to tune their empathy.

78

LET US SAVE THE HOLLOW MEN—SET YOUR PEOPLE FREE

Do well by doing good. But first get rid of old clichés and know what goodness means.

[M]inds of the strongest and most active powers . . . fall below mediocrity, and labor without effect, if confined to uncongenial pursuits. [But] when . . . each individual can find his proper element . . . [he] can call into activity the whole vigor of his nature.
Alexander Hamilton, "Manufactures," 1791[1]

As humans with a conscience, we have a right to make moral choices. Even if profits and paychecks don't favor it, we can choose to save our neighbors. We can choose to be truthful and just. We can choose to make profits from prophetic values, to put messianic leadership ahead of quarterly earnings, to use tuned empathy to find the secret needs and fantasies of others even before those needs have found words and before those fantasies have surfaced in daydreams. But in case moral arguments don't grab you, try this.

Do your business dishonestly, steal from your customer instead of serving and uplifting her or him, and you may well be brought down either by the market, by the media, or by the protest industry. These arms of the capitalist system generate their revenues by selling scandal, by telling the tales of folks who cheat. And they should. They are the businesses that humiliated J. D. Rockefeller for ten years and that made J. P. Morgan look like a monster.

Don't leave your emotions at the breakfast table. They are your most important asset, your scopes and your imagers, tuning you to the whispers of the public mood. Why? Because you are a part of that public too. What you want is likely to be what others want—especially if you've stayed in touch, especially if you've used tuned empathy.

But there's another payoff for taking your emotions to work with you. There's another reason to feel out the needs of those outside your company and to fill them. The son of a New England pencil manufacturer once observed that "the mass of men lead lives of quiet desperation." An early twentieth-century bank executive frustrated with his work and with the work of those around him called those he saw around him in the United States and in England "the hollow men, heads filled with straw." The manufacturer's son was Henry David Thoreau, author of *Walden*. The banker was the poet T. S. Eliot.

Why the desperation and why the sense of hollowness? Because we need to know we're working for something bigger than ourselves. We need to know we're contributing to the lives of others. We need to know that our contributions count. So do what you need to do— work for something bigger. Work to upgrade, console, and delight your fellow human beings. Feed their lust for novelty, even when it takes directions that seem crazy to you. Give them status symbols if they need them. Help them gain a feeling of identity. More important, give them new powers, new freedoms, new choices, and new guides through the nightmare of too much choice, give them new anxiety relievers. Give them more tools for mood control, emotional consolation, creativity, and elation.

Help others grow selfish on behalf of others too. Ask what your fixations and what your private passions can contribute to the lives of others. Get fervent about it. Crusade! If it's a better art-directed envelope for the mail room, one that will light up the people who find it in their mail box, if it's a service that will give your customers the honest sense that you care for their security, no matter what it is, do it! Forget the horse-puckey of lean and mean. Meanness is punished in the long run by the capitalist system. It's socked by a dive in long-range profits and in long-range value, long-range company capitalization. It's rocked by the hatred the meanness makers generate. Profit, value, and longevity come from caring, not from ruthless savagery. You are here—at your job, your forty or sixty hours a week—not to plunder but to please. You are here to give eight hours of meaning to those you work for, to those who work for you, and most of all to your public, to your audience, to the tens of millions or hundreds of millions you would like to reach and bring into your fold.

In the 1990s corporate leaders were taught to work on behalf of others—on behalf of investors and employees—their major groups of "stakeholders." But the concept of stakeholders missed the point. What many analysts failed to see was a deeper moral imperative at the heart of the Western system.

Feed your flock with more than loaves and fishes. Feed them with caring, sharing, warmth, and new tools for friendship. Feed their lust for amazement, their hunger for belonging, and their need for admiration and attention. Feed them entertainment and escape. Feed them meaning and commitment. Feed them the surprise of recognition that bursts from unconventional, unexpected truths. Feed the flames of identity hunger, feed the flames of those whose souls flicker in the way that yours does, too. Dare to be Promethean. Steal the fire of the gods and give it to those you brush past in the street.

Stop and talk to strangers. Visit neighborhoods and towns you've never seen. Do what saints and saviors do. Go among your people. People you've never imagined meeting. Get to know them. Stand up for them at meetings. Fight for them when plans are laid. Bring humanity new ways of being, new ways of seeing, and whole new forms of life and play.

Stretch the range of human powers, as the first stone toolmakers did.

Give us ways to show that we belong and yet stand out, as the creators of the first ground-stone makeup kits in Africa and India did.

Stretch the range of fantasy the way the makers of the first stone-walled city, Jericho, did.

Stretch the reach of comfort and security the way the makers of the first brick city, Catal Huyuk, did.

Give us new metaphors with which to puzzle out our mysteries—mysteries that range from private insecurities to the wheeling of the cosmos—as the first shepherds and the first explorers did.

Give us pride and higher aspirations the way the first pyramid builders did.

Turn our trash into treasure, as the Mesopotamian deal recorders who turned squabbles into writing did.

Give us goals and meaning, as Moses, Jesus, and Muhammad did.

Surprise us—satisfy our lust for novelty and choice—the way Phoenician merchant sailors did.

Give us power over our moods as David and the real-life equivalents of Orpheus did.

Give us new tools with which we can connect in global productivity teams, as Croesus of Lydia, inventor of money, and as the Roman and Venetian bankers did.

Validate us in our moments of confusion, as the Greek oracle creators and the Roman dream book publishers did.

Upgrade the convenience of the everyday as the Roman concrete creators and their aqueducts did.

Stretch the breadth of our horizons, as Marco Polo, Prince Henry the Navigator, and Christopher Columbus did.

Give us tools to win others to our ideas, as the pamphlet printers who empowered Christopher Columbus and Martin Luther did.

Satisfy our needs for the harmless but undignified, as Benvenuto Cellini and William Shakespeare did.

Give us new rituals to make sense of our day, new ways of coming together and of exciting each other as the importers of the afternoon tea ceremony from China and the importers of Yemeni coffee at the first cafés did.

Give us new frivolities and new openings to the formerly strange as the importers of tulips from Turkey did.

Give us new levels of reality, new virtual plateaus of possibility, as Daniel Defoe and novels did.

Give us new ways to share the phantasms drifting through our brains as Prince Ferdinando de' Medici and his instrument maker, Bartolomeo Cristofori, the inventors of the piano, did.

Give us your soul and bare your emotions, as Jean-Jacques Rousseau did.

Give us new tools of understanding, as Adam Smith and his *Wealth of Nations* did.

Turn luxuries into everyday commodities, as the mass-producers of cotton did.

Warn us of our failings, of our complacency, of our alternatives, and of our dangers, as Isaiah, Marx, and Ida Tarbell did.

Give us an ego-stake in your plans the way Linnaeus did and we will pull through for you. Add us to your brain trust—add us to your group IQ. Give us your visions, give us your obsessions, give us your heart, and give us your caring. Give us new tools, and we will give new visions, new obsessions, new fantasies, new realities, new powers, and new emotions back to you.

Help us serve a purpose higher than ourselves. Help us do what slime mold, bees, and ants achieve. Help us serve the interests of our fellow human beings. And help us serve the goals of biomass, the grand experiment of life. Help us achieve our destiny as antennae of creation, as explorers in an evolutionary search engine, as participants in a godlike process, as agents of creation in a secular genesis machine.

These are the imperatives of the Western system. These are the implicit commandments of third-millennium capitalism, of messianic capitalism. They've cried out silently for two and a half million years, waiting to be said, waiting to gain utterance through you.

This is a universe in search of her potential. And you are her next-step creator. May you exhilarate and prosper. May you do your job with passion, reason, empathy, and astonishment. May you do your job in ways exuberant and new.

ENDNOTES

These endnotes have been abridged to give you a book of reasonable size. To see the unabridged endnotes—and pictures—see howardbloom.net.

PROLOGUE

I. Does Soul Belong in This Machine?

1. Jean Baudrillard, *Selected Writings*, edited by Mark Poster (Palo Alto, CA: Stanford University Press, 1988), pp. 22–23; Anastasios S. Korkotsides, *Consumer Capitalism* (London: Routledge, 2007), p. xvii; Sallie Westwood, *Power and the Social* (London: Routledge, 2002), p. 121.

2. Raising the Poor and the Oppressed: Which Is the System That Does It Best?

1. Grizzly Adams—a nineteenth-century Wild West adventurer who inspired a 1977–1978 TV series and several TV specials and films—made the trip from California to New York in the 1850s, rounding Cape Horn in the Concorde of its day, the clipper ship *Golden Fleece*, in only three and a half months. Few ships were this swift. See Phineas Taylor Barnum, *The Humbugs of the World* (Amsterdam: Fredonia Books, 2001, reprinted from the original 1866 edition), pp. 38–39.

2. Karl Marx and Friedrich Engels, *The Communist Manifesto*, ed. Gareth Stedman Jones and trans. Samuel Moore (New York: Penguin, 2002), p. 11.

I THE MYSTERY OF MANIC-DEPRESSIVE ECONOMIES

4. The Great Crash of 2008

1. Pablo Martinez Monsivais, "Government Prepared to Lend $7.7 Trillion," *Bloomberg News*, November 24, 2008.

2. Gregor Peter Schmitz, "G-20 Meeting in Washington—The Good Intentions Summit," *Der Spiegel*, November 17, 2008.

3. Louis Uchitelle, Edmund L. Andrews, and Stephen Labaton, "U.S. Loses 533,000 Jobs in Biggest Drop since 1974," *New York Times*, December 5, 2008. America lost a total of 2.6 million jobs in 2008.

4. Gregg Farrell and Barbara Hansen, "Stocks May Fall, but Execs' Pay Doesn't," *USA Today* April 11, 2008.

5. HCL Finance invented the term *NINJA loan*. Another name in the finance business for NINJA loans was "liar loans." The formal titles for NINJA loans, liar loans, and other high-risk mortgage loans of this kind were "subprime loans" and "subprime mortgages."

6. Steven A. Holmes, "Fannie Mae Eases Credit to Aid Mortgage Lending," *New York Times*, September 30, 1999.

7. Jo Becker, Sheryl Gay Stolberg, and Stephen Labaton, "The Reckoning: White House Philosophy Stoked Mortgage Bonfire," *New York Times*, December 21, 2008.

8. Edmund Conway, "'Ninja' Loans Explode on Sub-prime Frontline," *London Telegraph*, September 22, 2008.

9. Bureau of the Census, "Census Bureau Reports on Residential Vacancies and Homeownership," *United States Department of Commerce News*, October 25, 2004.

5. Who Toppled the Titans?

1. Paul Rancatore, "Ten Steps to Save Obama's First Term (and Billions in Taxpayer Dollars)," unpublished manuscript, December 8, 2008.

2. CNN Money, "New Century Files for Chapter 11 Bankruptcy," CNN Money, April 3, 2007, http://money.cnn.com/2007/04/02/news/companies/new_century_bankruptcy/index.htm (accessed December 17, 2008).

3. JP Morgan Chase, "Strengthening Communities," http://www.jp morganchase.com/cm/Satellite?c=Page&cid=1159304834085&pagename =jpmc/Page/New_JPMC_Homepage (accessed December 17, 2008).

4. BBC News, "Sub-prime Stricken Sachsen Probed," BBC News, August 28, 2007, http://news.bbc.co.uk/2/hi/business/6967400.stm (accessed December 18, 2008).

5. UBS, "UBS Factsheet," http://www.ubs.com/1/e/media_overview/ media_asiapacific/corporate_factsheet.html (accessed December 19, 2009).

6. Reuters, "ICBC Tops Citigroup as World's Biggest Bank," July 24, 2007.

7. Eric Dash, "The Citigroup Bailout Came at a Cost," International Herald Tribune, November 24, 2008.

8. "Merrill Lynch," Fortune 500, 2006, http://money.cnn.com/magazines/ fortune/fortune500/snapshots/865.html (accessed December 15, 2008).

9. "Wall Street's Most Famous Bull for Sale," CNN.com, December 20, 2004, http://money.cnn.com/2004/12/20/news/newsmakers/nyse_bull/index .htm (accessed February 28, 2009).

10. Federal Reserve Bank, "Ben Bernanke," Board of Governors of the Federal Reserve System, http://www.federalreserve.gov/aboutthefed/bios/ board/bernanke.htm (accessed December 15, 2008); see, for example, Ben S. Bernanke, *Essays on the Great Depression* (Princeton, NJ: Princeton University Press, 2004); Ashley Seager, "'Helicopter Ben' and His 0% Remedy for Depression," *Guardian*, March 19, 2008.

11. Federal Reserve Board, Board of Governors of the Federal Reserve Bank, http://www.federalreserve.gov/ (accessed December 15, 2008).

12. "Timeline: Global Credit Crunch: A Quick Guide to How the Credit Crunch Unfolded," BBC News, December 19, 2008, http://news.bbc.co.uk/ 1/hi/business/7521250.stm (accessed December 26, 2008).

13. Walden Siew, "MBIA Details Huge Mortgage Exposure, Shares Collapse," Reuters, December 20, 2007.

14. Ben Bernanke, "Remarks by Governor Ben S. Bernanke before the National Economists Club, Washington, DC, December 2, 2004," Federal Reserve Bank, http://www.federalreserve.gov/BoardDocs/Speeches/2004/ 20041202/default.htm (accessed December 23, 2008); Hossein Askari and Noureddine Krichene, "The Mother of All Golden Parachutes," *Asia Times*, October 4, 2008.

15. Bernanke attributed the term helicopter drop of money to one of the fathers of free-market economics, Milton Friedman. See Ben Bernanke, "Remarks by Governor Ben S. Bernanke before the National Economists Club, Washington, DC, November 21, 2002," Federal Reserve Board, http:// www.federalreserve.gov/BOARDDOCS/SPEECHES/2002/20021121/

default.htm (accessed December 24, 2008). See also Dean Foust, "Will 'Helicopter Ben' Bernanke Ride to the Rescue?" *BusinessWeek*, August 16, 2008.

16. Jane Wardell, "Woolworths to Go into Administration," Associated Press, November 26, 2008; "Q&A: Bankruptcy Made Simple: Bankruptcy, Receivership and Administration Mean Different Things in Different Countries. BBC News Online Explains," BBC News Online, October 5, 2001, http://news.bbc.co.uk/1/hi/business/1578896.stm (accessed February 13, 2009).

6. The Music of Boom and Crash

1. Joshua Goldstein, *Long Cycles: Prosperity and War in the Modern Age* (New Haven, CT: Yale University Press, 1988); John Sterman and Dennis Lynn Meadows, "Strategem-2: A Microcomputer Simulation Game of the Kondratiev Cycle," working paper, MIT, 1985; Arno Tausch, *From the "Washington" towards a "Vienna Consensus"? A Quantitative Analysis on Globalization, Development and Global Governance* (Hauppauge, NY: Nova, 2006), p. 136.

2. Nikolai D. Kondratiev, N. A. Makasheva, Stephen S. Wilson, Warren J. Samuels, and Vincent Barnett, *The Works of Nikolai D. Kondratiev*, trans. Stephen S. Wilson (London: Pickering & Chatto, 1998).

3. For the technological interpretation of the Kondratiev wave and for the techno-interpretation's debt to the ideas of Joseph Schumpeter, see Byung-Rok Choi, *High Technology Development in Regional Economic Growth: Policy Implications of Dynamic Externalities* (London: Ashgate, 2003), p. 3; Christopher Freeman and Francisco Louçã, *As Time Goes By: From the Industrial Revolutions to the Information Revolution* (New York: Oxford University Press, 2001), p. 81; Karamjit S. Gill, *Information Society: New Media, Ethics, and Postmodernism* (New York: Springer, 1996), p. 12.

4. Carole Collier Frick, *Dressing Renaissance Florence: Families, Fortunes, & Fine Clothing* (Baltimore: Johns Hopkins University Press, 2002).

5. Paul Abbott Ketchum, *Microbiology: Introduction for Health Professionals* (New York: Wiley, 1984), p. 3; Ben Waggoner, "Antony van Leeuwenhoek (1632–1723)," University of California Museum of Paleontology, http://www.ucmp.berkeley.edu/history/leeuwenhoek.html (accessed December 28, 2008).

6. Niall Ferguson, *The Ascent of Money: A Financial History of the World* (New York: Penguin, 2008).

7. UK Parliament, "The Woolsack," http://www.parliament.uk/parliament/guide/woolsack.htm (accessed December 20, 2008).

8. John Kay's patent of the flying shuttle in 1733 would be one key to mechanized fabric production. Lance Day and Ian McNeil, *Biographical Dic-*

tionary of the History of Technology (London: Taylor & Francis, 1996), p. 393.

9. Mary Beggs-Humphreys, Hugh Gregor, and Darlow Humphreys, *The Industrial Revolution* (London: Allen & Unwin, 1975).

10. Watt took out his first steam engine patent in 1769, but he wasn't satisfied with the machine he'd built. He worked on the design for another fifteen years. In 1784 he finally took out his last patent. At last he felt he had a machine that, in the words of Perry Walton, "was applicable to power-driving of all sorts." Watt's 1784 design was in use for the next hundred years. See Perry Walton, *The Story of Textiles: A Bird's-Eye View of the History of the Beginning and the Growth of the Industry by Which Mankind Is Clothed* (Boston: John S. Lawrence, 1912), pp. 99–100; Roy Rothwell and Walter Zegveld, *Reindustrialization and Technology* (Armonk, NY: M. E. Sharpe, 1985); Andrew Carnegie, *James Watt* (New York: Doubleday, Page: 1905). Watt was not the inventor of the first widely used steam engine. Thomas Newcomen had that honor. Newcomen's steam engines were used to pump water out of mines and were installed in over one hundred locations in Britain and Europe. But they had to be housed in large, special-purpose buildings, they were expensive, they used huge amounts of fuel, they were slow, and they produced a jerky movement that was much too punishing to power most machines.

11. Jane Jacobs, *Cities and the Wealth of Nations: Principles of Economic Life* (New York: Vintage, 1985).

12. Piyapas Tharavanij, "Capital Market Development, Frequency of Recession, and Fraction of Time the Economy in Recession," Munich Personal RePEc Archive, September 9, 2007, MPRA paper no. 4954, November 7, 2007, p. 15, http://mpra.ub.uni-muenchen.de/4954/1/MPRA_paper_4954.pdf (accessed December 28, 2008).

7. The World Wide Web of 1931

1. Denis Twitchett, John King Fairbank, and Michael Loewe, "The Cambridge History of China: The Ch'in and Han Empires 221 B.C.–A.D. 220" (Cambridge: Cambridge University Press, 1987), p. 579.

2. Edgar Lawrence Smith, *Common Stocks and Business Cycles: A Practical Analysis of the Basic Causes and Patterns of Cyclical Behavior in Economic Series* (New York: William-Frederick Press, 1959), p. 174; Niall Ferguson, *The Ascent of Money: A Financial History of the World* (New York: Penguin, 2008).

3. Robert Sobel and Broadus Mitchell, *The Big Board: A History of the New York Stock Market* (Frederick, MD: Beard Books, 2000), pp. 8–9.

4. Walter Adolphe Roberts, *The French in the West Indies* (Indianapolis: Bobbs-Merrill, 1942); James Handasyd Perkins and James R. Albach, *Annals of the West: Embracing a Concise Account of Principal Events Which Have Occurred in the Western States and Territories, from the Discovery of the Mississippi Valley to the Year Eighteen Hundred and Forty-five: Compiled from the Most Authentic Sources* (Cincinnati: J. R. Albach, 1847), p. 34.

5. Charles MacKay, *Extraordinary Popular Delusions and the Madness of Crowds* (Petersfield, Hampshire, England: Harriman House, 2003, originally published 1841), p. 55.

6. Aurel Schubert, *The Credit-Anstalt Crisis of 1931* (Cambridge: Cambridge University Press, 1991), p. 8; Charles P. Kindleberger, "The Credit-Anstalt Crisis of 1931," book review, *Southern Economic Journal*, July 1993; Barry J. Eichengreen, *Globalizing Capital* (Princeton, NJ: Princeton University Press, 1998), pp. 78–79.

7. Arnold Joseph Toynbee, V. M. Boulter, and Veronica M. Toynbee, *Survey of International Affairs* (Oxford: Oxford University Press, 1931), p. 63.

8. For a more conspiratorial reading of the Creditanstalt crisis, see William Engdahl, *A Century of War: Anglo-American Oil Politics and the New World Order* (London: Pluto Press, 2004).

9. Bank for International Settlements, "Introductory Note on the Bank for International Settlements: 1930–1945," Bank for International Settlements, May 12, 1997, http://www.bis.org/publ/bisp02a.pdf (accessed March 2, 2009).

10. Schubert, *The Credit-Anstalt Crisis of 1931*, p. 13.

8. Why X-Ray a Boom?

1. Carl Cavanagh Hodge and Cathal J. Nolan, *U.S. Presidents and Foreign Policy: From 1789 to the Present* (Santa Barbara, CA: ABC-CLIO, 2006), p. 231; David Greenberg, *Calvin Coolidge: The 30th President, 1923–1929* (New York: Macmillan, 2007), pp. 146–47, 150.

2. Claude M. Fuess, *Calvin Coolidge: The Man from Vermont* (Boston: Little, Brown, 1940), p. 82.

3. Ben Bernanke, "Money, Gold, and the Great Depression, Remarks by Governor Ben S. Bernanke at the H. Parker Willis Lecture in Economic Policy, Washington and Lee University, Lexington, Virginia, March 2, 2004," Federal Reserve Board, http://www.federalreserve.gov/boarddocs/speeches/2004/200403022/default.htm (accessed January 2, 2009).

4. Elaine Hatfield, John T. Cacioppo, and Richard L. Rapson, *Emotional Contagion: Studies in Emotion & Social Interaction* (Cambridge: Cambridge University Press, 1994).

5. The phrase "irrational exuberance," Greenspan reports, came to him

while he was in the bathtub. Alan Greenspan, *The Age of Turbulence: Adventures in a New World* (New York: Penguin, 2007), p. 176.

6. Robert Sobel and Roger Lowenstein, *Crashes, Booms, Panics, and Government Regulations* (Ashland, OR: Blackstone Audio Books, 2006); Mark Skousen, *The Making of Modern Economics* (Armonk, NY: M. E. Sharpe, 2001).

7. Barbara Silberdick Feinberg, *Black Tuesday* (Brookfield, CT: Millbrook Press, 1995).

8. "The Great Depression," in *Teaching Eleanor Roosevelt*, ed. Allida Black, June Hopkins et al. (Hyde Park, NY: Eleanor Roosevelt National Historic Site, 2003), http://www.nps.gov/archive/elro/glossary/great-depression.htm (accessed December 15, 2008).

9. University of California, Berkeley Institute of International Studies, *Asian Survey* (Berkeley: University of California Press, 1988), p. 23.

10. Peter Haggett, *Encyclopedia of World Geography* (Tarrytown, NY: Marshall Cavendish, 2002), p. 193.

11. Richard J. Evans, *The Coming of the Third Reich* (New York: Penguin, 2004), p. 135.

12. Nassim Nicholas Taleb, *The Black Swan: The Impact of the Highly Improbable* (New York: Random House, 2007), p. 262.

II THE BIRDS AND THE BEES OF BOOM AND CRASH

9. The Pendulum of Repurposing

1. R. Kallenbach, T. Encrenaz, J. Geiss, K. Mauersberger, T. Owen, and F. Robert, eds., *Solar System History from Isotopic Signatures of Volatile Elements: Proceedings of an ISSI Workshop, 14–18 January 2002, Bern, Switzerland* (New York: Springer, 2003), p. 321; K. Altwegg, P. Ehrenfreund, Johannes Geiss, and W. F. Huebner, *Composition and Origin of Cometary Materials: Proceedings of an ISSI Workshop, 14–18 September 1998, Bern, Switzerland* (New York: Springer, 1999); Martha Haynes and Stirling Churchman, "The Evolution of the Sun," Cornell Astronomy Department, December 24, 2008, http://astrosun2.astro.cornell.edu/academics/courses//astro201/evol_sun.htm (accessed January 2, 2009).

2. The solar system including comets is 100,000 Astronomical Units in size. One Astronomical Unit is 93 million miles. $100,000 \times 93$ million $= 9.3 \times 10^{12}$ miles. The presolar nebula, the cloud of matter that gave birth to our sun, its planets, and its moons, was about three times that size. For the size of the solar system, see Amelie Saintonge, "What Is the Size of the Solar

System?" Cornell Astronomy Department, November 2002, http://curious .astro.cornell.edu/question.php?number=374 (accessed January 2, 2009).

3. The number of atoms in some protein chains is 240,243,785. Zoltán Szabadka and Vince Grolmusz, "High Throughput Processing of the Structural Information of the Protein Data Bank," *Journal of Molecular Graphics and Modeling* 25 (2007): 831–36; James K. Hardy, "DNA and RNA Structure and Function," 1998, http://ull.chemistry.uakron.edu/biochem/10/ (accessed January 2, 2009); R. Bennewitz, J. N. Crain, A. Kirakosian, J-L Lin, J. L. McChesney, D. Y. Petrovykh, and F. J. Himpsel, "Atomic Scale Memory at a Silicon Surface," *Nanotechnology,* July 13, 2002, pp. 499–502.

4. Ronald P. Jean, Christopher S. Chen, and Alexander A. Spector, "Finite-Element Analysis of the Adhesion-Cytoskeleton-Nucleus Mechanotransduction Pathway during Endothelial Cell Rounding: Axisymmetric Model," *Journal of Biomechanical Engineering,* August 2005, pp. 594–600.

5. Takashi Ohyama, *DNA Conformation and Transcription* (New York: Springer, 2005).

6. "How Many Genes Are in the Human Genome?" Oak Ridge National Lab, Genome Programs of the US Department of Energy Office of Science, September 19, 2008, http://www.ornl.gov/sci/techresources/Human _Genome/faq/genenumber.shtml (accessed January 3, 2009).

7. Fabia U. Battistuzzi, Andreia Feijao, and S. Blair Hedges, "A Genomic Timescale of Prokaryote Evolution: Insights into the Origin of Methanogenesis, Phototrophy, and the Colonization of Land," *BMC Evolutionary Biology* 4 (2004): 44; Heinrich D. Holland, "Evidence for Life on Earth More Than 3850 Million Years Ago," *Science* (January 3, 1997): pp. 38–39; Norman R. Pace, "A Molecular View of Microbial Diversity and the Biosphere," *Science* (May 2, 1997): 734–40; S. J. Mojzsis, G. Arrhenius, K. D. Mckeegan, T. M. Harrison, A. P. Nutman, and C. R. L. Friend, "Evidence for Life on Earth before 3,800 Million Years Ago," *Nature* (November 7, 1996): 55–59; "When Life Began on Earth," NASA press release, November 5, 1996; John M. Hayes, "The Earliest Memories of Life on Earth," *Nature* (November 7, 1996): 21–22; James F. Kasting, "Planetary Atmospheres: Warming Early Earth and Mars," *Science* (May 23, 1997): 1213–15.

8. R. Schodel, T. Ott, R. Genzel, R. Hofmann et al., "A Star in a 15.2-Year Orbit around the Supermassive Black Hole at the Centre of the Milky Way," *Nature* (October 17, 2002): 694–96.

10. Is the Business Cycle in Your DNA?

1. Sources on bacteria include Yves Brun and Lawrence J. Shimkets, *Prokaryotic Development* (Washington, DC: ASM Press, 2000); Dennis Bray,

"Bacterial Chemotaxis: Using Computer Models to Unravel Mechanism," speaker abstracts, Society of General Physiologists, Symposium 2006, http://www.sgpweb.org/Abstracts2006.pdf (accessed March 2, 2009); R. M. Harshey and T. Matsuyama, "Dimorphic Transition in *Escherichia coli* and *Salmonella typhimurium*: Surface-Induced Differentiation into Hyperflagellate Swarmer Cells," *Proceedings of the National Academy of Sciences of the United States of America* (August 30, 1994): 8631–35; B. Terrana and A. Newton, "Requirement of a Cell Division Step for Stalk Formation in *Caulobacter crescentus*," *Journal of Bacteriology* (October 1976): 456–62; C. J. Ong, M. L. Wong, and J. Smit, "Attachment of the Adhesive Holdfast Organelle to the Cellular Stalk of *Caulobacter crescentus*," *Journal of Bacteriology* (March 1990): 1448–56; J. Smit and N. Agabian, "Cell Surface Patterning and Morphogenesis: Biogenesis of a Periodic Surface Array during *Caulobacter* Development," *Journal of Cell Biology* (October 1982): 41–49; J. M. Sommer, A. Newton, "Turning Off Flagellum Rotation Requires the Pleiotropic Gene pleD: pleA, pleC, and pleD Define Two Morphogenic Pathways in *Caulobacter crescentus*," *Journal of Bacteriology* (January 1989): 392–401.

2. Mitsugu Matsushita, "Dynamic Aspects of the Structured Cell Population in a Swarming Colony of *Proteus mirabilis*," *Journal of Bacteriology* (January 2000): 385–93.

3. Jeanne S. Poindexter, Kanan P. Pujara, and James T. Staley, "In Situ Reproductive Rate of Freshwater *Caulobacter*," *Applied and Environmental Microbiology* (September 2000): 4105–11. See the photos of the stalked and flagellar forms of *Caulobacter crescentus* at "*Caulobacter*, Microbe Wiki," Kenyon College, http://microbewiki.kenyon.edu/index.php/Caulobacter (accessed December 25, 2008).

4. M. Kanbe, S. Shibata, Y. Umino, U. Jenal, and S. I. Aizawa, "Protease Susceptibility of the *Caulobacter crescentus* Flagellar Hook-Basal Body: A Possible Mechanism of Flagellar Ejection during Cell Differentiation," *Microbiology* (February 2005): 433–38.

5. Benoit B. Mandelbrot and Richard L. Hudson, *The (Mis)behavior of Markets: A Fractal View of Risk, Ruin, and Reward* (New York: Basic Books, 2004), pp. 207–208.

6. Anne Goldgar, *Tulipmania: Money, Honor, and Knowledge in the Dutch Golden Age* (Chicago: University of Chicago Press, 2007), p. 5.

7. Gabriel Abraham Almond, Scott C. Flanagan, and Robert J. Mundt, *Crisis, Choice, and Change: Historical Studies of Political Development* (Boston: Little, Brown, 1973), p. 152.

8. See, for example, Maite Narvarte, Raúl González, and Pablo Filippo, "Artisanal Mollusk Fisheries in San Matías Gulf (Patagonia, Argentina): An

Appraisal of the Factors Contributing to Unsustainability," *Fisheries Research* (October 2007): 68–76; David R. Montgomery, *King of Fish: The Thousand-Year Run of Salmon* (Boulder, CO: Westview Press, 2004), p. 43.

9. Peter J. Hudson, Andy P. Dobson, and Dave Newborn, "Prevention of Population Cycles by Parasite Removal," *Science* (December 18, 1998): 2256–58.

10. Marc Kirschner and John Gerhart, "Evolvability," *Proceedings of the National Academy of Sciences 95*, no. 15:8420–27; Marie-Thérèse Heemels, "Apoptosis," *Nature* (October 12, 2000); Pascal Meier, Andrew Finch, and Gerard Evan, "Apoptosis in Development," *Nature* (October 12, 2000): 796–801.

11. "The Visible Embryo," compiled from the National Institute of Child and Human Development's Carnegie Collection of Human Development, http://www.visembryo.com/baby/16.html (accessed December 2, 2008).

11. The Secret of Your Inner Fish

1. Credit goes to Neil Shubin for originating the phrase "your inner fish." See Neil Shubin, *Your Inner Fish: A Journey into the 3.5-Billion-Year History of the Human Body* (New York: Pantheon, 2008).

2. Ernst Heinrich Philipp August Haeckel, *The History of Creation, or, The Development of the Earth and Its Inhabitants by the Action of Natural Causes: A Popular Exposition of the Doctrine of Evolution in General, and of that of Darwin, Goethe, and Lamarck in Particular*, 8th German ed. of Ernst Haeckel, trans. L. Dora Schmitz and rev. trans. Edwin Ray Lankester (New York: D. Appleton, 1892), p. 219.

3. For the tale of how Haeckel's idea that "ontology recapitulates phylogeny" came into disrepute, see Hugo Tristram Engelhardt and Arthur L. Caplan, *Scientific Controversies: Case Studies in the Resolution and Closure of Disputes in Science and Technology* (Cambridge, England, 1987), pp. 82–83.

4. Stephen Jay Gould brought Haeckel, ontogeny, and phylogeny back on center stage in 1977 with his book *Ontogeny and Phylogeny* (Cambridge, MA: Belknap Press of Harvard University Press, 1977).

5. Alessandro Minelli, *The Development of Animal Form* (Cambridge: Cambridge University Press, 2003), p. 7.

12. Bionomics: Is Crash and Boom *in* Your Fingertips?

1. For a use of the term *bionomics* as early as 1905, see John Thomas Gulick, *Evolution, Racial and Habitudinal* (Washington, DC: Carnegie Institution of Washington, 1905).

2. Michael L. Rothschild, *Bionomics: Economy as Ecosystem* (New York: Henry Holt, 1992).

3. International Bionomics Institute, http://bionomica.ru/indexen.htm (accessed January 1, 2009).

4. International Bionomics Institute, "History," http://bionomica.ru/historyen4.htm (accessed January 1, 2009).

5. Lubomira Lencesova, Andrea O'Neill, Wendy G. Resneck, Robert J. Bloch, and Mordecai P. Blaustein, "Plasma Membrane-Cytoskeleton-Endoplasmic Reticulum Complexes in Neurons and Astrocytes," *Journal of Biological Chemistry* (January 23, 2004): 2885–93.

6. Ronald P. Jean, Christopher S. Chen, and Alexander A. Spector, "Finite-Element Analysis of the Adhesion-Cytoskeleton-Nucleus Mechanotransduction Pathway during Endothelial Cell Rounding: Axisymmetric Model," *Journal of Biomechanical Engineering* (August 2005): 594–600.

7. "About Dictyostelium," Dictybase: Online Information Resource for Dictyostelium, supported by NIH, http://dictybase.org/tutorial/about_dictyostelium.htm (accessed January 4, 2009).

8. John Tyler Bonner, *The Evolution of Culture in Animals* (Princeton, NJ: Princeton University Press, 1983).

9. If a mouse gives birth to ten pups every twenty-one days for a year, that's 17.3 litters a year. In other words, 173 pups per year. If she is able to have litters for three out of her four years of life, that's 519 pups. Per mouse mother!!!

10. James F. Willott, *The Auditory Psychobiology of the Mouse* (Springfield, IL: C. C. Thomas, 1983), p. 15; J. Panksepp and J. Burgdorf, "50-kHz Chirping (Laughter?) [sic] in Response to Conditioned and Unconditioned Tickle-Induced Reward in Rats: Effects of Social Housing and Genetic Variables," *Behavioural Brain Research* 115 (2000): 25–38; J. Panksepp and J. Burgdorf, "'Laughing' Rats and the Evolutionary Antecedents of Human Joy?" *Physiology and Behavior* 79 (2003): 533–47.

11. Jerry Wolff and Paul W. Sherman, *Rodent Societies: An Ecological & Evolutionary Perspective* (Chicago: University of Chicago Press, 2007), p. 318; Robert Thomas Mason, Michael P. LeMaster, and Dietland Müller-Schwarze, *Chemical Signals in Vertebrates 10* (New York: Springer, 2003), p. 8.

12. The concept of the fission-fusion strategy or of "fission-fusion dynamics" appears to have originated in 1971 in F. P. G. Aldrich-Blake, T. K. Bunn, R. I. M. Dunbar, and P. M. Headley, "Observations on Baboons, *Papio anubis*, in an Arid Region in Ethiopia," *Folia Primatologica* 15 (1971): 1–35. Fission-fusion dynamics were then discovered in chimpanzees, apes, elephants, dolphins, and whales. Most important, fission-fusion dynamics were discovered among human beings. The result? A renaissance in the use of the

concept from 2004 onward, complete with a conference dedicated solely to "Fission-Fusion Societies and Cognitive Evolution" in Siena, Italy, August 28–30, 2004. F. Aureli et al., "Fission-Fusion Dynamics: New Research Frameworks," *Current Anthropology* 49, no. 4 (August 2008): 627–54; Janet Mann, Richard C. Connor, Peter L. Tyack, and Hal Whitehead, *Cetacean Societies, Field Studies of Dolphins and Whales* (Chicago: University of Chicago Press, 2000).

13. Michael Patrick Ghiglieri, *The Chimpanzees of Kibale Forest: A Field Study of Ecology and Social Structure* (New York: Columbia University Press, 1984); Russell Tuttle, *Apes of the World: Their Social Behavior, Communication, Mentality, and Ecology* (Norwich, NY: William Andrew, 1985), p. 115.

14. Primate species that use the fission-fusion search strategy include the chimp, bonobo, the spider monkey, the red colobus, the gelada baboon, and the Hamadryas baboon. Ghiglieri, *The Chimpanzees of Kibale Forest*; Dorothy L. Cheney and Robert M. Seyfarth, *Baboon Metaphysics: The Evolution of a Social Mind* (Chicago: University of Chicago Press, 2007), pp. 278–79; Christophe Boesch and Hedwige Boesch-Achermann, *The Chimpanzees of the Taï Forest: Behavioural Ecology and Evolution* (Oxford: Oxford University Press, 2000), pp. 263–66; Margaret Power, *The Egalitarians—Human and Chimpanzee: An Anthropological View of Social Organization* (Cambridge: Cambridge University Press, 1991), pp. 128–31; Stuart A. Altmann, "The Structure of Primate Social Communication," in *Social Communication Among Primates*, ed. Stuart A. Altman (Chicago: University of Chicago Press, 1967), pp. 325–62.

15. Tuttle, *Apes of the World*, p. 115.

16. Christof Koch, *The Quest for Consciousness: A Neurobiological Approach* (Greenwood Village, CO: Roberts and Co., 2004), p. 63.

17. The visual cortexes in the brain are labeled V1 through V5. But those are not the only centers involved in "seeing." Other cerebral participants in the process include the lateral geniculate nucleus, the suprachiasmatic nucleus, the pretectum, the superior colliculus, and the pulvinar. See Bruno Dubuc, "The Brain from Top to Bottom," English trans. Al Daigen, Canadian Institute of Neuroscience, Mental Health and Addiction, Canadian Institute of Health Research, http://thebrain.mcgill.ca/flash/a/a_02/a_02_cr/a_02_cr_vis/a_02_cr_vis.html (accessed January 8, 2009); also see P. Dupont, G. A. Orban, B. De Bruyn, A. Verbruggen, and L. Mortelmans, "Many Areas in the Human Brain Respond to Visual Motion," *Journal of Neurophysiology* 72, no. 3 (1994): 1420–24.

18. Some clams are hermaphrodites. They're male and female simultaneously. But most clams settle into just one sex, male or female.

19. L. J. Davenport, "Sex and the Single Freshwater Mussel," *Alabama Heritage*, Spring 2006.

20. Mobile clam larvae are called *veligers*.

21. S. M. Bower and J. Blackbourn, "Geoduck Clam (*Panopea abrupta*): Anatomy, Histology, Development, Pathology, Parasites and Symbionts: Developmental Stages of the Geoduck Clam," Fisheries and Oceans Canada Science, May 2003, http://www-sci.pac.dfo-mpo.gc.ca/geoduck/develop_e.htm (accessed January 10, 2009).

13. The Tale of the Jobless Bees

1. Thomas D. Seeley, *The Wisdom of the Hive: The Social Physiology of Honey Bee Colonies* (Cambridge, MA: Harvard University Press, 1995); Thomas D. Seeley, *Honeybee Ecology: A Study of Adaptation in Social Life* (Princeton, NJ: Princeton University Press, 1985); Thomas D. Seeley and Royce A. Levien, "A Colony of Mind: The Beehive as Thinking Machine," *Sciences*, July/August 1987, pp. 38–42; E. O. Wilson, *The Insect Societies* (Cambridge, MA: Harvard University Press, 1971).

2. Seeley and Levien, "A Colony of Mind."

3. A six-kilometer trip to a flower patch takes one bee fifteen minutes. A hive of 30,000 bees has 10,000 foragers. And yanking the pollen and nectar from a single flower patch takes many trips. So just one trip by all the foragers takes an investment of 2,500 bee-hours. For the raw figures, see Seeley, *The Wisdom of the Hive*, p. 46.

4. According to the American National Honey Board, a single pound of honey is the fruit of 55,000 miles of bee-flight. Using that figure, if a hive made forty kg of honey per year, the total cost of that honey in bee-flight mileage would be 4,840,000 miles—close to 5 million miles. National Honey Board, cited at University of Minnesota's 4-H Camping Program Web site, www.fourh.umn.edu/Programs/camping/bug_camp/trivia.html. See also Seeley, *The Wisdom of the Hive*, pp. 36–51.

5. Gro V. Amdam, Angela Csondes, M. Kim Fondrkand, and Robert E. Page Jr., "Complex Social Behaviour Derived from Maternal Reproductive Traits," *Nature* (January 5, 2006): 76–78; Michael Price, "Social Bee-havior," ASU Research, Arizona State University, http://researchmag.asu.edu/stories/socialbees.html (accessed April 3, 2008).

6. Christof Koch, *The Quest for Consciousness: A Neurobiological Approach* (Greenwood Village, CO: Roberts and Co., 2004), p. 63.

14. Breakdancing with All Six Feet

1. Karl von Frisch, *Bees: Their Vision, Chemical Senses, and Language* (Ithaca: Cornell University Press, 1950), p. 50. Some of us humans use linden flowers to make a soothing tea. Volker Schulz, Rudolf Hänsel, Mark Blumenthal, and V. E. Tyler, *Rational Phytotherapy: A Reference Guide for Physicians and Pharmacists*, trans. T. C. Telger (New York: Springer, 2004), p. 193. Von Frisch calls a bee's carrying pouches *pollen baskets*. In reality, the hip pouches are specialized carrying hairs. See von Frisch, *Bees*, p. 70.

2. Thomas D. Seeley, "Thomas D. Seeley Research Interests," http://www .nbb.cornell.edu/Faculty/seeley/research2.html (accessed April 15, 2008).

3. "Honey sacks" carry liquids like water and nectar. Karl von Frisch, "Decoding the Language of the Bee," Nobel lecture, December 12, 1973, http://nobelprize.org/nobel_prizes/medicine/laureates/1973/frisch-lecture.html (accessed March 3, 2009).

4. Thomas D. Seeley, *The Wisdom of the Hive: The Social Physiology of Honey Bee Colonies* (Cambridge, MA: Harvard University Press, 1995), pp. 223–24.

5. Ibid., p. 122.

6. Neil Greenberg, James A. Carr, and Cliff H. Summers, "Ethological Causes and Consequences of the Stress Response," *Integrative & Comparative Biology* 42, no. 3 (2002): 508–16; Neil Greenberg, "Sociality, Stress, and the Corpus Striatum of the Green Anolis Lizard," *Physiology & Behavior* 79, no. 3 (2003): 429–40. Neil Greenberg, "Review of *The Executive Brain: Frontal Lobes and the Civilized Mind* by Elkhonon Goldberg," *Human Nature Review* 3 (2003): 422–31; Neil Greenberg, "Review of *Up from Dragons: The Evolution of Human Intelligence* by John R. Skoyles and Dorion Sagan," *Human Nature Review* 3 (2003): 142–48; personal communication with Neil Greenberg, March 30, 2008.

7. E. O. Wilson, *The Insect Societies* (Cambridge, MA: Harvard University Press, 1971), p. 265.

8. "Air Traffic Control," *New Scientist*, January 5, 2008, http://www .newscientist.com/backpage.ns?id=mg19726373.800 (accessed May 18, 2008).

9. Bees use dew, streams, wet rocks on a lake shore, and puddles for their supplies of water. Seeley, *The Wisdom of the Hive*, pp. 40, 231.

10. In his Nobel Prize lecture, Karl von Frisch calls the dances of bees "advertising" and "promotional messages." Von Frisch, "Decoding the Language of the Bee," pp. 78, 82. And Seeley says, "Each employed forager advertises her work site with waggle dances." Seeley, "Thomas D. Seeley Research Interests."

11. Karl von Frisch, *The Dance Language and Orientation of Bees*, trans. Leigh E. Chadwick (Cambridge, MA: Belknap Press of Harvard University Press, 1967).

12. Mandyan V. Srinivasan, Shaowu Zhang, Monika Altwein, and Jurgen Tautz, "Honeybee Navigation: Nature and Calibration of the Odometer," *Science* (February 4, 2000): 851–53; Harald E. Esch, Shaowu Zhang, Mandyan V. Srinivasan, and Jürgen Tautz, "Honeybee Dances Communicate Distances Measured by Optic Flow," *Nature* (May 31, 2001): 581–83.

13. *New York Times* science writer Natalie Angier describes the size of a bee's brain as no larger than the loop of a letter *b* on this page. Natalie Angier, "Honeybee Shows a Little Gene Activity Goes Miles and Miles," *New York Times*, May 7, 2002.

14. E. O. Wilson says the underlying math that allows a scout bee to remember her winding path, to derive the precise location of her find, then to calculate a straight path—a bee-line—back to her hive, is a "feat—which in our case would require a compass, a stopwatch, and integral vector calculus." Wilson, *The Insect Societies*, p. 216.

15. To try a bit of dynamic geometry, see "The Geometer's Sketchpad Resource Center," dynamicgeometry.com (accessed March 3, 2009).

16. Seeley, *The Wisdom of the Hive*, p. 90.

17. Von Frisch, *Bees: Their Vision, Chemical Senses, and Language*, pp. 27–28, 60–61. For a diagram of the honey stomach, see Seeley, *The Wisdom of the Hive*, p. 25.

18. Karl von Frisch calls this contagion of enthusiasm "excitement" and "arousal." Von Frisch, *Bees: Their Vision, Chemical Senses, and Language*, pp. 56, 61.

19. Seeley also says that when you, a forager bee, finally fix your attention on a winning dancer, your level of "arousal" and "enthusiasm" skyrocket. Seeley, *The Wisdom of the Hive*, p. 126.

20. Seeley says that a colony "optimizes" its "energy collection" with remarkable efficiency. Seeley, "Thomas D. Seeley Research Interests," http://www.nbb.cornell.edu/Faculty/seeley/research2.html (accessed April 15, 2008).

21. Seeley, *The Wisdom of the Hive*, pp. 226–25.

22. Seeley calls the hive a "large, diffuse, amoeboid entity which can extend itself over great distances and in multiple directions simultaneously to tap the flower patches in the surrounding environment" with an "impressive search ability." Seeley, "Thomas D. Seeley Research Interests," http://www.nbb.cornell.edu/Faculty/seeley/research2.html. (accessed April 15, 2008).

23. See ibid. and Seeley, *The Wisdom of the Hive*, p. 50.

III HOW PASSIONS POWER THE EVOLUTIONARY SEARCH ENGINE

15. You and Me and the Cycle of Insecurity

1. The research I'm about to cite does not come from Deborah Gordon, but many of the details on harvester ants do. For Gordon's overview of search strategies, communication, organization, and nonstop repurposing in the societies of ants, see Deborah M. Gordon, *Ants at Work: How an Insect Society Is Organized* (New York: Norton, 2000); Deborah M. Gordon, "The Regulation of Foraging Activity in Red Harvester Ant Colonies," *American Naturalist* 159 (2002): 509–18; Deborah M. Gordon, "Control without Hierarchy: Understanding How Particular Natural Systems Operate without Central Control Will Reveal Whether Such Systems Share General Properties," Gordon Lab Home Page, Stanford University, http://www.stanford .edu/~dmgordon/Gordon2007_Nature_Essay.pdf (accessed January 10, 2009); Deborah M. Gordon, "Networking Ants," *Natural History* 106, no. 7 (September 1997); Nathan Sanders and Deborah M. Gordon, "Resource-Dependent Interactions and the Organization of Desert Ant Communities," *Ecology* (April 2003): 1024–32. See also Rodrigo Cogni and Paulo S. Oliveira, "Recruitment Behavior during Foraging in the Neotropical Ant *Gnamptogenys moelleri* (Formicidae: Ponerinae): Does the Type of Food Matter?" *Journal of Insect Behavior* (July 2004); Bert Hölldobler and Edward O. Wilson, *The Superorganism: The Beauty, Elegance, and Strangeness of Insect Societies* (New York: Norton, 2008): 183–239; Edward O. Wilson, *Sociobiology: The Abridged Edition* (Cambridge: Harvard University Press, 1980); Douglas Foster, "An Ant's Life," *APF Reporter* 19, no. 4, Alicia Patterson Foundation, http://www.aliciapatterson.org/APF1904/ Foster/Foster.html (accessed January 10, 2009); Mitchell Leslie, "Life in the Colonies," *Stanford Magazine*, http://www.cs.princeton.edu/~zkhan/ popscience/ants.html (accessed January 10, 2009); Kitty Lanthrop and Bernadette Valdellon, "Argentine Ants," *Insecta Inspecta World*, http://www .insecta-inspecta.com/ants/argentine/index.html (accessed January 10, 2009); Evan Pellegrino, "Ants Don't Have to Be Specialists to Benefit Colony, UA Study Finds," *Arizona Daily Star*, December 1, 2008, http://www.azstarnet .com/sn/printDS/269584 (accessed January 10, 2009).

For ant architecture and agriculture—digging tunnels, building buttresses, and even raising their own grain—see this nineteenth-century source: Charles Anderson Dana, "Ant," in *The American Cyclopaedia: A Popular Dictionary of General Knowledge*, ed. Thomas Jefferson Conant and Blandina Conant (New York: Appleton, 1873), p. 54.

2. Michael J. Greene and Deborah M. Gordon, "Cuticular Hydrocarbons Inform Task Decisions," *Nature* (May 2003): 32; Jay W. Sharp, "Harvester Ants," *Desert USA*, July 10, 2007, http://www.desertusa.com/mag07/jul07/ant.html (accessed January 11, 2009).

3. The males of the colony do no work. In the words of Mitchell Leslie, who interviewed Gordon for Stanford University's *Stanford Magazine*, "The males are nothing more than sperm-delivering missiles: they cannot feed themselves, and they die right after mating." Leslie, "Life in the Colonies."

4. This ant pattern is called *circular column milling*. John Field, *Language and the Mind* (London: Routledge, 2005), pp. 103–105.

5. Anna Dornhaus at the University of Arizona has demonstrated that only 10 percent of the ants in a colony do the heavy lifting. Ninety percent hang around in the tunnels and relax. See Pellegrino, "Ants Don't Have to Be Specialists to Benefit Colony, UA Study Finds."

6. Ants on their own do *not* cycle through periods of excitability and rest like those of the human boom-bust cycle. But in groups ants do cycle through an analog of boom and bust. And the larger the group, the more regular the cycle. See Blain J. Cole, "Short-Term Activity Cycles in Ants: Generation of Periodicity by Worker Interaction," *American Naturalist* (February 1991) 244–59.

7. Ryohei Yamaoka, "The Communication and Community of Ants," http://www.natureinterface.com/e/ni06/P058-061/ (accessed January 11, 2009); William Morton Wheeler, "A New Case of Parabiosis and the 'Ant Gardens' of British Guiana," *Ecology* 2, no. 2 (April 1921): 89–103; William Morton Wheeler, "A Study of Some Texan Ponerinae," *Biological Bulletin* 2 (October 1900): 13; William Morton Wheeler, "The Compound and Mixed Nests of American Ants," reprinted from *American Naturalist* 35, nos. 414, 415, 417, and 418 (1901), http://www.archive.org/stream/ants_10488/ants_10488_djvu.txt (accessed January 12, 2009).

8. The ant has two stomachs, one to fuel its own metabolism and another to feed other ants. A few sources, a very few, call the trophylaxis stomach a "public stomach." E. O. Wilson and Bert Hölldobler call it a "social stomach." Walter Reinhart Tschinkel, *The Fire Ants* (Cambridge, MA: Harvard University Press, 2006), p. 332; Bert Hölldobler and E. O. Wilson, *Journey to the Ants: A Story of Scientific Exploration* (Cambridge, MA: Belknap Press of Harvard University Press, 1994), p. 52; Andrew Barto, Neil Bhatt, Jason Clarke et al., "Argentine Ants," *Insecta Inspecta World* (June 1, 2004), http://www.insecta-inspecta.com/ants/argentine/index.html (accessed January 13, 2009).

9. Susan Goldberg, Roy Muir, and John Kerr, *Attachment Theory: Social, Developmental, and Clinical Perspectives* (London: Routledge, 2000),

pp. 47–61; Klaus E. Grossmann, Karin Grossmann, and Everett Waters, *Attachment from Infancy to Adulthood: The Major Longitudinal Studies* (New York: Guilford Press, 2005), p. 100; Robert Karen, *Becoming Attached: First Relationships and How They Shape Our Capacity to Love* (New York: Oxford University Press, 1998), p. 148; "Attachment—Mary Dinsmore Salter Ainsworth and the Strange Situation," *Social Issues Reference*, http://social.jrank.org/pages/47/Attachment-Mary-Dinsmore-Salter-Ainsworth-Strange-Situation.html (accessed January 12, 2009); Inge Bretherton, "Mary Ainsworth: Insightful Observer and Courageous Theoretician," to appear in *Portraits of Pioneers in Psychology*, vol. 5, ed. G. A. Kimble, C. White, and M. Wertheimer (Hillsdale, NJ: Erlbaum, 2006), http://www.psychology.sunysb.edu/attachment/pdf/mda_inge.pdf (accessed January 12, 2009); Elizabeth D. Hutchison, *Dimensions of Human Behavior: The Changing Life Course* (Beverly Hills: Sage, 2007), p. 119.

16. Why Jealousy Drives You Crazy: The Othello Effect

1. William Shakespeare, *Othello: Complete and Unabridged*, ed. Cedric Watts (Ware, Hertfordshire, England: Wordsworth Editions, 1992); Emrys Jones, "'Othello,' 'Lepanto' and the Cyprus Wars," in *Shakespeare Survey: An Annual Survey of Shakespearian Study & Production*, ed. Kenneth Muir (Cambridge: Cambridge University Press, 2002), pp. 47–52; Hugh Bicheno, *Crescent and Cross: The Battle of Lepanto 1571* (New York: Sterling, 2005).

2. Ned B. Allen, "The Two Parts of Othello," in *Shakespeare Survey: An Annual Survey of Shakespearian Study & Production*, ed. Kenneth Muir (Cambridge: Cambridge University Press, 2002), p. 14.

3. Charles Mackay, *Extraordinary Popular Delusions and the Madness of Crowds* (1841; Petersfield, Hampshire, England: Harriman House, 2003).

17. Googling the Future: The Fabulous Russian Gets It Wrong

1. Eleanor Goltz Huzar, *Mark Antony: A Biography* (Minneapolis: University of Minnesota Press, 1978), p. 207.

2. Mary Taliaferro Boatwright, Daniel J. Gargola, Richard J. A. Talbert, *The Romans: From Village to Empire* (New York: Oxford University Press, 2004), p. 304.

3. Mark Antony married Cleopatra despite the fact he was still married to a Roman wife. He also declared that he would be buried in Alexandria. These acts spooked the citizens of Rome, who could see that Antony's interests were shifting east, shifting in a way that threatened their primacy. Huzar, *Mark Antony*, p. 208. Octavian took advantage of the Romans' suspicions to

turn them against Antony—not an easy task, since Mark Antony was extremely popular.

4. Roman plunder was so rich in the days of Augustus that he was able to mint in the neighborhood of a billion denarii from the spoils taken in Spain, Illyricum, and Egypt. Kenneth W. Harl, *Coinage in the Roman Economy, 300 B.C. to A.D. 700* (Baltimore: Johns Hopkins University Press, 1996), p. 78.

5. Craige Brian Champion, *Roman Imperialism: Readings and Sources* (Oxford: Blackwell, 2004), p. 34.

6. A. E. Astin, F. W. Walbank, and M. W. Frederiksen, *Rome and the Mediterranean to 133 B.C.* (Cambridge: Cambridge University Press, 1989), p. 41; C. Nicolet, "Economy and Society, 133–43 B.C.," in *The Cambridge Ancient History, Volume V: The Fifth Century B.C.*, ed. John Bagnell Bury et al. (Cambridge: Cambridge University Press, 2000), p. 624.

7. Like railroads, Rome's industrial farming on *latifundia* grew steadily from roughly 100 BCE until 100 CE. The Kondratiev wave model would predict that these massive farms would produce a depression by peaking and declining. But *latifundia* were nowhere near their peak in Augustus's time. See Pliny, *Natural History* 18.35, in Kathryn Lomas, *Roman Italy, 338 B.C.–AD 200: A Sourcebook* (London: Routledge, 1996), pp. 148–49.

8. Ernle Dusgate Selby Bradford, *Hannibal* (New York: McGraw-Hill, 1981).

9. Marie-Thérèse Heemels, "Apoptosis," http://www.nature.com/nature/insights/6805.html (accessed April 28, 2009).

10. Though science writers have often called DNA a blueprint, it's not. It contains no "picture" of the final product. It's more like an incredibly intricate computer program.

11. Thomas N. Habinek, *The World of Roman Song: From Ritualized Speech to Social Order* (Baltimore: Johns Hopkins University Press, 2005), p. 176.

12. Cornelius Tacitus, *Annals of Tacitus*, trans. Alfred John Church and William Jackson Brodribb (New York: Macmillan, 1906), p. 23.

13. Richard Duncan-Jones, *Money and Government in the Roman Empire* (Cambridge: Cambridge University Press, 1998), p. 11.

14. William Smith, "Augustus," in *A Dictionary of Greek and Roman Biography and Mythology* (London: J. Murray, 1880), pp. 420–30; Pat Southern, *Augustus* (London: Routledge, 1998), pp. 79–89; Plinio Prioreschi, *A History of Medicine* (Omaha: Horatius Press, 1995), pp. 12–13.

15. Here's how things had looked just four years earlier, in 40 BCE during a lull in the civil wars that followed the assassination of Julius Caesar: "Towns, and Rome in particular, were thronged by ruined farmers, bankrupt

merchants, artisans and freedmen without work . . . to these were added the learned freedmen . . . reduced to living upon the savings they had made in happier times. . . . Finally, everyone was suffering from the scarcity of money and the general depreciation of all securities. Those even who enlisted and were able to serve the triumvirs were often ill satisfied, and those who had been able to seize fields or houses during the revolutions had no money; expensive luxuries were therefore out of the question." In other words, economic downturns in ancient Rome were much like they are in modern depressions. The quote comes from Guglielmo Ferrero, *The Greatness and Decline of Rome*, trans. Alfred Eckhard Zimmern and Henry John Chaytor (New York: G. P. Putnam's Sons, 1910), p. 262.

16. Peter Levi, *Horace: A Life* (London: Routledge, 1998), p. 62.

17. Edward Gibbon, *The History of the Decline and Fall of the Roman Empire*, ed. Henry Hart Milman (New York: Harper & Brothers, 1850), pp. 189–91.

18. Colin Adams and Ray Laurence, *Travel and Geography in the Roman Empire* (London: Routledge, 2001), p. 53; Bruce Bartlett, "How Excessive Government Killed Ancient Rome," *Cato Journal* 14, no. 2 (Fall 1994).

19. William Warde Fowler, *The Religious Experience of the Roman People, from the Earliest Times to the Age of Augustus: The Gifford Lectures for 1909–10* (London: MacMillan, 1922), p. 428; Linda Stone, *Kinship and Gender* (Boulder, CO: Westview Press, 2000), p. 220.

20. Some land in the American West sold for as little as twelve and a half cents an acre. James West Davidson, William E. Gienapp, and Christine Leigh Heyrman, *Nation of Nations: A Narrative History of the American Republic* (New York: McGraw-Hill, 1998), p. 320; Willard Wesley Cochrane, *The Development of American Agriculture: A Historical Analysis* (Minneapolis: University of Minnesota Press, 1993), pp. 59–60; "Farmland Market on Rise in Area," *Bowling Green Daily News*, August 12, 2008.

21. Emerson Willard Keyes, *A History of Savings Banks in the United States from Their Inception in 1816 down to 1874: With Discussions of Their Theory, Practical Workings and Incidents, Present Condition and Prospective Development* (New York: Bradford Rhodes, 1878); H. Oliver Horne, *A History of Savings Banks* (Oxford: Oxford University Press, 1947).

22. "During the toll assessment period, the Erie produced revenue totaling $121,000,000. The total cost of the canal to 1883, including maintenance and repairs was $78,000,000, leaving a favorable balance on the books of the state treasury of some $42,000,000." "Chapter 1—History of the Canal," *State of New York Report of the Joint Legislative Committee on The Barge Canal*, Legislative Document 1961, March 21, 1961, in Morris

Pierce, *History of the Erie Canal*, Department of History, University of Rochester, http://www.history.rochester.edu/canal/bib/nys1961/historyc.htm (accessed January 17, 2009).

23. Wikipedia, "List of Canals in the United States," http://en.wikipedia .org/wiki/List_of_canals_in_the_United_States (accessed January 17, 2009).

24. Canal building was as exploratory a venture in its early days as was early railroad building. The Erie Canal was the most successful of the American waterways constructed in the canal-building era. Some others were apparently water courses to nowhere and turned out to be poor investments. William L. Barney, *A Companion to 19th-Century America* (Oxford: Blackwell, 2001), p. 131.

25. According to the Virginia Federal Writers Project, "In 1831 . . . there were little more than 100 miles of railroad completed in the United States." By the Civil War there were 1,290 miles of track, a spread that seemed gargantuan. And both sides fought to control this prize. But by 1885, Virginia alone had thirty-two railroad companies and 2,430 miles of track. Just one state had twice as much railroad track as the entire nation had had just twenty years earlier. Virginia Federal Writers Project, *Virginia: A Guide to the Old Dominion* (Murrieta, CA: US History Publishers, 1952), pp. 94–95.

26. According to John Newell Tilden, in 1875 the world had 185,000 miles of railway line. By 1895, that figure had ballooned to 406,000 miles. An increase of over 200,000 miles in a mere twenty years. See John Newell Tilden, *A Commercial Geography for Academies, High Schools, and Business Colleges* (New York: Thomas R. Shewell, 1900), p. 40.

27. David Prerau, *Seize the Daylight: The Curious and Contentious Story of Daylight Saving Time* (New York: Thunder's Mouth Press, 2006), p. 34; Peter Mathias and M. M. Postan, *Cambridge Economic History of Europe: The Industrial Economies: Capital, Labour and Enterprise, the United States, Japan and Russia* (Cambridge: Cambridge University Archive, 1983), p. 88.

28. John Steele Gordon, *An Empire of Wealth: The Epic History of American Economic Power* (New York: HarperCollins, 2004), pp. 235–36.

29. Amy Glasmeier, *Manufacturing Time: Global Competition in the Watch Industry, 1795–2000* (New York: Guilford Press, 2000), pp. 107–108.

30. Stuart Berg Flexner, *Listening to America: An Illustrated History of Words and Phrases from Our Lively and Splendid Past* (New York: Simon & Schuster, 1982), p. 16.

31. John Steele Gordon points out that just one state, Illinois, had twenty-seven time zones and Wisconsin had thirty-eight. When the government dithered over standardization, the railroad companies stepped in. Yes, it was the railroad companies that divided the nation into four time zones in

1883. And it was the railroad companies that established North American standard time. Gordon, *An Empire of Wealth*, pp. 235–36.

32. Quoted in Bruce Arnold, "Dot-com Bubble: Steam Age," *Caslon Analytics*, December 2008, http://www.caslon.com.au/boomprofile3.htm (accessed March 3, 2009).

33. Abraham Seldin Eisenstadt, *Carnegie's Model Republic: Triumphant Democracy and the British-American Relationship* (Albany: State University of New York Press, 2007), p. 22.

18. What Does Crash Create?

1. Until 1852, the etymologies in the *Oxford English Dictionary* suggest that the word *nation* was used for a single race that had shared a land from time immemorial. That began to change in 1822 when a new phrase entered the English language: *nation-making*. The idea that a nation could be fashioned voluntarily, not just born haphazardly, was new. *Oxford English Dictionary* CD-ROM, 2nd ed., additions and new ed. (Oxford: Oxford University Press, 2004). It appears that even in the view of the Founding Fathers of the United States, a nation was a people with a common heritage and a common hereditary territory. For example, in the *Federalist Papers*, no. 26, Alexander Hamilton refers to "those habits of thinking which we derive from the nation from whom the inhabitants of these States have in general sprung. . . . England." Lincoln's idea of a nation dedicated to a concept, no matter what the "derivation" of its people, was a new notion, one for which Lincoln was the great articulator. See Alexander Hamilton, John Jay, and James Madison, *The Federalist Papers* (New York: J. and A. McLean, 1788).

2. Abraham Lincoln, "The First Inaugural Address, March 4, 1861," *The Gettysburg Speech and Other Papers* (Boston: Houghton, Mifflin, 1899), pp. 43–44.

3. The image of amputation is in ibid., "Letter to A. G. Hodges, April 4, 1864," p. 75.

4. Ibid., p. 37.

5. Rufus Blanchard, *The Northwest* (Chicago: Cushing, Thomas, 1880), p. 352.

6. Ibid.

7. Rufus Blanchard, *Discovery and Conquests of the North-West, with the History of Chicago* (Wheaton, IL: R. Blanchard & Co., 1881), p. 340.

8. Robin L. Einhorn, *Property Rules: Political Economy in Chicago, 1833–1872* (Chicago: University of Chicago Press, 2001), p. xviii.

9. James William Putnam, *The Illinois and Michigan Canal: A Study in Economic History* (Chicago: University of Chicago Press, 1918), p. 62.

10. University of Illinois Eye and Ear Infirmary, "1858–1912: A Private Chicago Charity Blooms into an Illinois State Benefaction," University of Illinois Eye and Ear Infirmary, http://www.uic.edu/com/eye/Department/Publications/Department%20History/1858-1912.shtml (accessed January 15, 2009).

11. William H. Stennett and Chicago and North Western Railway Company, *Yesterday and Today: A History* (New York: Press of Rand, McNally & Company, 1905), p. 33.

12. Midwest High-Speed Rail Association, "What Is High-Speed Rail?" 2007, http://www.midwesthsr.org/promote_whathsr.htm (accessed January 15, 2009).

13. Walter Bagehot, banker and editor of London's *Economist* magazine, is generally credited with introducing the concept of lender of last resort in his 1873 work on banking, *Lombard Street*. See Frank C. Genovese, "Bagehot, Walter (1826–1877)," in *Business Cycles and Depressions: An Encyclopedia*, ed. David Glasner and Thomas F. Cooley (London: Taylor & Francis, 1997), pp. 30–31; Angela Redish, "Lender of Last Resort Policies: From Bagehot to Bailout," University of British Columbia, October 2001, preliminary draft, http://www.econ.ubc.ca/redish/llr.pdf (accessed December 29, 2008).

14. National Labor Relations Board, "About Us," http://www.nlrb.gov/about_us/index.aspx (accessed January 15, 2009).

15. Robert P. Flood and Peter M. Garber, *Speculative Bubbles, Speculative Attacks, and Policy Switching* (Cambridge, MA: MIT Press, 1994), p. 35.

19. The Battle of the Big Men

1. Edward S. Rogers, *New Guinea: Big Man Island* (Toronto: Royal Ontario Museum, 1970), pp. 118, 130.

2. New Guinean pork dishes can be cooked with bananas, sugar cane, and a spectrum of leafy vegetables. Rogers, *New Guinea*, p. 108.

20. The Brilliance of the Robber Barons and the J. P. Morgan Blues

1. Robert K. Merton, "The Matthew Effect in Science," *Science*, January 5, 1968, pp. 56–63.

2. *Possibility space* is a term coined by the Santa Fe Institute's Stuart Kauffman. For the ways in which the term has been used since Kaufman originated it, see Eric D. Schneider and Dorion Sagan, *Into the Cool: Energy*

Flow, Thermodynamics, and Life (Chicago: University of Chicago Press, 2005), p. 91; John Johnston, *The Allure of Machinic Life: Cybernetics, Artificial Life, and the New AI* (Cambridge, MA: MIT Press, 2008), p. 226.

3. E. Ray Canterbery, *A Brief History of Economics: Artful Approaches to the Dismal Science* (Singapore: World Scientific, 2001), p. 153.

4. The accusation that Morgan was milking an entire continent and pouring its profits into his own pocketbook came from Congress's Pujo Committee, which hauled Morgan in to testify in October 1912. Michael Burgan, *J. Pierpont Morgan: Industrialist and Financier* (Mankato, MN: Compass Point Books, 2006), p. 92; Ron Chernow, *The House of Morgan: An American Banking Dynasty and the Rise of Modern Finance* (New York: Grove Press, 2001), p. 150; James Grant, *Money of the Mind: Borrowing and Lending in America from the Civil War to Michael Milken* (New York: Macmillan, 1994), pp. 132–33; William B. McCash and June Hall McCash, *The Jekyll Island Club: Southern Haven for America's Millionaires* (Athens: University of Georgia Press, 1989), p. 127.

5. Thomas S. Ulen, "The Market for Regulation: The ICC from 1887 to 1920," *American Economic Review* 70, no. 2 (May 1980): 306–10; "Interstate Commerce Act (1887)," http://www.ourdocuments.gov/doc.php?flash=true&doc=49 (accessed January 16, 2009).

6. "Think of it—all the competing traffic of the roads west of Chicago and Saint Louis placed in the control of 30 men!" said Morgan to one of the many reporters staked out at his Manhattan home to see who attended what a *New York Herald* headline called a meeting to establish "A Gigantic Trust." Chernow, *The House of Morgan*, pp. 56–57; "Railroads in the United States in 1889," *Science* 14, no. 342 (August 23, 1889): 124; Eric J. Morse, "Grassroots Rebels: Municipal Power and Railroad Regulation in La Crosse, Wisconsin, 1883–1900," *Business History Conference Publications*, http://www.h-net.org/~business/bhcweb/publications/BEHonline/2005/morser.pdf (accessed January 16, 2009).

7. Charles R. Morris, *The Tycoons: How Andrew Carnegie, John D. Rockefeller, Jay Gould, and J. P. Morgan Invented the American Supereconomy* (New York: Macmillan, 2006), p. 235; "Francis H. Peabody Dead," *New York Times*, September 23, 1905.

8. Edwin Palmer Hoyt, *The House of Morgan* (New York: Dodd, Mead, 1966), pp. 29–35; Morgan Library & Museum, "Pierpont Morgan: Banker," http://www.themorgan.org/about/historyMore.asp?id=1 (accessed January 16, 2009).

9. Morgan was known as Pierpont to his friends, but something far more intimate to his schoolmates—"Pip." Samuel E. Moffett, "John Pierpont Morgan," *Pall Mall Magazine*, January–April 1903, p. 178.

10. Chernow, *The House of Morgan*, p. 22.

11. Stanley Jackson, *J. P. Morgan: A Biography* (New York: Stein and Day, 1983), p. 84.

12. K. R. Howe, Robert C. Kiste, and Brij V. Lal, *Tides of History: The Pacific Islands in the Twentieth Century* (Honolulu: University of Hawaii Press, 1994), p. 17.

13. Cynthia Clark Northrup calls "J. P. Morgan, the wealthiest banker in the United States," in *The American Economy: A Historical Encyclopedia* (Santa Barbara: ABC-CLIO, 2003), p. 222.

14. The Europeans had lost their faith in the US government. But they had retained their faith in J. P. Morgan. Robert Sobel, *Panic on Wall Street: A History of America's Financial Disasters* (Frederick, MD: Beard Books, 1999), pp. 263–63, 278; Gabriel Kolko, *The Triumph of Conservatism: A Re-interpretation of American History, 1900–1916* (New York: Simon & Schuster, 1977), p. 142; Milton Friedman and Anna Jacobson Schwartz, *A Monetary History of the United States, 1867–1960* (Princeton, NJ: Princeton University Press, 1971), pp. 111–12.

15. Paul Bairoch, *Economics and World History: Myths and Paradoxes* (Chicago: University of Chicago Press, 1995), pp. 42–46.

16. Wesley Clair Mitchell, *Business Cycles* (Manchester, NH: Ayer, 1970), pp. 51–60.

17. "Negotiations in Big Steel Deal Continue: Purchase of Carnegie Holdings May Be Concluded at Any Time," *New York Times*, February 8, 1901; Abraham Berglund, "The United States Steel Corporation: A Study of the Growth and Influence of Combination in the Iron and Steel Industry," PhD thesis, Columbia University, 1907, pp. 70–71; "History of US Steel," http://www .ussteel.com/corp/company/profile/history.asp (accessed January 16, 2009).

18. "International Harvester," *Antique Farming*, http://www.antique farming.com/internationalharvester.html (accessed December 23, 2008).

19. Robert F. Bruner and Sean D. Carr, *The Panic of 1907: Lessons Learned from the Market's Perfect Storm* (New York: Wiley, 2007), pp. 74–98.

20. In 1907, panic hit Europe, Asia, and Africa. Alexander Dana Noyes, *Forty Years of American Finance: A Short Financial History of the Government and People of the United States since the Civil War, 1865–1907* (London: G. P. Putnam's Sons, 1909), p. 362.

21. The Poet and the Escalator of Complexity

1. Edward Gibbon, *The Decline and Fall of the Roman Empire— Volume I: 180 A.D.–395 A.D.* (New York: Modern Library, n.d.); Paul

Veyne, ed., *A History of Private Life: I—From Pagan Rome to Byzantium* (Cambridge, MA: Harvard University Press, 1987): pp. 143, 154; Justine Davis Randers-Pehrson, *Barbarians and Romans* (Norman: University of Oklahoma Press, 1983); Albert A. Trever, *History of Ancient Civilization— Volume II: The Roman World* (New York: Harcourt, Brace, 1939); Daniel J. Boorstin, "Our Cultural Hypochondria and How to Cure It," in *Genius of American Politics* (Chicago: University of Chicago Press, 1953), pp. 161–89.

2. Dennis M. Welch, "Blake, the Famine of 1795, and the Economics of Vision," *European Romantic Review* (December 2007): 597–622.

3. Charles Aimé Dauban, *Paris en 1794 et en 1795: Histoire de la Rue, Du Club, de la Famine* (Paris: Henri Plon, 1869).

4. Victor George, *Social Security and Society* (London: Routledge & Kegan Paul, 1973), p. 10. The new system, "The Speenhamland system was an amendment to the old Poor Law or Elizabethan Poor Law." See Marjie Bloy, "The Speenhamland System," November 2002, http://www.victorian web.org/history/poorlaw/speen.html (accessed December 26, 2008).

5. Gerald Newman and Leslie Ellen Brown, *Britain in the Hanoverian Age, 1714–1837: An Encyclopedia* (London: Taylor & Francis, 1997), p. 151.

6. Kansas Department of Labor, "History—Unemployment Insurance," Kansas Department of Labor, May 16, 2006, http://www.dol.ks.gov/UI/ html/enhist_DBR.html (accessed December 26, 2008); David R. Francis, "Unemployment Insurance," *Concise Encyclopedia of Economics*, Library of Economics and Liberty, Liberty Fund, 2002, http://www.econlib.org/ library/Enc1/UnemploymentInsurance.html (accessed March 4, 2009).

7. Joseph Haydn and Benjamin Vincent, *Haydn's Dictionary of Dates and Universal Information Relating to All Ages and Nations*, 23rd ed. (London: G. P. Putnam's Sons, 1904), p. 461; Leslie A. Clarkson and E. Margaret Crawford, *Feast and Famine: Food and Nutrition in Ireland, 1500–1920* (Oxford: Oxford University Press, 2001), p. 131.

8. Shih-Rung Yeh, Barbara E. Musolf, and Donald H. Edwards, "Neuronal Adaptations to Changes in the Social Dominance Status of Crayfish," *Journal of Neuroscience* (January 15, 1997): 697–708; D. L. Glanzman and F. B. Krasne, "Serotonin and Octopamine Have Opposite Modulatory Effects on the Crayfish's Lateral Giant Escape Reaction," *Journal of Neuroscience* 3 (1983): 2263–69; Paul A. Moore and Daniel A. Bergman, "The Smell of Success and Failure: The Role of Intrinsic and Extrinsic Chemical Signals on the Social Behavior of Crayfish," *Integrative and Comparative Biology* 45, no. 4 (2005): 650–57; Jens Herberholz, Fadi A. Issa, and Donald H. Edwards, "Patterns of Neural Circuit Activation and Behavior during Dominance Hierarchy Formation in Freely Behaving Crayfish," *Journal of Neuroscience*

(April 15, 2001): 2759–67; Marcia Barinaga, "Neurobiology: Social Status Sculpts Activity of Crayfish Neurons," *Science* (January 19, 1996): 290–91.

9. Gerald P. Schatten, *Current Topics in Developmental Biology* (New York: Academic Press, 2006), pp. 177–202; Elena Tricarico and Francesca Gherardi, "Biogenic Amines Influence Aggressiveness in Crayfish but Not Their Force or Hierarchical Rank," *Animal Behaviour* (December 2007): 1715–24.

10. Donald H. Edwards, Shih-Rung Yeh, Barbara E. Musolf, Brian L. Antonsen, and Franklin B. Krasne, "Metamodulation of the Crayfish Escape Circuit," *Brain, Behavior and Evolution* 60, no. 6 (2002): 360–69.

11. Randy Joe Nelson, *Biology of Aggression* (New York: Oxford University Press, 2006), p. 49.

12. Yeh, Fricke, and Edwards, "The Effect of Social Experience on Serotonergic Modulation of the Escape Circuit of Crayfish."

13. Valerius Geist, *Life Strategies, Human Evolution, Environmental Design: Toward a Biological Theory of Health* (New York: Springer-Verlag, 1978); Valerius Geist, personal communication, 1998–2008.

14. Here's a sampling of the references used for this brief summary of the physiological effects of control and the role of stress hormones: Herbert M. Lefcourt, *Locus of Control: Current Trends in Theory and Research* (Hillsdale, NJ: Lawrence Erlbaum Associates, 1982), pp. 8, 18; William R. Miller, Robert A. Rosellini, and Martin E. P. Seligman, "Learned Helplessness and Depression," in *Psychopathology: Experimental Models*, ed. Jack D. Maser and Martin E. P. Seligman (San Francisco: W. H. Freeman, 1977), pp. 104, 130; T. J. Shors, T. B. Seib, S. Levine, and R. F. Thompson, "Inescapable versus Escapable Shock Modulates Long-Term Potentiation in the Rat Hippocampus," *Science* (April 14, 1989): 224, 226; Jay M. Weiss, "Effects of Coping Behavior on Development of Gastrointestinal Lesions in Rats," *Proceedings of the Annual Convention of the American Psychological Association* 2 (Washington, DC: American Psychological Association, 1967), pp. 135–36; Jay M. Weiss, "Effects of Coping Responses on Stress," *Journal of Comparative & Physiological Psychology* 65, no. 2 (1968): 251–60; Jay M. Weiss, "Effects of Predictable and Unpredictable Shock on Development of Gastrointestinal Lesions in Rats," *Proceedings of the Annual Convention of the American Psychological Association* 3 (Washington, DC: American Psychological Association, 1968), pp. 263–64; Jay M. Weiss, "Effects of Coping Behavior in Different Warning Signal Conditions on Stress Pathology in Rats," *Journal of Comparative & Physiological Psychology* (October 1971): 1–13; J. M. Weiss, "Influence of Psychological Variables on Stress-Induced Pathology," *Ciba Foundation Symposium* 8 (1972): 253–65; Jon Franklin, *Molecules of the Mind: The Brave New Science of Molecular Psy-*

chology (New York: Atheneum, 1987), p. 131; Leonard A. Sagan, "Family Ties: The Real Reason People Are Living Longer," *Sciences* (March/April 1988): 28; Robert M. Sapolsky, "Stress, Social Status, and Reproductive Physiology in Free-Living Baboons," in *Psychobiology of Reproductive Behavior: An Evolutionary Perspective*, ed. David Crews (Englewood Cliffs, NJ: Prentice Hall, 1987); Robert M. Sapolsky, "Stress in the Wild," *Scientific American*, January 1990, pp. 116–23; Robert M. Sapolsky, *Why Zebras Don't Get Ulcers: An Updated Guide to Stress, Stress-Related Diseases, and Coping* (New York: W. H. Freeman, 1998); Robert I. Scheinman, Patricia C. Cogswell, Alan K. Lofquist, and Albert S. Baldwin Jr., "Role of Transcriptional Activation of IκBα in Mediation of Immunosuppression by Glucocorticoids," *Science* (October 13, 1995): 283–86; R. Rupprecht, N. Wodarz, J. Kornhuber, B. Schmitz, K. Wild, H. U. Braner, O. A. Müller, and P. Riederer, "In Vivo and In Vitro Effects of Glucocorticoids on Lymphocyte Proliferation in Man: Relationship to Glucocorticoid Receptors," *Neuropsychobiology* 24, no. 2 (1990/1991): 61–66; Neil Greenberg, "Behavioral Endocrinology of Physiological Stress in a Lizard," *Journal of Experimental Zoology* 4 (1990): S170–S173; Robert M. Sapolsky, "Lessons of the Serengeti," *Sciences* (May/June 1988): 42.

15. Michael E. Thase, "Molecules That Mediate Mood," *New England Journal of Medicine* (December 6, 2007): 2400–2402.

16. Jay M. Weiss, "Somatic Effects of Predictable and Unpredictable Shock," *Psychosomatic Medicine* 32 (1970): 397–408.

17. Denise Schmandt Besserat, "Oneness, Twoness, Threeness: How Ancient Accountants Invented Numbers," *Sciences* (July/August 1987).

18. Bread made from barley was the norm in ancient Greece. But white bread made from wheat was a prized luxury. Otto Thomas Solbrig and Dorothy J. Solbrig, *So Shall You Reap: Farming and Crops in Human Affairs* (Washington, DC: Island Press, 1996), p. 112.

19. The Free Banking Act required that banks had enough high-grade bonds and mortgages on deposit with the state to cover the redemption of any banknotes they issued. The "high-grade bonds" were usually state bonds. In other words, the state effectively guaranteed the bank's notes. Here's how. Imagine that you walk into a bank in 1839 with one of that bank's ten-dollar notes and demand ten dollars in gold. If the bank can't cough up the gold on the spot, the state government will give you your ten dollars in gold. How? If worse comes to worst, it will sell ten dollars' worth of the bonds and mortgages the bank has deposited. In other words, the state has stepped in to be the ultimate guarantor of banknotes. This innovation helped pave the way for a national note—a "legal tender note"—the greenback, in 1862. David A. Moss, *When All Else Fails: Government as the Ulti-*

mate Risk Manager (Cambridge, MA: Harvard University Press, 2004), p. 108; Ray B. Westerfield, "Bases of Note Issue before the Civil War," in *Banking Principles and Practice* (New York: Ronald Press, 1928); John M. Dobson, *Bulls, Bears, Boom, and Bust: A Historical Encyclopedia of American Business Concepts* (Santa Barbara: ABC-CLIO, 2006), p. 79.

20. "A Look at Wall Street's Shadow Market: How Some Arcane Wall Street Financial Instruments Magnified Economic Crisis," *60 Minutes*, October 5, 2008, http://www.cbsnews.com/stories/2008/10/05/60minutes/main4502454.shtml (accessed January 17, 2009); Alaron Trading Corporation, "The U.S. Dollar Index Futures Contract," http://www.alaron.com/uploadedFiles/alaron/client_services/exchange_resources/NYBOT/USDX4.pdf (accessed January 17, 2009). For more on the role of complex financial instruments—symbols way up there on the symbol stack—in the Great Crash of 2008, see Ricardo J. Caballero and Arvind Krishnamurthy, "Musical Chairs: A Comment on the Credit Crisis," Banque de France Publications, February 2008, http://www.banque-france.fr/gb/publications/telechar/rsf/2008/etud2_0208.pdf (accessed January 17, 2009); Stephen G. Cecchetti, "Monetary Policy and the Financial Crisis of 2007–2008," April 3, 2008, http://fmwww.bc.edu/ec-j/sems2008/Cecchetti.pdf (accessed January 17, 2009).

21. "Congregation (Jamaat) Prayer," http://www.islam-laws.com/congregationprayer.htm (accessed January 17, 2009).

22. One of Pakistan's key political parties, its oldest "fundamentalist" Islamic religious party, is named the Jamaat-e-Islami. "Jamaat-e-Islami Pakistan," http://www.jamaat.org/ (accessed January 18, 2009). India and Bangladesh also have Jamaat-e-Islami political organizations. Says globalsecurity.org of Pakistan's Jamaat-e-Islami, "The JI ranks among the leading and most influential Islamic revivalist movements and the first of its kind to develop an ideology based on the modern revolutionary conception of Islam in the contemporary world." http://www.globalsecurity.org/military/world/pakistan/ji.htmll (accessed January 18, 2009).

23. Office of the Spokesman, US Department of State, "Addition of Aliases Jamaat-Ud-Dawa and Idara Khidmat-E-Khalq to the Specially Designated Global Terrorist Designation of Lashkhar-E-Tayyiba," April 28, 2006, http://www.state.gov/r/pa/prs/ps/2006/65401.htm (accessed January 17, 2009); "Jamaat-ud-Dawa," *USA Today*, October 31, 2008, http://content.usatoday.com/topics/topic/Jamaat-ud-Dawa (accessed January 18, 2009).

24. Dileep Padgaonkar, "Blood in Mumbai," *Washington Post*, November 28, 2008, p. A29.

25. Hugh Bicheno, *Crescent and Cross: The Battle of Lepanto 1571* (New York: Sterling, 2005), p. 43.

26. Sharada Srinivasan, "Sharada Srinivasan PhD Dancer," http://www.youtube.com/watch?v=LsfQy_5uvnA (accessed January 18, 2009).

27. Alice H. Amsden, *Asia's Next Giant: South Korea and Late Industrialization* (New York: Oxford University Press, 1992).

28. Walter Adams and James W. Brock, *The Bigness Complex: Industry, Labor, and Government in the American Economy* (Palo Alto, CA: Stanford University Press, 2004), pp. 275–76.

29. Amsden, *Asia's Next Giant*, p. 291.

30. Ibid., p. 304.

31. William H. McNeill, *Keeping Together in Time: Dance and Drill in Human History* (Cambridge, MA: Harvard University Press, 1997).

32. Stewart Clegg and David Dunkerley, *Organization, Class and Control: An Insider's Guide to Politics* (London: Taylor & Francis, 1980), p. 75.

33. Michel Foucault had a similar concept to scaffolds of habit: "regimes of behavior." These regimes, he felt, were created and hammered home by the institutions of what Foucault called "a disciplinary society." Among these institutions were the Catholic Church, insane asylums, prisons, and the military. Steven Seidman, *Contested Knowledge: Social Theory Today* (Oxford: Blackwell, 2004), p. 189; Rick Iedema, *Discourses of Post-bureaucratic Organization* (Amsterdam: John Benjamins, 2003), p. 91.

34. Tom Brokaw, *The Greatest Generation* (New York: Random House, 2004).

35. David Goldman, "The $8 Trillion Bailout," CNNMoney.com, January 6, 2009, http://money.cnn.com/2009/01/06/news/economy/where_stimulus_fits_in/?postversion=2009010610 (accessed January 18, 2009).

36. John L. Andreassi, *Psychophysiology: Human Behavior and Physiological Response* (London: Routledge, 2006), p. 339.

37. Marie-Thérèse Heemels, "Apoptosis," http://www.nature.com/nature/insights/6805.html (accessed April 28, 2009).

IV TRUTH IN THE CORRIDORS OF POWER

22. The Truth at Any Price Including the Price of Your Life

1. Karl Taro Greenfeld, "Voracious Inc.," *Time*, December 7, 1998.

2. Ibid.

3. "Joseph and the Amazing Technicolor Dreamcoat," 1991 Palladium production program, http://www.andrewlloydwebber.com/theatre/joseph.php (accessed March 4, 2009).

4. John Snelson and Geoffrey Holden Block, *Andrew Lloyd Webber* (New Haven, CT: Yale University Press, 2004); Andrew Lloyd Webber's thoughts on *Jesus Christ Superstar*, http://www.andrewlloydwebber.com/theatre/jcs.php (accessed January 19, 2009).

5. Albert Van Helden and Elizabeth Burr, "Pope Urban VIII," Galileo Project, Rice University, http://galileo.rice.edu/gal/urban.html (accessed January 19, 2009); James Reston, *Galileo: A Life* (Frederick, MD: Beard Books, 2000), pp. 24, 25, 261; Maurice A. Finocchiaro, *Retrying Galileo, 1633–1992* (Berkeley: University of California Press, 2007), pp. 60–61; Albert Van Helden and Elizabeth Burr, "Galileo and the Inquisition," Galileo Project, Rice University, http://galileo.rice.edu/bio/narrative_7.html (accessed January 19, 2009).

6. Harry Wain, *A History of Preventive Medicine* (New York: Thomas, 1970), p. 116.

7. Patrick Collard, *The Development of Microbiology* (Farnham Common, Buckinghamshire, England: Cambridge Archive Editions, 1976), p. 9.

8. Mark Ridley, *The Cooperative Gene: How Mendel's Demon Explains the Evolution of Complex Beings* (New York: Simon & Schuster, 2001), p. 2; Herbert Wendt, *The Sex Life of the Animals* (New York: Simon & Schuster, 1965), p. 57.

9. Stephen Hart, "Flashback/Flashforward: Black Orpheus," *CinemATL*, June 16, 2007, http://www.cinematl.com/index.php?option=com_content&task=view&id=385&Itemid=99999999 (accessed January 19, 2009).

10. James Baldwin, *Go Tell It on the Mountain* (1953; New York: Random House, 1985).

11. Sonny Carson, "Koreans and Racism," *New York Times*, May 8, 1990; Tamar Jacoby, "Sonny Carson and the Politics of Protest," *City Journal* (Summer 1991). When accused of racism and anti-semitism, Carson reportedly said, "I'm anti-white—don't limit my anti's to one group of people." Unfortunately this did not explain the demonstrations Carson led against Korean green grocers with shops in the black community. "Thugs Don't Deserve Honors," *New York Post*, April 14, 2007; Mark Santora, "Sonny Carson, 66, Figure in 60's Battle for Schools," *New York Times*, December 23, 2002.

23. How to Gain the Power of the Force

1. George Lucas, *Star Wars—Episode IV, A New Hope* (1977).

V THE GREATEST HITS OF HISTORY ...
AND HOW THEY GOT TO BE THAT WAY

24. Plato and the Name Game

1. Plato, *The Republic*, Library of the Future (R), 4th ed., ver. 5.0, CD-ROM, screen 121: 646.

2. See, for example, Allan Bloom, *The Closing of the American Mind* (New York: Simon & Schuster, 1987).

3. Herodotus, *History*, Library of the Future (R), 4th ed., ver. 5.0, CD-ROM, screen 59: 1130.

4. Plato, *Theaetetus*, Library of the Future, 4th ed., ver. 5.0; Will Durant, *The Story of Civilization: Volume 2, The Life of Greece*, ver. 4.0, CD-ROM (Irvine, CA: World Library, 1994), 147:1621.

5. F. Diamandopoulos, "Thales of Miletus," in *The Encyclopedia of Philosophy*, ed. Paul Edwards (New York: Macmillan, 1967): vols. 7 and 8; Aristotle, *Heavens*, Library of the Future, 4th ed., ver. 5.0; Aristotle, *Metaphysics*, Library of the Future, 4th ed., ver. 5.0.

6. Thucydides, *History of the Peloponnesian War*, trans. Richard Crawley, Library of the Future, 4th ed., ver. 5.0. (Irvine, CA: World Library, 1994); Xenophon, *Memorabilia* (Charleston: BiblioBazaar, 2007); Durant, *The Story of Civilization*, p. 445.

7. Thucydides, *History of the Peloponnesian War*, trans. Steven Lattimore (Indianapolis: Hackett, 1998).

8. Plato, *Charmides*, in Library of the Future, 4th ed., ver. 5.0. (Irvine, CA: World Library, Inc., 1996).

9. Plato, *Cratylus*, 402, in Plato, *The Dialogues of Plato Translated into English with Analyses and Introductions by B. Jowett, Volume I* (New York: Oxford University Press/MacMillan, 1892), p. 269.

10. Plato, *The Timaeus, and the Critias: Or Atlanticus*, trans. Thomas Taylor (New York: Pantheon Books, 1944).

11. S. Tebbich, M. Taborsky, et al., "Do Woodpecker Finches Acquire Tool-Use by Social Learning?" *Proceedings of the Royal Society of London B* (November 7, 2001): 2189; Susan Milius, "Finches Figure Out Solo How to Use Tools," *Science News*, November 10, 2001.

12. Lauren Kosseff, "Tool Use in Animals," in Dr. Robert Cook, *Animal Cognition*, http://www.pigeon.psy.tufts.edu/psych26/birds.htm (accessed March 15, 2004).

13. Irene Maxine Pepperberg, *The Alex Studies: Cognitive and Communicative Abilities of Grey Parrots* (Cambridge, MA: Harvard University Press, 2002).

14. Lyle B. Steadman, Craig T. Palmer, and Christopher F. Tilley, "The Universality of Ancestor Worship," *Ethnology* (December 1996).

25. The Stone Tool Evolution of Capitalism: What's in a Flake?

1. William H. McNeill, *Plagues and Peoples* (1976; New York: Anchor Books, 1998); Jared Diamond, *Guns, Germs, and Steel: The Fates of Human Societies* (New York: Norton, 1997). The date generally given for the closing of the American frontier is 1890. In reality, battles against Indian tribes continued until 1918.

2. Kenneth T. Jackson, *The Encyclopedia of New York City*, 2004, http://www.yale.edu/yup/ENYC/triangle_shirtwaist.html (accessed March 30, 2004).

3. Greenpeace, "The Disaster in Bhopal," http://www.greenpeace.org/international/campaigns/toxics/toxic-hotspots/the-disaster-in-bhopal (accessed March 5, 2009).

4. Stephanie Anderson Forest and Tom Lowery, "Is Clear Channel Hogging the Airwaves?" *BusinessWeek*, October 1, 2001, http://www.business week.com/print/magazine/content/01_40/b3751043.htm?mz (accessed March 5, 2009).

5. Jennifer Jordan, "Hawks' Nest," *West Virginia Historical Society Quarterly*, April 1998, pp. 1–3; John Flores, "Dusts and Pneumoconioses," Utah State University, September 11, 2002, www.biology.usu.edu/pubh 5310/2002/Particles2002.pdf (accessed March 13, 2004).

6. James K. Mitchell, "Improving Community Responses to Industrial Disasters," United Nations University, 2004, http://www.unu.edu/unupress/unupbooks/uu21le/uu21le03.htm (accessed April 3, 2004); "Deadly Toll of Chernobyl," *BBC News*, April 22, 2000, http://news.bbc.co.uk/1/hi/world/europe/722533.stm (accessed April 3, 2004).

7. Linda Schele and David Freidel, *A Forest of Kings: The Untold Story of the Ancient Maya* (New York: William Morrow, 1990).

8. Bernal Diaz Del Castillo, *The Discovery and Conquest of Mexico: 1517–1521*, ed. Genaro Garcia, trans. A. P. Maudslay (New York: Da Capo Press, 2004).

9. Ann Gibbons, "Archaeologists Rediscover Cannibals," *Science*, August 1, 1997; Jean Luis Arsuaga, "Requiem for a Heavyweight," *Natural History* (December 2002/January 2003): 635–37.

10. Michael Patrick Ghiglieri and Joshua Bilmes, *The Dark Side of Man: Tracing the Origins of Male Violence* (New York: Da Capo Press, 2000), pp. 116–17

11. S. Semaw, P. Renne, J. W. K. Harris, C. S. Feibel, et al., "2.5-Million-

Year-Old Stone Tools from Gona, Ethiopia," *Nature* (January 23, 1997): 333–36.

12. Julio Mercader, Melissa Panger, and Christophe Boesch, "Excavation of a Chimpanzee Stone Tool Site in the African Rainforest," *Science* (May 24, 2002): 1452–55.

13. Gretchen Vogel, "Chimps in the Wild Show Stirrings of Culture," *Science* (June 25, 1999): 2070–73.

26. Flash Isn't Frivolous—Why We Need the Identity Biz

1. Nancy Adajania, "Reaching Out: Between Static and Ghost Image: Art as Transmission," *Hindu*, special issue with the Sunday magazine, April 8, 2001.

2. UNESCO, "Consumer Education," *Across the Curriculum 9*, http://www.unesco.org/education/tlsf/pdf/theme_b_pdf/mod09.pdf (accessed April 28, 2004).

3. Randolph Blake and Robert Sekuler, *Perception* (McGraw-Hill Higher Education Online Learning Center), 2006, http://highered .mcgrawhill.com/sites/0072887605/student_view0/chapter3/glossary.html (accessed February 15, 2009).

4. Roy Lachman and Earl C. Butterfield, *Cognitive Psychology and Information Processing: An Introduction* (Hillsdale, NJ: Lawrence Erlbaum, 1979), p. 496.

5. Jeff Hawkins and Sandra Blakeslee, *On Intelligence* (New York: Holt, 2005).

6. D. Bray, M. D. Levin, and C. J. Morton-Firth, "Receptor Clustering as a Mechanism to Control Sensitivity," *Nature* (May 7, 1998): 85–88; T. A. J. Duke and D. Bray, "Heightened Sensitivity of a Lattice of Membrane Receptors," *Proceedings of the National Academy of Sciences USA* (August 31, 1999): 10104–108; Keith L. Moore, Arthur F. Dalley, and A. M. R. Agur, *Clinically Oriented Anatomy* (Philadelphia: Lippincott Williams & Wilkins, 2006), pp. 1132–33.

7. Frank J. Sulloway, *Born to Rebel: Birth Order, Family Dynamics, and Creative Lives* (New York: Vintage Books, 1997).

8. Frank Sulloway, "Born to Rebel," http://www.sulloway.org/bornto rebel.html (accessed March 5, 2009).

9. Sally McBrearty and Alison S. Brooks, "The Revolution That Wasn't: A New Interpretation of the Origins of Modern Human Behavior," *Journal of Human Evolution* (November 2000): 453–563; Peter Ward, "The Future of Man—How Will Evolution Change Humans?" *Scientific American*, December 2008.

10. Valerius Geist, personal communication, February 8, 2004.

11. Larry Barham, "From Art and Tools Came Human Origins," *British Archaeology Magazine* 42, March 1999, http://www.britarch.ac.uk/ba/ba42/ba42feat.html (accessed March 6, 2009).

12. Lawrence S . Barham, "Systematic Pigment Use in the Middle Pleistocene of South-Central Africa," *Current Anthropology* (February 2002): 182–90.

13. Karl Gröning and Ferdinand Anton, *Body Decoration: A World Survey of Body Art* (New York: Vendome Press, 1998), p. 32; Scott Craig, *Body Painting Gallery*, http://bodypainting.piercingmap.com/index.php ?showimage=3 (accessed February 21, 2009).

14. G. R. Wyatt, "The Biochemistry of Sugars and Polysaccharides in Insects," in *Advances in Insect Physiology*, ed. J. W. L. Beament and J. E. Treherne (New York: Academic Press, 1971), p. 295.

15. Johan Huizinga, *Homo Ludens: A Study of the Play-Element in Culture* (Boston: Beacon Press, 1986).

16. Here are two more tidbits on the power of play to yank the future into the present. The first financially successful railroad in the world was an amusement ride in London. See Jane Jacobs, "The Greening of the City," *New York Times Sunday Magazine*, May 16, 2004, http://www.nytimes.com/2004/05/16/magazine/16ESSAY.html?pagewanted=print&position= (accessed March 6, 2009). And for the philosopher Ludwig Wittgenstein, "Chess was his logic and systems abacus, always at the ready to work out a particular thought problem." David Shenk, *The Immortal Game: A History of Chess or How 32 Carved Pieces on a Board Illuminated Our Understanding of War, Art, Science, and the Human Brain* (New York: Doubleday, 2006), p. 186.

27. Why Neanderthals Couldn't Cut It— The Crucial Use of Vanity

1. Juan Luis Arsuaga, *The Neanderthal's Necklace: In Search of the First Thinkers*, trans. Andy Klatt (New York: Four Walls Eight Windows, 2002); Robert G. Bednarik, "Concept-Mediated Marking in the Lower Palaeolithic," *Current Anthropology* (August/October 1995): 606; Jeffrey Brainard, "Giving Neandertals Their Due: Similarities with Modern Humans Shift the Image of the Caveman Brute," *Science News*, August 1, 1998.

2. Valerius Geist, *Life Strategies, Human Evolution, Environmental Design: Toward a Biological Theory of Health* (New York: Springer, 1978); Valerius Geist, personal communication, 1997–2004.

3. Richard Law, "The Long Foreground: Human Prehistory," Wash-

ington State University, 2004, http://www.wsu.edu/gened/learn-modules/top_longfor/phychar/culture-humans-2two.html (accessed May 21, 2004).

4. Sigfried J. de Laet, Ahmad Hasan Dani, International Commission for the New Edition of the History of the Scientific and Cultural Development of Mankind, J. L. Lorenzo, R. B. Nunoo, UNESCO, *History of Humanity: Scientific and Cultural Development* (New York: Taylor & Francis, 1994), p. 645.

5. Jean Luis Arsuaga, "Requiem for a Heavyweight," *Natural History* (December 2002/January 2003): 635–37.

6. David White, *Social Studies for Kids*, http://www.socialstudies forkids.com/articles/economics/wantsandneeds1.htm (accessed May 3, 2004); Southern LINCS Workforce Education Lab, National Institute for Literacy, "Especially for Teachers: Needs vs. Wants," *Daytona Beach News-Journal*, http://www.nieworld.com/teachers/lessonplans/stetsonplans11.htm (accessed May 3, 2004); Carol Cheatwood, "Determining Needs vs. Wants," Tennessee Department of Human Services for the Fannie Mae Foundation, http://slincs.coe.utk.edu/gtelab/learning_activities/36chec.html (accessed Mary 3, 2004); Michael Scriven, "Foundations of Evaluation: Needs vs. Wants," Claremont Graduate University, http://fac.cgu.edu/~scrivenm/lectures/needwant/needs.htm (accessed May 3, 2004); Evelyn DeLoatch, "Needs vs. Wants," North Carolina State University and AT&T State University Cooperative Extension, http://www.ces.ncsu.edu/alamance/news letters/ Evelyn/money/01/needswants.html (accessed May 3, 2004); University of Georgia, "Needs vs. Wants," College of Agricultural and Environmental Sciences, University of Georgia, http://apps.caes.uga.edu/presentations/data/mrneedswants.ppt (accessed February 6, 2009).

28. Swapping Drops of Blood: The Animal Roots of Trade

1. Raghavendra Gadagkar, *Survival Strategies: Cooperation and Conflict in Animal Societies* (Cambridge, MA: Harvard University Press, 2001), p. 77; Joan Roughgarden, *Evolution's Rainbow: Diversity, Gender, and Sexuality in Nature and People* (Berkeley: University of California Press, 2004), p. 61; Julie Perry, "Reciprocal Altruism: Vampire Bats," Department of Biology, Davidson College, North Carolina, April 19, 2002, http://www.bio.davidson.edu/people/vecase/behavior/Spring2002/Perry/altruism.html (accessed January 20, 2009).

2. Steven Pinker, *The Language Instinct* (New York: William Morrow, 1994).

3. P. J. Zak, A. A. Stanton, and S. Ahmadi, "Oxytocin Increases Gen-

erosity in Humans," *Public Library of Science (PLoS) One,* November 7, 2007, e1128, http://www.plosone.org/article/info:doi/10.1371/journal.pone .0001128;jsessionid=2019B06B5958D0B9E938CB44CAF21AB0 (accessed February 15, 2009).

4. P. J. Zak and S. Knack, "Trust and Growth," *Economic Journal,* April 2001, pp. 295–321; Virginia Postrel, "Looking inside the Brains of the Stingy," *New York Times,* February 27, 2003, p. C2.

5. Zak and Knack, "Trust and Growth," p. 316.

6. Susan Milius, "Unfair Trade: Monkeys Demand Equitable Exchanges," *Science News* 162, no. 12 (September 20, 2003).

7. If you are 5'10", weigh 180 pounds, and are moderately active, your body will need 2,368 calories to maintain your current weight. To see exactly how many calories it takes per day to maintain your ideal weight, go to "Calories Per Day Calculator," http://walking.about.com/cs/calories/l/ blcalcalc.htm (accessed March 9, 2009).

8. Bruce Bower, "A Fair Share of the Pie: People Everywhere Put a Social Spin on Economic Exchanges," *Science News,* February 16, 2002.

9. Joseph Henrich, Robert Boyd, Samuel Bowles, Colin Camerer, Ernst Fehr, Herbert Gintis, Richard McElreath, Michael Alvard, Abigail Barr, Jean Ensminger, Kim Hill, Francisco Gil-White, Michael Gurven, Frank Marlowe, John Q. Patton, Natalie Smith, and David Tracer, "Economic Man in Cross-Cultural Perspective: Behavioral Experiments in Fifteen Small-Scale Societies," *Behavioral and Brain Sciences* 28, no. 6 (2005): 795–815.

VI THE INFRASTRUCTURE OF FANTASY

29. The Cannonball to the Moon

1. Jules Verne, *From the Earth to the Moon: And a Trip around It* (New York: Penguin, 1970); Marguerite Allotte de la Fuÿe, *Jules Verne* (New York: Coward-McCann, 1956).

2. George Dyson, *Project Orion: The True Story of the Atomic Spaceship* (New York: Macmillan, 2002), p. 59.

3. Charles D. Brown, *Spacecraft Propulsion* (Reston, VA: American Institute of Astronautics, 1996), p. 1.

4. Hermann Oberth, *Man into Space: New Projects for Rocket and Space Travel* (New York: Harper, 1957); Helen B. Walters, *Hermann Oberth: Father of Space Travel* (New York: Macmillan, 1962); A. Kosmodemyansky and X. Danko, *Konstantin Tsiolkovsky: His Life and Work,* trans. X. Danko (London: Minerva, 2000), p. 37.

5. Bob Ward and John Glenn, *Dr. Space: The Life of Wernher von Braun* (Annapolis, MD: Naval Institute Press, 2005), p. 14; Michael Neufeld, *Von Braun: Dreamer of Space, Engineer of War* (New York: Vintage Books, 2008).

6. Ward and Glenn, *Dr. Space*, p. 56.

7. "Chesley Bonestell," http://www.absoluteastronomy.com/topics/Chesley_Bonestell (accessed January 27, 2009).

8. Melvin H. Schuetz, *A Chesley Bonestell Space Art Chronology* (Boca Raton, FL: Universal-Publishers, 1999), p. xxii.

9. Willy Ley and Chesley Bonestell, *The Conquest of Space* (New York: Viking, 1949); Joseph Kaplan and Cornelius Ryan, *Across the Space Frontier* (New York: Viking, 1952); Wernher von Braun, Fred Lawrence Whipple, and Willy Ley, *Conquest of the Moon*, illust. Chesley Bonestell, Fred Freeman, and Rolf Klep, ed. Cornelius Ryan (New York: Viking Press, 1953); Kenneth Heuer, *The End of the World*, illust. Chesley Bonestell (New York: Viking, 1953; reprinted and revised, 1957, as *The Next Fifty Billion Years: An Astronomer's Glimpse into the Future*). And nine others—for the complete list see Wikipedia, "Books Illustrated by Bonestell," http://en.wikipedia.org/wiki/Bonestell#Books_illustrated_by_Bonestell (accessed January 27, 2009). See also "Bibliography," Bonestell Space Art, http://www.bonestell.org/biblio.html (accessed January 27, 2009).

10. Matthew Brzezinski, *Red Moon Rising*: Sputnik *and the Hidden Rivalries That Ignited the Space Age* (New York: Macmillan, 2007), p. 91.

11. John F. Kennedy, "We Choose to Go to the Moon," 1962 speech, http://www.historyplace.com/speeches/jfk-space.htm (accessed January 27, 2009); Eugene Cernan and Donald A. Davis, *The Last Man on the Moon: Astronaut Eugene Cernan and America's Race in Space* (New York: Macmillan, 2000), p. 251.

30. Inventing the City: Even the Walls Tell Tales of Soul

1. Yoonsoo Hahn and Byungkook Lee, "Human-Specific Nonsense Mutations Identified by Genome Sequence Comparisons," *Human Genetics*, March 2006, pp. 169–78.

2. Sean B. Carroll, *Endless Forms Most Beautiful: The New Science of Evo Devo and the Making of the Animal Kingdom* (New York: Norton, 2005), p. 277; Alan R. Rogers, "Meat in Human Evolution," Department of Anthropology, University of Utah, www.anthro.utah.edu/~rogers/ant1050/Lectures/hunting-2x3.pdf (accessed February 15, 2009).

3. Hillard S. Kaplan and Arthur J. Robson, "The Emergence of Humans: The Coevolution of Intelligence and Longevity with Intergenera-

tional Transfers," *Proceedings of the National Academy of Sciences of the United States*, July 23, 2002, pp. 10221–226; David Magnusson and Torgny Greitz, *The Lifespan Development of Individuals: Behavioral, Neurobiological, and Psychosocial Perspectives: A Synthesis* (Cambridge: Cambridge University Press, 1997), p. 425.

4. The phrase "stored labor" emerged from Marx's labor theory, his notion that all the value in something you buy comes from the sweat and toil of the laborers who made it. Let me repeat. Marx said ALL the value comes from labor. None from entrepreneurs, none from investors, none from inventors, and none from leaders. And none from the extent to which you hunger for your purchase, or the extent to which you're simply not interested in purchasing at all. Marx's labor theory was so obviously flawed that he promised to defend it against its critics in the second volume of his masterwork, *Das Kapital*. But he never got around to writing that second volume. For more on Marx's labor theory, see Edmund Wilson, *To the Finland Station: A Study in the Writing and Acting of History* (New York: New York Review of Books, 2003), pp. 212, 290–91; Mark Skousen, *The Making of Modern Economics: The Lives and Ideas of the Great Thinkers* (Armonk, NY: M. E. Sharpe, 2001), pp. 107–108. For uses of the term "stored labor" to sum up Marx's labor theory, see Amalgamated Meat Cutters and Butcher Workmen of North America, *Official Journal*, 6:4–7:2, 1905, p. 8; Lester D. Taylor, *Capital, Accumulation, and Money: An Integration of Capital, Growth, and Monetary Theory* (New York: Springer, 2000), pp. 147–48.

5. Douglas J. Kennett and Bruce Winterhalder, *Behavioral Ecology and the Transition to Agriculture* (Berkeley: University of California Press, 2006), p. 207.

6. Jon Elster, *Addiction: Entries and Exits* (New York: Russell Sage Foundation, 1999), pp. 80–83; Marvin Zuckerman, *Psychobiology of Personality* (New York: Cambridge University Press, 2005), p. 195; Gerd Kempermann, *Adult Neurogenesis: Stem Cells and Neuronal Development in the Adult Brain* (New York: Oxford University Press, 2006), p. 347; H. P. Lipp, H. Schwegler, B. Heinrich, A. Cerbone, and A. G. Sadile, "Strain-Specific Correlations between Hippocampal Structural Traits and Habituation in a Spatial Novelty Situation," *Behavioral Brain Research* 24 (1987): 111–23; C. Belzung, "Hippocampal Mossy Fibres: Implication in Novelty Reactions or in Anxiety Behaviours?" *Behavioral Brain Research* (November 15, 1992): 149–55.

7. Anna Belfer-Cohen and Offer Bar-Yosef, "Early Sedentism in the Near East: A Bumpy Ride to Village Life," in Ian Kuijt, *Life in Neolithic Farming Communities: Social Organization, Identity, and Differentiation* (New York: Springer, 2000), pp. 21–28; Arlene Miller Rosen, *Civilizing Cli-*

mate: Social Responses to Climate Change in the Ancient Near East (Walnut Creek, CA: Rowman Altamira, 2007), pp. 118–26; Iorwerth Eiddon Stephen Edwards, Cyril John Gadd, Nicholas Geoffrey Lemprière Hammond, and John Boardman, *The Cambridge Ancient History: Prolegomena and Prehistory, Vol. 1: Part 1* (Cambridge: Cambridge University Press, 1970), p. 95; Graeme Barker, *The Agricultural Revolution in Prehistory: Why Did Foragers Become Farmers?* (Oxford: Oxford University Press, 2006), p. 125.

8. Personal communication based on four days of brainstorming sessions for which Buckner flew from Texas to New York City and camped out in a Lower Manhattan hotel to spend evenings at the infamous Bloom Brownstone in Park Slope, Brooklyn. This crash session occurred in 2002, shortly after 9/11. Buckner was a $50,000-a-day CEO consultant at the time, with clients like Bank of America, Booz Allen, BP, Comsat, Deutsche Bank, Fujitsu, General Electric, Mitsubishi, Nabisco, Pillsbury, and Procter & Gamble. But his concepts have, alas, never been published.

9. Kathleen Mary Kenyon, *Digging Up Jericho: The Results of the Jericho Excavations, 1952–1956* (Westport, CT: Praeger, 1957).

31. Try a Little Craziness

1. For the manner in which the invention of city walls gave birth to subcultures and to your freedom and mine to pick our roles in society, see Howard Bloom, *Global Brain: The Evolution of Mass Mind from the Big Bang to the 21st Century* (New York: Wiley, 2000).

2. Sigfried J. de Laet, Ahmad Hasan Dani, International Commission for the New Edition of the History of the Scientific and Cultural Development of Mankind, J. L. Lorenzo, R. B. Nunoo, UNESCO, *History of Humanity: Scientific and Cultural Development* (New York: Taylor & Francis, 1994), p. 427; Dora Jane Hamblin with C. C. Lamberg-Karlovsky and the editors of Time-Life Books, *The Emergence of Man: The First Cities* (New York: Time-Life Books, 1979).

3. A grass operating without human help needs to spread its seed as widely as it can. That means it has to let go of its seeds so the wind or passing animals can spread them. But Jericho archaeological digs have turned up twelve-thousand-year-old wheat and barley kernels, grains from grasses that resisted giving up their seeds—a sign that their genes had been tinkered with by human beings. See Maguelonne Toussaint-Samat, *A History of Food*, trans. Anthea Bell (Oxford: Blackwell Publishing, 1994), p. 126.

32. Quantum Leaps of Fantasy

1. James Mellaart, the first and most famous archaeologist of the Catal Huyuk dig, a man whose name became synonymous with Catal Huyuk and its finds, taught his students at the Institute of Archaeology in London that the Catal Huyuk wall paintings showed the same patterns that would appear in Turkish carpets, *kilims*, for the next seven thousand years. Mellaart repeated this assertion in two books, *Catal-Huyuk: A Neolithic Town in Anatolia* and *The Goddess from Anatolia*. But rug specialists among his colleagues disagreed. Vehemently. They claimed that Mellaart had fabricated his evidence. The result was the "kilim hypothesis" rug controversy, a dust-up that roiled the Catal Huyuk scholarly community from the rug-battle's start in the 1980s to today. For Mellaart's views, see James Mellaart, *Catal-Huyuk: A Neolithic Town in Anatolia* (New York: McGraw-Hill, 1967) and James Mellaart, Udo Hirsch, and Belkis Balpinar, *The Goddess from Anatolia* (Milan, Italy: Eskenazi, 1989). For a more balanced telling of the story of the controversy, see Michael Balter, *The Goddess and the Bull: Catalhöyük: An Archaeological Journey to the Dawn of Civilization* (New York: Simon & Schuster, 2005), pp. 205–208, 245–46. Balter should know what he is talking about. He's the official biographer for the Catal Huyuk dig. For the views of the leader of the anti-rug hypothesis team, Marla Mallett, see "The Goddess from Anatolia: An Updated View of the Çatal Hüyük Controversy," http://www.marlamallett .com/chupdate.htm (accessed January 22, 2009). See also Pat Shipman, "At the Trowel's Edge," *Nature* (May 19, 2005): 278–79.

2. Dora Jane Hamblin with C. C. Lamberg-Karlovsky and the editors of Time-Life Books, *The Emergence of Man: The First Cities* (New York: Time-Life Books, 1979), p. 19.

3. Richard Dawkins calls the system that results when a species reinvents itself by reinventing its tools and its environment an "extended phenotype." Termites, for example, reinvented their species when they began to create palatial cities that housed millions. Thus the combination of termites and their architectural wonders formed an "extended phenotype." Richard Dawkins, *The Extended Phenotype: The Long Reach of the Gene* (New York: Oxford University Press, 1999). See also J. Scott Turner, *The Extended Organism: The Physiology of Animal-Built Structures* (Cambridge, MA: Harvard University Press, 2000).

33. The Flaws in the Concept of Consumerism and the Hungers in the Fissures of the Brain

1. The man leading the biopsychological charge to unearth the sources of desire in the brain is Kent Berridge at the University of Michigan. For a simple map of the locations of the bioplan of human needs and the taxonomy of desire in the brain, see K. C. Berridge and T. E. Robinson, "Parsing Reward," *Trends in Neurosciences* 26, no. 9 (2003): 507–13, http://www .lsa.umich.edu/psych/research&labs/berridge/publications/Berridge%20&%20Robinson%20TINS%202003.pdf (accessed January 22, 2009). See also Kent Berridge, "Research Projects," Affective Neuroscience and Psychology Lab, University of Michigan Psychology Department—Biopsychology Program, http://www.lsa.umich.edu/psych/research&labs/berridge/research/affectiveneuroscience.html (accessed January 22, 2009). See also Kathleen Stein, *The Genius Engine: Where Memory, Reason, Passion, Violence, and Creativity Intersect in the Human Brain* (New York: Wiley, 2007), pp. 135–42. And see Philip Winn, *Dictionary of Biological Psychology* (London: Taylor & Francis, 2001), p. 61.

2. Theodore Low De Vinne, *The Invention of Printing: A Collection of Facts and Opinions Descriptive of Early Prints and Playing Cards . . .* (New York: Francis Hart and Company, 1878), pp. 376–401. Low De Vinne gives extensive quotes from the primary sources for the story of Gutenberg's life— records of the testimony at Gutenberg's many legal battles. See also John Luther Ringwalt, *American Encyclopaedia of Printing* (Philadelphia: Menamin & Ringwalt, 1871), p. 191; Bryan H. Bunch and Alexander Hellemans, *The History of Science and Technology: A Browser's Guide to the Great Discoveries, Inventions, and the People Who Made Them, from the Dawn of Time to Today* (Boston: Houghton Mifflin Harcourt, 2004), p. 138; Henri-Jean Martin, *The History and Power of Writing*, trans. Lydia G. Cochrane (Chicago: University of Chicago Press, 1995), pp. 217–22; Anthony Day, "Threads of Gutenberg's Life Woven into a Tapestry," *Los Angeles Times*, June 21, 2002, p. E-3. And most intriguing and entrancing of them all, James Burke, *Connections* (Boston: Little, Brown, 1978).

3. Fran Rees, *Johannes Gutenberg: Inventor of the Printing Press* (Mankato, MN: Compass Point Books, 2006), pp. 22, 39; J. Michael Adams, David D. Faux, and Lloyd J. Rieber, *Printing Technology: A Medium of Visual Communications* (North Scituate, MA: Breton, 1982), p. 2; Christine L. Borgman, *From Gutenberg to the Global Information Infrastructure: Access to Information in the Networked World* (Cambridge, MA: MIT Press, 2003), p. ix; John H. Lienhard, *How Invention Begins: Echoes of Old Voices in the Rise of New Machines* (New York: Oxford University Press, 2006), p. 138.

4. Robert Raymond, *Out of the Fiery Furnace: The Impact of Metals on the History of Mankind* (University Park: Penn State Press, 1986), p. 106.

5. Bryan Jay Wolf, *Vermeer and the Invention of Seeing* (Chicago: University of Chicago Press, 2001), p. 256; Sabine Melchior-Bonnet, Katharine Jewett, and Jean Delumeau, *The Mirror: A History*, trans. Katharine Jewett (London: Routledge, 2002), pp. 5–6.

6. Richard Campbell, Christopher R. Martin, and Bettina G. Fabos, *Media and Culture with 2009 Update: An Introduction to Mass Communication* (New York: Macmillan, 2008), p. 356.

7. For the books printed by Gutenberg, see Thomas Frognall Dibdin, *Bibliotheca Spenceriana: A Descriptive Catalogue of the Books Printed in the Fifteenth Century and of Many Valuable First Editions, in the Library of George John Earl Spencer* (London: Longman, Hurst, 1815); "William Morris on the Printing of Books," *Publishers Weekly*, July–December 1893, p. 1065.

8. Low De Vinne, *The Invention of Printing*, p. 393.

9. Howard Bloom, "Instant Evolution: The Influence of the City on Human Genes," *New Ideas in Psychology* (September 13, 2001): 203–20.

10. "1974—Digital Watch Is First System-On-Chip: Integrated Circuit," http://www.computerhistory.org/semiconductor/timeline/1974-digital-watch-is-first-system-on-chip-integrated-circuit-52.html (accessed January 24, 2009).

11. David E. Hunter and Phillip Whitten, *Readings in Physical Anthropology and Archaeology* (New York: Harper & Row, 1978), p. 265.

34. The Spiritual Fruits of Material Things: How the Flock Became a Metaphor

1. Julian Roche, *The International Wool Trade* (Cambridge: Woodhead Publishing, 1995), pp. 1–2; Thomas Scott, *Concise Encyclopedia Biology* [*sic*], trans. Thomas Scott (Berlin: Walter de Gruyter, 1995), p. 394; Melinda A. Zeder, *Documenting Domestication: New Genetic and Archaeological Paradigms* (Berkeley: University of California Press, 2006), p. 211. See also Tetsu Yamazaki and Toyoharu Kojima, *Legacy of the Dog: The Ultimate Illustrated Guide* (San Francisco: Chronicle Books, 2005), p. 6.

2. Melinda Zeder's genetic evidence hints that dogs may have started hanging around with humans as early as two hundred thousand years ago. Zeder, *Documenting Domestication*, p. 281. See also Rodney P. Carlisle, *Scientific American Inventions and Discoveries: All the Milestones in Ingenuity—From the Discovery of Fire to the Invention of the Microwave Oven* (New York: Wiley, 2004), p. 38; John Paul Scott and John L. Fuller, *Dog*

Behavior: The Genetic Basis (Chicago: University of Chicago Press, 1974), p. 54.

3. Marshall Cavendish Corporation, *Endangered Wildlife and Plants of the World* (Tarrytown, NY: Marshall Cavendish, 2001), p. 1666.

4. Chris Witt, *Wolves: Life in the Pack* (New York: Sterling, 2003), p. 55.

5. L. David Mech, "Leadership in Wolf, *Canis lupus*, Packs," *Canadian Field-Naturalist* 114, no. 2 (2000): 259–63.

6. Barry Holstun Lopez, *Of Wolves and Men* (New York: Simon & Schuster, 2004), p. 80.

7. Olga Soffer and N. D. Praslov, *From Kostenki to Clovis: Upper Paleolithic Paleo-Indian Adaptations* (New York: Springer, 1993), p. 246.

8. Rolf O. Peterson, *The Wolves of Isle Royale: A Broken Balance* (Ann Arbor: University of Michigan Press, 2007), p. 134. For a shocking description of a battle in which the wolves of one pack kill the alpha male of a pack that competes with theirs for hunting territory, see Rolf O. Peterson, *The Wolves of Isle Royale*, p. 138.

9. American Pet Products Association, "Industry Statistics & Trends," http://www.americanpetproducts.org/press_industrytrends.asp (accessed January 26, 2009).

10. "Grey Wolf Returns to US Endangered Species List," *Guardian*, September 30, 2008, http://www.guardian.co.uk/world/2008/sep/30/usa.endangeredspecies (accessed January 26, 2009).

11. International Wolf Center, "Are Gray Wolves Endangered?" International Wolf Center, updated August 2005, http://www.wolf.org/wolves/learn/intermed/inter_mgmt/endangered.asp (accessed January 26, 2009).

12. Gabriel Horn, *Memory, Imprinting and the Brain: An Inquiry into Mechanisms* (New York: Oxford University Press, 1985); Jörg Bock and Katharina Braun, "Filial Imprinting in Domestic Chicks Is Associated with Spine Pruning in the Associative Area, Dorsocaudal Neostriatum," *European Journal of Neuroscience* 11, no. 7:2566–70; Konrad Lorenz, *On Aggression* (New York: Harcourt Brace Jovanovich, 1974).

13. Kathreen [*sic*] E. Ruckstuhl and Peter Neuhaus, *Sexual Segregation in Vertebrates: Ecology of the Two Sexes* (Cambridge: Cambridge University Press, 2005), p. 192; Marco Festa-Bianchet, "Site Fidelity and Seasonal Range Use by Bighorn Rams," *Canadian Journal of Zoology/Revue Canadienne de Zoologie* 64, no. 10 (1986): 2126–32; Marco Festa-Bianchet and Steeve D. Cote, *Mountain Goats: Ecology, Behavior, and Conservation of an Alpine Ungulate* (Washington, DC: Island Press, 2008), pp. 4, 74.

14. In many animal and human societies, males play a special role—and not a happy one—in the fission-fusion strategy. They are used as exploratory

probes, disposable test vehicles. C. N. Johnson, "Sex-Biased Philopatry and Dispersal in Mammals," *Oecologia* (Berlin) 69 (1986): 626; Maury M. Haraway, *Comparative Psychology: A Handbook* (Taylor & Francis, 1998), p. 441; Howard Bloom, *The Lucifer Principle: A Scientific Expedition into the Forces of History* (New York: Atlantic Monthly Press, 1997).

15. Yoshiaki Itō and Jiro Kikkawa, *Comparative Ecology* (Farnham Common, Buckinghamshire, England: Cambridge Archive Editions, 1980), pp. 314–15; Katherine A. Houpt, *Domestic Animal Behavior for Veterinarians and Animal Scientists* (Oxford: Blackwell, 2004), p. 49; Don E. Wilson, American Society of Mammalogists, and Sue Ruff, Smithsonian Institution, *The Smithsonian Book of North American Mammals* (Vancouver: University of British Columbia Press, 1999), pp. 348–49.

16. Marshall Cavendish Corporation, *Endangered Wildlife and Plants of the World.*

17. "Norman Rockwell's Four Freedoms," http://www.best-norman-rockwell-art.com/four-freedoms.html (accessed January 26, 2009).

18. Ernest S. Burch and Linda J. Ellanna, *Key Issues in Hunter Gatherer Research* (Oxford: Berg Publishers, 1996), p. 25; Robin Torrence, ed., *Time, Energy and Stone Tools* (Farnham Common, Buckinghamshire, England: Cambridge Archive Editions, 1989), p. 35.

35. Accounting and the Birth of the Written Word: The Art of Finding Wealth in Toxic Waste

1. Denise Schmandt Besserat, "Oneness, Twoness, Threeness: How Ancient Accountants Invented Numbers," *Sciences*, July/August 1987.

36. Meaning and Marketing: Moses and the Slogan

1. Barack Obama, "We Are Better Than These Last Eight Years," prepared remarks of Barack Obama to the Democratic National Convention, August 28, 2008, MSNBC, http://www.msnbc.msn.com/id/26446638/page/7/ (accessed January 26, 2009).

2. Deuteronomy 6–9.

3. Exodus 20:13–16.

4. Exodus 20:3–5.

5. Michael W. Eysenck and Mark T. Keane, *Cognitive Psychology: A Student's Handbook* (London: Taylor & Francis, 2005), p. 191; Bernard J. Baars, *The Cognitive Revolution in Psychology* (New York: Guilford Press, 1986), pp. 164–65.

37. The Positive Power of Novelty Lust:
The Phoenicians and Their Wonder Ships

1. Gregory S. Berns, Jonathan D. Cohen, and Mark A. Mintun, "Brain Regions Responsive to Novelty in the Absence of Awareness," *Science* (May 23, 1997): 1272–75; Gregory Berns, *Iconoclast: A Neuroscientist Reveals How to Think Differently* (Cambridge, MA: Harvard Business Press, 2008); Gregory S. Berns, personal communication, 2000 to 2009.

2. William Copeland Borlase, *Tin-Mining in Spain, Past and Present* (London: Effingham Wilson, 1897), pp. 25, 27.

3. Vincent C. Pigott, *The Archaeometallurgy of the Asian Old World* (Philadelphia: University of Pennsylvania Museum of Archaeology, 1999), p. 54.

38. Righteous Indignation—
The Western System's Protest Industry:
Isaiah's Swords to Plowshares

1. *The Holy Bible: Containing the Old and New Testaments Translated Out of the Original Tongues: And with the Former Translations Diligently Compared and Revised* (New York: American Bible Society, 1903); *The Bible* (King James Version), Library of the Future (R), 4th ed., ver. 5.0, CD-ROM; Emmet John Sweeney, *The Ramessides, Medes, and Persians* (New York: Algora Publishing, 2007), p. 108; Emil G. Hirsch, Thomas Kelly Cheyne, Isidore Singer, and Isaac Broydé, "Isaiah," *Jewish Encyclopedia*, http://www.jewishencyclopedia.com/view.jsp?artid=261&letter=I (accessed January 28, 2009); Richard Gottheil, Gotthard Deutsch, Martin A. Meyer, Joseph Jacobs, and M. Franco, "Jerusalem," *Jewish Encyclopedia*, http://www.jewishencyclopedia.com/view.jsp?artid=242&letter=J&search=jerusalem#910 (accessed January 28, 2009); Joseph Jacobs and J. F. McLaughlin, "Shalmaneser," *Jewish Encyclopedia*, http://www.jewishencyclopedia.com/view.jsp?letter=S&artid=542 (accessed January 28, 2009); "Neo-Assyrian Empire," *Encyclopædia Britannica*, http://www.britannica.com/EBchecked/topic/408611/Neo-Assyrian-Empire (accessed January 28, 2009); "Isaiah," *Encyclopædia Britannica*, http://www.britannica.com/EBchecked/topic/295133/Isaiah (accessed January 28, 2009); "Assyriology," *Encyclopædia Britannica*, http://www.britannica.com/EBchecked/topic/39634/Assyriology (accessed January 28, 2009); "History of Mesopotamia," *Encyclopædia Britannica*, http://www.britannica.com/EBchecked/topic/376828/Mesopotamia/55452/Assyria-and-Babylonia-from-c-1000-to-c-750-bc#ref=ref361392 (accessed January 28, 2009); "Tukulti-Ninurta II," *Ency-

clopædia Britannica, http://www.britannica.com/EBchecked/topic/608605/ Tukulti-Ninurta-II (accessed January 28, 2009); "Ashurnasirpal II," Encyclopædia Britannica, http://www.britannica.com/EBchecked/topic/38459/ Ashurnasirpal-II (accessed January 28, 2009).

39. The Mood-Shift Industry: David's Songs and Orpheus's Lyre

1. Joseph Jacobs, Ira Maurice Price, Isidore Singer, and Jacob Zallel Lauterbach, "Saul," *Jewish Encyclopedia*, http://www.jewishencyclopedia .com/view.jsp?letter=S&artid=275 (accessed January 28, 2009); "Saul," *Encyclopædia Britannica*, http://www.britannica.com/EBchecked/topic/ 525442/Saul (accessed January 28, 2009).

2. Samuel 15:1–24.

3. This calculation is based on the beeper studies of Mihaly Csikszentmihalyi and Reed Larson. For a complete report on the studies, see Mihaly Csikszentmihalyi and Reed Larson, *Being Adolescent: Conflict and Growth in the Teenage Years* (New York: Basic Books, 1984); see also Richard G. Condon, *Inuit Youth: Growth and Change in the Canadian Arctic* (New Brunswick, NJ: Rutgers University Press, 1988), pp. 196–97.

VII JACKING UP THE SYMBOL STACK

40. How Symbols Expand Our Powers—Croesus Invents Money

1. Sanford Holst, "Sea Peoples and the Phoenicians: A Critical Turning Point in History," based on the paper presented at Al Akhawayn University in Ifrane, Morocco, on June 28, 2005, http://www.phoenician.org/ sea_peoples.htm (accessed March 9, 2009); Glenn Markoe, *Phoenicians* (Berkley: University of California Press, 2001), p. 187.

2. David M. Schaps, *The Invention of Coinage and the Monetization of Ancient Greece* (Ann Arbor: University of Michigan Press, 2004).

3. Steve Harvey and Kerry Hull, "Neural Growth Hormone: An Update," *Journal of Molecular Neuroscience* (February 2003): 1–14.

4. Ruth Benedict, *Patterns of Culture* (1934; New York: New American Library, 1950).

5. Janet F. Werker and Renee N. Desjardins, "Listening to Speech in the 1st Year of Life: Experiential Influences on Phoneme Perception," *Current Directions in Psychological Science* (June 1995): 76–81; Janet F. Werker, "Becoming a Native Listener," *American Scientist* (January/February 1989):

54–59; Janet F. Werker and Richard C. Tees, "The Organization and Reorganization of Human Speech Perception," *Annual Review of Neuroscience* 15 (1992): 377–402; J. F. Werker and J. E. Pegg, "Infant Speech Perception and Phonological Acquisition," *Phonological Development: Research, Models and Implications*, ed. C. E. Ferguson, L. Menn, and C. Stoel-Gammon (Parkton, MD: York Press, 1992); Janet F. Werker, "Exploring Developmental Changes in Cross-Language Speech Perception," in *An Invitation to Cognitive Science—Part I: Language*, vol. ed. L. Gleitman and M. Liberman, series ed. D. Osherson (Cambridge, MA: MIT Press, 1995), pp. 87–106.

6. David Birdsong, *Second Language Acquisition and the Critical Period Hypothesis* (Hillsdale, NJ: Lawrence Erlbaum Associates, 1999).

7. Sarah T. Boysen and Karen I. Hallberg, "Primate Numerical Competence: Contributions toward Understanding Nonhuman Cognition," *Cognitive Science* 24, no. 3 (2000): 434–38; Alan Silberberg and Kazuo Fujita, "Pointing at Smaller Food Amounts in an Analogue of Boysen and Berntson's (1995) Procedure," *Journal of the Experimental Analysis of Behavior* (July 1996): 143–47; "Sally (Sarah) Boysen," Sally Boysen Homepage, Department of Psychology, Ohio State University, http://faculty.psy.ohio-state.edu/boysen/ (accessed January 29, 2009). The name the "candy game" is the contribution of Adrienne L. Zihlman. Adrienne L. Zihlman, *The Human Evolution Coloring Book*, illust. Carla Simmons (New York: HarperCollins, 2001), chs. 3–35.

41. The Might, Height, Right, and Glory Biz: The Seven Wonders of the World and How They Got to Be That Way

1. Charles Darwin, *The Formation of Vegetable Mould, through the Action of Worms: With Observations of Their Habits* (1881; New York: D. Appleton, 1907); Pat Vickers Rich, Carroll Lane Fenton, and Mildred Adams Fenton, *The Fossil Book: A Record of Prehistoric Life* (New York: Courier Dover Publications, 1996), p. 183.

42. This Dollar Is My Body and My Blood: Banking and Cicero's Family

1. William N. Goetzmann and K. Geert Rouwenhorst argue that ancient Rome also had its equivalent of corporations. William N. Goetzmann and K. Geert Rouwenhorst, *Origins of Value: A Document History of Finance* (New York: Oxford University Press, 2005).

2. Jean Andreau and Janet Lloyd, *Banking and Business in the Roman World* (New York: Cambridge University Press, 1999), p. 13.

3. For a detailed description of the Egypt-to-Rome grain trade, complete with an explanation of bread and circuses, see Michael Atkin, *The International Grain Trade* (Cambridge: Woodhead, 1995), pp. 13–16.

4. Egypt shipped 20 million *modi* of wheat to Rome each year, says *The Cambridge Ancient History*. Alan K. Bowman, Edward Champlin, and Andrew Lintott, *The Cambridge Ancient History* (Cambridge: Cambridge University Press, 1996), p. 694; Gregory S. Aldrete, *Daily Life in the Roman City: Rome, Pompeii and Ostia* (Westport, CT: Greenwood, 2004), pp. 198–200. For a description of the massive clipper ships built under Augustus for the Egypt-to-Rome run, see Lionel Casson, *The Ancient Mariners: Seafarers and Sea Fighters of the Mediterranean in Ancient Times* (Princeton, NJ: Princeton University Press, 1991), pp. 208–209. For the role of merchants and commercial shippers in the Egypt-to-Rome grain trade, see Walter Scheidel and Sitta von Reden, *The Ancient Economy* (London: Taylor & Francis, 2002), pp. 215–16; Geoffrey Rickman, *The Corn Supply of Ancient Rome* (Oxford: Clarendon Press, 1980), pp. 72, 150. For general money and trade matters in ancient Rome see Lionel Casson, *Ancient Trade and Society* (Detroit: Wayne State University Press, 1984) and Richard Duncan-Jones, *Money and Government in the Roman Empire* (Cambridge: Cambridge University Press, 1998).

5. Colin McEvedy and David Woodroffe, *The New Penguin Atlas of Medieval History: Revised Edition* (London: Penguin, 1992), p. 24.

6. Paul A. Samuelson, "Interactions between the Multiplier Analysis and the Principle of Acceleration," in *The Collected Scientific Papers of Paul A. Samuelson*, ed. Joseph E. Stiglitz (Cambridge, MA: MIT Press, 1966), p. 107.

43. Decision Panic and the Anti-anxiety Trade: The Roman Dream Book Industry

1. Roger Beck, *A Brief History of Ancient Astrology* (Oxford: Blackwell, 2007), p. 38; Leda Jean Ciraolo and Jonathan Lee Seidel, eds., *Magic and Divination in the Ancient World: Proceedings of the Conference on Magic and Divination in the Ancient World Held at the University of California at Berkeley in February 1994* (Boston: Brill, 2002), pp. 47, 51.

2. T. Dempsey, *Delphic Oracle: Its Early History, Influence and Fall* (Whitefish, MT: Kessinger Publishing, 2003).

3. Querist, "Caesar and the Delphic Oracle," *Notes and Queries*, London, January 14, 1865, series 3, vols. 7–8 (Oxford: Oxford University Press, 1865), p. 182.

4. Says Kelly Bulkeley, the dream book written by the professional dream interpreter Artemidorus in the second century BCE "has been copied

and translated so often that it could be the single most influential dream book in the world." Kelly Bulkeley, *Dreaming in the World's Religions: A Comparative History* (New York: New York University Press, 2008), p. 162; Artemidorus, *The Interpretation of Dreams*, in *Religions of Rome: A Sourcebook*, ed. Mary Beard, John A. North, and S. R. F. Price (Cambridge: Cambridge University Press, 1998), pp. 192–94; Patricia Cox Miller, *Dreams in Late Antiquity: Studies in the Imagination of a Culture* (Princeton, NJ: Princeton University Press, 1997); Peter Brown, *The Body and Society: Men, Women, and Sexual Renunciation in Early Christianity* (New York: Columbia University Press, 1988).

44. Turning Garbage into Gold: The Romans Invent Concrete

1. Marion Elizabeth Blake and Esther Boise Van Deman, *Ancient Roman Construction in Italy from the Prehistoric Period to Augustus: A Chronological Study Based in Part upon the Material Accumulated by Esther Boise Van Deman* (Washington, DC: Carnegie Institution of Washington, 1947); Derek Williams, *The Reach of Rome: A History of the Roman Imperial Frontier, 1st–5th Centuries* (London: Constable, 1996), p. 32.

45. Choice Production: Meet Me at the Medieval Fair

1. Gerald P. Schatten, *Current Topics in Developmental Biology* (New York: Academic Press, 2006), pp. 177–202; Elena Tricarico and Francesca Gherardi, "Biogenic Amines Influence Aggressiveness in Crayfish but Not Their Force or Hierarchical Rank," *Animal Behaviour* (December 2007): 1715–24; Donald H. Edwards, Shih-Rung Yeh, Barbara E. Musolf, Brian L. Antonsen, and Franklin B. Krasne, "Metamodulation of the Crayfish Escape Circuit," *Brain, Behavior and Evolution* 60, no. 6 (2002): 360–69; Shih-Rung Yeh, Russell Fricke, and Donald Edwards, "The Effect of Social Experience on Serotonergic Modulation of the Escape Circuit of Crayfish," *Science* (January 19, 1996): 366–69; Valerius Geist, *Life Strategies*. Valerius Geist, Personal Communication, 1998–2008. Herbert M. Lefcourt, *Locus of Control*, pp. 8–18.

2. Carol Zaleski, *Otherworld Journeys: Accounts of Near-Death Experience in Medieval and Modern Times* (New York: Oxford University Press, 1989), p. 28.

3. James F. Weiner, *Mountain Papuans: Historical and Comparative Perspectives from New Guinea Fringe Highlands Societies* (Ann Arbor: University of Michigan Press, 1988), p. 80.

4. Thomas Jefferson wanted a "device" to represent the United States with the pillar of fire that led the Hebrews on one side and on the other:

"Hengest and Horsa, the Saxon Chiefs, from whom we claim the honor of being descended, and whose political principles and form of government we have assumed." Those are Jefferson's words. Henry Stephens Randal, *The Life of Thomas Jefferson* (Philadelphia: J. B. Lippincott, 1871), p. 192. Hengest and Horsa were brutal, legendary Saxon invaders in the time of Aurelius Ambrosius, king of the Brittaines. See Leonard Hutten, "Antiquities of Oxford," in *Elizabethan Oxford: Reprints of Rare Tracts* by Charles Plummer (Oxford: Oxford Historical Society, 1887) pp. 87–88; Anthony Brundage and Richard A. Cosgrove, *The Great Tradition: Constitutional History and National Identity in Britain and the United States, 1870–1960* (Palo Alto, CA: Stanford University Press, 2007), p. 33.

5. T. J. Shors, T. B. Seib, S. Levine, and R. F. Thompson, "Inescapable versus Escapable Shock Modulates Long Term Potentiation in the Rat Hippocampus," *Science* (April 14, 1989): 224–26.

6. Robert A. Scott, *The Gothic Enterprise: A Guide to Understanding the Medieval Cathedral* (Berkeley: University of California Press, 2006), pp. 76–90. Regina Lenore Shoolman and Charles Eli Slatkin, *The Story of Art: The Lives and Times of the Great Masters* (New York: Halcyon House, 1940), p. 245.

46. Security Is an Emotion, Credit Is a Feeling Called Belief: Venice and the Resurrection of Banking and Accounting

1. Colin Camerer, George Loewenstein, and Drazen Prelec, "Neuroeconomics: How Neuroscience Can Inform Economics," *Journal of Economic Literature* (March 2005): 9–64. For experiments on the role that Brodmann area ten and the thalamus play in trust, see p. 47. For the role of oxytocin in trust, see p. 57.

2. For the financial details of Florence's fur trade in the Renaissance, see Carole Collier Frick, *Dressing Renaissance Florence* (Baltimore: Johns Hopkins University Press, 2002), p. 48. By 1400 CE, a million pelts a year were coming to Florence from Poland and Russia, says Frick.

3. Some say double-entry bookkeeping was invented by the Arabs. Others believe it was created thousands of years ago in India "in the form of the Bahi-Khata system of bookkeeping." J. R. Edwards says the only thing scholars agree on is that double-entry bookkeeping was developed and popularized in Italy, where the first double-entry bookkeeping was done using, of all things, Roman numbers. Arabic numbers were new, and state authorities distrusted their use in finance. In other words, Arabic numbers had not yet entered the scaffold of habit and the symbol stack. J. R. Edwards, *A History of Financial Accounting* (London: Routledge, 1989), pp. 11, 46–48.

VIII THE TRANSCENDENCE ENGINE

47. Quantum Shifts in the Scope of Dreams: Marco Polo, Author

1. Coleridge's opium was in the form of laudanum—opium dissolved in alcohol. Laudanum was sold over the counter in the nineteenth century as a common cure for whatever ailed you. But the cure was addictive, as Coleridge found out the hard way. Walter Jackson Bate, *Coleridge* (New York: Macmillan, 1968).

2. Samuel Taylor Coleridge, *The Complete Works of Samuel Taylor Coleridge: With an Introductory Essay upon His Philosophical and Theological Opinions,* ed. William Greenough Thayer Shedd (New York: Harper & Brothers, 1853), pp. 212–14.

3. Dante Alighieri, *Dante: De Vulgari Eloquentia,* trans. Steven Botterill (Cambridge: Cambridge University Press, 2005), p. i.

4. Frederick A. P. Barnard, ed., *Johnson's (revised) Universal Cyclopaedia: A Scientific and Popular Treasury of Useful Knowledge* (Davenport: A. J. Johnson, 1886), p. 392.

48. Visioneering: Lead with Your Fantasies— Prince Henry the Navigator

1. Ernle Dusgate Selby Bradford, *A Wind from the North: The Life of Henry the Navigator* (New York: Harcourt, Brace, 1960); John Scott Keltie, *The Partition of Africa* (London: E. Stanford, 1895).

2. Charles Raymond Beazley, *Prince Henry the Navigator: The Hero of Portugal and of Modern Discovery, 1394–1460 A.D. with an Account of Geographical Progress throughout the Middle Ages as the Preparation for His Work* (New York: G. P. Putnam's Sons, 1894), pp. 1–138.

3. Gene W. Heck, *Charlemagne, Muhammad, and the Arab Roots of Capitalism* (Berlin: Walter de Gruyter, 2006); Jenny Balfour-Paul, *Indigo in the Arab World* (London: Routledge, 1997), p. 30; Michael Edwardes, *East-West Passage: The Travel of Ideas, Arts, and Inventions between Asia and the Western World* (New York: Taplinger, 1971), p. 87; Daniel J. Boorstin, *The Discoverers: A History of Man's Search to Know His World and Himself* (New York: Vintage Books, 1985); C. Beazley, *Prince Henry the Navigator,* p. 204.

4. Sanjay Subrahmanyam calls Shihab al-Din Ahmad ibn Majid "the most celebrated Arab navigator and theorist of navigation of the fifteenth century." However, he also believes that the idea that Majid guided da Gama is a myth that grew up among historians in the twentieth century. In the

process of deconstructing that myth, Subrahmanyam gives an amazing trail of documentary evidence. See Sanjay Subrahmanyam, *The Career and Legend of Vasco Da Gama* (Cambridge: Cambridge University Press, 1998), pp. 122–28. For the traditional tale of Majid and da Gama, see Jesuits, Ateneo de Manila University, *Philippine Studies* (Philippines: Ateneo de Manila University Press, 1989), 37:135.

49. Change the World: Promote— Christopher Columbus, Mass-Market Pamphleteer

1. Konrad Lorenz, *King Solomon's Ring: New Light on Animal Ways* (London: Routledge, 2002); Konrad Lorenz, *On Aggression* (New York: Harcourt Brace Jovanovich, 1974); Konrad Lorenz, *Behind the Mirror: A Search for a Natural History of Human Knowledge* (New York: Harcourt Brace Jovanovich, 1977); Rom Harre, *Great Scientific Experiments: Twenty Experiments That Changed Our View of the World* (New York: Courier Dover Publications, 2002), pp. 65–71.

2. Lorenz, *King Solomon's Ring*, p. xvi.

3. Lorenz, *Behind the Mirror*, pp. 75, 78.

4. Bruce D. J. Batt, *Ecology and Management of Breeding Waterfowl* (Minneapolis: University of Minnesota Press, 1992), p. 229.

5. Paul McGreevy and R. A. Boakes, *Carrots and Sticks: Principles of Animal Training* (Cambridge: Cambridge University Press, 2007), p. 16.

6. Carla Rahn Phillips, *The Worlds of Christopher Columbus* (Cambridge: Cambridge University Press, 1993), p. 86.

7. Leslie Bethell, *The Cambridge History of Latin America* (Cambridge: Cambridge University Press, 1984), p. 345.

8. Daniel Boorstin gets the credit for making the point that the Vikings were not explorers despite the fact that they did, indeed, explore. Why? They didn't publicize. Daniel J. Boorstin, *The Discoverers: A History of Man's Search to Know His World and Himself* (New York: Vintage Books, 1985). See also F. Donald Logan, *The Vikings in History* (London: Routledge, 1992), p. 81.

9. Inga Clendinnen, *Ambivalent Conquests: Maya and Spaniard in Yucatan, 1517–1570* (Cambridge: Cambridge University Press, 2003), pp. 46, 56, 81; Matthew Bunson and Margaret Bunson, *OSV's Encyclopedia of Catholic History* (Huntington, IN: Our Sunday Visitor Publishing, 2004), p. 207; Manning Nash and Robert Wauchope, *Social Anthropology* (Austin: University of Texas Press, 1967), p. 385; Matthew Restall, *Maya Conquistador* (Boston: Beacon Press, 1999), p. 230; Philip Young, *History of Mexico, Her Civil Wars, and Colonial and Revolutionary Annals: From the Period of*

the Spanish Conquest, 1520, to the Present Time, 1847, Including an Account of the War with the United States, Its Causes and Military Achievements (Cincinnati: J. A. & U. P. James, 1850). The accounts in Young's book are suspect. They appear to be heavily slanted against the Catholic Spanish, in part because they were written as the United States was trying to justify a hard-to-swallow war against Mexico.

50. Messianic Accidents: The Spread of the Chili Pepper

1. E. N. Anderson, *The Food of China* (New Haven, CT: Yale University Press, 1988).

2. Graeme Barker, *Prehistoric Farming in Europe* (Farnham Common, Buckinghamshire, England: Cambridge Archive Editions, 1985), p. 167.

3. "Irish Potato Famine," *Encyclopædia Britannica*, http://www .britannica.com/EBchecked/topic/294137/Irish-Potato-Famine (accessed February 3, 2009); Wikipedia, "Irish Potato Famine—Death Toll," http://en.wikipedia .org/wiki/Irish_Potato_Famine#Death_toll (accessed February 3, 2009).

4. Biodiversity Explorer, "Solanacaea (Potato, Tomato, Tobacco Family): Genera Native or Naturalized in Southern Africa," *Biodiversity Explorer, the Web of Life in Southern Africa*, http://www.biodiversity explorer.org/plants/solanaceae/ (accessed February 3, 2009).

IX EMOPOWER: THE LIFT OF GENEROUS SELFISHNESS

51. He Who Feels Will Lead: The Power of Self-Revelation—Martin Luther

1. Rene Seindal, "Pontifex Maximus: The High Priests of Ancient Roman Religion," *Roman Religion and Mythology*, http://sights.seindal.dk/ sight/1244_Pontifex_maximus.html (accessed February 3, 2009).

2. Louis Duchesne and M. L. McClure, *Christian Worship: Its Origin and Evolution: A Study of the Latin Liturgy up to the Time of Charlemagne* (London: Society for Promoting Christian Knowledge, 1903), p. 24.

3. Hannah Chaplin Conant, *The English Bible: History of the Translation of the Holy Scriptures into the English Tongue. With Specimens of the Old English Versions* (New York: Sheldon, Blakeman, 1856), p. 45.

4. John Skoyles, London School of Economics Centre research associate in residence, neuroscience, personal communication, 1997–2003.

5. Erik Homburger Erikson, *Young Man Luther: A Study in Psycho-analysis and History* (New York: Norton, 1993), pp. 67–68.

6. Keith Thomas, *Man and the Natural World: A History of the Modern Sensibility* (New York: Pantheon Books, 1983).

7. Christopher Boyd Brown, *Singing the Gospel: Lutheran Hymns and the Success of the Reformation* (Cambridge, MA: Harvard University Press, 2005).

8. Luther relied on literacy in his pamphlet writing but eventually grew leery of putting the Bible in the hands of the people. Instead, he recommended teaching religion to the masses using his catechism. However, the genie was out of the bottle. Contemporaries of Luther like Britain's Reformation leader Thomas Cranmer wanted every man and woman to be able to read the Holy Book. Wrote Cranmer in his introduction to *The Great Bible of 1540*, "The Holy Ghost hath so ordered and attempered the scriptures that in them as well publicans, fishers, and shepherds may find their edification as great doctors their erudition. . . . The apostles and prophets wrote their books . . . [for] *every reader.*" John S. Pendergast, *Religion, Allegory, and Literacy in Early Modern England, 1560–1640: The Control of the Word* (Farnham, Surrey, England: Ashgate, 2006), pp. 45–46.

52. The Role of Sex and Violence: Benvenuto Cellini and Will Shakespeare

1. David P. Barash, *The Whisperings Within: Evolution and the Origin of Human Nature* (New York: Penguin, 1979).

2. San Diego Zoo, "Mammals: Ocelot," *Animal Bytes*, Zoological Society of San Diego, http://www.sandiegozoo.org/animalbytes/t-ocelot.html (accessed February 16, 2009).

3. Benvenuto Cellini, *The Autobiography of Benvenuto Cellini*, trans. John Addington Symonds (New York: P. F. Collier & Son, 1910).

4. Walter Kendrick, *The Secret Museum: Pornography in Modern Culture* (Berkeley: University of California Press, 1997).

5. Graham Holderness, *Shakespeare Recycled: The Making of Historical Drama* (Lanham, MD: Rowman & Littlefield, 1992); Richard Findlater, *Banned! A Review of Theatrical Censorship in Britain* (London: MacGibbon & Kee, 1967).

6. "Current Rate: Rate of Population Change (% over Previous 10 Years)," *A Vision of Britain through Time*, http://www.visionofbritain.org.uk/data_rate_page.jsp?u_id=10057218&c_id=10001043&data_theme=T_POP&id=1 (accessed March 6, 2009).

7. Steve Rappaport, *Worlds within Worlds: Structures of Life in Six-*

teenth-Century London (Cambridge: Cambridge University Press, 2002), p. 69; Caroline M. Barron, "London 1300–1540," in *The Cambridge Urban History of Britain*, ed. Peter Clark, D. M. Palliser, and Martin Daunton (Cambridge: Cambridge University Press, 2000), pp. 399–400; Barrie Dobson, "General Survey 1300–1540," in ibid., p. 276; Jennifer Kermode, "The Greater Towns 1300–1540," in ibid., p. 458.

8. Robert Green, "Greenes, Groats-Worth of Witte, Bought with a Million of Repentance, 1592," in *Cartae Shakespeareanae: Shakespeare Documents; A Chronological Catalogue of Extant Evidence Relating to the Life and Works of William Shakespeare*, ed. Daniel Henry Lambert (London: G. Bell and Sons, 1904), p. 16.

9. Stephen Greenblatt, *Will in the World: How Shakespeare Became Shakespeare* (New York: Norton, 2004), pp. 185–86.

10. Daniel J. Levitin, *This Is Your Brain on Music: The Science of a Human Obsession* (New York: Dutton, 2006), pp. 192–93, 202–203. Malcolm Gladwell also builds many of his key arguments in his book *Outliers: The Story of Success* on this pivotal bit of research. See Malcolm Gladwell, *Outliers: The Story of Success* (New York: Hachette Book Group USA, 2008).

11. Dean Keith Simonton, *Greatness: Who Makes History and Why* (New York: Guilford Press, 1994).

12. William Replingham, "Agreement Protecting Shakespeare against Loss of Tithe Income by Reason of Enclosures at Welcombe," in *Shakespeare of Stratford: A Handbook for Students*, ed. Tucker Brooke (Manchester, NH: Ayer, 1970), pp. 75–76.

13. "William Shakespeare," *Encyclopædia Britannica*, http://www.britannica.com/EBchecked/topic/537853/William-Shakespeare (accessed February 2, 2009).

14. Frances A. Shirley, *Swearing and Perjury in Shakespeare's Plays* (London: Routledge, 2005), p. 29.

15. Gordon Williams, *Shakespeare, Sex and the Print Revolution* (London: Continuum International Publishing Group, 1996).

16. F. L. Lucas, *Seneca and Elizabethan Tragedy* (Farnham Common, Buckinghamshire, England: Cambridge Archive Editions, originally published 1922); Peter Mercer, *Hamlet and the Acting of Revenge* (Iowa City: University of Iowa Press, 1987), p. 252.

17. Charles Derber, *The Wilding of America: Money, Mayhem, and the New American Dream* (New York: Macmillan, 2006).

18. National Center for Juvenile Justice, *Juvenile Offenders and Victims: 2006 National Report* (Pittsburgh: National Center for Juvenile Justice, 2006), p. 20.

19. James Robert Flynn, *What Is Intelligence? Beyond the Flynn Effect* (New York: Cambridge University Press, 2007).

20. Marguerite Holloway, "Flynn's Effect," *Scientific American*, January 1999.

21. Steven Johnson, *Everything Bad Is Good for You: How Today's Popular Culture Is Actually Making Us Smarter* (New York: Penguin, 2006).

22. Flynn, *What Is Intelligence?* p. 44.

23. Napoleon Hill, *Think and Grow Rich* (1938; Forgotten Books, 1962). Complete text at http://books.google.com/books?id=c86H36mgiM4C (accessed February 2, 2009).

24. Kinney, *Shakespeare by Stages*, p. 130.

25. For an example, see William Shakespeare, *Manga Shakespeare: The Tempest*, ed. Richard Appignanesi and illust. Paul Duffield (New York: Harry N. Abrams, 2008).

26. Katharina M. Wilson, *An Encyclopedia of Continental Women Writers* (London: Taylor & Francis, 1991), 1:241; Florimond-Claude Mercy-Argenteau, *The Guardian of Marie Antoinette: Letters from the Comte de Mercy-Argenteau, Austrian Ambassador to the Court of Versailles, to Marie Thérèse, Empress of Austria, 1770–1780*, ed. Lillian C. Smythe (London: Hutchinson, 1902), pp. 577–608.

53. New Deeds Lead to New Dreams . . . And to Virtual Realities: Robinson Crusoe

1. William James Roosen, *Daniel Defoe and Diplomacy* (Selinsgrove, PA: Susquehanna University Press, 1986), pp. 17–18. Edd [*sic*] Applegate, *Literary Journalism: A Biographical Dictionary of Writers and Editors* (Westport, CT: Greenwood, 1996), pp. 60–61.

2. IMDB, "Media from Robinson Crusoe (1954)," Internet Movie Database, http://www.imdb.com/find?s=all&q=robinson+crusoe&x=0&y=0 (accessed February 4, 2009); IMDB, "Media from Swiss Family Robinson (1960)," Internet Movie Database, http://www.imdb.com/find?s=all&q =swiss+family+robinson&x=0&y=0 (accessed February 4, 2009).

54. Cash Is Massed Attention, Coin Is Emotional Need: The Tulip Craze

1. Mark Frankel, "When the Tulip Bubble Burst," *BusinessWeek*, April 24, 2000.

2. Kenneth Katzner, *The Languages of the World* (London: Routledge, 2002), p. 153.

3. Robert B. Cialdini, *Influence: Science and Practice* (Boston: Allyn and Bacon, 2001), p. 204.

4. J. F. W. Lane, "Some Statistics of Small-Pox and Vaccination," *American Journal of the Medical Sciences*, ed. Isaac Hays, vol. 12 (1846): 122–23. See also William Hardy McNeill, *Plagues and Peoples* (New York: Anchor, 1989), p. 260.

5. Walter William Skeat, *A Concise Etymological Dictionary of the English Language* (New York: Harper, 1893), p. 610.

6. Katzner, *The Languages of the World*, p. 153.

7. Stanford J. Shaw, *History of the Ottoman Empire and Modern Turkey: Empire of the Gazis: The Rise and Decline of the Ottoman Empire, 1280–1808* (Cambridge: Cambridge University Press, 1976), pp. 234–35.

55. The Birth of Tea and the Rise of the Cup and Saucer: Mindmaps of the Day

1. According to author Isaac Disraeli, British prime minister Benjamin Disraeli's father, tea didn't come into general use until after 1687. Until then, the few who knew about it considered it "stinking hay water." As late as 1739, the Russian ambassador at the court of the Mongol Khan was offered tea as a present for his czar. He turned down the gift. Isaac Disraeli and Rufus Wilmot Griswold, *Curiosities of Literature: And, The Literary Character Illustrated* (New York: Leavitt and Allen, 1857), p. 205.

57. The Blessings (and the Curses) of Obsession: Inventing the Plantation

1. A. L. Rowse, *The Expansion of Elizabethan England* (London: Macmillan, 1955).

2. Angus Konstam and Tony Bryan, *Tudor Warships: Henry VIII's Navy* (Oxford: Osprey, 2008), p. 16.

3. Vivian Louis Forbes, *The Maritime Boundaries of the Indian Ocean Region* (Singapore: NUS Press, 1995), p. 43.

4. Angus Konstam and Roger Michael Kean, *Pirates—Predators of the Seas: An Illustrated History* (New York: Skyhorse, 2007), p. 18; Henry B. Culver and Gordon Grant, *The Book of Old Ships: From Egyptian Galleys to Clipper Ships* (Chelmsford, MA: Courier, 1992).

5. Martin L. Van Creveld, *Technology and War: From 2000 B.C. to the Present* (New York: Simon & Schuster, 1991), p. 133.

6. Maurice Daumas and Eileen B. Hennessy, *A History of Technology & Invention: Progress through the Ages* (New York: Crown, 1970), p. 370; Jeff

Kinard and Spencer C. Tucker, *Artillery: An Illustrated History of Its Impact* (Santa Barbara: ABC-CLIO, 2007).

7. John Ramsay McCulloch and Daniel Haskel, *M'Culloch's Universal Gazetteer: A Dictionary, Geographical, Statistical, and Historical, of the Various Countries, Places, and Principal Natural Objects in the World* (New York: Harper & Bros., 1845), p. 848.

8. "Fears . . . had already been excited in Henry VIII's day that the continued destruction of forests, in order to supply the iron-works with fuel, would lead to a timber famine." Edwin A. Pratt, *A History of Inland Transport and Communication in England* (New York: Dutton, 1912), p. 189. The fears in Henry's day were well founded. By the time Elizabeth was on the throne, England had broken out in a full-scale "timber crisis," one so severe that from 1558 to 1649 dozens of commissions were called to help understand and solve it. One big solution came from a grubby substance that could substitute for wood as a fuel—coal. Michael Williams, *Deforesting the Earth: From Prehistory to Global Crisis, an Abridgment* (Chicago: University of Chicago Press, 2006), p. 166; J. U. Nef, *The Rise of the British Coal Industry*, vol. 1 (London: Routledge, 1966) pp. 163–64.

9. Sylvie Nail, *Forest Policies and Social Change in England* (New York: Springer, 2008), p. 23.

10. Roger Sands, *Forestry in a Global Context* (Wallingford, England: CABI, 2005), p. 32; Diana Muir, *Reflections in Bullough's Pond: Economy and Ecosystem in New England* (Hanover, NH: University Press of New England, 2002), pp. 59–61.

11. For a revealing exaggeration of the British aristocracy's breeding fetish, see P. G. Wodehouse, *Pigs Have Wings* (London: Penguin, 2000).

12. Philip Curtin gives the range of eight to fifteen million slaves shipped from Africa to the Americas. See Philip D. Curtin, *The Atlantic Slave Trade: A Census* (Madison: University of Wisconsin Press, 1972), p. 87. Herbert Klein gives a total figure of eleven million slaves shipped from Africa across the Atlantic, of whom only nine and a half million lived to reach their destination. Herbert S. Klein, *The Atlantic Slave Trade* (Cambridge: Cambridge University Press, 1999), p. xx. See also "When Europeans Were Slaves: Research Suggests White Slavery Was Much More Common Than Previously Believed," *Ohio State University News*, March 8, 2004, http://research news.osu.edu/archive/whtslav.htm (accessed November 25, 2005); "The Scourge of Slavery," *Christian Action Magazine* 4, http://www.christian action.org.za/articles_ca/2004-4-TheScourgeofSlavery.htm (accessed November 25, 2005).

13. Zdzisław E. Sikorski, *Chemical and Functional Properties of Food Components* (Boca Raton, FL: CRC Press, 2007), p. 429; George H. Fried

and George J. Hademenos, *Schaum's Outline of Theory and Problems of Biology* (New York: McGraw-Hill, 1998), p. 210.

14. Ted Schmidt, "A Powerful History Lesson," *Catholic New Times*, September 25, 2005; Brycchan Carey, personal communication, March 1, 2008; Brycchan Carey, "John Wesley," July 12, 2008, http://www.brycchan carey.com/abolition/wesley.htm (accessed March 7, 2009).

15. Catherine Ella Blanshard Asher and Cynthia Talbot, *India before Europe* (Cambridge: Cambridge University Press, 2006), p. 130.

16. John S. Bowman, ed., *Columbia Chronologies of Asian History and Culture* (New York: Columbia University Press, 2000), p. 410.

17. Mahatma Gandhi did a brilliant job of planting the protest industry in the East—in India. But peaceful protest remained, like parliamentary democracy, primarily a Western implant.

58. Transubstantiation: Making Spirit Flesh— The Tale of the Piano

1. George Frederick Young, *The Medici* (New York: E. P. Dutton, 1911), pp. 459–60.

2. Stewart Pollens, *The Early Pianoforte* (Farnham Common, Buckinghamshire, England: Cambridge Archive Editions, 1995), pp. 42–43, 49; David Rowland, *The Cambridge Companion to the Piano* (Cambridge: Cambridge University Press, 1998), p. 7; James Parakilas and E. Douglas Bomberger, *Piano Roles: Three Hundred Years of Life with the Piano* (New Haven, CT: Yale University Press, 1999), pp. 26–34.

3. Georg Wilhelm Friedrich Hegel, *The Philosophy of History*, trans. John Sibree (New York: Collier, 1902).

4. For the evolution of chords, see William Henry Hadow, C. Hubert Parry, and Edward J. Dent, *The Oxford History of Music, Volume 3: The Music of the Seventeenth Century* (Oxford: Clarendon Press, 1902); Charles Hubert Hastings Parry, *The Evolution of the Art of Music* (New York: D. Appleton, 1920); Julius Klauser, *The Nature of Music: Original Harmony in One Voice* (Boston: Riverside Press, 1909); George Grove and Stanley Sadie, *The New Grove Dictionary of Music and Musicians* (New York: Macmillan, 1980).

5. Leonard Feather and Ira Gitler, *The Biographical Encyclopedia of Jazz* (New York: Oxford University Press, 1999).

59. Harnessing the Mass IQ: Offering an Ego-Stake—
Linnaeus and His Viral Meme

1. Saying that crop yields quadrupled because of chemical fertilizers is, in some ways, an enormous understatement. For a rough idea of the real increase, ponder these figures. In the 1860s, the British yield of wheat per acre was 4 bushels. By the early twentieth century, corn yield per acre in the United States was 26 bushels per acre. And in just the thirty years from 1964 to 1994, corn yields in America went from 62 bushels per acre to 139 bushels. Extrapolating from these figures, the land that produced a mere one bushel in the 1860s would have produced 9.5 bushels in 1994, a whopping increase. And the following sources attribute this productivity explosion to two major factors—improved tools and chemical fertilizers. See Waldo Rudolph Wedel, *Central Plains Prehistory: Holocene Environments and Culture Change in the Republican River Basin* (Lincoln: University of Nebraska Press, 1986), p. 120; Joel Mokyr, *The British Industrial Revolution: An Economic Perspective* (Boulder, CO: Westview Press, 1999), p. 215; Noel D. Uri, *Agriculture and the Environment* (Hauppauge, NY: Nova, 1999), p. 11.

60. Creative Capitalism vs. Criminal Capitalism:
The Rise of Stocks and Bonds

1. Jerry W. Markham, *A Financial History of Modern U.S. Corporate Scandals: From Enron to Reform* (Armonk, NY: M. E. Sharpe, 2006), p. 92.

2. Robert Lenzner, "Bernie Madoff's $50 Billion Ponzi Scheme," *Forbes*, December 12, 2008.

61. Self-Revelation and Secular Salvation:
Rousseau Goes to the Bone

1. Eugene L. Stelzig, *The Romantic Subject in Autobiography: Rousseau and Goethe* (Charlottesville: University of Virginia Press, 2000), p. 7; Paul A. Cantor, *Creature and Creator: Myth-Making and English Romanticism* (Farnham Common, Buckinghamshire, England: Cambridge Archive Editions, 1985), p. 11.

2. Jean-Jacques Rousseau, *The Confessions of Jean-Jacques Rousseau* (Edinburgh, Scotland: Oliver and Boyd, 1904), full text available at http://books.google.com/books?id=w3HlcgckBNAC (accessed February 6, 2009).

3. Shoshana Zuboff and James Maxmin, *The Support Economy: Why Corporations Are Failing Individuals and the Next Episode of Capitalism* (New York: Viking, 2002), p. 165–66.

62. Words Remake Reality: Adam Smith Sparks Economics

1. Robert Bittlestone, James Diggle, and John Underhill, *Odysseus Unbound: The Search for Homer's Ithaca* (Cambridge: Cambridge University Press, 2005), p. 482.

2. Adam Smith, *The Wealth of Nations: Books I–III*, ed. Andrew S. Skinner (New York: Penguin, 1999).

3. For the full text of the Declaration of Independence, see Alexander Hamilton, John Jay, and James Madison, *The Federalist Papers* (New York: Cosimo, 2006), p. 619.

4. Reuters, "Big Banks Owe Bosses $40 Billion in Bonuses, Deferred Comp: Report," *Financial Week*, October 31, 2008. See also AFL-CIO Corporate Pay Watch, http://www.aflcio.org/corporatewatch/paywatch (accessed May 29, 2009).

5. This quote is from United Nations Development Programme's *Arab Human Development Report 2002*, http://hdr.undp.org/en/reports/regional reports/arabstates/name,3140,en.html; see also Margareta Drzeniek Hanouz and Tarik Yousef, "Assessing Competitiveness in the Arab World: Strategies for Sustaining the Growth Momentum," *Arab World Competitiveness Report 2007*, World Economic Forum, http://www.weforum.org/pdf/Global _Competitiveness_Reports/Reports/chapters/1_1.pdf (accessed February 6, 2009).

X AN EXTRA TWENTY YEARS OF LIFE?

63. The Soap Revolution, Mass Marketing, and the Rise of Advertising: Messianic Capitalism

1. Fernand Braudel, *The Structures of Everyday Life: Civilization & Capitalism, 15th–18th Century, Vol. 1*, trans. Sian Reynolds (New York: Perennial Library, Harper & Row, 1981); Victoria Sherrow, *For Appearance' Sake: The Historical Encyclopedia of Good Looks, Beauty, and Grooming* (Westport, CT: Greenwood, 2001), p. 58.

2. Aaron John Ihde, *The Development of Modern Chemistry* (New York: Courier Dover, 1984), pp. 168–70; Albert B. Costa, *Michel Eugène Chevreul: Pioneer of Organic Chemistry* (Madison: State Historical Society of Wisconsin for the Department of History, University of Wisconsin, 1962); Campbell Morfit, *A Treatise on Chemistry Applied to the Manufacture of Soap and Candles: Being a thorough Exposition, in All Their Minutiae, of*

the Principles and Practice of the Trade, Based upon the Most Recent Discoveries in Science and Art (Philadelphia: Parry and McMillan, 1856), p. 20; Soap and Detergent Association, "Soaps and Detergents: History," http://www.sdahq.org/cleaning/history/ (accessed February 6, 2009).

3. "The Water-Butt," *Chambers's Edinburgh Journal*, January–June 1853, pp. 132–35; Joseph A. Amato and Jeffrey Burton Russell, *Dust: A History of the Small and the Invisible* (Berkeley: University of California Press, 2001), pp. 77, 78, 87.

4. Sherrow, *For Appearance' Sake*, p. 125.

5. Said the Duke of Wellington, "They wanted me to be president of another society for the cure of diseases of the skin, but I proposed the use of soap and water, and refused." Francis Egerton Ellesmere and Alice Byng Strafford, *Personal Reminiscences of the Duke of Wellington* (London: J. Murray, 1904), p. 119. See also Charles Wilson, *The History of Unilever: A Study in Economic Growth and Social Change* (Westport, CT: Praeger, 1968); Frank Atkinson, *The Industrial Archaeology of North-East England (The Counties of Northumberland and Durham and the Cleveland District of Yorkshire)* (Devon, England: David & Charles, 1974), p. 170; Arthur Wellesley Wellington, *Supplementary Despatches and Memoranda of Field Marshal Arthur, Duke of Wellington, K. G.* (London: J. Murray, 1860), p. 143; Dorothy Constance Bayliff Peel, *The Stream of Time: Social and Domestic Life in England, 1805–1861* (New York: Scribner, 1932), p. 67.

6. "Where Britons Are Holding Their Own: The Story of Pears' Soap," *Review of Reviews*, July–December 1901, pp. 437–46.

7. Richard Ayton, *Essays and Sketches of Character* (London: Taylor and Hessey, 1825), p. 27. Sales of soap were aided in the first half of the nineteenth century by variations of a new catchphrase, "the great moral influence of soap and water." See R. R. Madden, "Letter from R. R. Madden to Count O'Day," in Richard Robert Madden, *The Literary Life and Correspondence of the Countess of Blessington* (New York: Harper & Bros., 1855), pp. 462–63.

8. Theron Pond was one of those who worked through an army of peddlers, drummers who "sold his Pond's Extract skin cream in the 1840s. In Cincinnati, Ohio . . . then hired people to sell them. He shipped products as far as California via the Pony Express." Sherrow, *For Appearance' Sake*, p. 40.

9. Lawrence Lewis, John Houston Merrill, Adelbert Hamilton, William Mark McKinney, John Crawford Thomson, and James Manford Kerr, *American and English Corporation Cases: A Collection of All Corporation Cases, Both Private and Municipal (Excepting Railway Cases), Decided in the Courts of Last Resort in the United States, England, and Canada [1883–1894]* (Northport, NY: E. Thompson, 1888), p. 534.

10. Ann Anderson, *Snake Oil, Hustlers and Hambones: The American Medicine Show* (Jefferson, NC: McFarland, 2004), pp. 134–35.

11. Ibid.

12. Sidney A. Sherman, "Advertising in the United States," *Publications of the American Statistical Association* 7, no. 52 (December 1900): 1–44; Alecia Swasy, *Soap Opera: The Inside Story of Procter & Gamble* (New York: Simon & Schuster, 1994), pp. 107–108; Sherrow, *For Appearance' Sake*, pp. 2–100.

13. By the 1990s, soap-making giant Procter and Gamble's advertising budget was "larger than those of McDonald's, Kellogg, Anheuser Busch, and Coca-Cola combined." Swasy, *Soap Opera*, p. 107.

14. Thomas Wright, *The Great Unwashed: By the Journeyman Engineer* (London: Tinsley Brothers, 1868), pp. vii–viii.

15. Braudel, *The Structures of Everyday Life*.

16. P. E. Razzell, "An Interpretation of the Modern Rise of Population in Europe—A Critique," *Population Studies* 23, no. 1 (March 1974): 5–17; Robert Ornstein and David Sobel, *The Healing Brain* (New York: Simon & Schuster, 1987), pp. 21, 24; Leonard A. Sagan, "Family Ties: The Real Reason People Are Living Longer," *Sciences*, March/April 1988, p. 22.

17. B. Harder, "Scrubbing Down: Free Soap, Hygiene Tips Cut Kids' Illnesses," *Science News*, October 9, 2007, p. 230.

64. A Bourgeois Luxury: Rebellion— Karl Marx and His Manifesto

1. Adam Smith, *The Wealth of Nations: Books I–III*, ed. Andrew S. Skinner (New York: Penguin, 1999).

2. Karl Marx and Friedrich Engels, *Das Kapital: A Critique of Political Economy*, ed. Serge L. Levitsky (Lake Bluff, IL: Regnery Gateway, 1996).

3. Marx is very muddy about what labor is and is not. He states that labor is work that can be measured in hours, days, and weeks. And, he says, "For simplicity's sake, we shall henceforth account every kind of labour to be unskilled, simple labour." Karl Marx and Friedrich Engels, *Das Kapital: Kritik der politischen Ökonomie: Erster Band, Hamburg 1883*, ed. Rolf Hecker (Berlin: Akademie Verlag, 1989), p. 37. This implies that in Marx's view, brainwork doesn't count. But a lot depends on which English translation you use. In the English edition of *Das Kapital* edited by Ernest Mandel, Marx refers to "intellectual labor" four times. But he doesn't appear to define it as real labor. And he doesn't appear to regard it as something of "value." Mandel sums up Marx's dismissal of one aspect of imagination, invention, and insight with these words: "In and of itself, 'science' produces neither

value nor income." Karl Marx, *Capital: A Critique of Political Economy*, ed. Ernest Mandel, trans. David Ferbach (New York: Penguin Classics, 1993), p. 77; Marx and Engels, *Das Kapital: Kritik der politischen Ökonomie: Erster Band, Hamburg 1883*, pp. 21, 37, 39, 337. A review of three editions of *Das Kapital* produced no statements whatsoever on the value of the "labor" of philosophers, scientists, mathematicians, artists, and others of the thinking class. The closest to a clear statement is this opaque sentence from the Hecker edition of *Das Kapital*: "Science, generally speaking, costs the capitalist nothing, a fact that by no means hinders him from exploiting it. The science of others is as much annexed by capital as the labour of others. Capitalistic appropriation and personal appropriation, whether of science or material wealth, are, however, totally different things" (p. 337).

4. Marx and Engels, *Das Kapital: Kritik der politischen Ökonomie: Erster Band, Hamburg 1883*, p. 37.

5. In 1850, two years after Marx published *The Communist Manifesto*, the average Irish dockworker in London made 16s, 6d per week. That's 16 shillings, 6 pence. Or, in 2007 dollars, $98.31 a week. In 2009, the average personal assistant in London, another worker at the low end of the scale, made £28,183 a year. That's $38,750.84. In other words, the average London personal assistant in 2007 earned as much as seven and a half dockworkers had taken home in 1850. Or, to put it differently, by 2007, one low-end London worker earned as much as an entire tenement building of low-end London workers in 1850. Source for the average Irish dockworker: Lynn Hollen Lees, *Exiles of Erin: Irish Migrants in Victorian London* (Manchester, England: Manchester University Press, 1979), p. 100. Source for the conversion of 1848 shillings and pence to 1848 dollars: "The Coinage in England and the United States," *Hunt's Merchants' Magazine and Commercial Review, Journal of Banking, Currency, and Finance* 29, July–December 1853, p. 98. Source of current wages in London, including the low end of the totem pole, personal assistants: PayScale, "Salary Survey Report for City: London, PayScale," February 4, 2009, http://www .payscale.com/research/ UK/City=London/Salary (accessed February 7, 2009).

6. The phrase "greed is good" was taken from a speech given by Ivan Boesky to a class of graduating UCLA School of Business Administration students. "Greed is all right, by the way," Boesky said. "I think greed is healthy. You can be greedy and still feel good about yourself." In the film, this turned into, "Greed, for lack of a better word, is good," a phrase that wormed its way into *Bartlett's Familiar Quotations* in its street simplification: "greed is good." However, Boesky went to jail for financial crimes. The capitalist system stopped the crook, but not the catchphrase. Ralph Keyes, *The Quote Verifier: Who Said What, Where, and When* (New York: Macmillan, 2006), pp. 85, 152.

7. AFL-CIO, "Executive PayWatch 2008," *Corporate Watch*, http://www.aflcio.org/corporatewatch/paywatch/ (accessed February 6, 2009).

8. AFL-CIO, "Countrywide Financial Case Study," http://www.aflcio.org/corporatewatch/paywatch/retirementsecurity/case_countrywide.cfm (accessed February 7, 2009).

9. AFL-CIO, "Bear Stearns Case Study," http://www.aflcio.org/corporatewatch/paywatch/retirementsecurity/case_bearstearns.cfm (accessed February 7, 2009).

10. AFL-CIO, "Washington Mutual Case Study," http://www.aflcio.org/corporatewatch/paywatch/retirementsecurity/case_washmutual.cfm (accessed February 7, 2009).

11. AFL-CIO, "Morgan Stanley Case Study," http://www.aflcio.org/corporatewatch/paywatch/retirementsecurity/case_morganstanley.cfm (accessed February 7, 2009).

65. What Seduction Was Marx Selling?

1. Robert William Davies, Mark Harrison, and S. G. Wheatcroft, *The Economic Transformation of the Soviet Union, 1913–1945* (Cambridge: Cambridge University Press, 1994), pp. 78–79.

2. Bruce Gilley, *Model Rebels: The Rise and Fall of China's Richest Village* (Berkeley: University of California Press, 2001), p. 5.

3. Rory Carroll and Sibylla Brodzinsky, "Colombia Accuses Chávez of Funding Marxist Rebels," *Guardian*, March 4, 2008; Mexico's rebel force calls itself "Ejército Popular Revolucionario." See Latin American Data Base, "Ejército Popular Revolucionario Damages Pemex Pipelines Again, Causing Disruptions to Economy for Second Time in Two Months," http://www.thefreelibrary.com/EJERCITO+POPULAR+REVOLUCIONARIO+DAMAGES+PEMEX+PIPELINES+AGAIN,...-a0168661929 (accessed February 8, 2009); Associated Press, "Philippine Communist Rebels Pledge to Intensify Attacks amid Corruption Scandal, Protests," *International Herald Tribune*, February 13, 2008; Sinhalaya News Editor, "Sri Lanka Marxist Rebels Form New Party," Sinhalaya News Agency, February 8, 2009, http://www.sinhalaya.com/news/english/wmview.php?ArtID=15270 (accessed February 8, 2009).

4. Indo-Asian News Service (IANS), "After Mao, Marx and Lenin to Get Marching Orders in Nepal," *China National News*, October 19, 2008.

5. Helena Smith, "New Marxist President Seeks to Quell Cypriots' Economic Fears," *Guardian*, February 26, 2008; Reuters, "Cyprus: Akel Party Leader Steps Down," *New York Times*, January 21, 2009.

6. Stalin Society, "Stalin Society—Public Meeting—South West—Event

Notice," November 23, 2008, http://bristol.indymedia.org/article/689279 (accessed February 8, 2009).

66. The Heart Has Reasons Reason Never Knows: Saturated Intuition and the Culture Lift of P. T. Barnum

1. Sources for this portrait of Barnum include Phineas Taylor Barnum, *Life of P. T. Barnum* (London: Sampson Low, 1855); Phineas Taylor Barnum, *Struggles and Triumphs: Or, Forty Years' Recollections of P. T. Barnum* (Hartford, CT: J. B. Burr, 1869); Phineas Taylor Barnum, *The Humbugs of the World: An Account of Humbugs, Delusions, Impositions, Quackeries, Deceits and Deceivers Generally, in All Ages* (New York: Carleton, 1866); Phineas Taylor Barnum, *The Art of Money Getting* (LaVergne, TN: Ingram, 1999); A. H. Saxon, *P. T. Barnum: The Legend and the Man* (New York: Columbia University Press, 1995).

2. James A. Boon, "Showbiz as a Cross-Cultural System: Circus and Song, Garland and Geertz, Rushdie, Mordden—and More," *Cultural Anthropology* 15, no. 3, pp. 424–56.

3. Eric Foner and John Arthur Garraty, Society of American Historians, *The Reader's Companion to American History* (Boston: Houghton Mifflin Harcourt, 1991).

4. Barnum, *Struggles and Triumphs*, pp. 30–31.

5. Ibid., p. 474; Samuel Irving Bellman, *Constance M. Rourke* (Woodbridge, CT: Twayne, 1981), p. 76.

6. Barnum, *Struggles and Triumphs*, p. 71.

7. Barnum, *Life of P. T. Barnum*, p. 143; Rosemarie Garland Thomson, *Freakery: Cultural Spectacles of the Extraordinary Body* (New York: New York University Press, 1996), p. 97.

8. Barnum, *Struggles and Triumphs*, p. 143; Richard Crawford, *America's Musical Life: A History* (New York: Norton, 2001).

9. See the purchase contract for Heth in Barnum, *Life of P. T. Barnum*, p. 151.

10. Ibid., pp. 152–55.

11. LeRoy Ashby, *With Amusement for All: A History of American Popular Culture since 1830* (Lexington: University Press of Kentucky, 2006), p. 27.

12. Benjamin Reiss does his best to make Joice Heth sound exploited and oppressed. Rosemarie Garland Thompson, on the other hand, implies that the ruse was Heth's invention and that Heth was enthusiastic about being able to babble to a fascinated audience. If you were offered two choices for the eightieth year of your life, fame and the attention of an amazed crowd

or isolation in a comfortable hospital bed, which would you pick? Thomson, *Freakery*, p. 103. See also Benjamin Reiss, *The Showman and the Slave: Race, Death, and Memory in Barnum's America* (Cambridge, MA: Harvard University Press, 2001), p. 1. Garland, by the way, points out that Barnum was enthusiastic about revealing his hoaxes in his autobiographies. But he swears that when it came to Heth, he was taken in "by a forged bill of sale purporting to have been made by the father of George Washington."

13. Barnum, *Life of P. T. Barnum*, p. 153.

14. Ibid., p. 395.

15. Phineas Taylor Barnum, *The Colossal P. T. Barnum Reader: Nothing Else Like it in the Universe*, ed. James W. Cook (Champaign: University of Illinois Press, 2005), p. 125.

16. Joshua Brown, *Beyond the Lines: Pictorial Reporting, Everyday Life, and the Crisis of Gilded Age America* (Berkeley: University of California Press, 2006), p. 46.

17. Wikipedia, "P. T. Barnum," http://en.wikipedia.org/wiki/P.t._barnum (accessed February 9, 2009).

18. Neil Harris, *Humbug: The Art of P. T. Barnum* (Chicago: University of Chicago Press, 1973), p. 43; Francine Hornberger, *Carny Folk: The World's Weirdest Sideshow Acts* (New York: Citadel Press, 2005), pp. 13–15; Saxon, *P. T. Barnum: The Legend and the Man*, p. 10.

19. The newspapers of New York were moving from the 1810 average circulation of nine hundred to the tens and hundreds of thousands just as Barnum was cutting his teeth on press relations. The newspapers available to Barnum in 1842 included: the *New York Sun* (founded about 1801), *Journal of Commerce* (founded 1827), the *Evening Post* (William Cullen Bryant, editor, 1828), the *Herald* (founded 1835, James Gordon Bennett, editor), the *Tribune* (founded 1841 and headed by a man who would become one of Barnum's best friends, Horace Greeley), and the *Brooklyn Eagle* (founded 1841). Papers that Barnum would later work with included: the *New York Times* (founded 1851) and the *New York World* (founded around 1860, Joseph Pulitzer, editor). See "Newspapers, American," *Encyclopedia Americana: A Library of Universal Knowledge* (New York: Encyclopedia Americana, 1919), pp. 284–85.

20. Barnum, *Struggles and Triumphs*, p. 357.

21. Ibid., p. 359.

22. Barnum, *The Colossal P. T. Barnum Reader*, p. 7.

23. Barnum may have been alone in championing "the lower half million's" right to theatrical amusement at the beginning of the 1840s, but in 1846 the Boston Museum tried to follow Barnum's example by appealing to the "blood and thunder" tastes of Boston's lower half million. William War-

land Clapp, *A Record of the Boston Stage* (Boston: James Munroe, 1853), pp. 387–92.

24. Robert Michael Lewis, *Rational Recreation: The Ideology of Recreation in the Northern United States in the Nineteenth Century*, PhD thesis, Johns Hopkins University, 1980; Foster Rhea Dulles, *America Learns to Play: A History of Popular Recreation, 1607–1940* (Gloucester, MA: Peter Smith, 1959), p. 123.

25. Chang and Eng Bunker, *The Lost Museum*, American Social History Productions, Inc. American Social History Project, Center for Media & Learning, City University of New York, and the Center for History and New Media of George Mason University, http://chnm.gmu.edu/lostmuseum/chang/ (accessed February 10, 2009). See also *The Lost Museum*, http://www.lostmuseum.cuny.edu/home.html (accessed February 10, 2009).

26. Library of Congress, "What Was Chautauqua? Traveling Culture, Circuit Chautauqua in the Twentieth Century," Library of Congress American Memory, http://sdrc.lib.uiowa.edu/traveling-culture/essay.htm (accessed February 10, 2009).

27. Ronald A. Fullerton, "A Prophet of Modern Advertising: Germany's Karl Knies," *Journal of Advertising*, March 22, 1998.

28. Robert W. Rydell and Rob Kroes, *Buffalo Bill in Bologna: The Americanization of the World, 1869–1922* (Chicago: University of Chicago Press, 2005), p. 27.

29. Mark Sloan, F. W. Glasier, and Timothy Tegge, *Wild, Weird, and Wonderful: The American Circus 1901–1927, as Seen by F. W. Glasier, Photographer* (New York: Norton, 2002).

30. Joe Vitale, *There's a Customer Born Every Minute: P. T. Barnum's Secrets to Business Success* (New York: AMACOM, 1998).

31. James Trager, *The New York Chronology: The Ultimate Compendium of Events, People, and Anecdotes from the Dutch to the Present* (New York: HarperCollins, 2004), p. 84.

32. D. W. Meinig, *The Shaping of America: A Geographical Perspective on 500 Years of History: Volume 3—Transcontinental America, 1850–1915* (New Haven, CT: Yale University Press, 2000), p. 265.

33. James W. Cook, *The Arts of Deception: Playing with Fraud in the Age of Barnum* (Cambridge, MA: Harvard University Press, 2001), pp. 141–42.

34. Foner and Garraty, *The Reader's Companion to American History*, p. 84.

35. Author Andreas Schroeder is convinced that the words "There's a sucker born every minute" were those of George Hull, the man responsible for a nineteenth-century hoax that made scientific history—the Cardiff

Giant. Hull's phony prehuman giant was found out, discredited, and made headlines. Barnum drew crowds by exhibiting an "authentic fake" copy of Hull's giant. Said Hull in disgust, "There's a sucker born every minute." Andreas Schroeder, *Scams! Ten Stories That Explore Some of the Most Outrageous Swindlers and Tricksters of All Time* (Toronto: Annick, 2004), pp. 55–57. For two other hypotheses about who originated the saying, see Ralph Keyes, *The Quote Verifier: Who Said What, Where, and When* (New York: Macmillan, 2006), p. 215. The one thing Schroeder and Keyes agree on is that Barnum never uttered the infamous phrase.

36. Quoted in Saxon, *P. T. Barnum*, p. 57.

37. Here's what just one of Barnum's legacies, the circus, did for Americans in the dark days after 9/11. The words are those of the *New York Times*'s Glenn Collins: "The circus is promoting its show as 'the single most thrilling edition of the Greatest Show on Earth ever produced.' And for once the hokum is on target, because act after act—from six roaring motorcycles in the 16-foot-wide Globe of Death, to a fiery human cannonball and a star clown's high-wire pratfall—keeps spectators' shoulders tied in knots for two hours and six minutes." The circus appearance Collins was talking about came when 9/11 had shaken Americans—including Collins—to the core. New terror alerts were being issued every day. Barnum's circus was medicine to the soul. Collins wondered what the circus achieved. He knew it was salvation for his own emotions. But he needed some way to put that feeling into words. He wrote, "For 133 years, the circus has tapped into America's deepest fears and strongest desires, and audiences have often sought out the show in wartime." For what? Collins answer was a "lift" in "morale." And from Collins's article it was clear that one citizen whose morale the circus had lifted from gloom was Glenn Collins. But secular salvation was not enough for Collins. He wanted to understand its workings. "Why, in a time of chronic alert, are audiences rushing to take their anxiety up a notch?" Collins asked, referring to the constant stream of death-defying acts. "Professor [Peter W.] Meineck has an answer: 'Live performance is always connected with catharsis—and the pure translation of that word means healing.'" One grandmother who had come to the Manhattan performance with her adult daughters and with her two-year-old granddaughter may have done a better job of summing up the power of the experience: "It feels good to be around people who are enjoying this so much." Glenn Collins, "Running Away to the Circus; In Anxious Times, Crowds Get Thrills and Catharsis," *New York Times*, March 19, 2003.

38. Dulles, *America Learns to Play*, p. 126.

39. C. R. Snyder and Shane J. Lopez, *Handbook of Positive Psychology* (New York: Oxford University Press, 2005).

40. The key figure in hedonics is also one of the founders of behavioral economics, Noble Prize winner in Economics Daniel Kahneman. See Daniel Kahneman, Ed Diener, and Norbert Schwarz, *Well-Being: The Foundations of Hedonic Psychology* (New York: Russell Sage Foundation, 2003); Martin E. P. Seligman, *Authentic Happiness: Using the New Positive Psychology to Realize Your Potential for Lasting Fulfillment* (New York: Simon & Schuster, 2002).

41. Lyman Abbott, "P. T. Barnum, Showman, Snap-Shots of My Contemporaries," *Outlook: An Illustrated Weekly Journal of Current Life* 127, January–April 1921, p. 54.

67. The Art of Finding Wealth in Toxic Waste Part II: The Kitchen Sink, Indoor Plumbing, and the Crapper

1. William Safire and Leonard Safir, *Words of Wisdom: More Good Advice* (New York: Simon & Schuster, 1990), p. 213.

2. U.S. Army Corps of Engineers, "History of Lake Michigan Diversion," 4th Technical Committee Report, *Lake Michigan Diversion Accounting Information Website*, p. 1, http://155.79.114.198/divacct/Fourth_Technical\Fourth_Technical_intro.pdf (accessed February 11, 2009). Wikipedia claims the 1885 Chicago deaths are a myth. See Wikipedia, "Chicago 1885 Cholera Epidemic Myth," http://en.wikipedia.org/wiki/Chicago_1885_cholera_epidemic_myth (accessed February 11, 2009). See also Steven Johnson, *The Ghost Map: The Story of London's Most Terrifying Epidemic—And How It Changed Science, Cities, and the Modern World* (New York: Riverhead Books, 2006), pp. 214–15.

3. John H. Lienhard, *The Engines of Our Ingenuity: An Engineer Looks at Technology and Culture* (New York: Oxford University Press, 2003), p. 67; "Thomas Crapper: Myth and Reality," History of Plumbing, http://www.plumbingworld.com/historythomas.html (accessed May 29, 2009).

68. When Selfishness Is a Blessing: Kellogg and His Flakes

1. Richard W. Schwarz, *John Harvey Kellogg, M.D.: Pioneering Health Reformer* (Hagerstown, MD: Review and Herald Publishing Association, 2006), pp. 14–17; Scott Bruce and Bill Crawford, *Cerealizing America: The Unsweetened Story of American Breakfast Cereal* (London: Faber and Faber, 1995); Dave Hoekstra, "Cereal City Museum Spoons Up Kellogg's History," *Chicago Sun Times*, June 11, 2003.

2. Schwarz, *John Harvey Kellogg, M.D.*, p. 14.

3. Seventh-Day Adventist Dietetic Association, "The Seventh-Day Adventist Health Message," Seventh-Day Adventist Facts, http://www.sdada .org/sdahealth.htm (accessed February 11, 2009).

4. Schwarz, *John Harvey Kellogg, M.D.*, p. 32.

5. William Shurtleff and Akiko Aoyagi, "Dr. John Harvey Kellogg and Battle Creek Foods: Work with Soy, A Special Exhibit—The History of Soy Pioneers around the World," Soyinfo Center, Lafayette, CA, 2004, http ://www.soyinfocenter.com/HSS/john_kellogg_and_battle_creek_foods.php (accessed February 12, 2009).

XI IS GOSSIP GOOD FOR YOUR HEALTH?

69. How Rockefeller Lit the Night

1. In 1882 the government of Pennsylvania suspended the charters of a small army of companies for not paying taxes three years in a row. The list of suspended firms—firms that apparently had not made it—included 309 oil and petroleum companies. Pennsylvania Secretary of the Commonwealth, *Pennsylvania Archives* (Philadelphia: Pennsylvania Dept. of Public Instruction, Pennsylvania Secretary of the Commonwealth, Pennsylvania State Library, 1902), series 4, vol. 10, *Papers of the Governors of Pennsylvania, 1883–1891*, pp. 72–89.

By 1902 "more than fifteen hundred oil companies had been chartered" in the United States. Eric Foner and John A. Garraty, *The Reader's Companion to American History. The Columbia Electronic Encyclopedia*, 6th ed. (New York: Columbia University Press, 2003); Brian Black, *Petrolia: The Landscape of America's First Oil Boom* (Baltimore, MD: Johns Hopkins University Press, 2000), p. 56; Charles Franklin Dunbar, Frank William Taussig, Abbott Payson Usher, Alvin Harvey Hansen, Edward Chamberlin, William Leonard Crum, and Arthur Eli Monroe, *Quarterly Journal of Economics* 16, 1901–1902, p. 266 (Cambridge, MA: OCLC FirstSearch Electronic Collections Online, published for Harvard University by MIT Press), http:// books.google.com/books?id=n7MRAAAAYAAJ&pg=PA268&dq=standard +oil+competitors+1870&ei=SbyUScf3FJfUzASLz4mFCA (accessed February 12, 2009).

2. Ron Chernow, *Titan: The Life of John D. Rockefeller, Sr.* (New York: Random House, 1998); Denis Brian, *Pulitzer: A Life* (New York: John Wiley and Sons, 2001), p. 328; Peter Collier and David Horowitz, *The Rockefellers: An American Dynasty* (New York: Holt, Rinehart and Winston, 1976).

3. WGBH, "Rockefellers Timeline," *American Experience*, http://www.pbs.org/wgbh/amex/rockefellers/timeline/index.html (accessed March 7, 2009).

4. Gabriel Horn, *Memory, Imprinting and the Brain: An Inquiry into Mechanisms* (New York: Oxford University Press, 1985); Jörg Bock and Katharina Braun, "Filial Imprinting in Domestic Chicks Is Associated with Spine Pruning in the Associative Area, Dorsocaudal Neostriatum," *European Journal of Neuroscience* 11, no. 7, pp. 2566–70; Konrad Lorenz, *On Aggression* (New York: Harcourt Brace Jovanovich, 1974).

5. "Paraffin," *Encyclopaedia Britannica: A Dictionary of Arts, Sciences, Literature and General Information* (Edinburgh, Scotland: Encyclopaedia Britannica, 1911), 20:752–55; Tiverton Museum of Mid Devon Life and the Telematics Centre at the University of Exeter, "Virtual Victorians—Themes Gallery: Heating and Lighting," June 24, 2003, http://victorians.swgfl.org.uk/themes/heating_and_lighting/home.htms (accessed January 27, 2009).

6. This is assuming you are much poorer than King Louis XIV of France. At Louis' palace, Versailles, it took forty servants two hours to light all three thousand candles in just one room, the Hall of Mirrors. See Jacqueline Bouchard, "Let There Be Light," *The Secret Science of Everyday Things, What's That About?* Canadian Television Fund/Science Channel. See also Michael Bal and David Sunderland, *An Economic History of London, 1800–1914* (New York: Routledge, 2001), p. 132. And take a gander at the description of the candles in the Salle Blanche at the Winter Palace in St. Petersburg in John Lothrop Motley and George William Curtis, *The Correspondence of John Lothrop Motley* (New York: Harper & Bros., 1889), p. 82. Not to mention the description of the candles in the hall on "Lord Mayor's Day, 1773," in William Hone, *The Every-Day Book and Table Book: Or, Everlasting Calendar of Popular Amusements, Sports, Pastimes, Ceremonies, Manners, Customs and Events, Incident to Each of the Three Hundred and Sixty-five Days, in Past and Present Times; Forming a Complete History of the Year, Month, and Seasons* (London: Thomas Tegg and Son, 1837), p. 1385.

7. George G. Ramsdell, *Proceedings of the International Gas Congress Held at San Francisco, California, September 27–October 2, 1915* (Easton, PA: Press of the Chemical Publishing Company, 1915).

8. Thomas Webster and William Parkes, *An Encyclopædia of Domestic Economy* (New York: Harper & Bros., 1855), p. 158.

9. Ruth Sheldon Knowles, *The Greatest Gamblers: The Epic of American Oil Exploration* (Norman: University of Oklahoma Press, 1980).

10. Witold Rybczynski, *Home: A Short History of an Idea* (New York: Viking, 1986), p. 140; "Two kerosene lamp explosions on Saturday, and two

resulting fires, in one of which a woman was fatally burned, comprise the testimony of the week to the dangerous character of this household incendiary." *Chronicle: A Weekly Journal, Devoted to the Interests of Insurance, Manufacturers and Real Estate* (Chicago: John J. W. O'Donoghue, 1870), 5:12; Michigan Department of Health, "Why Lamps Explode," *State Board of Health—Report of Secretary, 1877*, Annual Report, Michigan State Board of Health, volume 5, 1877, pp. 77–78; *Chronicle: A Weekly Journal, Devoted to the Interests of Insurance, Manufacturers and Real Estate* 37 (1886): 211; C. H. Schmidt et al., *Respondents v. Union Oil Company of California*, civ. no. 1368, Third Appellate District, May 10, 1915, *Reports of Cases Determined in the District Courts of Appeal of the State of California* 27 (1915): 366; Michigan Supreme Court, "Explosion of Defective Oil," *Lawyers Reports Annotated* 48 (1914): 880.

11. "When John D. Rockefeller began to sell kerosene as an illuminant, he named his company Standard Oil as a way of assuring customers that the quality of his product met a certain standard." Peter Tertzakian, *A Thousand Barrels a Second: The Coming Oil Break Point and the Challenges Facing an Energy Dependent World* (New York: McGraw-Hill, 2007), p. 16.

12. Webster and Parkes, *An Encyclopædia of Domestic Economy*, p. 158.

13. Peter James George, *The Emergence of Industrial America: Strategic Factors in American Economic Growth since 1870* (Albany: State University of New York Press, 1982), p. 24.

14. Ida Minerva Tarbell, *The History of the Standard Oil Company* (New York: McClure, Phillips & Co., 1904), p. 88; Ron Chernow, *Titan: The Life of John D. Rockefeller Sr.* (New York: Random House, 1998), p. 443.

70. The Invention of Muckraking: The Ironies of Stirring Up Dirt

1. Tarbell's shares of *McClure's* were worth the equivalent of $344,000 in the currency of 2007. This was twice the initial investment with which S. S. McClure had started the publication.

2. For a sample of *McClure's*, see *McClure's Magazine*, October 1907, http://books.google.com/books?id=JKLmxJOsMIwC&printsec=frontcover &dq=mcclure's (accessed January 27, 2009).

3. The editor of one of the most acclaimed of the early magazines, the *Spectator*, wrote that the purpose of his publication was "to bring philosophy out of the closets and libraries, schools and colleges, to dwell in clubs and assemblies, at tea-tables and coffeehouses." The anonymous editor also recommended that you reshape your scaffolding of habit by reading his magazine—a daily—every

morning before you plunged into the chaos of the day. Quoted in Richard Keeble, *The Journalistic Imagination* (London: Routledge, 2007), p. 31.

The date of publication of the first issue of *The Collection for Improvement of Husbandry and Trade* was 1682. It was one of the first of a welter of news publications that flourished in Britain at the end of the seventeenth century. Alexander Andrews, *The History of British Journalism* (London: R. Bentley, 1859) p. 89.

4. "The Booksellers' League Discusses What Sells a Book," *Publishers Weekly*, January 2, 1904, p. 23; "Checking Up the Crowd," *Leslie's Monthly Magazine* 58, May–October 1904, p. 456; Peter Lyon, *Success Story: The Life and Times of S. S. McClure* (New York: Scribner, 1963), p. 36; H. W. Brands, *The Reckless Decade: America in the 1890s* (Chicago: University of Chicago Press, 2002), p. 95; Greg Gross, "'The Explosions of Our Fine Idealistic Undertakings'—The Staff Breakup of McClure's Magazine," Allegheny College, September 12, 2000, http://tarbell.allegheny.edu/mctable.html (accessed January 27, 2009).

5. Kathleen Brady, *Ida Tarbell: Portrait of a Muckraker* (Pittsburgh: University of Pittsburgh Press, 1989), p. 121.

6. We're still quite a distance from knowing exactly which hormones are associated with righteous indignation. Serotonin, dopamine, and testosterone have all been shown to accompany rises in rank. Opioids are our pleasure providers—not dopamine, as was once thought. For testosterone and a sense of winning, see Elizabeth Adkins-Regan, *Hormones and Animal Social Behavior* (Princeton, NJ: Princeton University Press, 2005), p. 96. For the way in which opioids provide our pleasure, even when dopamine is around, see Kent C. Berridge and Morten L. Kringelbach, "Review—Affective Neuroscience of Pleasure: Reward in Humans and Animals," *Psychopharmacology* 199 (2008): 457–80; K. C. Berridge and T. E. Robinson, "Parsing Reward," *Trends in Neurosciences* 26, no. 9 (2003): 507–13; Kent Berridge, "Research Projects," Affective Neuroscience & Psychology Lab, University of Michigan Psychology Department—Biopsychology Program, http://www.lsa.umich.edu/psych/research&labs/berridge/research/affectiveneuroscience.html (accessed January 22, 2009); Stein, *The Genius Engine*, pp. 135–42.

7. Lyon, *Success Story*, p. 206.

8. Theodore Roosevelt, *The Autobiography of Theodore Roosevelt, Condensed from the Original Edition, Supplemented by Letters, Speeches, and Other Writings*, ed. Wayne Andrews (New York: Charles Scribner's Sons, 1913, reprinted 1958), pp. 246–47.

9. Lyon, *Success Story*, p. 208; Robert M. Crunden, *Ministers of Reform: The Progressives' Achievement in American Civilization, 1889–1920* (Champaign: University of Illinois Press, 1985), p. 191.

10. Roosevelt, *The Autobiography of Theodore Roosevelt*, p. 247.

11. For bios of the key robber barons—Daniel Drew, Jay Cooke, Henry Frick, Jay Gould, Jim Fisk, J. P. Morgan, Collis Huntington, Andrew Carnegie, Henry Villard, William Rockefeller, and Thomas Mellon—see Matthew Josephson, *The Robber Barons: The Great American Capitalists, 1861–1901* (1934; New York: Harcourt, Brace & World, 1962). Josephson's 1934 Great Depression era book was the tome that drove the phrase "robber barons" home.

12. Steffens suggested to Tarbell that they turn *McClure's* into "a Socialist organ." Tarbell turned him down flat. Justin Kaplan, *Lincoln Steffens: A Biography* (New York: Simon & Schuster, 2004), p. 161.

13. "I have seen the future, and it works," said Steffens after a trip to the brand-new Soviet Union, just after the Russian Revolution of 1917. Kaplan, *Lincoln Steffens*, p. 8.

71. Don't Let Envy Get You: What Hath J. P. Morgan Wrought?

1. Bruce Bower, " A Fair Share of the Pie People Everywhere Put a Social Spin on Economic Exchanges," *Science News*, February 16, 2002; Virginia Postrel, "Looking Inside the Brains of the Stingy," *New York Times*, February 27, 2003.

2. Average GNP per capita was $324 in developed countries in 1860. It was $662 in 1913. Paul Bairoch, *Economics and World History: Myths and Paradoxes* (Chicago: University of Chicago Press, 1995), p. 95.

3. For figures on per capita GNP from 1750 to 1900, see Bairoch, *Economics and World History*, p. 95. For the GNP per capita figure of the United States in 2006, see Finfacts, Ireland's Business & Finance Portal, "From World Bank Development Indicators 2007," http://www.finfacts.ie/biz10/globalworldincomepercapita.htm (accessed January 26, 2009). In 1750, Western per capita GNP was $182. By 2007, the equivalent figure in American GNP per capita was $4,970. For a smorgasbord of mind-socking comparisons of this kind, see Gregg Easterbrook, *The Progress Paradox: How Life Gets Better while People Feel Worse* (New York: Random House, 2004).

72. The Secret of Tuned Empathy: Why Reason Is Insane

1. Helen Phillips, "Empathy May Not Be a Uniquely Human Quality," *New Scientist*, April 24, 2004; Emma Young, "Mind Theory," *New Scientist*, March 29, 2001; Helen Phillips, "'Mindsight' Could Explain Sixth Sense," *New Scientist*, February 4, 2004; Philip Cohen, "Humans Are Hardwired to Feel Others' Pain," *New Scientist*, February 19, 2004.

2. Sloan set the following example. "It is the duty of the Chief Executive Officer to be objective and impartial. He must be absolutely tolerant and pay no attention to how a man does his work, let alone whether he likes the man or not. The only criteria must be performance and character. And that is incompatible with friendship and social relations. . . . Loneliness, distance, and formality . . . are his [the CEO's] duty." In Peter Drucker with Joseph A. Maciariello, *The Daily Drucker: 366 Days of Insight and Motivation for Getting the Right Things Done* (New York: HarperCollins, 2004), p. 14.

3. Alfred P. Sloan, John McDonald, and Catharine Stevens, with a new introduction by Peter Drucker, *My Years with General Motors* (New York: Doubleday, 1972); David R. Farber, *Sloan Rules: Alfred P. Sloan and the Triumph of General Motors* (Chicago: University of Chicago Press, 2002), p. 87.

4. John Micklethwait and Adrian Wooldridge, *The Company: A Short History of a Revolutionary Idea* (New York: Modern Library, 2005), p. 104.

5. Michael S. Gazzaniga, *The Social Brain: Discovering the Networks of the Mind* (New York: Basic Books, 1985).

6. A. Bechara, H. Damasio, and A. R. Damasio, "Emotion, Decision Making and the Orbitofrontal Cortex," *Cerebral Cortex* (March 2000): 295–307; A. Bechara, H. Damasio, A. R. Damasio, and G. P. Lee, "Different Contributions of the Human Amygdala and Ventromedial Prefrontal Cortex to Decision-Making," *Journal of Neuroscience* (July 1999): 5473–81; A. R. Damasio, "The Somatic Marker Hypothesis and the Possible Functions of the Prefrontal Cortex," *Philosophical Transactions of the Royal Society of London (Biology)* (October 1996): pp. 1413–20; Oliver H. Turnbull, Cathryn E. Y. Evans, Alys Bunce, Barbara Carzolio, and Jane O'Connor, "Emotion-Based Learning and Central Executive Resources: An Investigation of Intuition and the Iowa Gambling Task," *Brain and Cognition* (April 2005): 244–47; Bruce Bower, "Hunches Pack Decisive Punches," *Science News*, March 22, 1997, p. 183. For Damasio's current activities, see Damasio's University of Southern California Brain and Creativity Institute Web site, http://www.usc.edu/schools/college/bci/whoweare.html (accessed January 23, 2009).

7. For the influence of the Iowa Gambling Task, see W. Russell Neuman, George E. Marcus, and Michael MacKuen, *The Affect Effect: Dynamics of Emotion in Political Thinking and Behavior* (Chicago: University of Chicago Press, 2007).

8. Here's how one neuroscientist, David M. Berson, describes the moment when intuition and reason meet to crack a tough problem: "I knew instantly that I'd been blessed with something every scientist dreams of—a moment when the expected and the unexpected, reason and intuition, coa-

lesce in an instant of pure, ecstatic discovery." David M. Berson, "Strange Vision," in *Neuroscience: Exploring the Brain*, ed. Mark F. Bear, Barry W. Connors, and Michael A. Paradiso (Philadelphia: Lippincott Williams & Wilkins, 2006), p. 614.

9. Michael Atherton, Jiancheng Zhuang, William M. Bart, Xiaoping Hub, and Sheng He, "A Functional MRI Study of High-Level Cognition: The Game of Chess," *Cognitive Brain Research* (March 2003): 26–31; William M. Bart and Michael Atherton, "The Neuroscientific Basis of Chess Playing: Applications to the Development of Talent and Education," paper presented at the American Educational Research Association Meeting, Chicago, April 2003, http://www.tc.umn.edu/~athe0007/BNEsig/papers/Neuroscientific BasisOfChess.pdf (accessed January 23, 2009); Jason Williams, "Grandmaster News Flash: Is Chess a Game of Spatial Processing?" *Psychology Today* 36, no. 2 (March–April 2003): 24.

10. Gazzaniga, *The Social Brain*; Jay Harris, *How the Brain Talks to Itself: A Clinical Primer of Psychotherapeutic Neuroscience* (New York: Haworth Press, 1998), pp. 2–5; Michael W. Eysenck and Mark T. Keane, *Cognitive Psychology: A Student's Handbook* (London: Taylor & Francis, 2005), pp. 524–31.

11. Rizzolatti tells the tale of how he discovered mirror neurons in a New York Academy of Sciences podcast: Vittorio Gallese, Giacomo Rizzolatti, et al., "Acting and Mirror Neurons," http://www.nyas.org/snc/podcasts .asp?pager_podcast=7& (accessed January 24, 2009). For more, see Giacomo Rizzolatti and Giovanni Buccino, "The Mirror Neuron System and Its Role in Imitation and Language," in *From Monkey Brain to Human Brain: A Fyssen Foundation Symposium*, ed. Stanislas Dehaene, Jean-Rene Duhamel, Marc D. Hauser, and Giacomo Rizzolatti (Cambridge, MA: MIT Press, 2003), pp. 213–34; Giacomo Rizzolatti and Laila Craighero, "The Mirror-Neuron System," *Annual Review of Neuroscience* 27 (July 2004): 169–92; David Freedberg, "Action, Empathy, and Emotion in the History of Art," in the series of talks titled "From Mirror Neurons to the Mona Lisa: Visual Art and the Brain," New York Academy of Science, http://www .nyas.org/ebriefreps/main.asp?intSubSectionID=3529 (accessed January 24, 2009).

12. Bruce Bower, "Repeat after Me: Imitation Is the Sincerest Form of Perception," *Science News Online*, May 24, 2003, http://www.science news.org/articles/20030524/bob9.asp (accessed March 21, 2004); L. Carr, M. Iacoboni, et al., "Neural Mechanisms of Empathy in Humans: A Relay from Neural Systems for Imitation to Limbic Areas," *Proceedings of the National Academy of Sciences* (April 29, 2003): 5497–5502; S. D. Preston and F. B. M. de Waal, *The Imitative Mind: Development, Evolution and*

Brain Bases (Cambridge: Cambridge University Press, 2002); "Empathy: Its Ultimate and Proximate Bases," *Behavioral and Brain Sciences* (February 2002): 1–19; P. Rochat, M. A. Umiltà, C. Keysers, G. Rizzolatti, et al., "I Know What You Are Doing: A Neurophysiological Study," *Neuron* (July 2001): 155–65.

13. Daniel Goleman, Richard E. Boyatzis, and Annie McKee, *Primal Leadership: Realizing the Power of Emotional Intelligence* (Cambridge: Harvard Business Press, 2002), p. 50.

14. Walter Karp, "Henry Ford's Village," in Editors of American Heritage, Byron Dobell, *A Sense of History: The Best Writing from the Pages of American Heritage* (Winter Park, FL: American Heritage Press, 1985), p. 667.

15. Drucker, introduction to *My Years with General Motors*, p. xxi.

16. "Alfred Sloan," *Economist*, January 30, 2009, http://www.economist.com/business/management/displaystory.cfm?story_id=13047099 (accessed February 22, 2009).

73. The Fall of the American Auto Industry: Breaking the Commodity Contract

1. "The Standard Oil Company of New York shipped its first kerosene to China in the 1880s. . . . By 1910 Standard Oil was shipping 15 per cent of its total exports of kerosene to China." John King Fairbank, Albert Feuerwerker, and Denis Twitchett, *The Cambridge History of China: Volume 12, Republican China, 1912–1949, Part 1* (Cambridge: Cambridge University Press, 1983), p. 196.

74. The Brilliant Demise of CBS: The Perils of Management by Walking Inside

1. Jane Jacobs, "The Greening of the City," *New York Times Sunday Magazine*, May 16, 2004.

2. Paul Flux, *Britain since 1930* (Portsmouth, NH: Heinemann, 2001), p. 9.

XII THE ROCKET FUEL OF EMPATHY

75. The Empathy Deep Inside of You:
More Management by Walking Outside

1. For van Leeuwenhoek's words on his discovery of animalcules, see Paul G. Engelkirk and Gwendolyn R. Wilson, *Burton's Microbiology for the Health Sciences* (Philadelphia: Lippincott Williams & Wilkins, 2007), p. 8.

2. Edna St. Vincent Millay, *Renascence and Other Poems* (New York: Mitchell Kennerley, 1921).

3. Robert Hazel, *Who Touches This: Selected Poems, 1951–1979* (Woodstock, VT: Countryman, 1980); Robert Hazel, *Soft Coal: Poems* (Woodstock, VT: Countryman, 1985); Robert Hazel, *American Elegies* (Fargo: North Dakota State University, 1968); Robert Hazel, *Poems, 1951–1961* (Morehead, KY: Morehead, 1961); Robert Hazel, "White Anglo-Saxon Protestant," in *Home and Beyond: An Anthology of Kentucky Short Stories*, ed. Morris Allen Grubbs (Lexington: University Press of Kentucky, 2002), p. 118. Robert Hazel mentored Ed McClanahn, Gurney Norman, Wendell Berry, Bobbie Ann Mason, and me.

4. Even in the age of the infinitely Googleable, it has been hard to track this book down. It may have been Albert Einstein, *Relativity, the Special & General Theory: A Popular Exposition* (New York: Methuen Wiley, 1931). Then again, it may not. See also Jeffrey Crelinsten, *Einstein's Jury: The Race to Test Relativity* (Princeton, NJ: Princeton University Press, 2006), p. 102.

5. For the story of the man who gave the rock-crit elite its name, *Village Voice* head music critic Robert Christgau, who called himself the "Dean of American Rock Critics," see Judy Rosen, "X-ed Out, the *Village Voice* Fires a Famous Music Critic," *Slate*, September 5, 2006, http://www.slate.com/id/2148997/ (accessed January 24, 2009).

6. Laurence Bergreen, *As Thousands Cheer: The Life of Irving Berlin* (New York: Da Capo Press, 1996).

76. What Hath Ochre Taught?
The Care and Feeding of Identity:
One More Way to Manage by Walking Outside

1. Jerry Useem, "Most Admired Company—Is Changing the Rules for Corporate America," *Fortune*, February 18, 2003.

77. You Owe Your Audience Your Life: The Curse of Losing Touch

1. Bob Shaye, personal communication, January 28, 2009.

2. Gina Keating, "Producer Sues New Line over 'Lord of the Rings,'" Reuters, December 14, 2007, http://www.reuters.com/articlePrint?articleId =USN1431993620071215 (accessed January 30, 2009).

78. Let Us Save the Hollow Men—Set Your People Free

1. Alexander Hamilton, "Manufactures, Communicated to the House of Representatives December 5, 1791," in *The Works of Alexander Hamilton: Containing His Correspondence, and His Political and Official Writings, Exclusive of the Federalist, Civil and Military: Published from the Original Manuscripts Deposited in the Department of State, by Order of the Joint Library Committee of Congress* Alexander Hamilton, ed. John Church Hamilton (New York: J. F. Trow, 1851), p. 209.

ACKNOWLEDGMENTS

To DARPA for mothering the Internet and to Google for turning the Net into one of the most important research tools since the invention of the library. To Frank Fox for research assistance on soap, P. T. Barnum, and the plantation. To James Burke for showing us a new way to think. To Michael Smolens and O. Woodward Buckner for kicking this book into existence. To the Tea Lounge's Jonathan Spiel, Greg Wolf, and Frieda Wolfe for creating a new form of community living room (complete with wi-fi). To Richard Metzger, Alex Burns, and Anat Levy for keeping me alive during an extremely challenging time. To Nancy Ellis and Linda Regan for making this book materialize.

To those who have stimulated and sustained me: Buzz Aldrin, Sabine Allaeys, Amy Alkon, Jill Andresevic, Amara Angelica, Barbara Annis, Jeremy Barr, Howard Baskind, Don Beck, Art Bell, Eshel ben-Jacob, Lawrence Joseph Berger, Berel Berko, Bonnie Bernstein, Richard Brodie, Bob Cavallo, Sol Charney, Alex Chislenko, Bob Citron, Michael Clauss, Andrew Cohen, Alan Corbeth, Joseph de Cuir, Bruce Damer, Tom Danheiser, Audrey Dawson, Gerry Delet, Daria Dorosh, Alexander Elder, Karen Ellis, Derek Enlander, Adam Fisher, Russell Gardner, Peter Garretson, Valerius and Renate Geist, Maya Gilbert, Jeffrey Gitomer, Bob Guccione Jr., Mark Hopkins, Steve Hovland, Feng Hsu, Barbara Marx Hubbard, Pascal Jouxtel, Jay Kenoff, Bob Krone, Mark Lamonica, Robert Largen, Stephen Lee,

Liza Lentini, Jason Liszkiewicz, David Livingstone, Michael Lockhart, Lisa Lyons, Sonia Mahendran, Rob McConnell, Chris McCulloch, Andy Meyer, Igal Moria, Gayil Nalls, George Noory, Nando Pelusi, Walter Petryk, Bala Pillai, David Pincus, Harold Pollak, Ian Punnett, Joe Quirk, Dennis Reinhart, Geraldine Reinhart, Lorraine Rice, Jessica Roemischer, Terry Jean Rosenberg, Judy Rubin, Jack Sarfatti, Linda Diane Scalf, John Skoyles, David Livingstone Smith, Harris "Bud" Stone, Mathew Tombers, Dana Toomey, Mel Toomey, Tina Turner, James Santagata, Amir Siddiqi, Jerry Sukinik, Sesh Velamoor, David Walley, Nancy Weber, Ira Weinstock, Paul Werbos, Ahmed Yehia, Robert Zubrin, and Steve Zuckerman.

To Gary Zamchick in New York, Kevin Hagell in Vancouver, Sabine Allaeys in Brussels, and Pigtail Pundits in Mumbai, India, for making the world's first biopolitical animation on behalf of the Big Bang Tango Media Lab.

Thanks for helping me infiltrate the entertainment business go to: Zohn Ardman, Dennis Arfa, Joan Armatrading, Dee Anthony, Don Arden, Bill Aucoin, Jeff Ayeroff, John Baruck, Philip Bailey, Frank Beard, Robert "Kool" Bell, Jim Belushi, Alvin Bennett, Chris Blackwell, Susan Blond, Marshall Blonstein, Jay Boberg, Bonnie Bruckheimer, Glen Brunman, Richard Burkhardt, Pamela Burton, David Byrne, Bob Cavallo, Ray Caviano, Janis Cercone, Lyor Cohen, Natalie Cole, Tom Consolo, Alice Cooper, Ian Copeland, Miles Copeland, Stewart Copeland, Bobbi Cowan, Jack Craigo, Peter Criss, Kevin Cronin, Cameron Crowe, Rick Davies, Freddy DeMann, Connie de Nave, John Denver, Joe Dera, Dennis De Young, Rick Dobbis, John Doumanian, Sheila E., Alan Edwards, Ken Emerson, Donna Fargo, Steve Fargnoli, Jim Foglesong, Peter Frampton, Chris Frantz, Harrison Funk, Peter Gabriel, Steve Gaines, Eric Gardner, Art Garfunkel, Billy Gibbons, Danny Goldberg, Lynn Goldsmith, Ron Goldstein, Shep Gordon, Mike Gormley, Bill Graham, Grandmaster Flash and the Furious Five, David Grisman, Alan Grubman, Dave Grusin, Daryl Hall, Jim Halsey, Jordon Harris, Annie Haslam, Peter Haycock, Jim Henke, Dusty Hill, Sam Holdsworth, Derek Holt, Dick Howard, Charles Huggins, Phyllis Hyman, Billy Idol, Arthur Indursky, Shelton Ivany, Jackie Jackson, Marlon Jackson, Michael Jackson, Randy Jackson, Tito Jackson, Joan Jett, Billy Joel, Geoff Jukes, Art Kass, Chaka Khan, Tony King, Martin Kirkup, Peter Knobler, Ken Kragan, Connie Kramer, David Krebs, Gary Kurfirst, Kenny Laguna, Ida Langsam, Carmen LaRosa, Larry Larson, Jay Lasker, Steve Leber, Anne Leighton, Ellen Levine, Aaron Levy, Nancy Lewis, Martin Lewis, Ralph MacDonald, Lou Maglia, Toby Mamis, Danny Marcus, Rhonda Markowitz, Bob Marley, Rita Marley, Ziggy Marley, Tony Martell, Doc McGhee, John Mellencamp, Bette Midler, Craig Miller, Andy Miele, Stephanie Mills, Tommy Mottola, Anne Murray, Ed Naha, Jack Nance, Terry Nunn, John Oates, John O'Donnell, Luke O'Reilly, Jim Pettigrew, George Pincus, I. Martin Pompadour, Bud Prager, Ed Pressman, Charley Prevost, Prince, Leonard Rambeau, Lou Reed, Bob Reno, Lionel Richie, Nelson Riddle, Sylvia Robinson, Larry Rosen, Jane Rosenthal, Sheldon Roskin, Carol Ross, Diana Ross, Gerald Rothberg, David Rubinson, Todd Rundgren, John Scher, Paul Schindler, Gina Schock, Marty Scott, Andy Secher, Russell Shaw, Bob Shaye, Jaime Shoop, Pat Siciliano, Mike Sigman, Robert Ellis Silberstein, Stan Silver, Gene Simmons, Russell Simmons, Paul Simon, Bob Small, Harry Spiro, Billy Squier, Paul Stanley, Harriet Sternberg, Charles Stetler, Tony Stratton-Smith, Mark Stern, Henry Stone, Derek Sutton, Sylvester, Mary Travers, Kathy Valentine, Luther Vandross, Vanity, Gabe Vigorito, Perry Watts-Russell, Wendy & Lisa, Jann Wenner, Tina Weymouth, Adam White, Jim White, Tim White, Paul Winter, Linda and Cecil Womack, Frank Yablans, Chuck Young, and James Young.

Thanks for teaching me the hidden art of building a superstar, the art of touring strategy, to Bill Ham.

Thanks for helping me slip into the corporate world to: Peter Bramley, Robert Hazel, Denny Hermanson, Brad Johanson, Stephanie Phelan, Linda Sampson, Matty Simmons Richard Skidmore, Bill Skurski, Gail Skurski, and Michael Sullivan.

Thanks to the first Omnologists: Morgan Kinney and Jim Watkin.

Super-sized thanks to my mentor in neurobiology, E. E. Coons; to my mentors in magazine publishing, Mary Peacock, Sally Freeman, and Gerald Rothburg; and to my mentors in the music world, Seymour Stein and Bob Cavallo.

And special thanks to the staff of The Howard Bloom Organization, Ltd.

INDEX